Decolonization and Dependence

About the Book and Author

After Nigeria's independence from British rule in 1960, the United States emerged, rather dramatically, as the most dynamic component in the determination of postcolonial Nigerian foreign, economic, and political policies. This book, the first definitive analysis of the emergent relationship between these two countries, examines the problematic development of this connection in the context of the twin challenges of the contemporary African situation: decolonization and dependence on the capitalist world economy.

From the Nigerian perspective, the evolving relationship has been determined above all by the combined requirements of domestic political security, economic advancement, and a perceived leadership obligation in the regional decolonization movement. The author claims that for the United States, mediation in Africa—a role greatly augmented by the complementary resources of the former British colonial power—is a function of U.S. interest in preserving the very colonial order Africans seek to transform. This interest has grown in the face of the Soviet challenge to Western dominion in Africa.

Dr. Ate juxtaposes the bilateral (largely economic) and regional (political) levels of Nigerian-U.S. ties to offer a structurally coherent explanation of the purpose and results of the relationship for the two countries.

Bassey E. Ate, a graduate of Harvard and Columbia universities, is a senior research fellow at the Nigerian Institute of International Affairs.

Decolonization and Dependence

The Development of Nigerian-U.S. Relations, 1960–1984

Bassey E. Ate

Westview Press / Boulder and London

Westview Special Studies on Africa

This Westview softcover edition is printed on acid-free paper and bound in softcovers that carry the highest rating of the National Association of State Textbook Administrators, in consultation with the Association of American Publishers and the Book Manufacturers' Institute.

Published in 1987 in the United States of America by Westview Press, Inc.; Frederick A. Praeger, Publisher; 5500 Central Avenue, Boulder, Colorado 80301

Library of Congress Cataloging-in-Publication Data
Ate, Bassey E.
   Decolonization and dependence.
   (Westview special studies on Africa)
   Bibliography: p.
   Includes index.
   1. United States—Foreign relations—Nigeria.
2. Nigeria—Foreign relations—United States.   I. Title.
II. Series.
E183.8.N6A84   1987   327.730669   85-22544
ISBN 0-8133-7137-6

Printed and bound in the United States of America

The paper used in this publication meets the requirements of the American National Standard for Permanence of Paper for Printed Library Materials Z39.48-1984.

6   5   4   3   2   1

To the memory of my father,
Ate Eyo Ate,
who instilled in me the value of
higher learning

Contents

Tables and Figures

Preface

This book is the first systematic analysis of the developing relationship between Nigeria and the United States during the dynamic era of African decolonization. A critical element in the drama of decolonization has been the interjection of the competitive interests of the United States and the Soviet Union: Whereas neither superpower has ever possessed an African colony, the influence of both countries has become crucial not only in the regional politics of decolonization, but also in the patterns of social formations and institution-building in the newly forming African nations. A specific dimension of the African drama is the progressive emergence of the United States as, tangibly, the main external focal point for Nigeria in the determination of its foreign economic and political policies, potentially set to eclipse the direct importance of the colonial sovereign country, the United Kingdom. Especially intriguing is the fact that the United States, in its attempt to control the currents of regional (political) change in the prevalent colonial relationship, lays great emphasis on manipulating the structures of its seedling bilateral (largely economic) ties with key African states and on the use of multilateral instruments. Hence, a concern throughout the study is to establish the connection between the bilateral and regional spheres of the evolving Nigeria-U.S. relationship. I hope thereby to offer a structurally coherent explanation of both the pattern of Nigeria-U.S. regional policy interactions and the substance of Nigeria's Africa policy in the period from 1960 to 1984.

The initial research for this work was done in connection with my doctoral program at Columbia University. I, therefore, acknowledge the invaluable assistance rendered by some individuals during that seminal period of my career. I thank, first of all, Professors William T.R. Fox and Jim Mittelman, both of whom provided ongoing intellectual stimulation and also personal encouragement, which resulted in the initial formulation of the subject of this study. To Professor Donald Puchala I owe an exceeding personal debt; his timely intervention and sustained guidance led to the successful completion of my program at Columbia.

There are numerous other persons in both the United States and Nigeria who, sometimes at utter inconvenience to themselves, assisted me in one way or another in bringing about this final product. To all of them I express profound gratitude. Three people in particular deserve special thanks: Marjorie D. Krome of the U.S. State Department's Freedom of Information Office, for her helpful cooperation during my persistent search for vital information, and my typists, Kenneth Jaja and Simeon Ugwu of the Nigerian Institute of International Affairs, for tolerating my incessant demands.

Most of all, I reserve for my wife, Delthyea Gautt Ate, the ultimate credit for making this work possible. I thank her not only for her helpful encouragement during the writing of the book in a very taxing environment, but also for her understanding companionship throughout and after my educational sojourn in the United States.

Finally, I acknowledge the assistance of the Nigerian Institute of International Affairs, which provided partial funding for the last phase of the research effort and under whose sponsorship this book was written. I owe the director of research of the institute, Professor Rafiu Akindele, gratitude for engineering this support.

Bassey E. Ate

Introduction

Unlike, for example, the long history of relations between the United States and Morocco, which dates back to U.S. independence, Nigeria and the United States had negligible ties prior to 1960. Early U.S. interest in the affairs of this former British colony was initiated largely by private organs. In 1920, for instance, the Phelps-Stokes Commission on Africa—the product of humanitarian efforts by private individuals—visited Nigeria to study the problems of education in the country and recommend ways of solving them.[1] Also, throughout the 1930s major U.S. cocoa dealers made serious efforts to buy cocoa directly from farmers in Nigeria (and Ghana), but their efforts were without success due to obstructionist tactics employed by established European firms and the British Colonial Office.[2]

There were, of course, some official contacts during this period, but they took place indirectly, between Washington and London. For example, although the United States opened its first consulate in Lagos in the early 1920s in response to the emerging interests of U.S. missionaries and trading organizations in the territory, the first major act by the United States before 1960 that had an impact on the decolonization process in Nigeria was the Consular Convention signed on June 6, 1951, between the Truman administration and the United Kingdom. The ratification of this convention in 1952 paved the way for the United States to initiate direct contacts with leading African nationalists and, specifically, made it possible for the U.S. State Department in 1954 to extend its Cultural Exchange Program to future Nigerian government leaders, such as the country's first prime minister, Abubakar Tafawa Balewa, who became a beneficiary of the program in 1957.[3] Further, the U.S. Congress showed keen interest in the future of Nigeria as an autonomous political entity by adopting, on August 27, 1954, a joint resolution that heralded the prospective attainment of "complete self-government" by that colonial territory.[4] Beyond these acts there were few tangible links between the United States and Nigeria on the eve of the latter's independence in October 1960.

Yet one year later, the political leaders of both countries became highly conscious of their mutual desire to cultivate an intensive relationship, each wishing to promote their own interests in the evolving postcolonial regional setting. The pace and extent of the developing links between the two countries was so rapid that by 1965 it was possible for Nigeria to diversify its foreign economic and political ties from exclusive dependence on Great Britain to a multilateral interrelationship embracing both the United Kingdom and the United States. Since 1970, the United States has emerged, in a most functional sense, as the dominant external focus of Nigeria's foreign economic and political policies, although the triangular relationship including Great Britain remains important. The following indicators illustrate this ongoing transformation.

On a bilateral (economic) level, Nigeria, by 1976, supplied about 40 percent of total U.S. imports from Africa as a whole. By comparison, the proportion for the Republic of South Africa, which until 1970 supplied one-third of all U.S. imports from the African continent, was only 7 percent. U.S. exports to Nigeria in the same year increased by 44 percent, while those to South Africa rose by only 1 percent.[5] Perhaps more significant, Nigeria, in 1973–1979, sold to the United States about 38–56 percent of its total oil exports (compared to 11 percent in 1965), and this accounted for about 18–26 percent of the total U.S. crude imports. The effect of these developments on the economies of the two countries was profound. On the one hand, Nigeria became, in a period of acute scarcity in the world energy supply, the second largest exporter of crude oil to the United States. On the other hand, U.S. market demand for Nigerian oil provided the major source of the immense accumulation of foreign exchange reserves available to Nigeria's federal governments in this period—the oil sector accounted for about 85–90 percent of total foreign reserves.

In the political sphere, Nigeria's regional diplomacy and U.S. Africa policy have become joined in a functional complementarity. Each nation regards the other, especially since the Angolan civil war of 1975–1976, to be of substantive relevance to its regional interests and objectives. Before 1966 Nigeria and the United States were indeed de facto allies, an alignment borne out of mutual necessity given the novel challenges facing them in the first decade of Africa's political independence. That early pattern of regional alignment was determined, in essence, by a bilateral context of dominance and dependence, which explained, to a great extent, Nigeria's celebrated "moderate" orientation in African affairs. As one indication of Nigeria's bilateral dependence, the United States, together with the United Kingdom, supplied more than 70 percent of all official economic aid received by that country before the political crisis of 1966. Witness the specific case of the 1962–1968 Nigerian national development plan in which the sum of US$949.2 million (for public expenditure, constituting 50 percent of the total cost of the plan) was expected to be raised through external loans and grants. Of that amount, the United States provided more than 50 percent (see Chapter 2). The United States also supplied 52.5 percent of the total technical assistance personnel available to Nigeria in the same period, followed by Great Britain with 37.5 percent.

From 1970 to 1979, however, Nigeria strained to relate to the United States in African (political) affairs from a position of relative economic independence. During this period, although the country remained substantially economically dependent on the United States (and Great Britain), the structure of its international economic relations had become modified in significant ways (see Chapter 5). As a result of greater economic growth and relative financial self-sufficiency—conditions that paradoxically were fueled by a new form of dependence on one export commodity (oil)—officials and the public at large no longer perceived their economic ties with the United States in terms of dependence but rather of interdependence. Many Nigerians, in the euphoric atmosphere of the period, were convinced that the "economic kingdom" was at last within their country's reach and that oil wealth was to be utilized in consolidating Africa's political emancipation.

Cultural and educational ties have served as a facilitative element in nurturing the more concrete economic and political dimensions in the Nigerian-U.S. relationship. Nigeria is the African state with the largest concentration of blacks (and one out of four Africans is a Nigerian); the United States is the only country in the world with a black population larger than that of any African country except Nigeria. This undoubtedly constitutes a strong cultural tie in the expanding contacts between the two societies. Quite early in the twentieth century, Booker T. Washington, the great Afro-American educator, demonstrated a crusading interest in the well-being of the African people when he urged Americans to contribute toward the improvement of the human condition on the African continent.[6] Another historical figure, Ralph J. Bunche, director of the Trusteeship Department of the United Nations, played a renowned role in guiding the department's progressive work in helping advance the demise of colonial rule in Africa. The historical preoccupation of such people as Washington, Bunche, W.E.B. Du Bois, Marcus Garvey, and others with the African situation illustrates the fact that the real cultural bond between Nigeria and the United States is established by the presence of about 30 million citizens of African descent in the United States. If the great nationalist upsurge in Africa proved to be a catalyst that ignited the Afro-American passion for cultural identity and self-determination within the United States, the resultant civil rights movement can be credited for spurring the United States under the

Kennedy presidency to cultivate direct links with the newly independent black African states.

This racial connection to the United States, along with U.S. egalitarian educational and political traditions, has historically lured African students to seek higher learning in the United States. Thus, the trail blazed by such pioneers as Nnamdi Azikiwe, Kwame Nkrumah, Nwafor Orizu, Mbonu Ojike, and Okechukwu Ikejiani has been followed over the years by thousands of U.S.-educated Africans. These individuals have enhanced the development of the Nigeria-U.S. relationship through both dissemination of ideas as educators and direct action as political and economic actors.[7]

Methodology

In a broad sense, this book is an assessment of the dramatic relations between Nigeria and the United States from 1960 to 1984. As such, it includes a critical examination of the factors that helped to mold the relationship, with emphasis on the first decade following Nigeria's independence. These factors are divided into two general areas: bilateral and regional. The first area consists of concrete measures of economic ties, such as official capital aid, technical assistance personnel, trade and private investment, and corresponding bilateral diplomatic relations. The second area embraces the political-diplomatic interactions concerning issues of African decolonization. These areas do not, of course, constitute independent processes that can be discussed in isolation; they are truly interrelated.

The bilateral structure of Nigeria-U.S. relations is of significance for two main reasons. First, by developing bilateral links with the core power of the capitalist world economy after 1960, Nigeria intensified the level of its earlier incorporation into and dependency within (through the United Kingdom) the global capitalist network. This meant, as will be shown, that the existing lopsided connections between the Nigerian economy and the external capitalist economy were reinforced by U.S. intervention in Nigeria in 1960, especially because the United States was the political fulcrum of that economy. Second, bilateral ties constitute the essential channels whereby influence dynamics in Nigeria-U.S. relations have occurred; pointedly, they provide the medium through which U.S. personnel and agencies have been able to exercise leverage on the Nigerian policymaking environment in a manner beneficial to U.S. interests and policy objectives. Moreover, through the same medium Nigerian state officials and other influential elites in the society have been able to convert U.S.-derived resources into power assets with which they have promoted their vital interests in both the domestic setting and the regional system.

From this point of view, what concerns the analyst of foreign policy even more than the existence of a dominance/dependence relationship is the dynamic processes by which this mode of coexistence is translated into actual advantages and disadvantages for the two entities. Of paramount interest to this study, consequently, is the critical impact of the bilateral structure on the patterns of Nigeria-U.S. regional (political) alignment and on Nigeria's Africa policy in the subperiods covered in the research.

As formulated in Chapter 1, the development of Nigerian-U.S. relations is best understood as an integral offshoot of the broader revolutionary movement of decolonization in Africa. The trend in U.S.-African relations in general and Nigerian-U.S. relations in particular during the overall period is examined from the perspective of the regional decolonization process. As other observers have generally acknowledged, the struggle for decolonization has been the dominant political reality in recent African history.[8] Roughly since 1956, the forces of decolonization have set the parameters for the resolution of every subissue in African interstate politics, including Pan-Africanism, apartheid, racism, irredentism, and regional economic integration. Further, the currents of decolonization have created numerous channels enabling extra-African forces and interests to seek competitive involvement in the region's economy and politics. Thus, decolonization provides the conceptual lenses through which one can address the dynamic intermeshing of postwar U.S. penetration of the African system, extended links between the Nigerian economy and the capitalist economic system, domestic politico-economic processes in Nigeria, and Nigeria's regional diplomacy.

By decolonization, one refers, of course, to the post–World War II movement wherein African societies have striven to transform their erstwhile colonial relationships to the Western-dominated capitalist world order. The role of the United States in Nigeria and in Africa in general, given the pivotal position of the United States in this world order, is conceived as the most crucial aspect of the overall Western drive to determine the direction of African decolonization in a manner that would sustain continued Western dominance in the continent and African dependence on the capitalist economy. This U.S. role was, during the 1960s, greatly augmented by the complementary resources of the United Kingdom.[9] Anglo-American policy collaboration in sub-Saharan Africa can be explained specifically by the countries' joint, if not always parallel, security, political, and economic interests in the region and generally by the special relationship between the two Anglo-Saxon nations in world affairs since 1914. Thus, the Anglo-American nexus has been another critical force in the evolving relationship between Nigeria and the United States.

Within the vortex of the decolonization movement in Africa, Nigeria's national role conception is clearly that of a core actor. Its position as a developing center of power in the regional system, relative to the interests of the metropolitan nations, approximates the experience of the United States in the North American system between 1783 and 1867. For the United States then, as it is for Nigeria now, the essential issue was how to reconcile the hegemonic presence of the European imperialist powers to the developing interests of an emerging regional state.[10] The inherent similarity in national self-perceptions is a powerful source of attraction for the two societies, but it also provides a built-in conflict in their relations within the African system, given the deep divergence in the national desires of the two entities in this environment as well as the U.S. connection to the excolonial powers. This factor, as distinct from the countervailing reality of international economic dependence, will likely remain a constant in the Nigerian-U.S. relationship in the foreseeable future.

The general methodology adopted here allows for an understanding of contemporary inter-African politics as well as of the African states' foreign policy relationships with the major capitalist powers. The focus on decolonization highlights the dominant motivating force in the political, economic, psychological, and cultural life of the people of the region over the past twenty-seven years. The emphasis on bilateral dependency, on the other hand, points to the most important external constraint on Africa's foreign policy behavior. In short, the focus of the study is the contradictions between the forces of decolonization and those of international dependency. The persistence of this conjuncture is truly paradoxical and underlines the predicament of African independence.

Organization and Sources

This book is organized, for analytical and substantive purposes, into four primary subperiods: 1960–1966, 1967–1976, 1977–1979, 1980–1983. These periods correspond in turn to the administrative tenures of four regimes in Nigeria as well as to variations in the political economy. This manner of periodization permits one to evaluate, conveniently, the structure of the bilateral relations (with indications of changes and continuities) under each regime and to relate the existing conditions to the corresponding pattern of Nigeria-U.S. relations at the regional level.

Major conflicts in the decolonization process provide a framework for assessing the prevailing patterns of Nigerian-U.S. political-diplomatic interactions. Treated as case studies, these conflicts include the Congo and Angola crises, the assassination of Sylvanus Olympio and the Nigeria-Ghana conflict, the Rhodesian conflict and United Nations sanctions, the Shaba incidents, Zimbabwe's independence settlement, and the Libyan problem. These cases embrace the spectrum of the conflict dimension of African decolonization between 1960 and 1983. Their selection is justified in that the different interests and objectives of Nigeria and the United States in Africa, as well as the essential character of their relations, are apt to be far more illuminated in the course of regional conflicts than in routine circumstances. Examining the actions of the two entities in these contexts should, it was considered, yield more conclusive results relative to the overall object of the study.

In Chapter 9 some remarks are made regarding the initial phase of the policy direction of the new military administration in Nigeria, which came to power in January 1984 at about the time this work was being completed. This is done within the process of recapitulating the central proposition of the study. Conclusions are also drawn about the future trends in Nigerian-U.S. relations.

Much of the data employed in this study was generated from primary sources that had not previously been available to researchers. For instance, official U.S. State Department memoranda, diplomatic dispatches, telegrams, and private files of former top government officials were extensively relied on for the analysis of the crucial first period. Many of these documents were made available by the timely declassification of the Kennedy Presidential Files and the State Department files of G. Mennen Williams (assistant secretary of state for African affairs under U.S. presidents John Kennedy and Lyndon Johnson). Other primary sources utilized for this period included records of parliamentary proceedings in Nigeria, U.S. congressional records, and private interviews conducted in Nigeria.

For the second, third, and fourth periods, primary data were drawn from extensive interviews with key officials in Lagos and Washington; the data were then joined with materials obtained directly from the U.S. State Department (under the Freedom of Information Act) and Nigerian government publications, as well as from press reports and statistical journals in both countries. Naturally the foregoing sources were supplemented by secondary commentaries in appropriate academic texts and journals.

Notes

The author acknowledges the benefit of information derived from a number of previous studies on some aspects of Nigeria-U.S. relations. These include Okoro

M. Ojiaku, "The Impact of American Academic Tradition on the Development of Higher Education in Eastern Nigeria" (Ph.D. Dissertation, University of California, Berkeley, 1968); Levi A. Nwachukwu, "U.S./Nigeria: An Analysis of U.S. Involvement in Nigeria/Biafra War of 1967–1970" (Ph.D. Dissertation, Michigan State University, Flint, 1975); George Obiozor, "The Development of Nigeria–United States Diplomacy—1960–1975" (Ph.D. Dissertation, Columbia University, New York, 1976).

1. Already in this period, U.S. missionary organizations were operating several hundred educational institutions in Nigeria. And before 1960, about 258 Nigerian students were enrolled in U.S. higher educational institutions.

2. Babalola Cole, "Cocoa Politics: Insights from the 'Pool' Crisis," *International Studies Notes of the International Studies Association* 8(2) (Summer 1981): 20–24.

3. Obiozor, "The Development of Nigeria-United States Diplomacy," pp. 48–50; also *U.S. Treaties in Force*, Office of the Legal Adviser, Department of State, Publication No. 8755, p. 186.

4. Senate Joint Resolution 183, August 27, 1954, cited in Arthur M. Schlesinger, Jr., *The Dynamics of Power: Documentary History of U.S. Foreign Policy 1945–1973* (New York: Chelsea House Publishers, 1973), Vol. 5, p. 739.

5. Gordon Bortolin, "U.S. Economic Interests in Africa: Investment, Trade, and Raw Materials," in Jennifer S. Whitaker, ed., *Africa and the United States: Vital Interests* (New York: New York University Press, 1978), pp. 30–32.

6. In 1912, Washington, for example, organized an international conference in the United States to consider what contributions Americans could make in this regard. The Phelps-Stokes Educational Commission on Africa, earlier cited, was one outcome of this conference. See Obiozor, "The Development of Nigerian–United States Diplomacy," p. 47.

7. Dr. Azikiwe, for example, returned to Africa in the early 1930s, imbued with the spirit of the American revolution, to lead the struggle for Nigeria's independence; later, as premier of the Eastern Region of Nigeria, he founded the University of Nigeria in Nsukka based on American tradition.

8. See note 1, Chapter 1.

9. The origin of Anglo-American cooperation on African decolonization issues, which is discussed in Chapter 2, can be traced to the collaboration of the United States and the United Kingdom in the disposition of the Italian colonies—Libya, Italian Somaliland, and Eritrea—between 1948 and 1949. See the various memoranda and diplomatic exchanges on "Proposals Regarding the Italian Colonies Question," State Department Files, Record Group 59, National Archives, Washington, D.C.

10. The term *regional state* is used in reference to those states in the developing regions of the world system that by virtue of their geographic dimension, population, and relative economic and military potentials usually perceive themselves and are so perceived by others as future leading powers in their regions of location. Other examples are Brazil in South America, India in South Asia, Indonesia in Southeast Asia, and Iran in the Gulf region. Nigerian policymakers and foreign policy public share this conception of their country's

position in sub-Saharan Africa; this role conception has served, since 1960, as a conscious determinant of Nigeria's regional relationship with the superpowers. See also Bassey Ate, "The Presence of France in West-Central Africa as a Fundamental Problem to Nigeria," *Millennium* 12(2) (Summer 1983), especially pp. 110–112.

1

Decolonization in African Politics: The Opening Phase

That decolonization has been the most profound political reality in Africa since the end of World War II is a fact hardly in dispute.[1] One can delineate two essential definitions of decolonization—one juridical, the other more substantive. In its juridical sense, decolonization denotes the transfer of sovereign political authority from the colonial rulers to indigenous nationalist leaders in conformity with United Nations rulings, most precisely stipulated in Resolution 1514 (XV), December 14, 1960, of the General Assembly.[2] Within the legal frame of the UN Charter, decolonization translates into the concrete exercise of the rights of colonized peoples to self-determination and independence. The satisfying criterion of this definition appears to be the relinquishing of formal, sovereign jurisdiction over colonial territories.

On the more substantive level, decolonization entails an awesome effort toward transformation of the political, economic, social, and psychological dimensions of the existing power relationships between the colonizing nations and the colonized peoples. This definition does not, by any means, presume a complete break in relations after independence between the former rulers and the ruled. The necessity of the power transformation follows from the very nature of the original colonial relationship. Even if we accept that colonization, according to one observer, entails only "the political control of underdeveloped people whose social and economic life is directed by the dominant power,"[3] then a fundamental change in this mode of relationship in all the crucial dimensions—in order to restore effective power of control to the people of the colonized society—becomes the basic object of decolonization. Put more concisely, decolonization involves the retrenchment of the control structures of the colonial system and the progressive development of autonomous systems of power in the new sovereign regions.[4] Consequently, decolonization should, if effective, result in wider decisionmaking freedom from foreign constraints for authorities of the independent states.

How can this desirable outcome materialize in practice? As is shown in this and the subsequent chapters, the process of decolonization has, as a consequence of contradictory and practical realities, been distorted and indeed confounding in its actual historical movement. The two definitions of decolonization are stressed at the outset because they were, in varying degrees, reflected in the conflicting conceptions and policies toward regional decolonization espoused by groups of independent African states and by nationalist movements in dependent territories, particularly between 1960 and 1974, and toward such ancillary issues as Pan-African unity and apartheid racism.

In this chapter, an attempt is made to identify, in broad outlines, the sources of this conflict in conceptions and policies and the effect of these differences on regional political relations, foreign policy alignments, and the collective commitment to terminate colonialism. The aim is twofold: to provide a conceptual clarification of the phenomenon of decolonization and to further develop the framework of analysis for the study.

Conceptions of African Decolonization

There were, broadly speaking, three conceptions of decolonization discernible in the pronouncements and actions of African governments and nationalist (liberation) movements in the first decade of the independence struggle. These can be identified as the *conservative*, *power*, and *people's* conceptions.

The Conservative Conception

The hallmark of the conservative (referred to as "moderate" by some Western analysts) conception in the political sphere is the implicit acceptance that an evolutionary or orderly transfer of sovereign authority from the colonial power to a national leadership is desirable. This means, in practice, the avoidance of intractable violence if possible as a catalyst to achieving independence. Advocates of the conservative conception prefer that the method of transition from colonial to national self-rule be instead one of constructive bargaining between colonial interests and a nationalist party or parties. Built into the bargaining would be political assets that the nationalist elites hope to harness after independence to protect their vital state interests.

Economically, conservative decolonization eschews radical nationalistic policies, preferring a national development strategy with a strong role for foreign capital and personnel as the most effective means for maximizing economic growth and generating material benefits for the citizenry.[5] The tendency, consequently, is to adopt an economic doctrine that is closer to neo–laissez-faire than a socialistic-type doctrine. In the social sphere, and perhaps a result of their economic philosophy, advocates of this conception tend not to support the necessity for a basic or radical change in the colonial social structure. They would not, for example, support redistributing socioeconomic benefits to the majority of the population or giving greater control to this segment of the citizenry in the production process.

Whether this orientation stems from conviction on the part of the new leadership arising from a perception of objective constraints (having become locked irredeemably into the colonial system through the historical process of "integration in the capitalist world economy"[6]) or from a perception of the desired transformation as antithetical to the security and material interests of the ruling stratum is an intriguing subject of discourse. Of immediate interest here is that there exist entities in the African international system that subscribe to this conception of decolonization and that this has critical consequences for collective regional diplomacy on decolonization. Outstanding examples of such state entities in the period of reference include the Ivory Coast, Senegal, Nigeria, and Kenya.[7] Ultimately, the designation "conservative" derives from the reality that this conception is more sympathetic to the preservation of the colonial status quo than the other conceptions. Even after independence, proponents of the conservative conception continue to extract material and political sustenance from the excolonialists in order to consolidate their position within the evolving regional system. This can also be regarded as the classical mode of African decolonization and, in general, accords more with the juridical definition of decolonization. The conservative conception, in essence, represents the firing target for critics who deny the claim of African decolonization and view Africa's post-independence relations with Western Europe and the United States in terms of neocolonialism and dependency.[8]

The Power Conception

The power conception of decolonization shares an essential tenet with the second definition—the requirement of a fundamental transition to independence—but it also has distinguishing characteristics. It proposes power transformation not within a single (balkanized) colonial territory but at a continental level. Under this conception, rapid decolonization is desired for the entire continent; but more than that, decolonization is sought within a framework of a single continental political entity. Above all, power proponents fervently regard the ultimate purpose of African independence to be the radical development and consolidation of a regional power capacity vis-à-vis forces in the global system.

The grand vision of proponents of the power conception is to transform the African continent immediately from a territorial jigsaw puzzle to a viable, autonomous, regional power colossus. Here, power is desired not in a Morgenthauan sense, as an end in itself, but as a weapon to bargain more effectively with other agglomerative centers of power in the world system, including nongovernmental economic organizations. In this view, contemporary Africa's material and political weakness in the world is the result of "balkanized sovereignty," which permits exploitation by imperialist and neocolonist forces. Salvation lies in a swift decolonization and amalgamation of the fragmented parts. The feasibility of attaining this political amalgamation is seen as a matter that fate would decide in due course.

In conventional analyses of inter-African diplomacy it is common to categorize this conception of decolonization as radical anticolonialism/ Pan-Africanism. Its proponents in the period 1960–1966 include Ghana, Guinea, Mali, Tanzania, Algeria, and the United Arab Republic (Egypt).[9] However, Kwame Nkrumah's (and thus Ghana's) idea of Pan-Africanism and its purpose had very early deviated, after the Fifth Pan-Africanist Congress, held in Manchester in 1945,[10] from the essentially sentimental, "Pan-Negro" concern of the early Pan-African movement, although with the continued blessing of two of its foremost pioneers, W.E.B. Du Bois and George Padmore. After leaving England for West Africa in 1947 Nkrumah declared that his mission was to fight for the independence of Ghana but only, in his words, as a "starting-off point" to secure the more herculean task of total African independence and political unity.[11] On the African continent Nkrumah's conception diverged sharply from the functionalist approach preferred by the conservative conceptionists. The Pan-Africanism that he propagated throughout his political life was distinctly power-oriented in the most operational sense. Professor Ali Mazrui agrees with what is here regarded as the basic Nkrumahist goal in advocating African unity. He wrote, "The ultimate inspiration behind Pan-Africanism is a desire to see Africa become powerful in the world. . . . An African determination to become a giant in its own right is the method prescribed by Pan-Africanism."[12]

Quite predictably, Nkrumah's conception of decolonization in terms of a radical transformation of the colonial power structure led him to a head-on collision with at least five other factions in this epic African development: (1) those colonial powers who had by 1960 accepted the principle of independence (Great Britain; France, to a large extent; and

Belgium); (2) Portugal, the only country in the European imperial system in Africa that (until 1974) denounced the concept of sovereignty for its colonial holdings (from the African perspective, and as the UN General Assembly and Security Council acknowledged in 1966 and 1970, respectively, South Africa—in regard to Namibia—also falls into this category); (3) the colonial settlers in the dependent territories such as Kenya before 1963, the former Southern Rhodesia, and Namibia; (4) the two superpowers, the United States and the Soviet Union, which had no history of colonialism in Africa but which, nevertheless, had emerged after 1945 as the dominant centers of the global power systems; and (5) the conservative (African) conceptionists, who constituted a formidable segment of actors in the regional political scene.

It seems clear, in hindsight, that Nkrumah's contribution to radical African nationalism has little to do with a belief in Marxist-Leninist socialism. His public espousal and devotion to this principle was at best "theoretical"[13] or instrumental, in order to raise what he thought to be the pallid consciousness of Africans about the need for a continental power transformation. At core, he was an advocate and admirer of immense power, as attested to by his internal and external policies; his burning desire was to redeem Africa's modern history by seizing the opportunity offered through the resurgence of independence to build a more secure collective regional power entity able to deal with the outside world in terms of power interdependence instead of continued dependence. As for the worth of this vision in the context of contemporary Africa, it is at the moment enough to, on the one hand, echo the words of Basil Davidson, one of Nkrumah's critical admirers: "History will have much to say about Nkrumah in the calm judgment of the future."[14] On the other hand, according to Davidson, Nkrumah's "sense of urgency far outstripped the times in which he lived."[15]

The People's Conception

Advocates of the third conception of decolonization, the people's conception, increasingly seem to question some of the fundamental precepts of the other two conceptions. They take issue with the type of classical transition that results from peaceful bargaining between colonial authorities and nationalist elites and that, in the words of Gary Wasserman, "represents the adaptive, cooptive, preemptive process of integrating a potentially disruptive nationalist party into the structures and requisites of the colonial political economy."[16] To them, such a transition would perpetuate the colonial socioeconomic value order, which they considered to be obstructive to Africa's material progress, and therefore would ensure continuance of Africa's historical situation of dependence. According to the people's conceptionists, decolonization should engender a "violent" mass involvement in which the basic productive system and sociopolitical structures are overhauled. In the now famous aphorism of their late intellectual inspirator, Frantz Fanon, success of decolonization requires that "the whole social structure [be] changed from the bottom up."[17] Decolonization, according to Fanon, is the "complete calling into question of the colonial situation,"[18] and this, in his view, cannot be achieved through the preemptive processes of compromise by peaceful bargaining, but only by thorough cleansing through a purposeful revolution.

Beyond what may seem to be an unrestrained adulation of Fanonian violence, the most creative requisite of this conception of decolonization is its unyielding demand that postcolonial development strategy be "people-oriented," not prescribed merely by the material needs of the new elites. As Davidson explains, development strategy in the context of true decolonization should place people at the center of its priorities, unlike the colonial concept of development, which he termed *elitist.* Further, the mass of the people should be involved in defining and deciding their needs, as well as in implementing those needs.[19] That this concept derives some of its assumptions and perceptions of social reality from the Marxist-Leninist postulates is obvious. This, however, is secondary to the conception's contribution of stressing the centrality of people in the development strategy. Advocates of this conception, quite naturally, support the need for rapid decolonization and presumably might also sympathize with the Nkrumahist power idea of regional political unification, provided these would be accompanied by the kind of internal (fundamental) social restructuring that is their primary concern. Says Amilcar Cabral, "We are for African unity, but we are for African unity in favour of the African peoples. We consider unity to be a means, not an end."[20] For Cabral the quest for independence becomes meaningless if the mass of the people are not involved in a real sense in the struggle and if independence does not bring about complete "identification with the hopes of the masses of the people."

In the 1960s this conception found a natural fertile ground—in both articulation and practice—in territories ruled by Portugal and France (the latter in regard to Algeria), powers that had proved most recalcitrant in coming to quick terms with the insurgents.[21] These environments, as in Guinea-Bissau, offered ample opportunity for the insurgents to systematically inculcate what they considered progressive, noncolonial values, those required to create a new society, among the largely traditional population as well as the partially modernized strata (e.g., the semi-bourgeoisie).

The proponents of the people's conception are persistent critics of Africa's continued structural ties to the Western political economy and, hence, of the strategy referred to as "growth without development," which they tend intuitively to link to the prevalence of this relationship. They are prone to be suspect of the de facto interests and influence of former colonial powers and of the United States in Africa and to see in the concentration of economic relations between African states and these more powerful Western countries a kind of neocolonial intrigue designed to keep Africa perpetually tied to the West. A final note on this conception is that some of its tenets have, since the mid-1960s, attracted more intellectual (or perhaps emotional) sympathy even among segments of the privileged social strata as a result of the frustrating performance of African states in the field of economic and social development after more than two decades of political independence.[22]

Decolonization and Regional Alignments: Internal and Global Dimensions

What was the implication of the conflicting conceptions of decolonization at the level of collective action against colonialism and related regional issues? Clearly, the highly charged atmosphere of African politics on decolonization was both a consequence and cause of basic differences in conceptual orientation, and hence practices, of regional entities. For example, during the first two crises of African decolonization—the Algerian and Congo crises—it became clear that the inherent contradictions between the conservative and power conceptionists posed a critical obstacle to a concerted mediation effort. The antagonisms provoked by this failure not only resulted, by the middle of 1961, in the formation of two broad rival regional alliances—the Casablanca and Monrovia groups—but it also helped to intensify and prolong those crises.[23]

Similarly, the conservative and power conceptionists attached fundamentally different purposes to Pan-Africanism, which involved the search for the form of African unity that would serve as a bulwark of regional strength and effective independence. To the conservatives, the approach to unity should be through functionalist cooperation between equal sovereign national partners. This meant, in effect, the building of regional, functionalist institutions for use in strengthening the parochial interests of regimes and powerful groups within each national frontier. Pan-African cooperation on this basis, with its emphasis on equality of national participation, would be an immediate device for enhancing the legitimacy of sovereignty within inherited colonial boundaries—a method that, as earlier indicated, power advocates opposed in both theory and practice. A functionalist approach to unity, in the view of the power group, meant, in essence, a fragmentation or decentralization, certainly not a consolidation, of regional power because each sovereign entity would exercise a veto over what action could or could not be taken on matters of interest to the entire region. Indeed this was to remain the reality of intraregional cooperation even after the amorphous compromise struck between the divergent camps under the umbrella of the Organization of African Unity (OAU) in May 1963. The dissatisfaction experienced to date with the structure and actions of the OAU, particularly with regard to its approach to the issue of unity, has led some Africanists to believe that the establishment of the organization under its existing charter constituted "an outright rejection of African unity."[24]

For the power conceptionists, political union was the heart of African unity. After political union was achieved, a set of functionalist arrangements could be instituted in the pattern of a federation. Note that this was in line with Nkrumah's often quoted adage: "Seek ye first the political Kingdom." To seek African unity through functionalist arrangements involving sovereign entities—as proposed by the conservatives—would mean, according to the power advocates, allowing time for new centers of interest within each state to expand and consolidate. This would make the idea of continental political unity in the future highly improbable. A major effort was made through the Lagos Conference of All Independent African States, held January 25–30, 1962, to smooth out the differences between the two groups on the issue of unity. The effort failed partly because members of the Casablanca group boycotted the meeting.[25] At the subsequent Addis Ababa Conference in May 1963, Nkrumah was isolated and the conservative conception and norms prevailed and became entrenched in the OAU Charter.[26]

But if Ghana could not successfully sell its vision of decolonization to the majority of African governments through persuasion or legal means, it was determined to adopt nonlegitimate methods to press its case. One such controversial technique was political subversion of those states considered here to be conservative because they presented the most reactionary obstacles. Ghana attempted to use sympathetic opposition elements in those states to replace the existing neocolonialist regimes, thereby reaping the advantage of projecting its mode of decolonization in an African diplomatic environment of more independent-minded states. One immediate result was intensified hostility between Ghana and its West African neighbors, disrupting collective efforts to solve crucial regional issues even at the OAU level.

The setting assessed above leads to the following conclusion: The contradictory conceptions of decolonization—shaped by conflicting images of regional priorities, opposing group interests within national boundaries, different views of how postcolonial state structures should be organized, incompatible personal ambitions of the new "sovereign" statesmen, and the sheer novelty of operating an interstate system of near-equal powers—helped transform the necessity for concerted action into personal and political competition within the regional system in a most inchoate manner. Regional (collective) diplomacy over decolonization thus became enmeshed in traditional diplomacy, involving competing alliances and intrigues and maneuvers to advance parochial interests and belief systems over those of rivals.[27]

In a formal sense, colonial disengagement involves direct negotiation and bargaining exclusively between officials of the metropolitan entity and nationalist elites. But decolonization as a process of transforming the complex system of colonial relationships is amenable, to an important extent, to influences emanating from global centers apart from the colonial metropoles. The United States and the Soviet Union are two such centers.[28] But in addition to the metropolitan countries and the two superpowers, transnational business corporations constitute another global force whose impact on African decolonization has been crucial. In the period under review, these extraregional forces acted, through their mediation of the regional political and economic processes, to strengthen the diverse conceptions and practices of the African actors on decolonization. The following section gives an indication of the general pattern of the extraregional interaction in the overall process.[29]

Extraregional Forces in Decolonization

It is clear, in hindsight, that the implementation of the UN mandate on decolonization did not entail, for the metropolitan countries, the dismantling of all imperial structures, nor did it envisage outright disengagement from acquired holdings in the old colonies. The decisions of Great Britain, for example, to enter into military pacts with the nationalist regimes of Nigeria and Kenya and of France to do the same with Gabon, Cameroon, the Ivory Coast, and other countries were proof of the intent to continue the colonial marriage. By dominating and influencing the new state institutions of these emerging countries, whether in the educational, financial, economic, or political sectors, Great Britain and France used less overt means to entrench and expand their former interests.

From the position of the metropolitan countries, therefore, the implications of the power and people's conceptions of decolonization were unacceptable. For instance, Ghana's concept of a monolithic continental entity posed a potential problem not only to the metropolitan countries but also to the regional conservatives. To the former, it meant at the very least the prospect of bargaining for future concessions with a more assertive, psychologically less pliant political entity. To the latter, one main disadvantage would be a fragmentation of the power assets and privileges secured from the departing colonialists. Thus the two entities now shared common interests that would be threatened should Ghana's radical decolonization become effected. Similarly, to the colonial powers and the large business companies associated with their economies, the decolonization ideas of the people's conceptionists were self-destructive. The areas of conflict were the people's conceptionists' radical opposition to the pro-capitalist system of economic production and class exploitation and their advocacy of greater public control of resources and mass involvement in economic decisions. The contradiction was between militant socialism and dominant capitalism.

The Role of Transnational Corporations. Transnational corporations have clearly become a vital agent of African decolonization (or neocolonialism) in at least three respects: They are now more important than direct official channels in the exchange of economic resources between African countries and the world economy; they serve as the conduit through which transnational class linkages between ruling African elites and dominant social strata in the former metropoles are maintained and reinforced; and they participate internally, sometimes directly, in the political processes in African countries, using their superior resources to influence the pattern of power and authority conducive to their operations.[30] It can be said that the confluence of interests and goals of the metropolitan countries, transnational corporations, and postcolonial conservative African elements foments an alignment among them, at both the bilateral and the regional diplomatic levels. It is also noteworthy that this form of internal-external interaction evidently has tended to entrench—regardless of any immediate growth value to the local economies and other short-run advantages for the regimes in power—the colonial pattern of Africa's relationship to the world political economy. It is basically for this reason that it became the object of severe attack by proponents of the power and people's conceptions.

The Role of the United States. The United States, it is often charged by those African and foreign observers who upheld Ghana's power conception of decolonization, was chiefly responsible for diverting "incipient African nationalism from the path of its historical development into sterile enclaves of neo-colonialism."[31] According to such critics, although the United States might be credited with prodding the majority of the colonial powers to accept the wisdom of early decolonization for their imperial territories, it was through U.S. connivance that African independence was subsequently doctored in a manner that left the emergent nations still structurally tied to the former metropoles. The

United States, it was said, used its overwhelming material affluence to entice conservative African groups to oppose regional unity because this mode of decolonization was judged to be too radical (or potentially destabilizing) vis-à-vis Western resource and strategic interests and the ideological competition with the Soviet system.

A serious flaw in this contention is the implicit attempt to assign a passive role to the African actors. A one-sided explanation based on external determinacy, which portrays the African elites merely as straws in the wind, lacking any autonomous capacity to judge what is in their self-interest, is without merit. Surely, it could be argued that the foreign strategy the elites adopted must have been grounded in their interpretation of the objective realities confronting them. Their immediate concern was how to manipulate those realities to advance their interests. The conservative conceptionists, for instance, condoned the penetration of the regional decisionmaking processes by external forces such as those linked to the United States (and vehemently opposed the countervailing efforts of the Soviet Union) because in their judgment these actions contributed to the enhancement of their interests. If this strategy later proves to be faulty and earlier policies found to be retrogressive in advancing African independence and real development, the villains are as much the responsible African elites as their foreign "manipulators."

The United States appeared to have exhibited genuine concern between 1941 and 1945 in ending Western European colonialism in Africa and other world regions. Evidence of U.S. interest is demonstrated not only by President Franklin Roosevelt's insistence that the broad problem of alien rule be addressed in the Atlantic Charter (1941), but more significantly by Roosevelt's subsequent articulation in a message to Congress on February 23, 1942, that the issues addressed by the charter included "self-determination of nations and peoples" worldwide, not just in enemy-occupied territories—a view held by the colonial powers.[32] By this, one is not suggesting that the United States was historically immune from the colonial impulses that underlay West European expansion in Africa and elsewhere in the nineteenth century. In occupying Spanish possessions, especially in the Pacific, and in exercising colonial overlordship, even if reluctantly, in the Philippines, the United States confirmed its disposition, earlier demonstrated in North America, for imperial expansion and control.

However, we are talking about a different period in international relations in which the United States was beginning to feel the weight of a more colossal responsibility—that of managing, along with the Soviet Union, the new balance of forces in a nuclearized world system in order to contain the danger of total destruction. After 1945, the U.S. commitment to decolonization under Roosevelt did not end; it was reformed: Henceforth, a different orientation on decolonization became instituted. The new orientation, in its specific African focus, accorded priority to preserving the vital interests of U.S. European NATO allies in the colonies; to preventing Soviet control of valuable resources, pivotal territories, and allegiance of people in Africa;[33] and to projecting the interests of the U.S. economy and U.S. corporations in trade, direct investments, and access to industrial raw materials in areas that in the past had remained exclusive reserves of the colonial powers. These considerations and their perception by policymakers in Washington inevitably predisposed the U.S. government under presidents Kennedy and Johnson (as well as subsequent administrations) toward courting and sustaining (materially and politically) those African entities of conservative persuasion—i.e., those that were also championed by the former metropoles and their associated business organizations. U.S. interaction with the regional advocates of the two transformative conceptions remained, at base, fitful and conflictual throughout the period. Proponents of these latter conceptions regarded the United States not as a neutral broker but as the guiding force behind a Western resolve to resist fundamental decolonization.

The Role of the Soviet Union. The general objective of the Soviet Union in Africa after 1945 was to capitalize upon the momentum of the decolonization movement as part of its strategy to redress the global balance of forces, which was still very much against the socialist system the USSR championed. When the imperial subjects in Africa and Asia revolted after the war against colonial rule and sought to reassert their independence, they found that they could draw inspiration and support from the Soviet Union. There was, to some extent, a spiritual affinity between the Bolshevik Communist revolution of October 1917 in the USSR and the later liberation struggles in the African and Asian colonies. Lenin and his comrades saw the institution of the Russian socialist system as the start of the colonial crisis. Even before the revolution was established, Lenin had taken a clear stand on decolonization. He wrote in May 1917 that Great Britain "must relinquish, immediately and unconditionally, not only the territories she has seized from others . . . , but all her own colonies as well."[34] Indeed one cannot doubt that the Russian socialist experiment had an infectious hold on certain groups of African nationalists in the formulation of their strategies for gaining independence and for postcolonial socioeconomic development.

When, however, we consider the colonial situation following World War II, we must view the role and attitude of the Soviet Union in the context of its new position in the emerging global scheme (as manifested in the period of the cold war). The anticolonialism of the Kremlin in the post-1945 era, coated as it was by ideological slogans, had a transparent design—to create opportunities for intrusion of Soviet in- fluence and power in the excolonies. And one must quickly stress that the reality of the new Soviet power has remained thus far a formidable political weapon in the ongoing process of decolonization in Africa.

In the strategic rationalization of the Soviets, decolonization would, at the very least, sharply increase the costs to the West of continued attempts to control the material resources, military bases, and populations in colonial territories. Better still, these assets could be denied the West, if the emergent nations insisted on their rights to exercise complete independence of the former colonial powers. Either possibility would result in eroding Western predominance and augmenting the Soviet presence. But the most desirable outcome of decolonization for Soviet purposes was the possibility that some of the new nations (perhaps emerging as a result of armed struggle) would adopt the Marxist-Leninist system of socioeconomic development. This would not only ensure an increase in the ranks of fraternal socialist states worldwide, but would serve as a natural vehicle for the expansion of the Soviet Union's influence. Through decolonization, the Soviet Union saw the likelihood of fulfilling its long-range aim to supplant Western control over the strategic assets of territories such as southern Africa.

In a substantial sense, these prospective advantages could explain the ardent interest of the USSR in backing the attempts of the Afro- Asian states at the United Nations to terminate colonial rule.[35] In Africa, both the power and people's conceptionists relied on the tactical, though cautious, support of the Soviet Union. In the short run at least, there appeared to be a convergence in the decolonization objectives of the Soviet Union and these two factions in the African struggle.

The Role of China. Analysts generally accept that the modest but strident role of the People's Republic of China (PRC) in African de- colonization (starting from 1960) resulted in part from the Sino-Soviet conflict. No one can deny this as an explanatory factor—one symptom of the ensuing rivalry between the two Communist powers was the comparative degree and type of support given by each to the anticolonial movement. The Chinese had charged by this period that the USSR had become a status quo global power concerned with peaceful coexistence with the Western imperialists and that it had consequently relented its support of world revolution. (One is by no means suggesting that this was the only or even the chief cause of their conflict.)[36] In Africa, the two powers competed in demonstrating their material and ideological interest in rapid decolonization. The early Chinese role was to provide aid to radical liberation groups operating mostly in territories engaged in armed revolts for independence, for example, the National Liberation Front (FLN) in Algeria and the Front for the Liberation of Mozambique

(FRELIMO). Chinese assistance was also extended to people's-oriented sovereign entities, notably Tanzania. The PRC naturally preferred to align, in this period, with the proponents of people's decolonization in the African regional system. Thus, Chou En-lai's caustic declaration, "Africa is ripe for revolution," during his 1963 tour of the continent had practical significance mainly for this class of conceptionists.

Nigeria and African Decolonization

Nigeria's policymakers in the period 1960–1966 found the management of a conservative leadership on African decolonization, most distinctly marked by an advocacy of an orderly, nontransformative transition to independence, to be subjected at home to incessant stresses. The great majority of the foreign policy public felt that the regional status of Nigeria, with its "manifest destiny" content, required its government to pursue an aggressive, mobilizing leadership in the struggle to retrench colonialism, at least in the Nkrumahist "power" sense.[37]

An early indication of the public's preference was demonstrated in 1961. In August of that year, all three hundred delegates to the All-Nigeria People's Conference pressed, among other resolutions, "that Nigeria [should] make an unequivocal declaration in favor of the political union of African states." Though they agreed with the government that Nigeria should initiate concrete cooperative arrangements in the fields of economics, science, culture, and so forth, with its African neighbors, they nevertheless agreed with Ghana that these links should be forged within a framework of an African political union.[38] However, from the more practical point of view of the ruling federal regime, adopting such a course on decolonization was clearly at variance with a number of realities, among which were the structure of the country's socioeconomic and political systems (which derived from Nigeria's own pattern of decolonization, described in Chapter 2); the interests—security, political, and financial—of conservative and powerful elements in the federal coalition; and, above all, the necessity to secure Anglo-American support (financial, political, and military) in the regime's perennial contest with domestic and regional forces of opposition. Nigeria's leadership could not operate in a material vacuum; it had to contend with these imperatives.

The country's bilateral relationships with the United States and Great Britain constituted critical external factors in the conceptualization and pursuit of its decolonization policy in the regional context. The Balewa government had to balance the necessity of external dependence in the realization of crucial state interests against the virtue of domestic pressures regarding the desirability of a mobilizing, radical anticolonial regional posture that would threaten Anglo-American interests and objectives in

Africa. The two Anglo-Saxon powers, it should be recalled, were in this period Nigeria's dominant foreign economic partners in the areas of capital aid, technical assistance, private investment, and trade.[39] The United States, as indicated in the Introduction, had by 1963 emerged as the most important external source of financial aid and high-level technical personnel in connection with the implementation of the first national development plan. The United States also complemented the United Kingdom in its political and diplomatic support of the Balewa regime's regional policy and domestic security interests.

What implication Nigeria's international dependency would have on its foreign policy was of interest to critical observers of the Nigerian scene even at this early period. Analysts generally contended that Nigeria's exclusive economic and political dependence on the Western powers—particularly the United States and Great Britain—imposed prohibitive effects on its freedom of action in foreign affairs.[40] Critics of the Nigerian policy noted that the interplay of such ties made it impossible for the national government to pursue the country's national interests and declared policy of nonalignment.[41] The following composite statement is representative of the views of these critics:

> Sir Abubakar [the country's first prime minister] throughout his tenure of office stuck to the bankrupt policy of seeking and accepting capital investment and economic aid only from [the] Western powers. [Consequently] apart from re-asserting a special friendship with the Anglo-American bloc and concluding a defence treaty with Britain, the fashioners of Nigerian foreign policy displayed a deep sense of sympathy for, and understanding of, the Western powers' international positions. [Thus] the government's all-out attempt to maintain close and increasing economic relations with the West contradicted and undermined Nigeria's foreign policy of non-alignment.[42]

Given the existing cold war environment of international relations, this view about Nigerian policy had as its premise, and was reinforced by, two underlying assumptions. One was that there existed a nexus of U.S.-British political-security interests in Africa. The second was that as a result of its economic and political dependence on this Anglo-American force, Nigeria was compelled to identify and comply with Western policy positions in Africa, thereby jeopardizing its national as well as collective African interests. The critics were arguing, in essence, that within a structure of vastly unequal economic and political relationships, Nigerian leaders could not conceive, much less sustain, an autonomous foreign policy directed at serving the country's best interests. Adopting the same general line of reasoning, Patrick McGowan and

Klaus-Peter Gottwald concluded that "African foreign policy, while adaptive, is more influenced by national attributes and linkage phenomena than the traditional emphasis on personalities and ideologies suggests."[43]

As pointed out earlier in this chapter, the practical challenge for the Balewa regime was how to contain the diverse pressures, both domestic and external, on the development of its foreign policy—that is, how to reconcile the basic conflict between carrying out its national responsibility in the regional decolonization movement and constraining external dependency without becoming seriously victimized by the inherent contradictions.

For this purpose, the regime sought to conduct its overall foreign policy relationship with the United States on two broad tactical planes. To convince domestic critics that its regional leadership capacity was in no way hampered by the emerging structural ties to the United States, it attempted to pursue a calculated (not balanced) nonalignment position on cold war issues at the United Nations.[44] However, where its vital concerns were directly involved—for example, on issues of African security and decolonization—the regime strained to exercise its leadership through steadfast cooperation with the United States, be it at the UN or in African diplomatic councils.

A specific case underscored Nigeria's approach to decolonization in this period. In October 1961, the Nigerian foreign minister, Jaja Wachuku, submitted a draft resolution at the UN General Assembly that proposed December 1, 1970, as the terminal date for colonialism. Observers have tended to explain Wachuku's action as a reflection of his and Prime Minister Balewa's concern to avoid the chaotic transition experience of the Congo (Zaire). As Wachuku subsequently explained in defense of his proposal, following a barrage of harsh condemnation within the UN Africa Group and in Nigeria,[45] the period from 1961 to 1970 was needed for adequately training an indigenous leadership corps in the colonial territories before independence. But a more revealing explanation for Wachuku's action could be linked to an understanding reached earlier the same year between him, U.S., and British officials. In that agreement, the Nigerian foreign minister formally committed his government to taking a temporizing position on African decolonization and indeed had pledged to mobilize other African states to act likewise if the colonial powers (especially Portugal) would publicly declare their acceptance of the principle of independence (or merely that of self-determination) as a future goal for their territories.[46] Although the idea of setting any timetable on decolonization, no matter how vaguely couched, was at the time unpalatable to the colonial nations (including Great Britain), the U.S. government was sympathetic to Wachuku's recommendation, specifically because it was considered far less radical than other proposals emerging from various Third World forums (e.g., the Belgrade Nonaligned Conference had proposed 1962 as the target date, and the All-Africa People's Conference in Accra in 1958 had proposed 1963).

Nigeria also demonstrated its basic attitude of permissiveness on decolonization through direct relations with Portugal. Despite the fact that the Portuguese had failed to concede to the minimal condition sought by Wachuku and instead proceeded to suppress, by armed measures, internal movements agitating for independence, the Balewa government permitted Portugal to operate a diplomatic post in Lagos from 1961 to 1965. What made this action even more puzzling was that a 1963 OAU resolution on decolonization pointedly forbade member states from maintaining any type of diplomatic links with Portugal because of its colonial policies. The Nigerian regime, a founder of the OAU, was willing to flout a canon of the organization because its more vital interests required policy harmonization with the United States. Portugal was, of course, a coveted NATO ally of the United States and had granted NATO base rights in the Azores. In conventional NATO thinking, Portugal was a crucial, even if costly, asset in southern Africa— an area of strategic and economic significance to the United States and its major allies. All this explained America's restrained criticism of Portuguese colonial policy, and Nigerian policymakers could not prudently ignore this reality.[47]

Synthesis: Decolonization and Dependency

The three conceptual models outlined above are designed to show how categories of African states attempted to rationalize, by means of ideas and actions, the outstanding contradictions of the postcolonial era. One may ask if it is relevant to categorize African states into three separate groups on the basis of certain exclusive characteristics, whereas, in fact, these states share common features of underdevelopment and dependence that are of decisive significance in their relations to the dominant capitalist world economy.[48] In reference to this, liberal academicians McGowan and Gottwald remarked that "within a context of powerlessness and dependence, character and ideas alone cannot overcome a passive-subordinate role in international affairs [for African states]."[49] According to Professor Claude Ake, African leaders in the postcolonial era have faced similar objective situations and, therefore, have thought and acted "in roughly the same way."[50] In Ake's opinion, any visible difference between "progressive" and "reactionary" states is more apparent than real.

Two comments will be made in response to this objection. First, this book affirms that external dependency is a formidable reality of the

African experience. The unfinished task for foreign policy scholars concerned with Africa, nonetheless, is to undertake systematic and properly focused studies of foreign policies of individual dependent states or categories of such states, with the aim of empirically determining the relative impact of the dependency relationship on the foreign policy dispositions of the governments and leaders concerned.[51] This, for example, would seem to be the proper approach toward verifying the contention that a dependency relationship leads to a subversion of the legitimate interests of a Third World country. From a foreign policy perspective, such an approach should yield insight into (1) how complex processes of foreign policy relationships between dominant and dependent states might be conditioned by the structure of bilateral dependency ties;[52] (2) what external interests elites of a dependent state might have and how these interests are conceived, advanced, or constrained by the dependency relationship; (3) the compelling interests of the dominant state both within the weaker entity and in its region of location; (4) variations in the modes of conflict and cooperation in the foreign policy relationships of dominant and dependent states over time; and (5) the potency of internal forces of the dependent state in shaping the patterns of bilateral dependency and, hence, foreign policy outputs. The present study attempts to respond to this need in the literature of the foreign policy of the African states by concentrating on the experience of one dependent but developing regional state with a superpower in the former's regional setting.

The second comment is that dependency, as significant as it is, depicts only one side of the contemporary experience for Africans. The other side of the equation is the persistence of the impetus toward true decolonization amid the prevailing crisis of political and economic development. The relevant question is not whether what is occurring in the continent is decolonization or dependency but rather what is the historical connection between decolonization and dependency? Real change is anticipated to emerge from the dynamics of the conflict between the two forces, for decolonization is a historical movement with deep currents whose endpoint is yet undetermined.[53]

The specific importance of the three conceptual models sketched in this chapter is that the differentiations noted corresponded to overt actions of, as well as ideas propounded by, the regional actors. Clearly there were empirical differences in the manner in which actors in the various groups reacted to such issues as the role of foreign private capital and personnel, foreign military bases, foreign intervention in regional conflicts, apartheid in South Africa, and regional political integration. These differences affected their relationships both with each other and with the major extraregional powers. Certainly the preferences and experiences of Ghana, Guinea, and Tanzania in this period were in contradistinction to those of Nigeria, the Ivory Coast, and Kenya.

The overall perspective of this study leads to the contention that the strategic essence of decolonization is a progressive transformation in the colonial power relationships involving Africa and the Western political economy. Decolonization is, at core, a power phenomenon with economic and political dimensions. The original colonial relationship with Western Europe was possible not by choice but through the imposition of political control using military coercion for the purpose of managing the economic exploitation of the colonial territories in the interest of the metropolitan economy and state. Thus, the critical factor in the establishment of this dominant-subordinate relationship was the unfavorable power differential between the African states and the European metropoles.

The previous analysis of conceptual interpretations points to the necessity of linking proposals of regional actions (either through multilateral organs like the OAU or the Economic Community of West African States [ECOWAS] or through unilateral effort) with the appropriate theoretical orientation in order to effectively pursue the substantive change. The question then is, which of the three conceptual approaches best qualifies as a guidepost of regional decolonization? What are the attributes of each? What are the short-falls? Quite clearly, proponents of the power perspective have addressed the dependency problem at the level of causation. To them, the objective basis of Africa's subordinate relationship to the West before and under colonial rule was the power imbalance magnified most glaringly by technological-economic underdevelopment and political fragmentation in Africa. Decolonization, in their view, provides opportunities for rectifying this traditional power imbalance against Africa.

Whereas the power proponents confront the strategic issue of power relationships, the conservative and people's conceptionists are basically concerned with tactics of survival and of insulation and equity, respectively. The conservative conceptionists argue for a policy of survival through continued deference and dependence; the people's conceptionists seek to evade historical constraints by advocating disengagement from the capitalist world system and by turning attention to issues of equity in the domestic economy and polity. Both approaches direct attention to the practical problems and basic conditions that need to be manipulated in order to achieve the central object, but they are misleading when posed as ends in themselves. A policy of mere survival within the system—as a long-term regional agenda—is retrogressive; it is a policy that is without virtue because it denies a regenerative capacity. The Ivory Coast or the Senegalese experience translated into a permanent regional model is untenable to postcolonial generations of Africans who yearn for fundamental changes. On the other hand, the people's conception approach, although its ethical objectives are crucially defensible and necessary, is impractical in its implicit demand for a disengagement from world capitalism. Socialist Africa, just as socialist Europe and China, cannot sever its links to the capitalist world economy, generally because capitalism has successfully integrated the economies of the world. It provides the only mechanism of economic exchange between all components of the world system. Marxist Angola and Mozambique, just as capitalist Kenya and Nigeria, know that they need the capitalist trading sytem and financial institutions, as well as services provided by transnational corporations, to maintain domestic economic viability and tangible growth. For all three conceptions, internal development cannot be engendered in total disregard of the forces in the external economy.

The inherent virtue of the proponents of power decolonization, it has been said, is their correct identification of the strategic issue. Their tactical recommendation, which centered on continental political unification, was flawed because it seemed monumentally idealistic considering the global and regional political situations of this period. But the basic goal of power transformation in the regional system can be pursued through alternative approaches that exclude a prior and divisive attempt at unifying the continent administratively.

In the post-1970 era, individual national entities are emerging that may be capable of acting as growth centers in mobilizing collective effort in the regional system. Whether these are referred to as regional states or subimperial states, they possess those requisite structural attributes that, by a process of concerted internal development coupled with pragmatic global alignments, could eventually be transformed into modern power assets through industrialization. Nigeria stands, in the context of sub-Saharan Africa, as a model of such a possibility. Ultimately this is the perspective that underpins the development of Nigeria-U.S. relations in Africa.

Notes

1. For an incisive account of the evolution and underlying sources of what has accurately been termed "one of the revolutions of the twentieth century," refer to the following: Immanuel Wallerstein, *Africa: The Politics of Independence* (New York: Vintage Books, 1961); Thomas L. Hodgkin, *Nationalism in Colonial Africa* (London: Oxford University Press, 1956); Basil Davidson, *Which Way Africa?* 3rd ed. (Harmondsworth, Middlesex, England: Penguin Books Ltd., 1971).

2. Yassin El-Ayouty, in *The United Nations and Decolonization* (The Hague: Martinus Nijhoff, 1971), offers an in-depth analysis of the struggle of Afro-Asia

to institutionalize decolonization, as a collective global responsibility, in the UN system. For a detailed and enlightening assessment of the workings of the major UN instrument for effecting decolonization—the 24 Committee—see James H. Mittelman, "Collective Decolonization and the U.N. Committee of 24," *The Journal of Modern African Studies* 14(1) (1976): 41–64.

3. T. R. Adam, *Modern Colonialism: Institutions and Policies* (Garden City, N.Y.: Doubleday and Company Inc., 1955), p. 3, quoted in El-Ayouty, *The United Nations and Decolonization*, p. 3.

4. In theory, the two definitions seem to be not mutually exclusive since the assumption of formal political authority is a prerequisite of transforming the effective power relationships in a postcolonial society. In fact, I. W. Zartman, in "Europe and Africa: Decolonization or Dependency," *Foreign Affairs* 54 (1976): 325–343, sees this as an actuality. However, in this analysis, one is impressed by the contrasting structural conditions that underly the two definitions and the consequent effect on social interaction among national groups and regional entities relative to important global forces.

5. Aristide R. Zolberg, "Political Development in the Ivory Coast Since Independence," in Philip Foster and Aristide R. Zolberg, eds., *Ghana and the Ivory Coast: Perspectives on Modernization* (Chicago: The University of Chicago Press, 1971), p. 27.

6. See, for example, Immanuel Wallerstein, "Dependence in an Interdependent World: The Limited Possibilities of Transformation Within the Capitalist World Economy," *African Studies Review* 17(1) (April 1974): 1–23. Wallerstein's thesis applies equally to the two definitions of decolonization noted above.

7. For analyses of the development problems of these countries, refer to the following: Colin Leys, *Underdevelopment in Kenya: The Political Economy of Neo-Colonialism* (Los Angeles: The University of California Press, 1975); Samir Amin, *Neo-Colonialism in West Africa* (Harmondsworth, Middlesex, England: Penguin Books, 1973); Garvin Williams, ed., *Nigeria: Economy and Society* (London: Rex Collings, 1976).

8. Refer to Zartman, "Europe and Africa."

9. Although all six states listed here were consistent in their support for immediate and unconditional decolonization, the same cannot be said of their attitude to the idea of a continental political union. On this, their support varied and was often ambiguous, if not self-serving. Guinea, for example, showed interest (as per the Ghana-Guinea-Mali Union) as a means of countering its isolation in the French-speaking African community; the UAR used continental political union more as a slogan for extending Egyptian influence into the sub-Saharan region; Algeria went along with the current because it sustained its image as a revolutionary regime; Nyerere can be said to have been a true Pan-Africanist of this genre until his disappointment with the East African Federation in 1963-1964, after which he turned inward. Of the six states, Nkrumah's Ghana was the most steadfast advocate, passionately unyielding in its defense of this conception, as discussed in the text. In this crusade, its true allies were the radical opposition elements in the conservative independent states.

10. The Fifth Pan-Africanist Congress was the last such assembly held outside the African continent.

11. Kwame Nkrumah, *Africa Must Unite* (New York: International Publishers, 1963). For the author's detailed economic defense of this conception, see *Neo-Colonialism: The Last Stage of Imperialism* (New York: International Publishers, 1965); also see R. H. Green and Ann Seidman, *Unity or Poverty: The Economics of Pan-Africanism* (Baltimore, Md.: Penguin Books, 1968), especially Part 3.

12. Ali Mazrui, *Towards a Pax Africana: A Study of Ideology and Ambition* (London: The Trininty Press, 1967), pp. 165–166.

13. For a trenchant critique, see Bob Fitch and Mary Oppenheimer, *Ghana: End of an Illusion* (New York: Monthly Review Press, 1966), especially Chapters 7 and 8.

14. Basil Davidson, *Black Star: A View of the Life and Times of Kwame Nkrumah* (New York: Praeger Publishers, 1974), p. 13.

15. Ibid., p. 187.

16. Gary Wasserman, "The Independence Bargain: Kenya, Europeans and the Land Issue: 1960–1962," *Journal of Commonwealth Political Studies* 11(2) (1973): 99.

17. Frantz Fanon, *The Wretched of the Earth* (New York: Grove Press Inc., 1963), p. 35.

18. Ibid., pp. 35–106.

19. Basil Davidson, *Can Africa Survive? Arguments Against Growth Without Development* (Boston: Little, Brown and Company, 1974), passim.

20. Amilcar Cabral, *Revolution in Guinea,* translated and edited by Richard Handyside (New York: Monthly Review Press, 1969), p. 80.

21. Most of these movements have since been transformed into ruling regimes, for example, Guinea-Bissau (under PAIGC), Mozambique (under FRELIMO), and Angola (under MPLA). Other independent territories that had earlier advanced this conception are Algeria, Tanzania, Guinea, Mali, Congo Brazzaville, and Zimbabwe. Of these states, Mozambique, Angola, and Congo Brazzaville have officially adopted the Marxist-Leninist ideology as their national system of development.

22. The distinction made here between the three conceptions departs from the conventional classification, which usually distinguishes between moderate (actually conservative) and radical on African colonial issues. It is my view that the classification "radicals" is inappropriate since there were two strains of radical actors (at least until 1966)—one concerned with unconditional decolonization and continental political unification, the other with revolutionary socioeconomic-political transformation of the colonial system as a corollary of decolonization. Nonetheless, it must be noted that the main struggle for political supremacy in the period of this study was waged between the conservative and power conceptionists as sovereign entities. The real impact of the people's proponents in regional politics was to be felt in the 1970s as the decolonization process intensified in southern Africa.

23. Immanuel Wallerstein, *Africa: The Politics of Unity* (New York: Vintage Books, 1967), particularly pp. 42–82; also refer to contrasting resolutions on the Congo and Algeria situations adopted by the Casablanca and Monrovia meetings of January 3–7, 1961, and May 8–12, 1961, respectively, in Colin

Legum, *Pan-Africanism: A Short Political Guide,* rev. ed. (New York: Praeger Publishers, 1965), pp. 209–210, 217.

24. See Bolaji Akinyemi, "Can the OAU Lead to African Unity?" *Afriscope* (Nigeria) (June 1971): 25–26.

25. The ostensible reason for the boycott was the failure to invite the provisoire de la Republique Algerienne (GPRA) to the conference due to pressure by the broad association of independent French-speaking states—the Union Africaine et Malagache (UAM). In truth, it was the irreconcilable character of the charters of the two alliances on a range of issues, particularly the Congo crisis and African decolonization in general, that frustrated the original purpose of the conference.

26. See "The Organization of African Unity (OAU)," in *Keesing's Research Report,* Vol. 6 (New York: Charles Scribner's Sons, 1972), pp. 1–6.

27. See I. William Zartman, "Africa as a Subordinate State System in International Relations," *International Organization* 31 (Summer 1967): 545–564, and W. Scott Thompson and Richard Bissell, "Legitimacy and Authority in the OAU," *African Studies Review* 15 (April 1972): 17–42.

28. In a more detailed manner, the following references depict the interests and role of these external actors: On the attitude of the colonial powers at the UN in the period 1945–1950, see A. B. Fox, "The United Nations and Colonial Development," *International Organization* 4(2) (May 1950), 199–218; also see El-Ayouty, *The United Nations and Decolonization.* On how multinational business corporations shape the decolonization transition and after, see Richard L. Sklar, *Corporate Power in an African State* (Berkeley: University of California Press, 1975), and Suzanne Cronge et al., *The Lonrho Connections: A Multinational and Its Politics in Africa* (Encino, Calif.: Dellwether Books, 1976). For a condensed view of the effect of cold war dynamics on the attitude of the superpowers on decolonization, see Inis L. Claude, Jr., *The Changing United Nations* (New York: Random House, 1967), pp. 49–72.

29. In order to understand more fully the ideological dynamics of Soviet-U.S. power competition in the liberation process in Asia and Africa in this period, it becomes of import to explain the mediating effect of China's policy under Mao. It is in this light that China's role in the African context is mentioned in this study. See below.

30. See Sklar, *Corporate Power in an African State;* also James H. Mittelman, "Underdevelopment and Nationalization: Banking in Tanzania," *The Journal of Modern African Studies* 16(4) (1978): 597–617.

31. See, for example, P. F. Wilmot, "African Nationalism and Superpower Rivalry," *Afriscope* (August 1977): 9–10.

32. *The Atlantic Charter and Africa from an American Standpoint: A Study by the Committee on Africa, the War, and Peace Aims* (New York, 1944).

33. See the interesting analysis of this factor by Winston S. Churchill (grandson of the great Churchill), "Africa: The Challenge to the West," *R.U.S.U. and Brassey's Defence Yearbook* (London: The Royal United Services Institute for Defence Studies, 1977), pp. 62–69.

34. Cited in Anatoly Gromyko, ed., *Africa Today: Progress, Difficulties, Perspectives* (Moscow: USSR Academy of Sciences, 1983), pp. 10–11. Lenin's statement

should, of course, be regarded in its true context. It was largely a measure of wartime propaganda aimed at the socialist parties in the capitalist countries whom the Bolsheviks exhorted to revolt against their governments in order to end the ongoing war as well as related pressures against Russia. See George F. Kennan, *Russia and the West Under Lenin and Stalin* (New York: The New American Library, 1961).

35. Perhaps the first momentous Soviet action on decolonization—significantly occurring in the midst of the Congo crisis—at this forum was its submission of a draft declaration calling for an immediate and complete end to all colonial administration in the fall of 1960. The final adoption of General Assembly Resolution 1514(XV) derived (in modified form) from the initial Soviet draft.

36. For a detailed explanation of China's Africa policy, refer to Alaba Ogunsanwo, *China's Policy in Africa, 1958–1971* (Cambridge, England: University Press, 1974).

37. There were a number of politically active and articulate groups in Nigeria—most of them formally organized, while others were informal associations—that served somewhat as the foreign policy public. Their importance in this respect did not rest on any clearcut ideological foundation. For the purpose of the study, one is impressed by how they repeatedly challenged the government's stated positions on foreign policy, particularly on Africa or the East-West conflict. Though in most cases the ruling government pursued its basic policies despite opposition from such groups, it often did so at great costs to its legitimacy both at home and in the regional political environment. On quite a few occasions, the government was forced to alter its tactics on policies so as to accommodate these critics.

The most important of these were the Nigerian Youth Congress (NYC), the National Union of Nigerian Students (NUNS), the Nigerian Trade Union Congress (NTUC), the Nigerian Socialist Group, and the Nigerian University Teachers. Note that the Nigerian press also played a role as a medium of pressure in regard to foreign policy. But, by and large, the role of the newspapers was circumscribed because of their formal association with the major political parties either in government or in opposition.

38. This conference is historically significant for two main reasons: First, the conference provided a forum of debate for a cross section of the public concerned about Nigeria's foreign policy and was attended by representatives of trade unions, women's organizations, political parties, and Parliament, and by war veterans, intellectuals, students, and members of the clergy. Second, the conference was sponsored by the personal advisor to the prime minister on African affairs for the purpose of seeking "all shades of opinion in the country" on Nigeria's role in Africa, and indeed the opening address at the conference was read by the prime minister. See Claude S. Phillips, *The Development of Nigerian Foreign Policy* (Illinois: Northwestern University Press, 1964), pp. 54–62.

39. See Chapters 3 and 4 for detailed discussion.

40. For early views on the constraining effect of economic dependence on the foreign policies of Nigeria in particular and African states in general, refer, respectively, to James S. Coleman, "The Foreign Policy of Nigeria," in Joseph

E. Black and Kenneth W. Thompson, eds., *Foreign Policies in a World of Change* (New York: Harper and Row, 1963), and to the chapters by Andrew Kamarck and C. T. Thorne, Jr., in Vernon McKay, ed., *African Diplomacy* (New York: Praeger Publishers, 1966).

41. Gordon J. Idang, *Nigeria: Internal Politics and Foreign Policy* (Ibadan, Nigeria: Ibadan University Press, 1973), p. 145. See also an early attempt to deal with this criticism by Douglas G. Anglin, "Nigeria: Political Non-alignment and Economic Alignment," *Journal of Modern African Studies* 2(1) (July 1964): 247–263.

42. Idang, *Nigeria*, pp. 135, 146.

43. Patrick J. McGowan and Klaus-Peter Gottwald, "Small State Foreign Policies," *International Studies Quarterly* 19(4) (December 1975): 469–497.

44. According to one calculation, between October 1960 and January 1966, Nigeria abstained in votes on twenty-five cold war issues to which the United States and its allies assented and to which the Soviet Union opposed. On the other hand, Nigeria sided with the United States in four votes and with the Soviet Union in an equal number of votes, while casting two negative votes with the Soviet Union against the United States.

On closer scrutiny, however, one learns that three of the four Nigerian "yes" votes that favored the USSR related either to issues on which the United States was ambivalent and, hence, abstained (e.g., the resolution on preventing wider dissemination of nuclear weapons, December 20, 1960) or to issues that were collectively sponsored by the Afro-Asian group, making it difficult for Nigeria to oppose (e.g., the Afro-Asian sponsored draft resolution calling for a ban on the use of nuclear weapons, September 24, 1961). Furthermore, most of the issues on which Nigeria either abstained or absented during voting were those in which the United States had more than enough voting strength to prevail; Nigeria often used such tactics for domestic consumption, with U.S. understanding.

See O. J. Ojo, "Nigerian-Soviet Relations," *African Studies Review* 19(3) (1976): 53, working with data contained in David A. Kay, *The New Nations in the United Nations, 1960–1967* (New York: Columbia University Press, 1970): pp. 226–241.

45. See *General Assembly Official Records*, 1050th Plenary Meeting (A/PV/1050), Thursday, November 9, 1961, pp. 607–611. In Nigeria, opposition to the proposal was raised by the Nigerian Youth Congress and (significantly) the NPC party chief-whip in government, Sarkin Bai, as well as others.

46. Wachuku's plea, urging U.S. cooperation in mediating with the Portuguese authorities in particular, is gleaned from a number of U.S.-Nigerian communication sources. See, for example, Rusk to Palmer, July 31, 1961, Telegram no. 201, N.S.C. Files (Angola), John F. Kennedy Presidential Library, Waltham, Massachusetts. Given this background, Nigeria's vote at the General Assembly, for example, in support of an Afro-Asian resolution of January 30, 1962, on the right to independence of Angola was not a contradiction of basic policy.

47. For a description of Nigeria's uncooperative attitude toward individual nationalist movements in non–self-governing territories, see Okwudibia Nnoli, "Nigerian Policy Toward Southern Africa," *Nigerian Journal of International Affairs* 2(1–2) (1976): 22–23.

48. Refer to the following: Immanuel Wallerstein, "Africa in a Capitalist World," *Issue* 3 (Fall 1973): 1–10; also by the same author, "Dependence in an Interdependent World: The Possibilities of Transformation Within the Capitalist World Economy," *African Studies Review* 17(1) (April 1974): 1–23; Basil Davidson, *Can Africa Survive?* (Boston: Little, Brown and Company, 1974).

49. See note 43 above.

50. Two situations experienced by all African countries identified by the author in the economic realm are "customary" dependence on the West and "exploitation of the masses." See "The Congruence of Political Economies and Ideologies in Africa" in Peter C. W. Gutkind and Immanuel Wallerstein, eds., *The Political Economy of Contemporary Africa* (Beverly Hills, Calif.: Sage Publications, 1976), pp. 206–207.

51. On this approach, see also the effort of Ken W. Grundy, "Intermediary Power and Global Dependence: The Case of South Africa," *International Studies Quarterly* 20(4) (December 1976): 553–578, and Richard Vengroff, "Neo-colonialism and Policy Outputs in Africa," *Comparative Political Studies* 8(2) (July 1975): 234–248.

52. Barbara B. Stallings defines dependency operationally as the extent of concentration of economic ties with one or a few advanced countries, whether in terms of aid, private direct investment, technical assistance personnel, or trade. See *Economic Dependency in Africa and Latin America* (Beverly Hills, Calif.: Sage Publications 1972), p. 7; also see T. Dos Santos, "The Structure of Dependence," in K. T. Fann and D. C. Hodges, eds., *Readings in U.S. Imperialism* (Boston: Porter Sargent Publishers, 1971), pp. 225–236, and V. I. Lenin, *Imperialism: The Highest Stage of Capitalism* (New York: International Publishers, 1939).

53. B. E. Ate, "Black Africa: A Generation After Independence" (review article), *Nigerian Journal of International Affairs*, 8(2) (1982): 125–133; also *Daedalus* (Spring 1982).

2

The Bases of Nigeria's Foreign
Economic and Political Relations:
1960–1961

The object of this chapter is fourfold: to review Nigeria's relationship on the eve of its independence to the Western political economy through the mediation of Great Britain; to show how issues of external economic dependence became interwoven with domestic political struggles; to depict the significance of the Anglo-American nexus of interest in the development of Nigeria-U.S. direct relations; and to illustrate the proposition that the post-independence ruling elite in Nigeria consciously sought to cultivate a relationship of dependence with the United States primarily in order to guarantee the attainment of vital state interests both internally and externally. In sum, this chapter sets the stage for understanding the concrete dynamics of Nigerian-U.S. relations discussed in Chapters 3 and 4.

The Essential Features of the Colonial Economy

As Nigeria's political independence became a certainty early in 1960, the focus of attention in its Federal House of Representatives (the National Assembly) shifted to the state of the nation's economy and the question of which strategies it should adopt in order to secure national economic independence. Related to this long-term concern was the more immediate question of how to implement, rapidly, a program of economic development designed to fulfill the material aspirations of the masses, a major object of political independence.

However, after 1960, efforts by the country's leaders to define these problems and to adopt concrete measures for their solutions would assume intense political and psychological significance, particularly because of the nature of the domestic economy and its relationship to the international political economy. The larger issue for the country would

TABLE 2.1

Some Basic Indicators of Nigeria's External Economic Dependency (1960)

1. Foreign trade as percentage of GDP	41.4
2. Percentage of three leading primary exports	65.7
3. Percentage of dependence of government revenues on foreign sector	67
4. Percentage of foreign personnel to total high-level manpower	30
5. Gross capital formation as percentage of GDP	15.4

Sources: Gerald K. Helleiner, *Peasant Agriculture, Government, and Economic Growth in Nigeria* (Homewood, Ill.: Richard D. Irwin, Inc., 1966), pp. 27, 217; Central Bank of Nigeria, *Economic and Financial Review* 3(2) (December 1965): 5; Angus Maddison, *Foreign Skills and Technical Assistance in Economic Development* (Paris: Development Center of the Organization for Economic Cooperation and Development, 1965), p. 20, n. 1.

be the historical dilemma faced by almost all former colonies: how to achieve sovereign status under a condition of extreme economic dependence on the former colonial power. The colonial experience imposes an acute psychological burden on the former colony that can be exacerbated by continued forms of dependence after formal independence. In Nigeria, as in other former colonies, the succeeding national regime must grapple with that condition of dependence in governing the new polity.

In the five years prior to independence, Nigeria, with a population of about forty million inhabitants and a per capita income of about $84, was a typical underdeveloped country. Its principal economic features showed their colonial determination. The economy was, characteristically, based on the production of primary commodities, geared to the international market in the form of exports. The country exported a large variety of agricultural items, unlike mono-export countries such as Senegal and Ghana; those items constituted about 85 percent of total exports.[1] Agriculture contributed about 60 percent of the gross national product (GNP), whereas industrial activities, begun in the late colonial period, contributed only about 2 percent. Further, the metropolitan country provided the principal market for Nigeria's exports and was the major source of its manufactured imports, accounting for 51 percent and 46 percent, respectively, in 1959.[2] (See Table 2.1 for other indexes of Nigeria's international dependence.)

This trade pattern was reinforced through Nigeria's membership in the Sterling area; through this association, Nigeria's external financial lifeline was closely linked to Great Britain. Membership, for example, placed an obligation on a country to contribute its foreign exchange earnings to a common pool of reserves "from which it could only withdraw specifically allocated quotas."[3] Nigeria had accumulated, especially from the end of World War II to the late 1950s, a great deal of sterling assets in London, in the absence of feasible investment outlets in the local economy. One significant effect of the restriction associated with membership in the Sterling area was that it discouraged diversification of export and import trading outside the Sterling areas.

Nigeria's domestic economy was, through a similar logic, dominated by a small group of oligopolistically organized foreign firms, largely British-owned but with a sizable participation by other West European nations such as France and the Netherlands. Among these firms were the United Africa Company (UAC), John Holt, Paterson Zochonis (PZ), Union Trading Company (UTC), and the Nigerian Tobacco Company (NTC). The influence of these firms, particularly the UAC, was strongly felt in the country's export-import trade system. For example, at the beginning of World War II, the UAC alone controlled more than 40 percent of Nigeria's import-export trade. As late as 1949 "it handled 34 percent of commercial merchandise imports into Nigeria and purchased, on behalf of Nigerian Marketing Boards, 43 percent of all Nigerian non-mineral exports."[4]

In addition to exercising control over wholesale trading, most of the same foreign companies also exercised control over other sectors, such as maritime shipping, aviation, banking, and even large-scale retail. As can be expected, such a predominant foreign presence left little scope for the growth of an indigenous entrepreneurial class. Local businessmen not strong enough to compete found themselves progressively pushed to the margin of the economic system, operating mainly as petty commercial agents dependent on commissions from the powerful expatriate firms for their profits. From this experience emerged the resentments felt by the Nigerian business class specifically toward the foreign firms and commercial banks. Nigerians bitterly accused the banks of engaging in restrictive credit practices against the Nigerian business community. Of course, from the perspective of the foreign banks, Nigerian businessmen may simply not have been credit-worthy—a problem that might have been aggravated by different standards of business ethics. Nonetheless, the local business community, correctly or not, saw the foreigners as working malevolently and deliberately against its interest by manipulating their concentrated financial power and competitive economic advantage.[5]

Predictably, this feeling of resentment was later projected onto the colonial administration. The colonial government was perceived as systematically supporting the economic status quo through various devices, such as the allocation of trading licenses, the administration of trade controls, and the formulation of tax policies. According to James Coleman, the suspicion "of a close association between alien political control and an alien economic oligopoly" gave rise to "a popular image of alien collusion and exploitation."[6]

Still another factor, though strictly noneconomic, that strengthened this perception was the vivid presence of foreigners occupying top administrative and military positions in the government bureaucracy and the security agencies. Although Nigerianization in these important state organs had been stepped up in anticipation of independence, this picture remained a reality of the Nigerian experience even after 1960.

This setting in due course supplied the flame that ignited Nigerian nationalism. The image of alien collusion and exploitation was to be seized upon by disaffected intellectuals and translated into a broad nationalist slogan in the course of demands for complete self-government. The same developments led the business and intellectual strata in Nigeria to share a nationalist platform against colonial rule and help explain the close partnership that ensued between Nigerian businessmen and all the governments of the federation after independence was achieved. But the point should be made that contrary to what the nationalists had promised, political self-rule by itself did not, after 1960, end the central problem of foreign economic dependence, although it might have enhanced economic diversification.

At the beginning of its independent existence, Nigeria remained dependent and economically underdeveloped. Consequently, the immediate domestic task confronting its leadership was to initiate an appropriate development strategy that would at least minimize the extent of the dependency while engendering rapid industrial growth for a rapidly expanding population. However, for a capital-poor country such as Nigeria, these two designs are critically interwoven. For instance, Nigerian leaders found that any massive development effort on the scale planned[7] by the federal government would entail extensive mobilization and reallocation of available domestic investment resources and a significant transfer of domestic economic control to the state and to aspiring Nigerian entrepreneurs. Both processes would necessarily involve difficult bargaining with the entrenched foreign firms who controlled much of those assets. Also, given the short-run limitation on investible domestic resources, progress on such a program might indeed depend on a steady inflow of further external capital, with related technical expertise.

Thus, it seemed that an effective solution to these issues of concern to the country might very likely prove impossible without the collaboration of the same foreign economic forces from whom independence was sought. Without a conscientious and imaginative leadership, the dynamic processes in that collaboration could in the long run intensify the original conditions of dependency without achieving the desired objectives. Given this prospect, the available strategic choice seemed to be between an idealistic, radical disengagement from the colonial power, with all its immediate baffling consequences (examples: Ghana, Guinea, Mali in the 1960s), and a realistic acceptance of dependent development with hope in the future (examples: the Ivory Coast, Kenya).

To show how the Nigerian leadership perceived these development concerns, we now focus on the first national development plan, 1962–1968, and the highly controversial debate on the question of nationalization. The specific purpose of this discussion is to clarify (1) the views of both government and opposition politicians on the nature of the development plan, preferable sources of development capital, and the role of private foreign investment in national development; and (2) the basic interests underlying the positions of the government and opposition groups. The aim is to indicate the considerations that, as will be argued, forced the Nigerian policymakers to adopt a foreign economic strategy that stressed intensified ties with the West, particularly the United States and Great Britain.

The National Development Plan, 1962–1968

The Six-Year National Development Plan[8] was, according to the Nigerian government, to be the first phase of a comprehensive and coordinated development effort that would lead to a self-sustaining national economy. Under colonial rule, there had been other attempts to execute conscious economic planning in Nigeria; the two previous attempts were the Ten-Year Plan of Development and Welfare for Nigeria, 1946, and the 1955–1960 development plans (later extended to 1962).[9] These were not, however, plans in the strict sense and were not directed toward a national objective. The 1946 plan, for example, consisted of a number of uncoordinated projects for the construction of transport and communication systems and for developing a narrow range of export crops. Similarly, the 1955–1960 development plans, which evolved from a report of the World Bank Mission to Nigeria in 1953, suffered from lack of national focus. The programs the mission recommended were designed to serve separately the individual needs of the three regions as well as the federal government.

It is this background that gives the 1962–1968 plan its unique significance in the history of economic planning in modern Nigeria. As one observer noted, the plan

constituted the first attempt in Nigeria at comprehensive, integrated planning. For the first time, projections were made and targets were formulated for the performance of the entire Nigerian economy—both public and

private sectors, both current and capital needs. The resource and foreign
exchange implications were calculated and conclusions for policy drawn.[10]

From the specific standpoint of this study, the plan serves as a developmental framework within which one can understand the nature of
Nigeria's economic (and indeed political) ties to the international economic
system in the post-independence period. As will be shown below, it
clearly defined the interests of the Nigerian economy vis-à-vis foreign
aid and technical assistance, private foreign investment, and foreign
trade. And it pointedly demonstrated the desire of the national and
regional governments to fulfill those interests through close cooperation
with the major Western nations and international financial institutions.
The relevant aspects of the plan for the present discussion are the role
envisaged for the private sector of the economy and the projected
contribution of foreign capital toward the finance of public and private
expenditures.

The Role of the Private Sector

The plan displayed the federal government's strong belief in private
enterprise by devoting more than half of the projected total investment
to the private sector. This interest is declared in the following clause
of the plan:

> . . . in formulating the National Plan, the Governments of the Federation
> have fully recognized the importance of the contribution which will be
> made by the private sector of the economy towards the Nation's economic
> growth. To this end, it is intended to pursue vigorous policies by which
> private industry and other business will be stimulated.[11]

But whose private enterprise would be promoted by the plan? Or
rather, who would control the private sector of the Nigerian economy?
In 1961, this question was raised and passionately debated in the Federal
House as well as in the media. The question was raised, specifically,
in the context of whether the government should uphold the state's right
to nationalize certain sectors of the economy. But to say that the issue
of nationalization had provoked a great deal of intense public debate
might give a wrong impression regarding the disposition of Nigerians
toward private enterprise. The fact was that all three major political
parties in the country espoused, nearly equally, a strong private sector
for the economy.[12] And indeed it has been said by many foreign observers
that Nigerians in general are capitalists by instinct. The real political
issue in the controversy was whether the federal government should
use its new powers to enhance the growth of indigenous private enterprise

or should continue, as a priority, to promote the interest of foreign investors in the economy. Because local businessmen owned less than 5 percent of direct investment capital in the country, nationalization (of foreign enterprises), in the view of proponents, should be used essentially to transfer economic control to Nigerian citizens. This, after all, was a major factor in the decolonization struggle, according to these proponents. In sum, nationalization, for its advocates, was a means of strengthening Nigerian capitalism and safeguarding the state against foreign economic (and political) control. Seen in this way, the real motivating force of nationalization was economic. Beyond this, however, there was the related and no less important question of the extent of state intervention in the economy.

On November 29, 1961, Chief Obafemi Awolowo, the leader of the opposition party in the Federal House (the Action Group party) moved that the House approve "in principle the nationalization of basic industries and commercial undertakings of vital importance to the economy of Nigeria."[13] Awolowo's central argument for nationalization was in essence an invocation of the pre-independence populist viewpoint concerning the "evil" effect of foreign investments, only now it was applicable to a newly independent nation. He maintained, "An untramelled [foreign] capitalist system, of necessity, places a newly emergent and underdeveloped nation, such as ours, in a state of defenceless economic servitude and unduly prolongs the regime of poverty, ignorance and disease among the bulk of our people."[14] In the manner of dependency theorists, he proceeded to list the methods by which he alleged foreign enterprisers manipulated the Nigerian economy:

> They have a monopoly on the purchase of our export commodities and so dictate the prices at which they are bought. Equally, they have an undisputed monopoly on all our imported goods, the prices of which they dictate. . . . It is they who . . . determine the types and locations of our industries, the pattern of our exchange and consumption . . . and the share of our national products which goes to each of the factors of production. Because they control the bulk of our financial institutions, they accordingly influence . . . the availability of capital and credit and their eventual direction.[15]

Furthermore, the proponents of nationalization questioned what foreign policy implications would arise from the predominance of foreign control of the economy. The foreign policy public was already pressing the government to adopt an assertive nonaligned foreign policy. Thus, Awolowo argued that the government was misguided in its attempt to "tie the development of Nigeria to the self-interest of the foreign investor," whose interests, he asserted, were "not always in accordance with our national interest." He presented the possibility that Nigeria's foreign policy might, for instance, be constrained by the predominant British interest in the national maritime industry:

> Suppose Britain did something which angered us . . . in the way that South Africa has done. . . . Suppose [then] we decided to impose certain sanctions. Are we going to impound all the ships belonging to Elder Dempster [a British-owned shipping line] . . . before we proceed with the sanctions?[16]

The decision of the opposition party to press for a debate on nationalization in the House was largely a response to pressures from most of the press, university students, university teachers, radical intellectual groups, trade unions, and others. These groups, along with what might be called the radical nationalists within the major political parties, had become highly critical of the evolving foreign economic policy of the government. The Action Group party was thus, in essence, exploiting the public's sentiment to score a point against the government on a highly sensitive matter.[17] Awolowo's views on this issue, it should also be indicated, tended to reflect the ideological pull of the left wing of his party; the rightist elements of the party shared the philosophical perceptions of the government on economic policies. Indeed, the divergent ideological pulls within the party resulted in its break-up in 1962.

The formal position of the federal government on nationalization is reflected in the following statement:

> It is the intention of the government[s] to enable Nigerian businessmen to control increasing portions of the Nigerian economy, not through *nationalisation* [emphasis added], but by the accelerated training of businessmen, the provision of advisory and training services, and the improved flow of capital and technical and market information.[18]

The minister of finance, Festus Okotie-Eboh, vigorously defended the government's antinationalization policy on a number of grounds. First, he argued that nationalization presented no effective solution to dependency. He pointed out that experience in other dependent countries "has shown that, quite apart from the loss of individual freedom and liberty, widespread state ownership and control do not necessarily lead to rapid economic development, nor to the material betterment of the mass of the people."[19] Second, he argued that there would be considerable practical constraints in any attempt to nationalize foreign enterprises. He noted the obvious fact that Nigeria was "desperately short of technical and managerial talent and of persons with modern business experience [and that it] would be grossly uneconomic . . . to recruit expatriate managers and technicians to manage the nationalized concerns."[20] It was also clear that the government was pathologically concerned about the impact that any "loose" talk of nationalization might have on potential foreign investments and on the government's ability to attract foreign aid for the development plan. Consequently, Okotie-Eboh warned Nigerians,

> It would be difficult indeed for us to attract any sympathy . . . from the international financial institutions or other friendly governments if they felt that we were using our own limited resources to buy out undertakings rather than deploy them in ways which would contribute directly to the growth of our economy.[21]

The federal government's policy was "Nigerianization" rather than nationalization. Nigerianization involved state ownership and operation of public utilities of strategic importance; adoption of regulatory measures to ensure that private enterprise was directed toward the interest of Nigerians; and encouragement of Nigerians to participate to an increasing extent in the ownership and direction of industry and commercial undertakings in Nigeria.

An earlier warning warrants repetition: One should not be misled by the tenor of this debate or the views expressed therein into concluding that there was a fundamental gap in the ideological outlooks of the government and the opposition coalition. It is true that both the Action Group (the opposition party) and the National Council of Nigerian Citizens (NCNC, a government party) had left-leaning factions who, at least in their public rhetoric, defended socialistic positions. It is also true that both parties were generally more liberal and welfare-oriented ideologically than the Northern People's Congress (NPC, the senior government party), which was the most conservative of the Nigerian parties. (NPC conservatism stemmed from the largely feudal social structure of its Northern base.) Yet, in practice, the mainstreams of both the government and the opposition coalition claimed to subscribe to "democratic socialism." Both professed a preference for a "mixed economy" as opposed to a strictly socialist or laissez-faire economic system. What was made clear from the debate was that the government showed stronger support for the primacy of the private sector without undue state intervention and an enthusiastic interest in the role of private foreign investment. In contrast, the opposition sought a more active and direct role for the state in an essentially capitalist economy, with a strong preference for locally owned over foreign investments.

The government, as might be expected under Nigeria's Westminster parliamentary system, used its large majority in the House to defeat Awolowo's motion 123 to 43. Thereafter, the regime methodically executed its "open door" policy on private foreign investment, using various attractive institutional devices. At the same time, it was impossible for the government to completely ignore the concerns expressed by the opposition party and the constant protests emanating from segments of the public. In that same year (1961), the government bought (with due compensation) British shares in the Nigerian National Shipping Line and the Nigerian Airways Corporation, making both companies fully public corporations. The following year, the government took a similar action against Cable and Wireless, Ltd., resulting in the incorporation of Nigerian External Telecommunications, Ltd. Apparently, these companies had been reclassified within the area of "strategic" importance to the public interest. Significantly, these government actions marked the beginning of the decline of traditional British predominance in Nigeria's economic life.

The Need for External Financing

The most crucial aspect of the development plan from the viewpoint of its subsequent impact on domestic politics and on Nigeria's relationship with the United States concerned the prospective sources of capital for its private and public programs. At the plan's inception, its total cost was projected to be $1,892,800,000. It was then estimated that over 50 percent of the planned expenditure in the public sector ($949.2 million) would be raised through foreign loans and grants; the remainder would be secured by private investments. About 30 percent of this ($560 million) was projected to be derived from foreign investments.[22] In all, over 50 percent of the public (capital) expenditure and two-thirds of the private investments were expected to be externally derived.

The nature of this projection immediately led critics to raise a number of questions. Was it realistic for the government to expect outsiders to assume such a disproportionate burden of the cost of the plan? Would it not have been more judicious, and honorable, to emphasize optimal exploitation of domestic sources before supplementing them with available foreign assistance? Given the very large projection for external loans in the plan, what effect would subsequent loan-servicing obligations have on the country's balance of payments position? Indeed, was it a prudent national policy to rely exclusively on Western-bloc nations for capital aid, shunning completely any aid contacts with the socialist bloc? Finally, the critics questioned whether any consideration had been given to the political costs that might accompany such extensive foreign capital involvement.[23]

The government attempted to respond, rather lamely one might say, to some of these questions during its budget presentation of March 29, 1962. As to whether the projected size of foreign capital assistance was realistic, the government offered the following circuitous explanation:

Nigeria is not a beggar country as some would have us believe. Among the less developed countries of the world our record of domestic savings and effort is very high indeed. By far the greater part of our present Economic Programme [i.e., 1960–1962] has been financed from our own resources. . . .

. . . We have a right [therefore] to expect that our friends overseas . . . will appreciate our efforts and have sympathy with our legitimate aspirations.[24]

This underlying expectation was not without substance, for by this time Nigeria had already received some firm offers of foreign capital assistance from friendly Western governments and international institutions. Foremost among these was the U.S. government, which, on December 12, 1961, announced an offer of $225 million in long-term development aid specifically for the Nigerian plan. This figure represented only direct U.S. assistance (and not indirect aid from nongovernmental sources, which was also promised), but the understanding in Nigeria was that this first U.S. aid pledge would be readily augmented as the initial sum became exhausted. Indeed, in the period 1959–1962—before the official inception of the plan—the United States extended a total sum of $43 million in concrete economic and technical assistance to Nigeria. Officials in Nigeria were highly impressed by the large U.S. aid commitment, prompting the finance minister to "pay a very warm tribute to the President and people of that great country for the generous assistance which they have already undertaken to make available." The minister found even more remarkable that the aid "was made freely and spontaneously at a time when [Nigeria's] planning was a long way from finality."[25]

By 1962, other major governments and nongovernment institutions had also promised assistance to the Nigerian plan, including the governments of Great Britain, West Germany, Switzerland, and the Netherlands, and the World Bank. By the first year of the plan, Nigeria had obtained about 50 percent of the projected foreign aid commitment toward public expenditure, all from Western sources. (It is important to note that aid commitment was merely a pledge to offer assistance up to the amount pledged and that payment would be made only after mutually acceptable terms had been worked out.)

The expectations of the Nigerian government leadership were so buoyed up by the immediate and positive response of the international community that the government erroneously assumed that future complications in the practical implementation of the aid so pledged would not occur. Further, in its enthusiasm it did not anticipate the possibility that additional aid commitments might not be forthcoming.

With such an effusive attitude toward foreign assistance, the government did not seem to regard very seriously the need to exhaust domestic resources. Rather, the public was informed that "it is an inescapable fact that if Nigeria is to move ahead with the speed all of us want to see, capital must be imported from abroad." According to the government, an inevitable gap was bound to exist "however much we . . . apply domestic resources to the development of industry and public services."[26] Furthermore, the government explained that importing capital from abroad was indispensable for the continued operation of a liberal economy in Nigeria. Such funds would, for example, make it unnecessary for the government to adopt restrictive exchange control and import licensing measures as alternative means for conserving foreign exchange and inducing domestic savings. In the same vein, a large influx of foreign capital in the form of loans would serve in the long run to stimulate substantial growth in the national income. It would, similarly, provide greater foreign exchange earnings either by reducing the nation's imports or by increasing its exports. Consequently, "these advantages will far outweigh the increased amount required to service the capital inflow [loans]." Using such a neo-liberal view of capital flows, the government sought to discount the concern that future debt-repayment obligations could have a harmful effect on the nation's balance of payments.

And what about the likely political costs of economic dependence? Unlike the clamourous agitations of the "economic nationalists" within the opposition party and in the public at large, the government's view, as on previous questions, was equally nonalarming. Placidly and simply, the government declared that it was not prepared to accept those forms of foreign transactions that involve political strings.[27]

The government's reluctance to solicit Soviet-bloc economic assistance and thus diversify its sources of development capital was, according to domestic critics, one of the most serious paradoxes of the regime's foreign economic policy. Given the urgency for economic expansion necessary to ensure political stability following independence, why, asked the critics, would the government place all of its aid expectations on Western-bloc sources, to the extent of ignoring the political underpinning of foreign aid in the cold war international environment? The regime's negative attitude to socialist-bloc aid had, indeed, been revealed before independence in public statements made by the leaders of all three parties. It was, ironically, Awolowo, the aspirant to the office of federal prime minister, who made it known then that his preference among the "two ideological camps in the world today" was "unhesitatingly for the Western democracies."[28] He had thought then that to woo both East and West for aid "is a tactic both disreputable and dangerous." Sir Ahmadu Bello, the powerful leader of the NPC and premier of the Northern Region, expressed a similar disinterest in Soviet aid—even at low interest rates—insisting, "We have to work with those we are accustomed to"[29] (meaning the West).

State Interests and External Dependence

As the foregoing discussions show, the Nigerian government had, after 1960, embarked deliberately and forcefully on a strategy of national economic development that not only sanctioned the strengthening of the old colonial links, but more crucially strengthened the expansion of economic channels with other Western nations, chiefly the United States. The leadership regarded this strategic development option, through its rationalizations, as the sine qua non of rapid progress, the option that would eventually promote greater economic independence.

The issue, however, is not so easily disposed of. In order to understand the more critical justification for this choice of strategy, one must penetrate the rationalizations offered by the regime. This requires discussion of critical factors outside the realm of strict development economics, for economic development decisions were rarely made in a political or security vacuum. More specifically, apart from their strict development value, decisions about foreign economic alignment were also based on the political and security interests of the regime, both at home and in the regional environment.

To appreciate properly this interconnection, one should remember that the evolution of the Nigerian plan occurred within a context of turbulent political developments in Africa as well as in Nigeria itself. In Africa, the Congo crisis was threatening to inject the global cold war conflict into the continent. The Algerian revolution was raging concurrently, and both decolonization crises, through the passions they evoked and the outside interests they attracted, helped produce two politically polarized blocs in the African regional system. Within Nigeria, the pre-independence decolonization arrangement had clearly failed its first serious constitutional test with the breakdown of parliamentary government in the Western Region and the subsequent declaration of emergency rule by the federal government—developments that presaged a threat to the very existence of the national political system. These problems and others in Africa as well as in Nigeria were extremely disturbing to the governments in Washington and Lagos because of the potential adverse effects they could have on their separate but complementary interests, and, as will be explored in the rest of this chapter and in the next two chapters, this was part of the general political environment in which decisions about Nigeria's foreign economic arrangements were made.

Preferred sources of economic development were also expected to generate indispensable political and security assets for the regime in the domestic and the regional arenas. Consequently, two vital interests that the Nigerian regime sought to promote (in addition to national economic development) were domestic political security—the country's sheer political survival in the face of determined hostile forces in both the domestic and regional environments—and a leadership role in African decolonization. Together, these three state interests constituted the major imperatives underlying the pattern of Nigeria's foreign economic and political alignments. A fourth factor—significant in reinforcing this pattern—was the particularistic commitment by important strata within the ruling political "class" to the maintenance of the pre-independence socioeconomic structure.

It is perhaps closer to reality to refer to "regime interest" than to the more conventional and elusive "national interest" when talking about interests of states, particularly new and institutionally weak states. There is, indeed, a sense in which the very notion of a nation for such incipient entities is far more ephemeral than for more established systems, though even in the latter case the validity of a "national interest" is controversial.[30] The problem of sorting out a new state's national interest is not linked so much to difficulty in identifying what constitutes the state; "in any given situation, the decision-makers acting on behalf of a state are quite clear about its identity and its delimitation from the universe."[31] The analytical questions are rather, what constitutes the national interest the decisionmakers seek to promote? How is this conceived? To what extent is there a national consensus about the type of interest sought? Or, is national interest simply whatever the more powerful nationals say it is?

The state's national interest, in the final analysis, will probably depend on the relative weight of such factors as the power attributes of the state, its system of government, the nature of sociopolitical forces in the society, forces in its immediate external environment, and above all the degree of its dependency relative to the global environment. It is generally the interplay of these factors that determines the interests a weak state will consider vital (especially in the absence of a direct external threat to its territorial integrity and independence). But it is also certain that the specific interpretation and manner of execution of those interests will ultimately reflect the predominant preferences of the most powerful strata (including the government) in the society.

National Economic Development

The significance of economic development as a high priority of national policy to the Nigerian government leadership has already been stressed. What follows is a concise identification of some of the concrete steps the government has systematically taken for the purpose of executing the economic strategy it adopted.

To attract private foreign investment, in particular, the government had to provide highly favorable incentives. Before 1960 the colonial administration enacted a number of income tax relief ordinances designed to guarantee exemptions from company taxes and import duties for "pioneer" industries (established by foreign investors).[32] Under these ordinances, other advantages such as allowances for capital depreciation and for buildings and plants were offered. During the 1957 Constitutional Conference in London (an outcome of this conference was the granting of internal self-government to the Eastern and Western Regions), foreign investors were assured unimpeded freedom to repatriate profits, dividends, and initial capital. All these measures were retained and strengthened after 1960.

Under the guidelines provided by the 1962–1968 development plan, foreign investors were promised equal access to all the incentive policies and facilities available to the Nigerian investor. The Republican Constitution of 1963 went even further and made the right of the foreign investor "fundamental."[33] Early in 1965, Nigeria became the first state to ratify the World Bank's convention on the settlement of investment disputes between states and nationals of other states. This convention guarantees third-party arbitration in any investment disputes.

One potential impediment to Nigeria's development effort—the dearth of high-level manpower critically needed to provide the necessary technical expertise in the Nigerian labor force—was identified early on by experts. Although in absolute terms, Nigeria had more indigenous civil servants and more highly trained manpower than the other new African nations, in relative terms the availability of this critical resource was far below the level required to implement the plan. In a 1960 study, Frederick Barbison of Princeton University concluded that "Nigeria has not now, nor will she have in the next few years, the capacity to generate the high-level manpower necessary to make rapid economic growth possible."[34] He calculated that between 1960 and 1970, Nigeria would require a high-level workforce capacity of 85,000 if its development goals were to be met.

In order to effect a long-term solution to this problem, postsecondary education was given high priority in the plan. However, for the short-term purpose of meeting the needs of the economy under provisions of the existing plan, Nigeria had to rely heavily on expatriate technical assistance. Indeed, the plan itself was produced under the direction of Wolfgang Stolper of the Massachusetts Institute of Technology (MIT) and his associates, under the auspices of the Ford Foundation.

After 1961, Nigeria was to turn dramatically toward the United States to secure its high-level manpower needs and to obtain new sources of public and private foreign capital. In the process, it would alter significantly its pre-1960 exclusive ties to Great Britain.

Domestic Power Struggle and Regime Security

Just before independence, Nigeria's incoming national government sought to strengthen its bilateral alignment with the United States and Great Britain as a bulwark against perceived internal threats to its existence and authority. The nature of the threats faced by the regime took two main forms. The first form of threat was that described by Howard Wriggins, what he called the "ruler's imperative" in new states. According to Wriggins, the rulers' positions in these states are precarious essentially because their

> political supports are uncertain. Offices they hold lack the legitimacy of having been long established. . . . Political institutions often appear to be insufficiently established to contain the political forces that the independence struggle, popular politics, and new communications have generated. Dissidence is widely expected; political disruption is all too easy. Searching for the means to stay in power is a more urgent matter for these real political actors than it is for rulers in more established politics.[35]

This particular threat was, in part, linked to the antipathy felt by the opposition party toward the ruling government coalition[36]—an attitude more intense than the usual critical but accommodative relationship between government and opposition parties in more established parliamentary systems. The hostility of the opposition toward the government resulted, in general, from the zero-sum game character of Nigerian politics between 1960 and 1966, in which the winner was believed to win everything, leaving the loser with no real institutional means to assert its interests. The defeat of the Action Group (the Western party) in the 1959 federal election and its subsequent exclusion from the national government appeared to signify to its Western supporters that their legitimate interests and aspirations within the federal structure would be jeopardized. (This fear was reinforced because the two ruling parties, for separate reasons, were archenemies of the Action Group.) The Action Group perception, however, was in no small degree aggravated by a personal factor—the deep personal disappointment experienced by its leader, Awolowo, in his failure to capture the position of federal prime minister (a position he highly coveted). Further, the opposition party could not even take solace in the possibility of a future electoral victory. That option seemed to be foreclosed by a serious anomaly (explained below) in the constitution left behind by the British, thus intensifying the party's frustration.

Given this outlook, the NPC/NCNC government became extremely concerned that the opposition might attempt to engineer a coup d'etat as an alternative means of installing itself in power. It was mainly in anticipation of this ever-present danger that the government passed into law, shortly before independence, the Royal Nigerian Military Forces Act.[37] It was also suspected that part of the justification for the abortive military pact that Nigeria had signed with Great Britain was to ensure against internal insurrection.[38] And one specific objective of U.S. economic policy in Nigeria was to support development programs with the potential for defusing political conditions of instability, thereby insulating the ruling regime against subversive pressures.

A more crucial dimension of the first form of threat was linked to the North-South polarization of Nigerian politics. Fundamentally, the constitutional arrangement worked out with Great Britain as part of the decolonization bargain tended, effectively, to ensure Northern dominance (through the Northern party, the NPC) of the federal legislature because of the Northern Region's numerical majority in the country.[39] This contributed to a serious contradiction in the body politic because the South as a whole was educationally and technologically more advanced than the North (an outcome of contrasting exposures of the two regions to modern influences during the colonial era).[40]

This disparity produced a deeply ingrained insecurity in the psyche of the Northern leadership and people. The Royal Nigerian Military Forces Act noted earlier was designed not only to safeguard the security of the state against possible subversion by the opposition groups, but also to ensure Northern control of the state. The Northerners needed to maintain firm control over the management of the state in order, first, to prevent the more egalitarian Southerners from subverting their sociocultural system and, second, to assure the North a veto over federal financial resources that would be used to bridge the development gap between areas of the country. Relatedly, because the federal government had exclusive jurisdiction over foreign economic contacts and distribution of foreign capital, the North had an additional potential leverage it could use to strengthen its political authority over the Southern regions.

Indeed, the conservative nature of Nigeria's foreign economic and political policies stemmed from the predominant influence of the NPC in the federal coalition. The general sensitivities in the North-South relationship served as a constant source of instability within the government. This inherent tension led to the final break-up of the NPC/NCNC federal coalition just before the 1964 national elections.

The second form of threat to the regime's existence was perceived to emanate from the regional environment, specifically through alleged subversive activities by the Republic of Ghana. Evidence obtained from prosecution witnesses during the celebrated treason trials of 1963 was regarded as conclusive proof that both Ghana and the Soviet Union had collaborated with domestic dissidents to overthrow the Nigerian government. Therefore, in the perception of the regime, there was a link between internal and regional sources of threat, and this only helped to worsen its general sense of insecurity.

Ghanaian disaffection with the regime in Lagos stemmed from two sources. The first was Nigeria's conservative (and to the Ghanaians reactionary) posture regarding African decolonization, especially as this became translated into a determined opposition to Nkrumah's grand design of establishing a continental political union. Throughout Nkrumah's tenure, Ghana regarded Nigeria's government as a collaborative instrument of Western resistance to true African decolonization. The second source of tension was linked to a long-standing rivalry between the two countries for political preeminence in the West African subregion. From the early 1950s, Nigerians seemed to have convinced themselves that Ghana's nationals treated them with condescension based on "a feeling of political superiority [because] . . . Ghana had achieved a higher stage of political development . . . [while] Nigerian politics were still dominated by ethnicity."[41] More important, Ghana's earlier attainment of independent statehood in sub-Saharan Africa served to confer on it a logical right to regional leadership until the Nigerian giant, with its superior structural attributes, took over this role in 1960. Henceforth, the leadership role once enjoyed by Ghana became progressively dissipated. Thus, on both grounds the Ghanaian leadership might have been tempted to subvert the Nigerian system from within.

Regional Leadership

The basis of a state's conception of its role in the international environment (regional or global) is a composite of ideals and realities, both borne of its concrete interests and material capabilities. But idealistic impulses are engendered by inherited values and beliefs or nurtured by compelling national attributes that impose a sense of noble mission on the state outside its own domain.

A discussion of Nigeria's role conception[42] in African politics must necessarily begin with a consideration of endogenous factors associated with the state's national attributes in relation to the total African setting. From about 1955, Nigerian politicians became imbued with visionary images about the messianic mission of an independent Nigeria in the continent of Africa. Comparing their territory to the other colonial enclaves around them, they came to link this mission to the relative virtue of Nigeria's size, population, and natural and human resources. In January 1960, Okotie-Eboh, who prided himself throughout the period under study as a realist, articulated this vision:

> Nigeria must show that by her size, . . . population, . . . economic potentialities and all the resources at her command, she is prepared to lead Africa so that Africa can be seen as a principal personality and a nation that will be recognized not as a second-class nation but as a first-class [nation] in the comity of nations.[43]

It is, indeed, hard to overemphasize the extent to which such a vision evoked a type of "manifest destiny" psychology among the Nigerian leadership and the more enlightened public, not dissimilar to the early American self-image in the North American continent. Between 1959 and 1961, public discussions inside and outside the Nigerian House of Representatives were replete with litanies about Nigeria's prime interest in African decolonization. For example, Prime Minister Balewa, a man of modest temperament, asserted, one month after independence, "It is our policy to fight for the liberation of all states in Africa which are still under colonial rule."[44] In a more strident manner, a number of opposition MPs (members of the Nigerian parliament), displaying the penchant of Nigerians for comparing their politico-historical evolution to that of the Americans even when inapplicable, actually urged the government to declare a Nigerian equivalent of the Monroe Doctrine in order to force the rapid liquidation of colonialism in the continent. That Nigeria was materially powerless to enforce such a regional fiat was to them inconsequential. Their vision derived from the calculation that the U.S.-Soviet power rivalry in Africa, if properly cultivated, could serve as an effective guarantor of that doctrine, permitting Nigeria to advance its historic destiny in Africa. Notice the historical similarity between this strategic thinking and the experience of the United States during much of the eighteenth century both before and after President James Monroe made his famous speech: The underlying goal of the Monroe Doctrine was given effect not because of the military capability of the United States but because of the mutual suspicions of Europe's imperial powers, which negated interimperial coexistence in the Western Hemisphere, and because of the naval protection of Great Britain.

An essential consequence of the public perception of Nigeria's natural role in Africa—a perception that was in 1960 prominently bolstered by official and private Western organs in an attempt to build Nigeria's influence as a Western ally in Africa—was the creation of a powerful foreign policy constituency in Nigeria whose self-assigned function was to serve as a watchdog over the regime's role performance on decolonization issues. Here lies the source of the contentious relationship between the government and the more radical segment of the foreign policy public over Nigeria's Africa policy, for in practice, the government's regional leadership performance was seriously compromised by the requirements of the other state interests—domestic security and economic development.

The logic of domestic security ultimately involved opposition to the radical decolonization that Ghana championed. The need for an assertive regional leadership had to be reconciled to the necessity of containing Ghana's hostile influences in the continent and in Nigeria in particular. On the other hand, the demands of economic development, and hence the need for Western capital, also necessitated the now-celebrated moderate leadership of the Balewa regime on African decolonization. Furthermore, Nigeria needed a U.S. and Western alignment in order to achieve its modest leadership objectives in Africa.

Particularistic Commitment by Strata in the Political Class

Of the standard definitions of a "political class," the definition provided by Gaetano Mosca[45] comes closest to approximating the operational experience in Nigeria in the first Republic.[46] This definition is appropriate, moreover, because it captures the general tendency in Nigeria as in most newly independent nations whereby acquired political power becomes "the primary force which created economic opportunity and determined the pattern of social stratification."[47] Members of the Nigerian political class of this time, as numerous official enquiries have revealed, were especially flagrant in the manner they manipulated political power and subverted state institutions for personal material gains.

The important stratum of this class (at both federal and regional levels) comprised principally the top politicians, professional groups, and heads of big business. These groups had constituted the leadership core of the nationalist movement, and they remained, after independence, the elder political patrons of the ruling political parties. Paradoxically, they became the group most committed to strengthening the colonial socioeconomic order and, concomitantly, maintaining a strict pro-Western foreign orientation. Now that they had complete control over state power, they could conveniently use that power to negotiate lucrative economic advantages with the former, vilified, foreign economic exploiters.

What emerged, in essence, after independence was a close partnership between the politicians in the major parties and the local and foreign businessmen in which the latter groups served as the prime sources of financial benefaction for the political parties in power in return for lucrative public contract awards.[48] Prominent local businessmen reaped other rewards from this arrangement, as well. They were, for instance, appointed directors and management board members by foreign firms. Furthermore, politicians and local businessmen benefited personally from contract negotiations on development-related projects sponsored through U.S. and other foreign loans and grants.

The specific influence of the Nigerian business community on foreign policy in this period has not been properly documented. However, the presence and role in the federal government of some powerful members of this class provides an indication of this influence. One such figure at the apex of the decisionmaking center was Chief Okotie-Eboh, perhaps the richest of Nigeria's businessmen.[49] As the principal government spokesperson on economic affairs, he had, as earlier mentioned, strenuously defended the government's development plan and general economic strategy. An indication of Okotie-Eboh's personal stake in the nation's foreign economic policy came to public attention in 1964. He was reported to have recommended sharply increased import and excise duties on all types of footwear materials except rubber and canvas; the reason for the exclusion of these two materials was his financial interest in rubber and canvas shoe production.[50]

In the absence of further concrete evidence of the possible direct influence of Nigerian business on foreign policy, one is inclined to share Marshall Singer's judgment. According to Singer, the more a country is economically dependent on another, the more the decisionmaking elite of the dependent nation will also probably depend on that relationship "for the maintenance of its own personal economic interest."[51] Consequently, there is a strong incentive for such an elite to see the dependency relationship strengthened.

The Significance of the Anglo-American Nexus

Beginning with the Kennedy administration, the United States moved more resolutely than in the previous Eisenhower administration to become directly involved in the African decolonization process. The official U.S. attitude through the 1950s regarded Colonial Africa as the primary responsibility of the European metropolitan powers. (With the exception of Spain, all these powers were NATO allies.) This attitude was reflected both in the substantive U.S. policy (where any existed) toward the continent and in the jurisdictional handling of African affairs in the U.S. State Department. Colonial Africa was treated by the European Bureau of the State Department as an annex to Europe until 1958 (when the African Affairs Bureau, established in 1956, was officially sanctioned by the House of Representatives).[52]

This official noninvolvement policy on Africa should, however, be kept in perspective, for it stemmed not from U.S. disinterest in developments in the continent but rather from a necessity to concentrate policy attention and material efforts in other world areas of more critical security interest, such as Western Europe, East Asia, and the Middle East. It was only economical and rational to allow the colonial powers—with the advantage of established links—to assume immediate responsibility for safeguarding Western purposes in Africa.[53]

The impetus toward direct U.S. involvement derived substantially from the dramatic events that occurred in Africa between 1958 and 1961 and the implications those events held for general Western as well as potential U.S. interests. For example, the crises in the Congo and Algeria demonstrated vividly to the U.S. leadership a number of African realities, among which were the violent determination of local nationalism to terminate colonial rule; the potential dangers of violent anticolonial struggles in creating opportunities for Soviet penetration—particularly in the southern tier of the continent with its abundance of strategic raw materials and potential markets; and indeed, the very limited capacity of the metropolitan powers, acting alone, to contain a combined nationalist and Soviet challenge and thus ensure continued Western dominance and influence.

Another contributing factor was the emerging significance of African voting strength in the UN General Assembly. The sudden appearance of seventeen independent African states in 1960 alone as members of the United Nations (raising the total African voting strength to twenty-two) generated a desire on the part of the United States to exercise tangible leverage on the voting behavior of these nations with regard to cold war issues.

Yet another factor was the necessity to resolve the political and psychological dilemma confronted by Africans arising from their continued and exclusive economic dependence on former metropoles, a relationship that evoked domestic charges of neocolonialism and demands to establish alternative foreign contacts with the socialist bloc. From this perspective, a U.S. posture that encouraged perpetuation of a restrictive relationship between former metropoles and independent

African states could only create a liability for the West. What was required of the United States in the era of decolonization was an approach that recognized the new realities of Africa and the need for a more imaginable basis of Euro-American cooperation in the continent.[54]

Under the specific guidance of such officials as G. Mennen Williams, Wayne Fredericks, and Harlan Cleveland and with the sympathetic ear of President Kennedy, a new Africa policy emphasizing direct action was developed. Williams argued the case for direct U.S. involvement in a memorandum to the secretary of state, Dean Rusk. The United States, he pointed out, "can perform an important function both for the independent African countries and their former metropoles by providing an expanded association within which they can comfortably continue to do business with each other without being suspected of neo-colonialism."[55] The reason, Williams explained, was that for most African states it was a domestic political imperative to expand their non-African contacts despite important "cultural and social ties with their metropoles." In particular, those states that valued their "independence or reputation for independence" had to "seek associations either with the United States or the Soviet Union."[56] As evidence to support this contention, Williams pointed to the existing controversy in Nigeria, Kenya, and Tanganyika (Tanzania) over the issue of association with the European Economic Community (EEC); the overwhelming opposition in Nigeria to the Anglo-Nigerian Defence Agreement of 1960; and the "compulsive urge" of the Ivory Coast's leaders to secure economic aid from the United States "so that they wouldn't be completely dependent upon the mother country, [and] because not to do so would lower their prestige in . . . Africa."[57]

To be certain, the United States would continue to acknowledge Western Europe's important interests in Africa and even exhort that region to assume primary responsibility in certain countries because it was ultimately in America's security interest to encourage a Western European economic presence in Africa. But for the sake of collective Western self-interest, Williams felt it was vital that "this compulsive urge on the part of independent Africans to widen their horizons find fulfillment in the U.S., which will seek to support West European presence, rather than the Soviet bloc, which will seek to reduce or terminate . . . that presence."[58] From this exposition emerged Williams' accurate conclusion that a strong U.S. presence in Africa was a prerequisite for sustaining Western Europe's historical interests there.

The metropolitan powers, not surprisingly, were not easily convinced of the rationale for a new basis of cooperation with the United States in Africa. To the more suspicious countries—such as Charles de Gaulle's France and Portugal—only selfish interest explained the insistence of the United States that it assume direct involvement in the African continent and its urging for rapid decolonization. The United States, they charged, had "ulterior economic designs" and was merely interested in supplanting their control in areas they regarded as a natural extension of the metropolitan domain. Their attitude was very often abetted by the views of the "Europeanists" in the U.S. State Department who acted more or less as their allies in restraining what they perceived as the extreme pro-Africa enthusiasm of the African Bureau. Until the Kennedy Africa policy became fairly established as a worthwhile U.S. option, the Europeanists persistently argued in favor of the old line "leave-it-to-the-Metropole" policy approach of the 1950s.[59] Nonetheless, chafed as they were, the metropolitan countries came to appreciate the increasing impotence of their power against both nationalist and socialist forces and, hence, the inevitability of an active U.S. cooperation in Africa.

Anglo-American Interdependence in Nigeria

The foregoing discussion offers a general indication of the basis for U.S.-British policy interdependence in Nigeria since 1960. This particular aspect of the U.S.-Western relationship is, however, reinforced by the unique nature of Anglo-American collaboration on matters affecting their common security and political interests in Africa since the end of World War II.

The special relationship between the two Anglo-Saxon nations was based, according to W.T.R. Fox, on the "assumption of a fundamental community of interest," one that has permitted U.S. and British assets to complement each other—through regional specialization—in promoting their joint security.[60] Although it is not certain that this common identity was always recognized to the same extent by the peoples and governments of both nations, the fact remains that its basic motif was strong enough to sustain their joint policy efforts toward African decolonization problems. Examples of such collaboration include their efforts in the Italian colonies, the Rhodesias, the Congo, and Kenya.[61] Indeed, once Great Britain officially acknowledged the necessity of direct U.S. involvement in Africa (at least in critical countries such as Ghana and Nigeria), British economic and political assets in its former colonies came to serve U.S. policy objectives by making the U.S. involvement cost-effective and thereby efficient.

In Nigeria itself, developing U.S. economic ties after 1960 complemented the structure of the traditional British presence. (See Tables 2.2–2.5, which show that the United States and Great Britain by 1966 were the most important sources of Nigeria's foreign aid, technical assistance personnel, and private foreign investments, as well as its dominant trade

TABLE 2.2

Aid Concentration, 1966: U.S.-U.K. Contribution as Percentage of Total (value in millions of U.S. dollars)

Donor	Value	Percentage of Total
United States	172,615,700[a]	49.5
United Kingdom	59,290,000	15.0
Total	231,905,700	64.5

[a]Excludes the value of U.S. assistance through multilateral agencies, the Peace Corps Volunteer program, etc.

Sources: U.S. *Technical and Capital Assistance in Support of Development in Nigeria, 1967* (Lagos, Nigeria: USAID, 1967), p. 5; O. Ojedokun, "Anglo-Nigerian Entente and Its Demise, 1960–1962," *Journal of Commonwealth Political Studies* 9 (November 1971): 232, n. 71.

TABLE 2.3

Concentration of Technical Assistance Personnel, 1966: U.S.-U.K. Contribution as Percentage of Total

Source	Contribution	Percentage of Total
United States	1,200[a]	52.5
United Kingdom	731[b]	37.5
Total	1,931	90.0

[a]Includes the Peace Corps Volunteer program but excludes U.S. experts on non-AID assignment.
[b]Excludes British civil servants on temporary duty in Nigeria.

Sources: U.S. *Technical and Capital Assistance in Support of Development in Nigeria, 1967,* pp. 1, 25; Angus Maddison, *Foreign Skills and Technical Assistance in Economic Development* (Paris: Development Center of the Organization for Economic Cooperation and Development, 1965), p. 21; O. Ojedokun, "The Changing Pattern of Nigeria's International Economic Relations: The Decline of Colonial Nexus," *The Journal of Developing Areas* 6 (July 1972): 551.

partners.) Another outcome of this development was the consolidation of Nigeria's historical economic links to the Western political economy. What is significant about the data in Tables 2.2–2.5 is that in terms of the scale of the investment capital and technical machinery needed to develop the infrastructural basis of a truly national economy, Nigeria's ties to the United States were clearly more critical than its ties to Great Britain after 1960. Thus, while Great Britain retained its colonial (though sharply declining) advantage in terms of direct private investment and trade concentration, the United States was responsible, by 1966, for the bulk of the capital aid and technical assistance personnel utilized within the framework of the Nigerian development plan. Indeed, the U.S. ties to Nigeria are even stronger than indicated in the tables when the U.S. role in generating additional aid through the International Bank for Reconstruction and Development (IBRD), the International Development Agency (IDA), the International Finance Association (IFA), and other

TABLE 2.4
Private Investment Concentration, 1966: U.S.-U.K. Contribution as
Percentage of Total (value in millions of U.S. dollars)

Source	Value	Percentage of Total
United States	183.96	17.0
United Kingdom	636.16	52.0
Total	820.12	69.0

Source: *Economic and Financial Review* (Central Bank of Nigeria) 6 (December 1968): 14.

TABLE 2.5
Trade Concentration, 1966: U.S.-U.K. Share as Percentage of Total

Partner	Percentage of Total Imports	Percentage of Total Exports
United States	16.2	8.0
United Kingdom	29.7	37.7
Total	45.9	45.7

Source: *Review of External Trade, 1966* (Lagos, Nigeria: Federal Office of Statistics, 1966), p. 11.

multilateral agencies is taken into account. At any rate, given the interrelated nature of U.S.-British political objectives in Nigeria and the U.S. leadership of the Western alliance, the United States became, after 1960, potentially the primary Western beneficiary of the British imperial economic (and political) legacy in Nigeria. That meant, for example, that in its direct foreign policy relationship with the ruling Nigerian regime, the United States would derive potential influence not only through the dynamics of its emerging economic (bilateral) links with Nigeria, but also from the historical British economic presence in the country.

This tripartite pattern of Nigeria-U.K.-U.S. interaction in foreign affairs warrants further discussion. There is reason to suggest that in implementing its vital regional policies the Nigerian regime found its direct ties to the United States to be, in a very real sense, more crucial and relevant than the declining colonial and Commonwealth links with Great Britain. The explanation lies partly in the structure of the regime's overall interests. Essentially, it was through the United States, with its enormous arsenal of material resources and global political-diplomatic muscle, that the Nigerian leaders hoped, perhaps with reckless idealism, to attain those interests. The explanation also lies in the dynamic role of the United States as the de facto senior partner and guardian of U.S.-British diplomacy in Africa. The United States, as the leader of the capitalist social system in the worldwide crusade against Soviet power and ideology, was naturally more captivated than Great Britain by the prospect of influencing the regional orientation of an emerging Nigeria as part of that mission.

Further, by 1962 British economic and political leverage in Nigeria was becoming modified in response to a number of factors both in Nigeria and in Great Britain. First, Great Britain, with its dwindling resources, could not adequately satisfy the development needs and interests of an independent Nigeria. Second, the articulate opposition groups and some public officials in Nigeria vehemently resisted a continuation of the British hegemony. And third, the British economy was still experiencing serious problems of contraction, caused by the structural dislocations of World War II and, more crucially, by the increasing loss of exclusive resources in its former colonies. However, one should not think that the British henceforth exercised no significant influence on Nigeria's foreign policy. Indeed, as is shown below, the intertwining nature of U.S.-British political objectives in Nigeria worked, by a cruel logic, to give the British an indirect veto over important aspects of Nigeria-U.S. relations. On the one hand, the minimum price of the British concession to the United States for direct access to its former colonies seemed to be an understanding that the residual influence of the United Kingdom would not be undermined. On the other hand, Americans greatly appreciated the value of the British imperial relationship as a vehicle for retaining overall Western control of African resources and territory. Besides, the Nigerian government, in other respects, found Great Britain to be a critical mediating asset in its direct diplomacy with the United States.

There is good indication from the available sources that the United States and Great Britain sought, jointly, to advance certain basic objectives in Nigeria after the British withdrew from that country in 1960.[62] One objective was to strengthen the development of democratic-parliamentary institutions, which would perhaps enhance the assimilation of other Western values by Nigerians. Although the British had, prior to their departure, laid a fair groundwork in the sense of creating basic parliamentary structures in the political system and in educating the Nigerian political elite in the operation of parliamentary procedures, there were indications seen as early as 1959 that this alien experiment might be threatened by the eruption of multiple contradictions inherent in the process of national decolonization.[63] To preempt this possibility and thus ensure Nigeria's pro-capitalist socioeconomic system, the United States and Great Britain thought it particularly necessary to undertake a concerted program of economic and technical assistance in conjunction with the Nigerian development plan. Such a program would also ensure the internal security of the Nigerian society against the possibility of infiltration by Communist forces.

A second objective was to bolster the image of the ruling national regime in Lagos and sustain its regional leadership capacity in Africa. The primary aim was to nurture Nigeria's pro-Western orientation and moderating capacity in African diplomacy.

A third objective, clearly in the mutual interest of the two allies, was to stem a precipitous decline in Great Britain's economic advantages in Nigeria. Although the British had lost a formal channel of political influence in that country, existing economic ties still provided a tangible medium of political leverage. The official U.S. policy, as earlier clarified, was aimed at cushioning the British economic position in Nigeria as a basis for retaining Great Britain's political presence, which then served as a supplementary asset of U.S. diplomacy. Moreover, given the still substantial British investments in Nigeria and the crucial Nigerian-U.K. commerce in industrial and raw materials, the United States was concerned lest a radical disruption of those links should cause economic dislocations in the economy of its most important NATO ally.

The interlocking structure of Anglo-American political ties in Africa posed a dilemma for Nigeria's foreign policy autonomy on critical issues. The issue of post-independence foreign military alignment was one particular policy area that became greatly sensitized by the reality of Anglo-American interdependence. The specific problem presented by the Anglo-Nigerian Defence Agreement of 1960 casts some light on the foreign policy implication of Nigeria's dependency as defined by that imperial relationship.

In January 1962, the Nigerian government succumbed, or so it seemed, to persistent public pressures and agreed to formally abrogate the defense agreement it had signed with Great Britain in 1960 as part of the independence bargain.[64] That agreement had been condemned in Nigeria on a number of grounds, one of which, as already indicated, was linked to the domestic political struggle. But the most emotionally charged argument against the agreement was that it would militarily consecrate Nigeria's dependence on the Anglo-American bloc. Critics also contended that the regime wished, for its exclusive purposes, to turn Nigeria into a military outpost of NATO in Africa, thus limiting the country's capacity for dynamic leadership on decolonization.[65] Because the issue came to a head just one year after Nigeria's independence, it was an early demonstration to the United States and Great Britain that Nigerians generally were extremely touchy about any foreign ties that seemed to tarnish their country's newly won sovereignty. (Witness, in this connection, the point made in Williams' thesis earlier cited.) It also revealed, in a practical manner, the end of British political preeminence in Nigeria clearly signified that unlike weaker former colonies of Great Britain in Africa, Nigeria was less disposed to compromise its foreign policy autonomy, even within a context of extreme international dependency, because of its regional role conception.

But if Nigeria could afford to resist a relatively weak Great Britain acting alone, could it also maintain a similar independent stance against Great Britain operating under a concerted Anglo-American nexus? In resisting an exclusive military dependence on Great Britain, Nigerians had expected that their leaders could safely diversify such dependence to embrace other sources, perhaps including even the United States. The practicality of that expectation was tested the following year, when Nigeria seemed to have faced an external emergency. In that year, following a military uprising in the Republic of Togo in which the country's first president was assassinated,[66] Prime Minister Balewa and his cabinet concluded that Ghana had engineered the crisis as part of its design to topple nonprogressive West African regimes. Nigeria, he decided, had to strengthen its armed forces in preparation for a possible military confrontation with Ghana. As part of this effort, Balewa sought to institute military links with the United States and specifically approached the U.S. government for the purpose of acquiring military assistance. But the U.S. government expressed strong reluctance, despite an equal concern over increasing evidence of Ghanaian subversive activities in the pro-Western states of the subregion. An explanation for the U.S. attitude was that the United States needed Great Britain's approval before attempting to displace its ally as the primary source of Nigeria's military aid.[67] The British, no doubt, were equally unwilling to relinquish that role; with it and their remaining economic ties, they hoped to retain some leverage in Nigeria.

The practical result was that until the outbreak of its civil war in 1967, Nigeria remained substantially dependent on Great Britain for its military needs. Between 1961 and 1967, about 1,151 Nigerian military personnel were trained in British military institutions. Moreover, most of the equipment used by the Nigerian armed forces in this period was supplied by the United Kingdom.[68] Yet another important indicator of Nigerian-British military ties was the fact that until 1965, the commanding officer of the Nigerian army was a British national—Major-General C. E. Welby Everard. By 1966, the value of U.S. military assistance to Nigeria—in dramatic contrast to its contribution in capital and technical aid—was a mere $1.3 million,[69] confirming the views expressed above.

During the Nigerian civil war, the U.S. government once again affirmed Great Britain's military responsibility in Nigeria by refusing to respond positively to the federal government's request for arms with which to suppress the rebellion. At this historic juncture, however, the U.S. policy achieved only partial success. Because the British were willing to supply only limited military assistance in accordance with their national goals in the Nigerian conflict, the wounded federal government reacted in desperation by approaching a very willing Soviet Union for the critical weapons it needed to end the secession—an act that ended the traditional British role as the exclusive supplier for the Nigerian military establishment.

Through experiences such as these, especially in the immediate post-independence years, Nigerian policymakers learned that they could not simply discount the opinion and interest of Great Britain, even in their direct dealings with the United States. These experiences were also some of the concrete sources of the popular perception in Nigeria of a homogeneous U.S.-British nexus of interests in Africa. Thus, it is accurate to say that the essential reality of a de facto division of labor in Nigeria between the United States and Great Britain worked to enhance Great Britain's role as an arbiter in Nigeria-U.S. relations. Chief Simeon Adebo, Nigeria's permanent delegate to the UN from 1961 to 1967, observed that Nigerian officials at the UN often received instructions from Lagos "to take their cue from Britain and the U.S. on vital cold war issues, by either voting along with [the two powers] or abstaining, rather than opposing a Western position."[70]

Summary

Nigeria's attainment of political independence pushed the issue of national economic development and economic independence into the center of domestic politics most intensively from 1961 to 1962. The vigorous national debates over foreign financing for the first development plan and over the issue of nationalization illustrate how factors of foreign economic dependence became intermeshed with domestic political and power processes.

The foreign economic strategy proposed by the ruling regime had the effect of strengthening Nigeria's colonial ties to the Western political economy. Also, the preference of this strategy by Nigeria's policymakers was related to a strong desire to safeguard the other two regime interests— domestic security and regional leadership—as well.

After 1961, the critical investment capital and technical expertise needed for Nigeria's development within the framework of the first national development plan were secured mainly through the assistance of the United States, but also through the assistance of Great Britain.

British colonial ties to Nigeria constituted, after 1960, a valuable asset to U.S. foreign policy. This was facilitated by the common nature of Anglo-American political-security interests and strategy in Nigeria and Africa generally. The emergent U.S. economic involvement in Nigeria in this period resulted in consolidating Nigeria's ties to the U.S.-British nexus—a process nurtured by Nigerian policymakers—and to the Western political economy in general. From their vantage position, the British were able to play a mediating role in the overall Nigerian-U.S. diplomacy.

Notes

1. Important Nigerian primary exports were cocoa, cotton, palm oil, palm kernels, groundnuts (peanuts), rubber, oil seeds, and timber; major minerals were tin, columbite, crude petroleum, coal, zinc, and iron ore.

2. A. A. Okolo, in "International Political Economy and Nigeria's Development: 1945–1975" (Unpublished Ph.D. Dissertation, Purdue University, 1978), has provided an interesting account of the processes of Nigeria's progressive incorporation in the capitalist world economy.

3. Olasupo Ojedokun, "The Changing Pattern of Nigeria's International Economic Relations: The Decline of the Colonial Nexus, 1960–1966," *Journal of Developing Nations* (July 1972): 535–554.

4. James Coleman, *Nigeria: Background to Nationalism* (Berkeley: University of California Press, 1958), p. 80; also Peter Kilby, *Industrialization in Open Economy: Nigeria* (Cambridge: The University Press, 1969), pp. 59–65.

5. In 1937, nearly all the major commercial firms entered into a cartel-like arrangement known as the "Pool," designed to stabilize the price of cocoa. This led to the charge by cocoa farmers of Nigeria and the Gold Coast (Ghana) that the Pool policy sought to enrich the international corporations at the expense of the poor countries. More pointedly, the *West African Pilot* charged in an editorial that "the Pool and the 'stabilization' of prices stemming from the agreement among the European firms worked against the interests of the Africans." Babalola Cole, "Cocoa Politics: Insights from the 'Pool' Crisis," *International Studies Notes of the ISA* 8(2) (Summer 1981): 20–24.

6. Coleman, *Nigeria: Background to Nationalism*, p. 81.

7. This is in reference to the Six-Year National Development Plan launched in 1962. See discussion below.

8. *National Development Plan, 1962–1968*, Sessional Paper No. 1 of 1962 (Federal Ministry of Economic Development, 1962).

9. Gerald K. Helleiner, *Peasant Agriculture, Government, and Economic Growth in Nigeria* (Homewood, Ill.: Richard D. Irwin, Inc., 1966), pp. 332–334.

10. Helleiner, *Peasant Agriculture*, p. 335.

11. *National Development Plan*, p. 50.

12. The three main political parties after independence were the Northern People's Congress (NPC), the National Council of Nigerian Citizens (NCNC), and the Action Group (AG). After the 1959 national elections, the NPC (having the largest number of seats in the national legislature) and the NCNC formed a coalition as government parties. This coalition ruled the country until 1964. Meanwhile, the AG (in coalition with some minor parties) became the official national opposition party in the assembly.

It should be added that the essential base of support for all these parties was their political (and, indeed, ethnic) region: The NPC had its main base of support in the North, the NCNC in the East, and the AG in the West.

13. *House of Representatives Debate* (hereinafter cited *HRD*), November 29, 1961, p. 346.

14. Ibid., p. 347; also David R. Mummery, *The Protection of International Private Investment* (New York: Praeger Publishers, 1968), pp. 18–31.

15. *HRD*, November 29, 1961, p. 347.

16. Ibid., April 6, 1960, p. 607.

17. This point seems further supported by the report that the Action Group, conjointly with the other two major parties, had in 1957 made a public pledge against nationalization. Sam Epele, *The Promise of Nigeria* (London: Pan Books, Ltd., 1960), p. 244.

18. *National Development Plan*, p. 24.

19. *HRD*, November 29, 1961, p. 352.

20. Ibid., p. 353.

21. Ibid., p. 354.

22. James S. Coleman, "The Foreign Policy of Nigeria," in Joseph E. Black and Kenneth W. Thompson, eds., *Foreign Policies in a World of Change* (New York: Harper and Row, 1963), p. 385; also Helleiner, *Peasant Agriculture*, pp. 336–338.

23. See O. Aboyade, "A General Critique of the Plan," and O. Olakanpo, "Foreign Aid and the Plan: A General Appraisal," both in *The Nigerian Journal of Economic and Social Studies* 4 (July 1962): 110–130. Also see Sayre P. Schartz, "Nigeria's First National Development Plan (1962–1968): An Appraisal," *The Nigerian Journal of Economic and Social Studies* 5 (July 1963): 221–235.

24. Okotie-Eboh, *HRD*, March 29, 1962, p. 283.

25. *HRD*, March 29, 1961, p. 285.

26. Ibid., April 6, 1961, p. 183.

27. Ibid., March 29, 1962, p. 284.

28. E. A. Ajayi, "Nigeria-Soviet Aid Relations," *Nigeria: Bulletin on Foreign Affairs* 1 (January 1972): 1–9.

29. Ibid.; also Ojedokun, "Changing Pattern of Nigeria's International Economic Relations," p. 540.

30. On another level, the movement toward increasing interdependence among the industrial nations is supposed to result in greater obfuscation of state boundaries. James Rosenau has suggested the potential effect of this trend on the continued utility of the concept of "national interest." *International Encyclopedia of Social Science*, Vol. 11, 1968, p. 39.

31. Joseph Frankel, *The Making of Foreign Policy* (London: Oxford University Press, 1971), p. 54; also Warner R. Schilling, "The Clarification of Ends: Or, Which Interest Is the National?" *World Politics* 8 (April 1956): 566–578.

32. Mummery, *Protection of International Private Investment*, pp. 6–10.

33. Thomas J. Biersteker, *Distortion or Development: Contending Perspectives on the Multinational Corporations* (Cambridge: M.I.T. Press, 1978), p. 71.

34. See Coleman, "Foreign Policy of Nigeria," p. 386; also Frederick Barbison, "Human Resources and Economic Development in Nigeria," in Robert O. Tilman

and Taylor Cole, eds., *The Nigerian Political Scene* (Durham, N.C.: Duke University Press, 1962), pp. 198–219.

35. W. Howard Wriggins, *The Ruler's Imperative* (New York: Columbia University Press, 1969), p. 4.

36. In a historical sense, the uncompromising relationship between the government and opposition parties derived primarily from the fragmentary nature of the Nigerian nationalist movement prior to independence. The emergence of regionalized political parties from about 1951 was a result, essentially, of regional mistrust and subsequent rivalry in 1959 among the three largest ethnic blocs to dominate a post-independence national government.

37. "This Act not only provided for the operational use of the armed forces for national security and the maintenance of public safety and . . . order, it also gave the Prime Minister authority to give direct orders to the Commanding Officer to use the Army for internal security purposes." (See Olatunde Ojo, "Nigeria's Foreign Policy" [Unpublished Ph.D. Dissertation, University of Connecticut, 1974], p. 102.)

38. Indeed, the government's premonition was proved correct about thirty months after independence. In 1963, the leader of the Action Group and some of his close associates were arrested, charged with treasonable felony against the state, and sentenced to long terms of imprisonment.

39. Of the estimated national population of 55.7 million in 1963, 29.8 million were in the North; 12.4 million were in the East; 10.3 million were in the West; 2.5 million were in the Midwest; and 675,000 were in the federal territory of Lagos. See R. L. Sklar, "Contradictions in the Nigerian Political System," *Journal of Modern African Studies* 3(2) (1965): 208.

40. The following indexes illustrate this reality: In 1963, 2,485,676 pupils were in elementary school in the South; the number in the North was 410,706. Also the amount of electricity used in the two regions—as an index of technological development—varied widely. At the end of March 1964, about 270,000,000 kwh were sold in the South as opposed to 40,000,000 sold in the North. See Sklar, "Contradictions in the Nigerian Political System," p. 209.

41. A. B. Akinyemi, *Foreign Policy and Federalism* (Ibadan, Nigeria: University Press, 1974), p. 75; also Ojo, "Nigeria's Foreign Policy," p. 202–223.

42. K. J. Holsti, "National Role Conceptions in the Study of Foreign Policy," *International Studies Quarterly* 14 (September 1970): 233–319.

43. *HRD*, January 15, 1960, p. 74.

44. Ibid., November 25, 1960, p. 250.

45. This refers to an "organized minority" that rules the majority through control of the dominant values and institutions of society. Consequently, "the class that rules . . . monopolizes power and enjoys the advantages that power brings." See Gaetano Mosca, *The Ruling Class*, trans. Hannah D. Kahn, ed. and rev. Arthur Livingston (New York: McGraw-Hill Book Co., 1939), pp. 50–53.

46. One necessarily becomes cautious in applying this concept to Nigeria in the period of study. It can be argued that the extremely regionalized nature of political competition made it difficult for members of this group to develop sufficient consciousness of their common interests. But the usage is justified

because of the special socioeconomic status enjoyed by the top stratum of this group despite their allegiance to different ethnic communities. Moreover, the stability of this group in national politics from 1951 to 1966 marked the group off from younger aspirants to top political positions, whose access was effectively closed off.

47. Sklar, "Contradictions in the Nigerian Political System," pp. 201–213; see also James O'Connell, "The Political Class and Economic Growth," *Nigerian Journal of Economic and Social Research* 8 (March 1966): 129–140.

48. The intertwining web of interests between Nigerian government ministers and business leaders is discussed by O'Connell in "Political Class," pp. 132–134.

49. As minister of finance, Okotie-Eboh was, after the prime minister, perhaps the most influential member of the cabinet. His durability in that post—1954 to 1966—enhanced further his influence in the government. Still another source of influence derived from his enormous economic wealth.

50. Reginald H. Green, "Economic Policy of the Political Class," *Nigerian Opinion* 6 (December 1965): 6–8.

51. Marshall R. Singer, *Weak States in a World of Powers* (New York: The Free Press, 1972), pp. 226–227.

52. Vernon McKay, *Africa in World Politics* (New York: Macfadden-Bartell Corp., 1964), pp. 254–262.

53. An important exception to this general posture was the direct operation by the United States, since World War II, of a number of air bases and communications facilities in Morocco, Libya, Liberia, and Eritrea.

54. For the Kennedy administration there were, in addition, certain domestic considerations. The president, for example, needed to strengthen his liberal image among black Americans and to establish his civil rights credentials by taking overt actions to demonstrate new American friendship toward black African states. Part of this thrust was Kennedy's drive to recruit blacks into the foreign service.

55. G. Mennen Williams, "U.S., Europe, and Africa," October 30, 1962, Memorandum, G. Mennen Williams Files, General Records of the Department of State, Record Group 59, National Archives, Washington, D.C. (Hereinafter, records in the National Archives building are indicated by the abbreviation NA.)

56. Ibid.

57. Ibid.

58. Ibid.

59. In a private interview, Williams acknowledged the struggle for jurisdictional supremacy on Africa between the African and European bureaus. But unlike the impression one gains from the available secondary literature on this issue, Williams claimed to have had a good working relationship with top Europeanists in the department, such as George Ball. He explained, for instance, that "the George Ball . . . I knew and worked with, I found situation after situation that in some cases he was . . . a better advocate on Africa than I could be myself." Interview with G. Mennen Williams, recorded by W. W. Moss, January 27, 1970, Oral History Program, John F. Kennedy Library, Waltham, Massachusetts.

60. W.T.R. Fox, *The Superpowers* (New York: Harcourt Brace, 1944), pp. 50–69; also by the same author in collaboration with Annette B. Fox, "Britain and America in the Era of Total Diplomacy" (Center of International Studies, Princeton University, March 25, 1952).

61. In fact, on some occasions, U.S. and British private business interests had been at odds with each other in some former British colonies, including Nigeria, indicating that private interests do not always share official enthusiasm regarding the prudence of collaboration. Joseph Palmer II, the U.S. ambassador in Nigeria, was forced more than once to write to Washington in an attempt to exonerate British economic interests in Nigeria against charges by private U.S. business groups that such interests were used prejudicially against them. See, for instance, J. Palmer to G. Williams, May 8, 1963, Williams Files, NA.

62. Consult the following, for example: "U.S.-U.K. Talks, December 3–4, 1964" (briefing notes), and "Parliamentary Conference on British and American Policies Toward Africa," June 24–27, 1965, both contained in G. Mennen Williams Files, RG 59, NA.

63. By 1962, the precariousness of the Nigerian parliamentary experiment had become quite obvious to responsible officials in both nations, although in public they persisted in extolling the country as a successful Western democratic model. See remarks in "Parliamentary Conference on British and American Policies Toward Africa," p. 13.

64. See a discussion of the political dynamics surrounding both the ratification and abrogation of the agreement by Gordon T. Idang, "The Politics of Nigerian Foreign Policy: The Ratification and Renunciation of the Anglo-Nigerian Defence Agreement," *African Studies Review* 13 (September 1970): 227–250.

65. Ibid., pp. 235–236.

66. This event and its impact on Nigerian-Ghanaian relations are discussed fully in Chapter 4.

67. The United States also seemed to have been concerned about the prospect of a West African arms race, which might produce greater instability in the subregion. See G. Williams (in Lagos) to Wayne Fredericks, February 13, 1963, Telegram no. 1167, Williams Files, NA.

68. Olasupo Ojedokun, "The Anglo-Nigerian Entente and Its Demise, 1960–1962," *Journal of Commonwealth and Political Studies* 19 (November 1971): 229: also Olajide Aluko, *Essays in Nigerian Foreign Policy* (London: George Allen and Unwin, 1981), pp. 62–63.

69. *U.S. Overseas Loans and Grants: July 1, 1945–June 30, 1966* (Washington, D.C.: Department of State, 1966), p. 100.

70. Interview with Chief S. O. Adebo, Lagos.

3

The Emerging Structure of
Bilateral Dependence: 1960–1966

Between 1960 and 1966, the Nigerian-U.S. relationship hinged on two tangible conditions. One was the concrete economic aid and technical assistance that the Nigerian political leadership hoped to obtain and actually received from the United States toward the execution of its national development program. The other was the political-diplomatic support that each country sought and gained from the other in promoting its regional objectives in Africa.

No doubt, other nontangible factors—e.g., cultural, sentimental, elite, and ideological ties—played a role in the development of the relationship. These factors, as noted in the Introduction, nurtured a facilitative environment in which the more substantive links operated. Moreover, Nigerian leaders engaged in what seemed to be a conscious propagandistic effort "of emphasizing their cultural and ideological similarities with America and Western nations" as a tactical device for attracting Western investment capital.[1] Economic and political connections were crucial in binding the real interests and actions of the two countries in their overall relationship. To the Nigerian leadership, economic ties, especially, assured Nigeria's access to the most valuable external development and political assets. To U.S. policymakers, these ties provided a functional and regulated channel through which they could affect both the general decisionmaking environment of Nigeria's foreign policy and specific Nigerian policies on regional issues of mutual concern.

That these economic ties existed does not, however, automatically connote a monocausal explanation of behavior based on economics, nor does the condition imply simplistically that economic ties inexorably worked to induce Nigeria's political compliance with the United States. Indeed, it seems futile and unnecessary to search for explicit effects of economic ties in discrete foreign policy actions of dependent states.[2] In the Nigerian experience, a more relevant observation is that these links, because of their immense value to the national economy and the ruling strata in the society, served to integrate all other areas of interest in the Nigerian-U.S. relationship. For the United States, in particular, the resultant medium became indispensable in its primary desire to "influence Nigerian policies and actions and establish a broad area of agreement to common objectives."[3]

U.S. interest in Nigeria's economic development was bound closely to its emerging political objectives in Nigeria (and in sub-Saharan Africa). In 1961, the broad political premise of U.S. economic initiative in Nigeria was explained by the State Department as follows:

> The basic . . . [economic] problem in our relations with Nigeria is to come up with a program of technical and economic assistance of sufficient scope to convince the Nigerians that, with the help they are currently receiving from the British, they can depend upon the West, rather than communist-bloc countries, for their development needs.[4]

In the previous fall, Prime Minister Balewa had called for precisely such a joint U.S.-British effort in Nigeria's development. The message to this effect was conveyed to the U.S. government through Governor Nelson Rockefeller of New York, who had been in Nigeria, attending that country's independence celebration, as the personal representative of President Eisenhower.

Two more specific political objectives underlay the U.S. economic policy in Nigeria. First, as indicated above, it was the desire of the United States to engage the active cooperation of the Nigerian regime in resisting Soviet-Communist penetration of Nigeria by contributing to the strengthening of its independence and institutions. Hence, the domestic economic and political stability of Nigeria was a priority of U.S. policy. Second, "because of its responsible leadership, . . . economic viability and political stability," the United States strongly favored and was willing to take appropriate measures to support "Nigeria's effort to assume a position of leadership in African affairs."[5] In this regard, U.S. officials had, since 1959, displayed unbounded optimism in their estimation of Nigeria's potential as a dominant and stabilizing regional force in the turbulent seas of African decolonization. An early recognition of this potential underlay such symbolic U.S. gestures as the decision of U.S. secretary of state Christian Herter to sponsor Nigeria's admission to the United Nations.

In addition to these central political objectives, the United States wished to expand its trading and private investment contacts with Africa's most populous nation. Between 1957 and 1961, successive U.S. economic missions (official and private) to Nigeria reported tremendous investment and trade opportunities available in the burgeoning Nigerian economy. U.S. businesses were exhorted to promptly seize these opportunities, especially by investing in the development of Nigeria's industrial infrastructure and mineral resources such as petroleum. A Commerce Department economic mission in 1961, for instance, remarked on the positive disposition of the Nigerian leadership toward U.S. investment: "Nigerian government officials recognize the vital role that overseas capital and managerial and technical skills must play in expanding the country's economy." In consequence the mission reported, "Federal and Regional governments are prepared to invest with foreign capital in worthwhile industrial enterprises."[6] Regarding trade, the mission reported, "The prospects for U.S. exporters to supply goods to the Nigerian market appear limitless. Practically any product is a potential export because of Nigeria's present limited industrialization."[7]

Therefore, on both grounds—the more critical and immediate political objectives and the long-term interest in establishing a larger American presence in the Nigerian economy—the U.S. government decided to make Nigeria a major recipient of its economic development aid in Africa. Thus, Nigeria emerged, by 1964, as one of four nations that together received 50 percent of all U.S. assistance to Africa (the others were Tunisia, Liberia, and Zaire). Nigeria also was among nine Third World nations that, according to Joan Nelson, since 1962 "received the lion's share of [U.S.] A.I.D.'s development funds, and roughly half of all A.I.D. assistance."[8]

Foreign Aid and Technical Assistance

The Six-Year Development Plan provided the essential vehicle of Nigerian-U.S. economic diplomacy between 1961 and 1966. Before 1961, the United States had extended various forms of economic aid to Nigeria worth about $43 million. The early aid was mainly in the form of technical assistance in the fields of education, public administration, investment and industrial development, and communications.

In 1961, the U.S. government formally announced its aid offer of $225 million (i.e., as a long-term commitment) for the Nigerian plan. But that decision was only approved after two exploratory visits to Washington were made by high-level Nigerian officials and one special U.S. economic mission, led by Arnold Rivkin, was sent to Nigeria, all in 1961, for the specific purpose of studying the prospects of U.S. participation in the implementation of the plan.[9]

During one of these visits to the United States, Prime Minister Balewa focused the important part of his discussions with President Kennedy on convincing the White House of the importance of U.S. development assistance for Nigeria's stability and growth. However, Balewa also used the occasion to caution the United States, and at the same time reassure his Nigerian and other African critics, that by accepting U.S. aid Nigeria would not necessarily sacrifice its foreign policy principle of nonalignment[10] in the East-West conflict. The Nigerian prime minister stressed this point while addressing a joint session of the U.S. Congress:

> Of course, it goes without saying that Nigeria must seek overseas aid in order to ensure her economic growth. But Nigeria is determined to remain on friendly terms with every nation which recognises and respects its sovereignty, and we are not prepared to follow blindly the lead of anyone. We prefer to remain on the path of truth. It is in this spirit that we shall seek and expect aid from abroad.[11]

This rather courageous statement reflected the desire of most Nigerians that their country should maintain an independent stance in the cold war. But how would a foreign policy of untainted nonalignment (especially if this was meant to apply as well to East-West power competition in Africa) square with the regime's strongly felt need for U.S. cooperation in promoting the three state interests discussed in Chapter 2? The extent of U.S. commitment sought by the Nigerian government could only be guaranteed, if at all, as an exchange for Nigeria's political alignment to the West. Balewa recognized this contradiction and sought to reconcile it. His resolution was to assure U.S. officials, in private, that an espousal of a policy of nonalignment "should not affect Nigeria's close relations with the . . . West, especially the United States."[12]

Meanwhile, the Rivkin Special Mission noted in its report that "Nigeria, perhaps more than any of the new independent African states . . . meets the new aid criteria of the President, and offers a good opportunity . . . to achieve economic development in a democratic framework."[13] In addition to recommending direct U.S. assistance, the report strongly urged the U.S. government to consult with the IBRD "with a view to coordinating possible U.S. contributions . . . with those which may come from the IBRD" for sponsoring, specifically, large-scale Nigerian development projects such as the Niger hydroelectric dam, projected in 1961 to cost $189 million.[14] Another recommendation was that the United States should lead immediate efforts to form a consortium of Western aid donors for Nigeria on the model of the consortiums already active for India and Pakistan. In a formal sense, it was the strong support given to the Nigerian plan by the Rivkin Report, along with the impact of Balewa's visit to Washington, that led to Kennedy's public announcement of the U.S. aid commitment a year before the official launching of the plan.

This aid commitment was primarily in the form of grants and technical assistance personnel, with a smaller proportion in the form of loans. The U.S. development projects were coordinated principally by the newly created Agency for International Development (USAID) but were under the political direction of the State Department (through the U.S. embassy and country team in Nigeria).

From about 1953 to the early 1960s, most U.S. economic assistance to Third World nations had been in the form of grants. This practice was, in part, a carryover from the experience with the Marshall Plan aid to Europe.[15] Partly, also, it was based on a consideration in Washington that because grants do not have to be repaid as such, aid in the form of grants would "relieve the poor recipient of the burden of future debt obligations." Further, many recipient governments, it was thought, would rather accept grants than loans because of a need to preserve their limited foreign reserves that otherwise would be expended on costly loan servicing.[16]

Although aid given on the basis of these considerations alone might normally engender goodwill in the recipient country toward the United States, the preference for grant over loan aid had a more immediate foreign policy justification. While both loan and grant aids—due to their intrinsic values and the fact that both involve direct transactions between governments—can be used as instruments of foreign policy, the political payoffs of loans, from the perspective of a dominant donor, are neither as profound nor as instantly attractive as those deriving from grant aid. In the parlance of international development, loans are used, normally, to sustain long-term economic programs; they are awarded on condition of future repayment plus interest. Theoretically, therefore, they should be utilized to finance sound economic schemes, without undue compromise by immediate political considerations, in order to assure future recovery by the donor. Grants, by contrast, are used to support more direct development projects; but more crucially, they are linked to the operations of foreign technical personnel from the donor country within the recipient society. Hence, they have the advantage of creating more direct and effective channels of influence relationships,[17] a fact that, paradoxically, causes certain recipients to prefer loans to grants—especially multilaterally sponsored loans. Thus, the official U.S. preference for grant aid was justified on the need to affect the decisionmaking environment and elite opinions in strategic recipient Third World nations both in the immediate sense and in the longer term.

Within one year of the formal launching of the Nigerian plan, the United States had obligated (i.e., to be negotiated for actual expenditure on feasible development projects) the sum of $62.8 million of its $225 million aid commitment to Nigeria. About $39 million of this was actually spent as grants; at the start of 1963, no funds had yet been expended as loans. In mid-1963, the number of U.S. technical personnel in Nigeria was about 795 (including Peace Corps volunteers but excluding personnel from other U.S. government agencies), having increased by more than 200 percent from 1961.[18] A few years later, the picture was different. By December 1966, total U.S. development aid to Nigeria amounted to $172,615,700. This did not include the cost of assistance through the Peace Corps Volunteer (PCV) program (the cost of the PCV program was not included in the $225 million commitment), nor did it reflect the value of U.S.-supported aid to Nigeria by the IBRD, IDA, IFA, and other international agencies. Of this sum, $58,860,000 was in loans, $110,324,900 was in grants, and $3,430,000 was in PL. 480-Title III (food) (see Table 3.1). Correspondingly, the number of U.S. technical personnel in Nigeria had risen to 1,200 by 1966. Significantly, Nigeria had also, in the same general period, attracted a sizeable amount of aid from the three international financial institutions listed above: IBRD, $213.2 million; IDA, $35.3 million; IFA, $2.7 million.[19]

U.S. loan aid was generally used to finance long-term capital programs, i.e., programs that affected the economic infrastructure upon which future development depended. The construction of roads, power plants, and telecommunications and higher education facilities, among other projects, fell into this category. The loans were mostly long-term, repayable after forty years with a ten-year grace period before principal repayment and with an annual interest rate of 1 to 2.5 percent (see Figure 3.1). In contrast, U.S. grants were used to finance projects having more immediate returns, for example, activities in such areas as development, public and business administration, teacher education, engineering, and feasibility studies (see Figure 3.2). These institution-building projects were supervised by AID-sponsored technical personnel. Other AID-sponsored technical personnel served as advisers in government ministries responsible for education, finance, economic development, commerce, and industry (see discussion in the next section). In another type of U.S. technical assistance, Nigerians were assigned to work under AID experts and Nigerian personnel were sent to the United States for further training—referred to as "participant training." At the end of 1966, about 1,265 Nigerians had been or were being trained in the United States.[20]

Mechanisms of Aid, Foreign Personnel, and Influence Relationships

Short of outright attempts by a donor to explicitly link aid to desired political objectives in the recipient nation,[21] there are a number of direct

TABLE 3.1
Statistical Summary of USAID Program in Nigeria Through December 1966[a]

Development grant assistance		
Technical assistance	£36,535,000	$102,297,900
Other grant assistance	2,866,800	8,027,000
Total	£39,401,800	$110,324,900
Development loans		
FY 1962 and prior		
Apapa Warehouse	£ 237,000	$ 663,600
Railway Corporation	1,070,400	2,997,200
FY 1963		
Ibadan Water Supply	4,321,400	12,100,000
FY 1964		
Calabar-Ikom Road	3,071,400	8,600,000
Niger Dam	2,500,000	7,000,000
Port Harcourt Comprehensive Secondary School	643,000	1,800,000
Northern Nigeria Teacher Training Colleges	1,357,000	3,800,000
National Telecommunications Development–		
Engineering Services	1,143,000	3,200,000
FY 1965		
Port Harcourt–Umuezeala Road	2,714,300	7,600,000
Umudike Agriculture School	1,000,000	2,800,000
FY 1966		
Telephone Instruments	571,400	1,600,000
Export-Import bank loans	2,392,900	6,700,000
Total	£21,021,800	$ 58,860,800
Food for peace shipments (Title III)		
FY 1962 and prior	£ 164,000	$ 460,000
FY 1963	147,000	411,000
FY 1964	154,000	431,000
FY 1965	367,000	1,028,000
FY 1966	393,000	1,100,000
Total	£ 1,225,000	$ 3,430,000
Grand total	£61,648,600	$172,615,700

[a]U.S. government assistance to Nigeria not listed includes the Peace Corps Volunteer program and regional projects in which other African countries and/or other donor countries cooperated.

Source: U.S. *Technical and Capital Assistance in Support of Development in Nigeria, 1967* (Lagos, Nigeria: USAID, 1967), p. 5.

and indirect ways by which the method of aid provision and project management can affect the environment of decisionmaking and hence the orientation of a recipient nation's domestic and foreign policies. There were many instances in the Nigerian experience where, for example, the practice of assigning foreign personnel to work in government ministries might have had a direct impact on policy output.

A case in point involved the Federal Ministry of Education. A U.S. expert who was assigned as the chief official of the Bureau of Foreign

FIGURE 3.1 Summary of USAID Development Loans to the Government of Nigeria Through December 1966 (in millions of dollars)

	MILLIONS OF DOLLARS	
LOAN AND DATE OF AGREEMENT	1 2 3 4 5 6 7 8 9 10 11 12	

Loan and Date	Bar	Amount
Apapa Warehouse December 1959		$663,600 £237,000
Nigeria Railway Corporation August 1961		$2,997,200 £1,070,400
Ibadan Water Supply December 1963		$12,100,000 £4,321,400
Calabar-Ikom Road December 1983		$8,600,000 £3,071,400
Telecommunications Instruments February 1966		$1,600,000 £571,400
National Telecommunications Development Engineering Services February 1964		$3,200,000 £1,143,000
Niger Dam June 1964		$7,000,000 £2,500,000
Port Harcourt Comprehensive Secondary School December 1964		$1,800,000 £643,0000
Northern Nigeria Teacher Training Colleges August 1965		$3,800,000 £1,357,000
Umudike Agricultural Research and Training Station August 1965		$2,800,000 £1,000,000
Port Harcourt - Umuezeala Road August 1965		$7,600,000 £2,714,300

Total USAID Development Loans: $52,160,800 £18,628,700

Source: U.S. Technical and Capital Assistance in Support of Development in Nigeria, 1967
(Lagos, Nigeria: USAID, 1967), p. 16.

FIGURE 3.2 Total USAID Grant Technical Assistance by Type of Activity Through December 1966 (in millions of dollars)

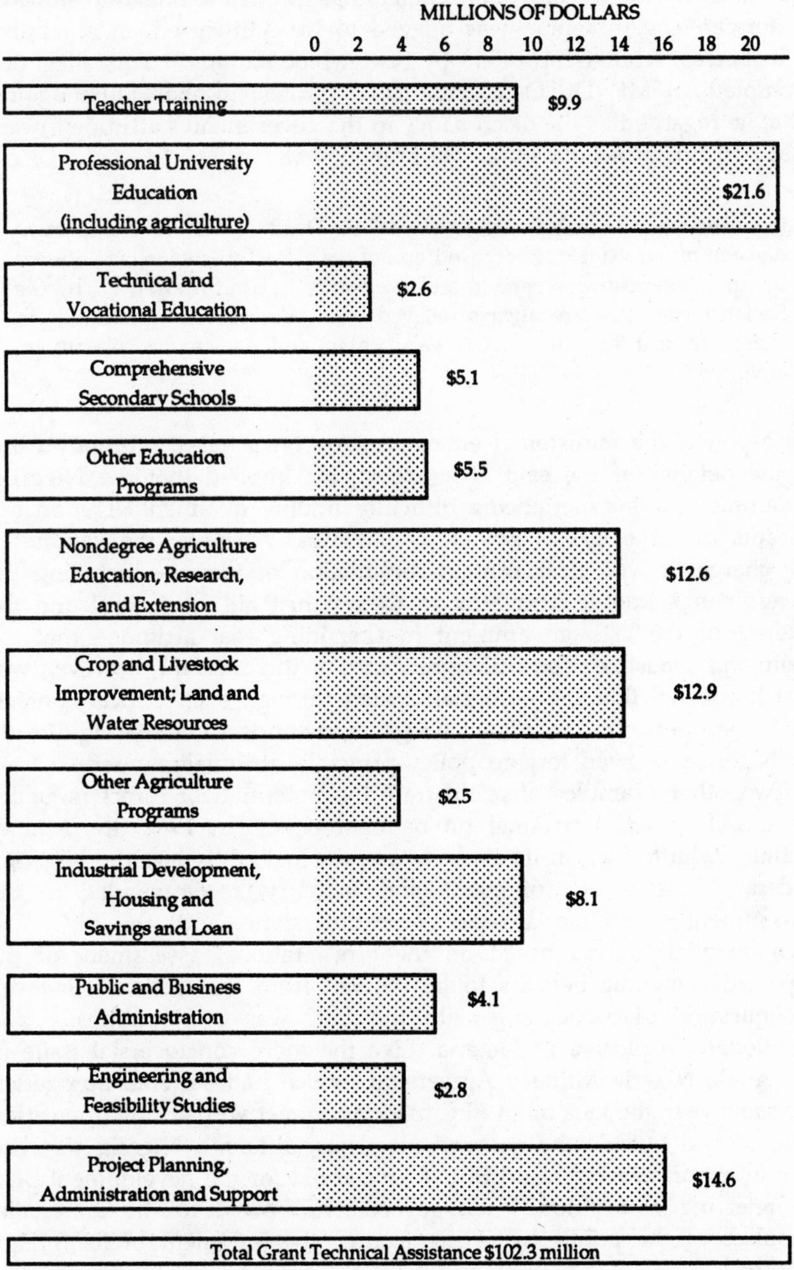

MILLIONS OF DOLLARS

| | 0 | 2 | 4 | 6 | 8 | 10 | 12 | 14 | 16 | 18 | 20 |

Teacher Training — $9.9

Professional University Education (including agriculture) — $21.6

Technical and Vocational Education — $2.6

Comprehensive Secondary Schools — $5.1

Other Education Programs — $5.5

Nondegree Agriculture Education, Research, and Extension — $12.6

Crop and Livestock Improvement; Land and Water Resources — $12.9

Other Agriculture Programs — $2.5

Industrial Development, Housing and Savings and Loan — $8.1

Public and Business Administration — $4.1

Engineering and Feasibility Studies — $2.8

Project Planning, Administration and Support — $14.6

Total Grant Technical Assistance $102.3 million

Source: U.S. Technical and Capital Assistance in Support of Development in Nigeria, 1967 (Lagos, Nigeria: USAID, 1967), p. 24.

Aid—the division in control of scholarships granted to Nigerian students by foreign governments—was alleged to have thwarted, in a number of instances, scholarship offers by Soviet-bloc nations.[22] This allegation prompted an MP, Dr. O. E. Ememe, to protest in the House against what he regarded as the discrepancy in the government's attitude toward U.S. and Soviet scholarships. He argued that

> it is necessary to have a Nigerian as the Head of this very important division of our Ministry, because I do not see . . . why scholarships offered by [the] American government are taken fully . . . but [those] . . . by the Socialist countries are always delayed . . . because an American is in charge of that Bureau. This is very unfair and we cannot tolerate [it] anymore.[23]

In response, the minister of education, Aja Nwachuku, promptly came to the defense of the said U.S. expert. He implied that the Nigerian government was experiencing difficulty finding qualified Nigerian applicants to make use of Soviet scholarships. Whatever the validity of the charge, it was clear from a conjunction of factors—including the government's known antipathy to Communist aid in general and the interest of the U.S. government in sustaining that attitude—that the claim was plausible. The real significance of this incident, however, was that it showed that the potential existed through such critical contacts for foreign personnel to influence a government decision bearing directly on Nigeria's avowed foreign policy principle of nonalignment.

Two other examples also illustrate the potential for direct influence by U.S. technical personnel on national policy. In 1962, the firm of Arthur D. Little Inc., in its capacity as principal adviser to the Nigerian Federal Ministry of Commerce and Industry, recommended to the government that Nigeria seek association status with the EEC. The recommendation was based on the firm's rational assessment of the expected economic benefits to be derived from that action. However, the question of associating with the EEC was both politically and emotionally explosive in Nigeria. Like the more controversial issue of the Anglo-Nigeria Military Agreement, which had suffered abrogation the same year, the idea of an EEC association met with strong opposition both in and outside the government. Thus, although Nigeria stood to lose in export revenues and EEC financial aid for the development plan by rejecting association,[24] the government bowed to the nationalist impulses of the public by acting against the judgment of its foreign adviser.

The second example involves adviser Wolfgang Stolper, the head of the economic planning unit of the Ministry of Economic Development, and his associates, and their role in designing the national development plan. Although Dr. Stolper was not directly accountable for all the concrete projects that emerged from the plan, many of which could only be politically justified, he and his colleagues made their mark on the future direction of Nigeria's economy through the very liberal economic ideas and recommendations that underpinned the plan.[25]

Despite what is said above, the probable leverage of U.S. aid strategy on Nigeria's foreign policy disposition most likely assumed a less direct, more subtle form. It should first of all be recalled that the formal U.S. aid offer to Nigeria was announced in 1961 in the nature of a prospective long-term commitment. Indeed, as earlier noted, this aid was actually to be obligated (and drawn upon) in installments from 1962 to 1968 as viable development projects could be designed. Contrary to what responsible Nigerian officials most likely expected at the outset, the aid commitment did not involve an automatic obligation that the aid would, at one moment, be turned over to the Nigerian government "to be spent as we think fit," as Okotie-Eboh later lamented.

From the perspective of the U.S. government there was nothing particularly insidious about the offering of development aid on a long-term basis. The practice had a rational premise; the purpose behind linking aid allocation to the availability of properly designed development projects over the course of the plan period was to avoid inefficient use of the aid and possible transformation of U.S. aid funds into nondevelopment purposes. Moreover, the practice was in compliance with a congressional guideline; the Foreign Assistance Act of 1961 stringently stipulated that U.S. development aid for inducing ultimate economic growth in the recipient country should be extended on a long-term basis. Further, it is to be expected that the business of U.S. policymakers in dealing with development aid is to reconcile formal development values to the more pressing political requirements of economic policy. Economic aid and related programs have to be conducted in the manner that will produce the maximum political policy impact.

In Nigeria, the acceptance of the U.S. long-term aid offer imposed, correspondingly, long-term obligations and restraints on the policymakers and society at large. As time progressed, it became clear that actual implementation of the committed aid over the six-year period would have to be predicated on a number of intractable conditions, some general, others more precise. Among these were the maintenance of a continuous state of domestic political stability, necessary for attracting foreign capital; moderation in foreign policy positions, necessary for preventing adverse public opinion and congressional attitude in the United States; the design of "acceptable" development projects and especially the conduct of proper feasibility studies on those projects;

and finally, the adequate preparation of loan applications. In order to assure the implementation of the aid offer and given the important value of the promised foreign aid to the ruling regime, it became essential for Nigerian policymakers to strive toward compliance with these conditions. The incentive to do precisely that was strengthened because the U.S. aid commitment (and that of other Western aid offers, in general), considering its timing, had the additional result of foreclosing a determined attempt by Nigerian officials to consider non-Western sources of foreign assistance for the development plan. The preemptive announcement of Western readiness to fulfill this need contributed in no small degree to consolidating the nonchalant disposition of the Nigerian leadership toward Soviet-bloc aid offers.

Note, also, that the original projection in the plan of the sizeable contribution by foreign capital was based on a calculation that Western nations—the United States in particular—were predisposed to offer that amount of assistance. Once this expectation was built into the plan, both the success and rate of implementation of the planned expenditures became linked critically to the rate at which the United States, as the principal donor, released the needed funds. Indeed, serious difficulties emerged in 1963 over what Nigerians regarded as the tedious pace of U.S. aid implementation (see discussion below), a problem that proved desperate enough to prompt some high officials to charge publicly that they had been misled by Western nations into inflating the objectives in the plan. The eastern regional minister of finance, Chief E. Emole, for example, despondently admitted that unless "external aid" was more urgently forthcoming, "the future of our Development Plan is distressingly bleak and gloomy."[26]

In a more specific sense, the conditions that aid implementation be linked to (1) the design of acceptable projects, (2) the conduct of proper feasibility studies, and (3) the adequate preparation of loan applications "which would meet the full documentation required by the Congress" resulted, in their practical application, in giving the United States effective control over the processes of implementing the public expenditure aspects of the Nigerian plan. The nature of these conditions presented the Nigerian government with two immediate and difficult choices. Fulfilling the stated conditions, as innocuous as they sounded, turned out to require the type of specialized knowledge in which Nigeria at the time had few qualified personnel. Thus, the government had to either appeal to the United States to provide the manpower needed for the performance of the tasks or repudiate the pre-aid requirements. Indeed, the United States had anticipated the manpower constraint and had, in more than one instance in the past, offered to provide the needed technical assistance, a gesture to which suspicious Nigerian officials had then been unresponsive.[27] The second choice, repudiating the pre-aid requirements, carried with it the inherent threat of forfeiting not only direct U.S. aid but also other related Western assistance—a connection very real in the thinking of the Nigerian leadership. This choice was all the more too risky, for by now the stakes in foreign aid for the Nigerian economy were looming fatefully larger than had before been anticipated. Aid flows, for instance, were becoming increasingly necessary for the general maintenance of a satisfactory balance of payments position, for the continued procurement of capital goods for the plan, as well as for meeting the escalating costs of imported consumer items. Faced with this dilemma, the government felt constrained to seek accommodation with the United States in order to minimize existing obstacles in their aid diplomacy while simultaneously attempting to justify its behavior to a frustrated and critical public.

By early 1963, the problems associated with U.S. aid conditions and the negative reaction to those conditions in Nigeria were regarded in Washington as sufficiently serious to warrant a "problem-solving" visit by G. Mennen Williams. Following discussions between Williams and high-level government officials, the federal minister of finance, Okotie-Eboh, came out publicly to re-echo what was the central U.S. view about the slow process of aid implementation. "The shortage of fully prepared projects," Okotie-Eboh asserted, "is the major cause of delays in executing new projects and in drawing down offers of external aid already made."[28] As one means for rectifying this handicap, he announced that the "staff of the planning and major executing Ministries and Corporations are already being expanded . . . and outside foreign assistance has already been obtained for the detailed preparation of a wide variety of new projects."[29] Another remedy suggested during Williams' visit and reluctantly accepted by the Nigerian authorities was the establishment of a regular consultative channel between the Nigerian External Aid Coordinating Committee[30] and technical representatives of the U.S. embassy and USAID. In addition, there were to be regularly scheduled meetings, at the cabinet level, between the U.S. ambassador and his top aides and the Nigerian federal and regional ministers of economic development. These multilayered consultative channels were to provide a structured medium through which both countries could identify obstacles in the implementation process, clarify each other's viewpoints on those obstacles, suggest practical solutions, and generally seek to harmonize their mutual interests in the aid relationship.

However, one major consequence of the U.S. aid strategy was that it lengthened considerably the gap between project identification and final project execution. Indeed, even after appropriate projects had been identified and properly appraised, and the relevant grant or loan agreement signed, no actual funding could occur until other subconditions required by the donors were fulfilled, an act that often took a considerable period of time. One such condition was finding an acceptable corporate contractor, either locally or abroad, to execute the project. An extreme example of how protracted and time-consuming the project-funding process could be was that of the Niger dam project, regarded as the cornerstone of the development plan because of its various ancillary advantages to the economy.[31] This project was formally approved in 1961, when extensive research and engineering work, which had begun in 1954 with funds from the World Bank, was completed. The U.S. government in consultation with the World Bank had agreed then (1961) to form a "Consultative Group" of Western donors to finance the dam, estimated initially to cost about $189 million. However, from 1961 to 1964, the fate of the project dangled in suspense as uncertainty mounted in Nigeria as to when the promised foreign assistance would materialize. Official anxiety was especially great because failure to secure the expected foreign assistance for this most vital aspect of the plan would be incisive evidence not only of the plan's failure, but of a misplaced trust in the good intentions of the Western donors. It was not until March 1965 that the government was able to announce that loan agreements for the first part of the project had been signed.[32] (By 1964, the cost of the project had risen to about $209 million.)

In sum, the overall result of the lengthy aid process and its complex requirements and procedures, referred to as aid mechanisms, was to create a conditioning effect on the Nigerian government and its officials. The aid mechanisms tended to firmly lock both recipient and donor (i.e., their relevant officials, groups, and institutions), at different points through the duration of the plan, into a close, ongoing effort to implement the aid commitment made at the plan's inception. In addition, they made it very costly, politically and economically, for Nigeria to switch in midstream to alternative sources of external aid. There was, so to say, an interlocking of obligations, responsibilities, and expectations in Nigeria-U.S. aid relations. And relations in this issue area, it is argued, served as an essential barometer of the foreign policy relationship between the two countries.

Politics of Aid Implementation

From the beginning of fiscal year 1963, the Nigerian federal regime was beset by two critical concerns with regard to the capital (public) expenditure aspect of its development strategy. First, the total foreign aid commitments up to that time were still under half that projected in the plan for this particular purpose. Second, the rate of actual implementation of the aid already pledged by the major donors was laboriously slow, with the practical result that in the first year of the plan, only a tiny percentage of the capital expenditure incurred was contributed by foreign aid funds (17 percent as opposed to the 50 percent annual foreign aid contribution anticipated in the plan).[33] The contribution of the United States—the major donor—was still at $62.8 million, and only some proportion of this amount had actually been expended on projects. This general situation did not improve very much by the end of the second year of the plan, to the consternation of the government leadership.

Ironically, the government was compelled in the first two years of the plan to resort to internal means for financing a large proportion of public expenditure that it had expected would be funded through foreign aid. One of these was the use of the country's own foreign reserves. This, along with substantial repayments on (pre-independence) external loans, contributed to a steep decline in the stock of foreign reserves from a level of £146 million in 1962 to £70 million in 1965.[34] Another device was the increased use of "medium-term, relatively high interest debt obligations to private foreign suppliers' credits," a very costly measure that according to the first progress report of the plan had reached "an alarming scale" by 1965.[35] The total effect of this alternative financing, aggravated by continued deterioration in primary export earnings, was that between 1962 and 1965 Nigeria experienced a persistent deficit in its balance of payments.

In strict development terms, the above context structured in the 1963–1964 period, the environment of the Nigerian-U.S. political tussle over the issue of how to implement the $225 million U.S. aid commitment. But the domestic politics of economic development also contributed in making the aid diplomacy with the United States even more complicated. More than ever, it was politically imperative for the ruling government to prove to its critics not only that foreign capital could be relied on to supplement domestic resources, but that the development effort would bear tangible results in improving the material lot of the citizens. As the federal minister of economic development, Waziri Ibrahim, realized, the people "expected too much benefit too soon from the development plan." Both counts, the poor record of foreign aid up to date and the resultant necessity to resort to prohibitive emergency measures, did not serve the regime's cause.

In 1963, it should be recalled, Nigeria was also reeling from its first serious internal security crisis linked to the "treasonable felony trials" involving the leaders of the national opposition party. In that same year, the country also experienced a demographic crisis: The outcome of the national census had been rejected because its conduct was alleged to be questionable and because the results had preserved the numerical predominance of the Northern Region, a fact detested by Southern politicians. Furthermore, the previous year had witnessed a constitutional crisis in the Western Region, which ended with the assumption of emergency rule by federal authorities. Likewise, within the West African subregion, it was in 1963 that the president of Togo, Sylvanus Olympio, was assassinated, an event the Nigerian regime regarded as posing a serious security threat to its existence because of alleged Ghanaian involvement. These, then, were some of the pertinent political and security uncertainties that confronted the Nigerian leadership simultaneously with the development problem of scarce foreign aid. The problems reinforced one another and made the regime ever more sensitive to the sudden and baffling complexities in its aid transaction with the United States.

U.S. officials were not unaware of the political ramifications facing the Nigerian leaders due to the foreign aid situation and prompting their increasing critical attitude toward U.S. aid policy. Writing from Lagos to the U.S. secretary of state on February 13, 1963, Williams noted,

> It is my own assessment and that of the Embassy that the action of the Premiers was at least as much political as economic. There seems to be an urgent need . . . to show concrete progress in the 6-year development plan, particularly under increasing financial stringencies imposing limitations on [the] government's own abilities to provide needed development, and to meeting [the] problem of unemployment and under-employment.[36]

But if the failure of economic development posed domestic political dangers for the Nigerian leadership, it was also a potential policy problem for the United States, considering its avowed stake in Nigeria's political stability and economic growth. Williams realized this connection and alluded to it in a subsequent dispatch to Washington:

> Nigeria for all its quiescence and apparent stability is not free of the general African problem which is that political structures remain stable . . . only in so far as the administration is able to reasonably meet the material aspirations of the peoples. While I do not believe Nigeria has reached a crisis condition by any means, I do believe that politicians have felt the possibility of popular resentment unless concrete progress is visible. Questions [put to Williams] from the Press and students as well as public officials indicate an uneasiness that . . . *somehow the U.S. is not living up to its bargain.*[37] (emphasis added)

Caught in their development dilemma, top Nigerian officials (including the three regional premiers) concertedly sought to use the opportunity of the Williams visit to voice their frustrations and to mount pressure on the U.S. government to modify its aid requirements and thereby expedite the implementation process. In Lagos, all five federal ministers in charge of economic affairs met with the U.S. assistant secretary of state and Ambassador Palmer. The ministers first expressed Nigeria's appreciation for "U.S. generosity" in extending aid, particularly in the form of grants, but they then expressed their concern "that not one loan [agreement] had been completed . . . since the long-term [aid] commitment" was announced.[38]

In Enugu, the eastern regional premier, Michael Okpara, stressed to Williams "the urgency of hastening the implementation of the U.S. aid commitment." While admitting that his own officials "had much to learn" with regard to the proper method of project appraisal and loan application, and while also welcoming U.S. proffered assistance in overcoming these obstacles, he nonetheless warned that the plan's objectives "might have to be cut by 50 percent if more [U.S.] help [is] not received [in 1963]."[39] Williams was also confronted by a cynical attitude regarding the aid problem in Kaduna. There, the northern premier, Ahmadu Bello, began his plea routinely by stating his appreciation for past U.S. offers and for the U.S. lead in pledging the "aid package" to Nigeria. But then he proceeded to appeal for faster implementation of the aid program because of the "depths of our needs."[40] Within the Nigerian House of Representatives, one heard repeated complaints to the effect that Western aid donors were unwilling to offer loans to Nigeria without imposing conditions "unbearable to the sovereignty of this country and to the positive development of our projects."[41] However, other members of the House, including the venerable Okotie-Eboh, remarked apologetically that Nigerians could not expect to attract Western aid while insisting on a foreign policy of nonalignment in the cold war.

What the United States considered to be the specific practical constraints impeding a speedier processing of the Nigerian aid program were discussed in the last section. What remains to be done is to trace, briefly, some of the underlying causes that might have obstructed a more energetic effort in Washington toward removing those obstacles. Considering the significance the United States attached to Nigeria in its overall Africa policy and the initial U.S. demonstration of interest in Nigeria's development plan, one becomes as puzzled as the Nigerian leaders about the general degree of complacency shown by the U.S. government in the face of the regime's existent predicament.

One clue to the U.S. complacency lies in the political atmosphere that surrounded the issue of foreign aid in the United States. The Clay Committee, appointed by President Kennedy late in 1962 to study the foreign aid program, had recommended in its report a general reduction in U.S. aid activities in Africa. Its main justification was that African nations as a rule were not "adjacent to the communist bloc" and hence did not serve any "immediate security interest" to the United States.[42] Referring to Nigeria specifically (as well as to a few other states), the report urged, "We should fulfill specific programs in Nigeria . . . to which we are committed. . . . As these commitments are completed, further U.S. aid should be confined to participation in multi-laterally-supported programs."[43] Although the Nigerian aid commitment, as such, was not affected by the Clay recommendations, the spirit of the Clay report, as of the subsequent more restrictive Foreign Assistance Act of 1963, had surely dampened the disposition of responsible State Department and USAID functionaries to push Nigeria's aid process more forcefully.

In addition, one could argue quite correctly that the indifferent atmosphere in Washington, and the specific perspective adopted by the Clay report, toward African aid represented an instinctive response to the political and security situation in Africa at that time. The first major crisis of African decolonization (the Congo crisis) which had threatened to inject Soviet influence into southern Africa, had seemingly been resolved with the end of Katangese secession. "Soviet-Communist" designs in this crisis had clearly been neutralized. The Republic of Guinea, which earlier had seemed a potential beachhead for Soviet penetration of West Africa, had convincingly demonstrated its independence of the Kremlin by denying the Soviet Union landing rights during the Cuban Missile Crisis. Nigeria had sufficiently projected, by this time, its pro-Western leadership in African diplomacy through its policy in the Congo crisis and in the formation of the Organization of African Unity (OAU). Nigeria had also exhibited, in the domestic arena, its determination to resist Soviet bilateral approaches. All of these factors probably contributed to the U.S. government's political apathy on African aid.

But as 1963 drew to a close, the complacent perception about events in Africa was being cast in doubt. Not only was the Congo astir again, with renewed instability leading to rebellions in two of its provinces, but there were armed uprisings in other countries as well, for example, in Togo. Further, the Soviets and the Chinese were more aggressively expanding their aid programs in the African continent. In July 1963, Nigeria's federal government, faced with mounting pressures and in light of the slow pace of Western aid entered into its first major trade agreement with the Soviet Union; trade agreements with other East European socialist countries soon followed. The Nigerian-Soviet trade agreement was significant in at least one respect: The list of Nigeria's exports to the Soviet Union included columbite, a strategic material covered by the U.S. Battle Act of 1951.[44] In conjunction with this agreement, Nigeria opened an embassy in Moscow and symbolically accepted some Soviet scholarships allowing students to study in the Soviet Union. These overt, pro-Soviet actions by the ruling regime did not put an end to Nigeria's basic bilateral coldness toward the Soviets; the acts were partially meant to register a point in Washington. During this same period, the Nigerian government also began to express discernible coolness toward U.S. requests to build additional communication and space-tracking facilities in that country.

These actions helped generate renewed interest for African aid in the State Department. In particular, they bolstered the viewpoints of Africanists in the Bureau of African Affairs, who had consistently argued that the political reality of Africa required greater U.S. aid effort, not less. Henceforth, both the bureau and AID administrations, under Williams' leadership, showed greater disposition to coordinate their efforts in resolving the practical obstacles that had previously slowed the drawing-down of obligated grant and loan funds. For example, USAID personnel in Washington began to take the initiative in conducting feasibility studies on projects that would meet the required criteria. The staff of the "country team" in Nigeria was expanded and urged to recommend a larger volume of "approvable" projects, for which funds could be released for execution. This expanded activity of USAID in Nigeria showed up in the fact that by 1965 (until overtaken by its operations in South Vietnam), USAID's technical assistance program in Nigeria "was the largest anywhere."[45] In terms of actual dollar value, total U.S. aid expenditure in Nigeria increased considerably after December 1963. As regards development loans alone, whereas no agreements had been signed before December 1963, by August 1965 the value of loan funds actually expended was $46,300,000.

The renewed U.S. enthusiasm toward Nigeria's economic development program (perhaps coming too late) did not put an end to Nigeria's dilemma with regard to "conditional aid" nor did it translate into real success in terms of economic and political stability. However, it did help facilitate a modest flow of external capital and technical skills into the domestic economy; it also resulted in mobilizing greater aid response from multilateral institutions and from other Western nations for Nigeria's development. By the end of 1965, the contradictions generated by the regime's past socioeconomic policies, fueled by incessant political and constitutional strains, had pushed the national system to the brink of disintegration.

Aid and Private Investment Ties

> Last year it became clear that Congress and important sectors of the business
> community considered that the Department of State and its representatives
> abroad were not giving adequate attention to problems relating to operations
> of American business overseas. The feeling was expressed that we treated
> important business complaints as if they were routine matters of little or no
> concern in the conduct of foreign policy. The charge was made that all too
> frequently business interests were sacrificed to international political consid-
> erations.
>
> —W. J. Crockett, Department of State
> September 10, 1963

The importance of the Six-Year Development Plan in laying the
foundation for Nigerian-U.S. private investment ties cannot be denied.
One must remember that there was very little direct U.S. investment
in Nigeria on the eve of Nigerian independence. For this reason, whatever
influence relationships later ensued via private investment ties, as such,
were located not in the attempt of U.S. investors to protect their established
interests in Nigeria but rather in their efforts to create those interests,
often through the mediation of the U.S. government with Nigerian
intermediaries.

The Nigerian government made strenuous efforts to attract U.S. private
investment, partly to counterbalance the predominant British position,
but more essentially to achieve the target for private foreign investment
projected in the development plan. The numerous incentive schemes
discussed in Chapter 2 were designed to bolster that objective. U.S.
investment was also deemed valuable because (unlike the bulk of existing
foreign investment, which was concentrated in commercial undertakings)
it was expected to be directed toward the establishment of the industrial
infrastructure, which would undergird future industrial growth of the
Nigerian economy. It is also significant that the bulk of the private U.S.
investment effort in Nigeria, from about 1961, rode on the back of
USAID economic and technical assistance schemes.

The U.S. contribution to the growth of private investment in Nigeria
was enhanced in two ways—one direct, the other indirect. Directly, U.S.
corporations and other private institutions (such as Western Electric,
International Telephone and Telegraph, and Lockheed Aircraft Corporation) were either awarded contracts for AID-sponsored projects or
provided government guaranteed loans for the purpose of establishing
new business lines or expanding old plants. The high concentration of
private U.S. corporations and institutions in AID-related activities in
Nigeria is revealed by the sharp increase in their numbers, from a low

of twelve in 1963 to forty-one in 1966 (see Appendix A). Private companies also benefited through the institutional medium of "tied aid"—aid linked to the requirements of U.S. foreign assistance laws. Thus, these companies and institutions enjoyed a monopoly in supplying the capital equipment and services needed for USAID projects. This connection was singularly responsible for tripling the value of U.S. exports to Nigeria from 1960 to 1966 ($39,000,000 in 1960; $116,200,000 in 1966).[46]

The role of technical assistance personnel provided an indirect channel for private U.S. economic contribution. These personnel, as shown earlier, were commissioned by the Nigerian government and USAID to conduct preinvestment feasibility, survey, and other specialized studies whose findings aided the activities of investors, both foreign and Nigerian. The following examples illustrate these interconnected processes.

The firm of Arthur D. Little Inc. was commissioned in 1963 to survey Nigeria's energy and fuel resources and to screen those "resources for potential investment opportunities." The specific objectives of the project in this vital sector were to (1) determine the history of Nigerian energy demand and project this demand to 1970; (2) establish the nature, location, availability, and cost of Nigerian resources; (3) identify problems of energy imbalance, involving interfuel competititon, domestic fuel alternatives, and refinery product pattern flexibility; and (4) elicit the best early opportunities for taking advantage of Nigeria's fuel and energy resources to stimulate industrial investment.[47] This effort certainly paid off in the sense of invigorating domestic Nigerian and private U.S. investment interest in the Nigerian petroleum industry. U.S. involvement is attested to by the number of U.S. companies that have participated, since the mid-1960s, in the sector that has become the staying-power of the Nigerian economy.

In May 1961, U.S. experts conducted a study on the "improvement of industrial management and technical services" in Nigeria. The project was designed, according to the final report, to "help improve the climate in Nigeria for both foreign and indigenous private capital, by providing technical services to Nigerian business managers and entrepreneurs, and advising government departments concerned with stimulating private investment."[48] Running concurrently with this was another study, which was geared specifically to the provision of investment promotion advisory services to prospective investors. The study took into consideration the interest of the Nigerian government in "achieving maximum industrial growth through private enterprise"; its aim was to encourage investment "of private capital by both Nigerian and foreign . . . business interests."[49] The concrete accomplishments of this effort, among others, were the creation within the Ministry of Commerce and Industry of an Economic Analysis and Statistics Division, which served to provide national industrial advisory services to Nigeria and to promote abroad opportunities for foreign investment in the country, and the preparation of concrete proposals for profitable enterprises in Nigeria.

These U.S. efforts, in conjunction with the private investment incentive schemes instituted by the Nigerian government, actually paid off very well, as far as they went. Within the first two years of the plan's inception, and in contrast to the poor record of capital (public) aid, the flow of private foreign investment into Nigeria was at the rate of about $7 million a month.[50] Between 1962 and 1963, private investment as a whole proceeded at a considerably faster rate than had been projected in the plan. By 1966, the nominal value of U.S. contribution to this growth was about $183,960,000, from a low of about $54,320,000 in 1962 (see Table 2.4).

U.S. investors were urged to respond vigorously to the private investment needs of the Nigerian development plan because of the unique opportunity such investments offered to influence the industrial base of an independent Nigeria. The most perceptive and cogent argument to this effect was made by Robert I. Flemming, the resident director (in Nigeria) of the Rockefeller Brothers Fund. The following was his reasoning:

> These years following independence constitute a "watershed period" during which those firms, hopeful of playing a major role in Nigeria's future, must establish their footholds.
>
> . . . This is the time when the "seeding industries" are being established, those on which other industrial developments depend: iron and steel, textiles, cement, salt and chemicals, petroleum refining, flour, etc.
>
> Inevitably, those nations which win control of these industries enjoy a great advantage in the struggle to dominate the many ancillary developments which follow. . . . Whoever dominates industry will enjoy great commercial advantages as well.[51]

This statement was made for the benefit of prospective U.S. investors, but it was also more specifically directed toward members of the U.S. diplomatic mission in Lagos in an attempt to convince them to be more supportive of private U.S. business interests in that country.

The background to Flemming's statement concerned a larger issue, regarding the proper role of private business in the management of U.S. foreign policy in developing countries. Between 1962 and 1963, the business community in the United States, both directly and through Congress, petitioned the State Department over what it regarded as the unsatisfactory attention paid to its special concerns by U.S. diplomats in developing countries. They charged particularly that "all too frequently

business interests were sacrificed to international political considerations."[52] It was in response to this collective protest (of which the
Flemming letter was symptomatic) that the State Department in 1963
decided to set up two institutional channels for dealing with this
problem.[53]

In Nigeria, the issue in its specific character emerged from a basic
conflict in the perceptions of members of the African Bureau (through
the embassy in Lagos) and private business groups (as articulated by
the Rockefeller Brothers Fund) about the comparative value of foreign
aid per se and private investment in serving U.S. foreign policy objectives.
The bureau and the embassy seemed to act on the presumption that
U.S. political objectives in Nigeria (as in the rest of Africa) constituted
a short-range rather than a long-range problem. Certainly the Communist
threat, to them, posed a "present danger." The course of African
decolonization and regional diplomacy had to be influenced by winning
the minds and hearts (and stomachs, one might add) of the African
leaders. These objectives, they considered, could best be achieved with
the use of foreign aid, especially grants. Aid provides more tangible,
immediate material and political payoffs than private investment, they
seemed to reason.

The business groups, by contrast, took a longer-range view of U.S.
interests and policy requirements. For them, failure to establish an
effective U.S. presence through private investment initiative would
diminish U.S. interests and chances for policy success in the future. In
this sense, U.S. business groups seemed to have invoked (because it
was in their favor) the original intent of the Foreign Assistance Act of
1961—that U.S. development aid be used as a long-term undertaking
to stimulate economic growth of underdeveloped nations. The Africa
Bureau and the mission in Lagos, however, treated aid more as a short-
term foreign policy device.

The relations between the two groups were also strained on another
ground. The embassy personnel were concerned not to overwhelm
Nigerian government officials with too many business propositions,
which could risk what Ambassador Palmer called "over-loading the
circuit," thus provoking a psychological reaction. This, they feared, might
introduce strains in their relations with the Nigerians at the political
level. Hence, they were often cautious in pressing private requests and
grievances on the government authorities.

This review of the dynamics between private U.S. business interests
and official U.S. concerns in Nigeria demonstrates that business and
official priorities in foreign policy do not always converge. Both sides
in Nigeria did not necessarily have similar conceptions, at least in the
short run, of the priorities of U.S. policy nor of the means to promote

it. This does not mean that the private interests of U.S. business groups were distinct from the overall U.S. interests in Nigeria, nor that their interests did not enhance U.S. policy objectives. Indeed, Nigerians did not see any distinction between private and official U.S. interests. To them, both the diplomatic mission and the private business groups constituted part and parcel of the U.S. diplomatic arsenal in Nigeria.

The Diplomatic-Political Dimension:
The Anti-Soviet Logic

Considering the nature of Nigerian state interests in the period from 1960 to 1966, it should not be surprising that the pattern of Nigeria's diplomatic-political ties in the same period evolved in response to its foreign economic links, for a country's decision to establish diplomatic relations abroad, and with whom, is determined primarily by the type of interests those relations are supposed to serve. The need for discrimination becomes even greater when the country in question is deficient both in financial resources and in trained diplomatic personnel.

The object of this section is to show how closely the two dimensions— diplomatic and political—of Nigeria's bilateral ties with the United States conformed to and reinforced one another. That this should have occurred in such a strict manner signified, above all, the critical relationship between the state interests and the ruling regime's extraordinary concern with survival in power. The central focus of analysis is the issue of the contrasting foreign orientation of Nigeria toward the Soviet Union (and the socialist bloc) and the United States (and its Western allies).

Mutual Suspicions of Nigerian and Soviet Leaders

On the surface, early Nigerian-Soviet bilateral contacts seemed merely to have been a victim of mutually harmful impressions held by authorities in the two countries. Until about 1962, the Soviet Union hardly thought of Nigeria as a "progressive" or even a "national-democratic" African state with whom it could expect to join forces for its anti-Western crusade in the African continent. In sharp contrast to their impression of the leaders of such states as Ghana, Guinea, and Mali, Soviet analysts fell that the Nigerian leadership constituted an amalgam of " 'bourgeois reactionaries' and 'local feudals' incapable [of], and unwilling to, engineer a widespread national liberation movement."[54] Contemptuously, Soviet spokesmen viewed the entire country as still being under the grips of the Western "imperialists."[55] In addition, individual Nigerian political parties and their leaders came under the critical scrutiny of Soviet writers. Interestingly, both the Action Group and NCNC leaders, Awolowo and Azikiwe, were as late as 1961 labeled "bourgeois reactionaries" by Soviet observer L. N. Pribtkovskiy. Sir Ahmadu Bello was, of course, the leader of the most feudal and reactionary of the three main Nigerian parties.[56]

However, it should be noted that the Nigerian political leaders themselves contributed in provoking this negative Soviet attitude through their public and essentially self-serving expressions of pro-Western sentiments, hardly promotive of the Soviet Union's own desires in Africa. In 1959, during the course of the pre-independence election campaigning, leaders of the three parties competed ardently to woo Western support for their causes. For example, Awolowo, after describing the Communist ideology as "atheistic materialism" that was "threatening to destroy or stifle all that is best and noblest in man," declared his party's intention "to bind Nigeria firmly to the Western bloc."[57] The NPC more steadfastly indicated its determination that an independent Nigeria under its leadership must "maintain the closest relationship with the United Kingdom and should aim at retaining and expanding her existing ties and friendship with the United States of America."[58]

In October 1960, the Soviet Union initiated efforts to reverse its previously unfriendly stance toward Nigeria. Apparently, the Soviet leadership had read a positive trend in the abruptly changed environment of Nigeria's domestic politics after the 1959 general election. It seemed that perhaps internal pressures might after all prove strong enough to force the ruling Nigerian regime to adopt at least a "positive neutralist" or independent orientation to global East-West political issues. Consequently, the Soviets decided to present Nigeria with an alternative to complete reliance on Western economic and diplomatic support. Upon Nigeria's independence, the Soviet government announced its hope that "friendly relations based on mutual understanding and close cooperation would be established."[59] And while in Lagos for the independence celebration, Joseph Malik, the leader of the Soviet delegation, informed Prime Minister Balewa of his country's desire to open an embassy in Lagos and its readiness to offer economic assistance for Nigeria's development.

There are a number of cogent reasons for why the Nigerian leadership, quite part from its subjective disposition, should have reacted with caution to these Soviet moves. With regard to the Soviet Union's request for an exchange of diplomatic missions, the Nigerian government might have reasoned, correctly, that financial and manpower stringencies in the first year of independence would make it prudent to establish embassies initially in those nations with which it had inherited established economic and social ties and to consider other countries only as conditions in the future permitted. In the specific case of the Soviet Union, there were at the time scarcely any Nigerians proficient in the Russian language.[60] As for Soviet economic offers, the Nigerian government was clearly unimpressed, partly because of the more substantial aid pledges coming from more familiar Western sources. Besides, Nigerian leaders were, in 1960, thoroughly convinced that any public flirtation with "Communist aid" on their part would harm prospects of receiving Western aid rather than enhancing them. The Nigerian leaders also had misgivings about the developmental effectiveness of Communist aid. They were well aware of communism's ideological prescriptions for the socioeconomic transformation of underdeveloped societies, in particular the emphasis on the socialization of the primary means of production preferably under the political leadership of the working class. Such prescriptions conflicted with the liberal-capitalistic social order the Nigerian leaders championed.

It was to some extent because of these considerations that Nigeria failed to establish an embassy in Moscow until 1963, although the Soviet Union was permitted to open its mission in Lagos in early 1962 (after considerable public clamouring). By contrast, at independence, four of the five diplomatic posts opened by Nigeria outside Africa were in Western nations.[61] The fifth was in Jeddah, Saudi Arabia (due to the large number of Nigerian Muslim pilgrims that visit there annually). As late as 1965, Nigeria had only one diplomatic post in the socialist bloc, that in Moscow, out of a total of thirty-nine posts. Perhaps reflecting its functional view of the purpose of diplomatic accreditation, the Nigerian government restricted the number of Soviet diplomatic personnel in Lagos to ten, while placing no restriction on the number of U.S. and British personnel.[62] In the aid sphere, the government refused to utilize a Soviet credit of forty million rubles (about $44.5 million) extended in mid-1961.

The Fear of "Communist Subversion"

The foregoing notwithstanding, there was indeed a more potent constraining factor in the Nigerian-Soviet relationship throughout the period under discussion. And that was the strong belief held by important elements in the Nigerian leadership that any close contacts with the Soviet Union would directly or indirectly provide an opportunity for the subversion of both the Nigerian state and the ruling regime. The very name of the Soviet Union, in the regime's mind, was synonymous with a mindless destruction of the existing political system. To cultivate close economic and political ties with such a power, especially when the new leadership was still struggling to establish its control over the entire system, was regarded as tantamount to committing national suicide.

"There is sufficient evidence to show," the minister of foreign affairs, Jaja Wachuku, claimed in 1961, "that if this country commits that indiscretion, this country will not last for two years before it is destroyed."[63] Chief Adebo offered his intimate view on this issue in a 1978 interview:

> The federal government was very much afraid of the Soviet Union, particularly given the image of the Soviet Union as a force of subversion. The North (as the dominant force in the federal government) was uncertain about the legitimacy of its control over the South. And the North needed such control in order to ensure its survival in the federation. Hence, it was very sensitive to any foreign relationship that would threaten its domination of the government. As a result, its attitude toward the Soviet Union was one of extreme caution.[64]

Soviet disposition for subversion was thought to operate directly through infiltration by political and security functionaries posing as economic experts and indirectly through indoctrination and exhortation of opposition elements in the society to destabilize the ruling government. In Nigeria, opposition elements included the pro-Soviet Nigerian Trade Union Congress (NTUC) and disenchanted youth groups. For the Nigerian government, it therefore became necessary to adopt measures to forestall any of these possibilities. In consequence, the government decided, after independence, to retain a ban originally imposed by the colonial administration in 1955 against importation of Communist-related literature. It also prohibited Nigerian citizens from traveling to East European nations or to the People's Republic of China.

These anti-Soviet dispositions had less to do with Communist ideology (though this aspect could not entirely be ruled out) than with the perception of the Nigerian regime that the Communist states had the potential to threaten its physical security. When, for instance, the regime decided to cooperate with the United States to check Soviet influence in Africa, it was not influenced so much by the prospect of communism spreading throughout the continent as by its perception that the Soviet Union was an ally of its regional and domestic opponents bent on destroying its political authority. Clearly, both Nigeria and the United States regarded the expansion of Soviet influence in Africa as a security threat. But the two countries had different perceptions of the essence of that threat. Nigeria took a narrow view, concerned with how such a development could affect its immediate domestic and regional security interests; the U.S. view was far more encompassing, linked to its global ideological concerns with the spread of communism.[65]

Also pertaining to the contrasting images of threat that the Nigerian leadership associated with U.S. and Soviet aid was the fact that the Nigerian regime was, on balance, more willing to condone the political-security implications of the U.S. economic program than that of the Soviet Union—a measure of the value the Nigerian regime attached to its basic links with the United States. This was even more revealing because U.S. development aid, as earlier shown, was mostly in the form of grants, which created opportunities for foreign technical personnel to directly influence domestic policies. Soviet offers of economic assistance, on the other hand, stressed loan credits at very low interest.[66] Thus, to the Nigerian leadership, the potential risk to its security perceived to emanate from U.S. aid ties was less worrisome than that associated with a prospective Soviet contact.

This diabolical world view of the Soviet Union, and Communist states in general, was not completely fanciful. There were a number of concrete incidents, some no doubt trivial, that helped reinforce this view. On July 16, 1961, a report in the British press stated that a Nigerian student in London had been invited to Moscow by Soviet authorities to undergo subversive training, with the specific aim of "overthrowing the Nigerian government."[67] On July 23 of the same year, yet another report, this time confirmed by the British Foreign Office, stated that young Africans were receiving training in "sabotage and guerrilla warfare" in the People's Republic of China.[68] Also, in apparent violation of Nigeria's passport law on travel to Communist states, many Nigerians were said to have undertaken such visits with Ghana's consular assistance. Nigerian authorities, no doubt, interpreted such nocturnal visits as having a clandestine purpose. There was, furthermore, a strong allegation made in 1962 that the Nigerian Trade Union Congress (NTUC) received financial support from Ghana's All-African Trade Union Federation (AATUF), an affiliate of the pro-Soviet World Federation of Trade Unions (WFTU), for the purpose of enhancing a Communist takeover of the Nigerian labor movement.[69]

It was, however, during the great treason trials of 1963 that more tangible evidence emerged regarding a probable Ghana-Soviet plot against the Nigerian regime. In those trials, three prosecution witnesses testified to the effect that Soviet nationals helped in training the would-be Nigerian "revolutionaries" inside Ghana and that "direct contacts were to be made with Moscow for financial and propaganda support."[70]

Nigeria's resolve to resist Soviet pressures for expansion in their bilateral relations was bolstered in no small degree by U.S.-British exhortation and direct support. Without such support, it is probable that Nigeria's resistance would have broken down much earlier under concerted domestic-regional battering perhaps nurtured by the covert application of Soviet resources. Washington officials considered Lagos to be "second to none" among U.S. Africa diplomatic posts. Through regular public declarations of approval for Nigeria's internal and regional policies (and by more discreet means), U.S. officials sought to strengthen the domestic position of the ruling regime and to enhance its regional leadership capacity. In the immediate post-independence period, the Nigerian government readily granted permission for the installation in Nigeria of U.S. communication facilities such as Project Mercury, the Foreign Broadcasting Information Service monitoring station (FBIS), and the SYNCOM (satellite communications) land station. The regime's expectation was that these facilities would, among other advantages, serve their security interests by helping to obtain vital information about activities of unfriendly foreign powers in neighboring countries (with Ghana and Mali in mind).[71]

On the occasions of the Monrovia Conference of May 1961, the Lagos Conference of January 1962, and the Inter-African and Malagasy Conference in Addis Ababa in May 1963 (out of which the OAU was born), the United States consistently buttressed Nigeria's effort to assume regional leadership.[72] And, interestingly, in all these forums, Nigeria's positions won majority approval, which in turn represented success for U.S. objectives. But although such U.S. support was a valuable asset in enabling Nigeria to execute its regional policy, it was also a continual political millstone around the neck of the Nigerian government. To its domestic and regional detractors, Nigeria was acting as the "chosen instrument" for the perpetuation of Western influence in Africa. Especially at the domestic level, the evident Nigerian-U.S. collaboration contributed to increasing the pressure on the regime to expand contacts with the Soviet Union. For example, the report of the All-Nigeria People's Conference strongly condemned Nigeria's discriminatory concentration of diplomatic ties with Western nations.[73] Two recommendations of the report were that the government accord the Soviet Union "equal facilities to those granted to other diplomatic Missions, particularly the U.S.A. and U.K.," and that it prevent any foreign nation from holding a conference in Nigeria, "e.g., the Conference of the American Diplomats recently held in Lagos."[74]

It was, therefore, a combination of continued public pressure and the regime's growing self-doubt and dilemma about the credibility of Western aid that, around the middle of 1963, produced the slight alteration in Nigeria's anti-Soviet orientation. Initial disappointment with the flow of Western aid seemed to have been a very significant factor. By early 1963, a growing number within the government's own rank had voiced strong skepticism about the very premise of a policy that, without reservation, required putting all of the nation's economic eggs in one ideological basket. Such opinion had not, of course, been entirely absent in the government in the past. It was, after all, the minister of commerce and industry, Zana Bukar Dipcharrima (of the NPC), who in 1961 urged trading with the Soviet Union and China because, according to him, both "could offer a stable and expanding market to Nigeria."[75] More than ever, the new aid reality in 1962–1963 called at least for a tactical shifting of gears to a different policy approach—one that required the government to attempt to place one foot, however shakily, inside the Soviet economic door as a hedge against greater future uncertainties with the West.

The concrete outcomes of this reassessment included the Nigerian-Soviet Trade Agreement of July 1963 and Nigeria's decision to establish full diplomatic relations with the Soviet Union by opening a Nigerian embassy in Moscow in the same year. Similar agreements to that with the USSR were signed with Bulgaria in September 1962, Hungary in June 1963, Yugoslavia in June 1964, and Czechoslovakia in September 1964. In February 1964, a nine-member Soviet delegation led by Y. V. Piene, chairman of nationalities of the Supreme Soviet of the USSR visited Nigeria and expressed desire for closer cooperation between the two nations. Resulting from this trip was the renewal of the forty-million-ruble loan credit offer and the award of forty-five and forty-six Soviet scholarships in 1964 and 1965, respectively.[76]

The flurry of these bilateral activities starting in 1963 might have led, at least, to some modest improvement in Nigerian-Soviet ties except for two significant neutralizing developments. One was the reported Soviet role in the treason conspiracy of the Action Group in 1963—a development that solidified the regime's awareness of the risk involved in courting the Soviets. The second was the resurgence of U.S. aid activities starting in late 1963. U.S. economic assets were still far more valuable than Soviet ties to the Nigerian regime. Besides, the costs of disengagement from U.S. ties even at this juncture were highly prohibitive, given the regime's real interests and the composite investments already made. Indeed, the renewed Soviet loan offer was not utilized until 1967. By 1965, Nigerian imports from the Soviet bloc (Eastern Europe) as a whole constituted about 2.9 percent of total imports; its exports to these countries likewise remained minimal, at 3.8 percent of the total. Thus, Nigerian-Soviet bilateral relations remained frozen until the end of 1965. A significant change was possible only within the new set of historical circumstances in Nigeria in the period 1966 to 1969.

The Psychology of Dependence and Policy Behavior

No discussion about the possible effects of a dependency relationship on foreign policy behavior is complete without an attempt to account for the (subjective) psychological costs involved.[77] At the very least, this provides one useful method for linking the generalized concept to concrete outcomes in the aspect of behavior being examined. Of interest here is the possibility that despite the basic value of the dependency interaction, if policymakers consistently incur a high psychological cost due to the interaction, they may react in a manner that could minimize the influence potential of the dominant partner in that relationship. Frustrations and anxieties experienced in the structure of dependence may not only generate instability in the relationship but, specifically, may distort the normal processes of influence as the subordinate entity attempts to reduce the total cost of itself.[78] Reactive behavior, or, as Singer refers to it, "counterdependence," may take the form of increased disposition to resist compliance with specific bilateral demands of the dominant partner or greater inclination to assert an independent stance on foreign policy issues.

The Sources of Resistance by Nigeria

The problem of psychological dependence does not derive solely from the situation of an asymmetrical relationship; it can, additionally, be stimulated through definite negative actions or omissions by the dominant party or through yet other forces. With respect to Nigeria, the problem could be traced to at least three essential stimuli. These reinforced one another in intensifying the psychological dilemma that confronted the policymakers in the aid experience with the United States.

First, as was stated in a previous section, one consequence of the overall U.S. aid strategy in Nigeria was to lock the relevant officials, groups, and institutions of both nations into an ongoing effort to implement the Nigerian aid. Although such interlocking procedures might have provided the United States with invaluable opportunities for applying leverage on Nigerian officials, certain risks were also inherent. For instance, through close and regular interactions between the U.S. technical advisers and the Nigerian advisers and bureaucratic superiors, a more vivid consciousness of Nigeria's dependence as well as technical inferiority was established. The result was the development of a complex of ambivalence in which foreign experts were at once needed and feared. This outcome was even more probable as a result of the pervasiveness of the U.S. "presence" in strategic federal and regional government ministries. It should be noted that apart from technical personnel directly affiliated with the State Department/AID program, many experts from other U.S. government institutions were also working in Nigerian public and private agencies.

By February 1963 Ambassador Palmer became so concerned about the dangers that this "presence" problem might create for him and his team in Nigeria that he cautioned Washington against further expansion in the number of U.S. personnel in Nigeria. In one specific instance, Palmer was "lukewarm" to a suggestion made by a visiting State Department official, W. Trimble, to the effect that a "small [AID] team [be sent] to Lagos to help process loan applications through the Nigerian Ministries."[79] Palmer's concern reflected an understanding of the sensitivities of the federal government's cabinet to this particular mode of U.S. assistance, a barrier that was reluctantly removed only when the aid situation deteriorated further in that year. Recall, also, the ambassador's caution about "flooding" the Nigerian officials with a rush of private business propositions.

Second, the psychological problem created through the physical presence of U.S. personnel within the country was, of course, compounded by more substantive difficulties associated with the slow aid process and the attendant constraint in implementing the development plan. If foreign aid is seen in its strict political context as a form of exchange in which reciprocity is highly valued,[80] then the Nigerian leadership must indeed have felt, as Assistant Secretary Williams put it, that the United States had not "lived up to its own side of the bargain." As already illustrated, the Nigerian regime in 1960–1962 was very strongly and favorably disposed to the West in its bilateral and foreign policies. As a price for this orientation, the regime had endured constant domestic villification and embarrassments.

To add to their consternation, Nigerian government officials observed that at the same time that they were having difficulty drawing down the U.S. loan aid offer, Ghana—a publicly pro-Soviet state and an arch political rival to Nigeria—had successfully obtained a U.S. loan guarantee for the Volta dam project, without suffering any loss to its national esteem. With obvious bitterness at this discovery, some Nigerian officials, including the finance minister, questioned whether the best way to obtain prompt U.S. economic assistance was to exhibit open hostility to its African policies, as the Ghanaians had done. The general frustrations of the Nigerian government were, as earlier shown, specifically channeled through Williams to the U.S. government. But in addition, U.S. personnel in Nigeria found themselves the immediate, visible target of passions released by this experience even at the highest official level.

A third contributing stimulus derived from the extensive and persistently deprecatory criticisms mounted against the regime's foreign policy orientation by the articulate public and the official opposition party. One central and persistent theme in these criticisms was the plausible charge that the government's public espousal of nonalignment was a farce. In actual practice, according to this charge, Nigeria was merely a "stooge" of the "Anglo-American bloc," especially with regard to the East-West conflict.[81] The Nigerian Prime Minister and his foreign affairs minister were, throughout the first two years of independence, crudely painted in the public eye as lacking any decisionmaking autonomy—leaders who hardly adopted an independent decision on serious foreign policy questions without prior reference to Washington or London.[82]

Moreover, the regime's leadership performance in Africa was frequently condemned as too conservative, unimaginative, as well as "undynamic," incessantly characterized by a fatal inclination to accommodate Western preferences. To the more radical nationalists, Ghana's assertive, anticolonialist role was the model upon which Nigeria's performance was to be judged. And this was despite the fact that Nigeria's policies were manifestly far more successful than Ghana's in terms of concrete achievement. Overall, most Nigerian critics of the government sought not an anti-Western foreign orientation, but an independent government that would unleash the bubbling energies of its human resources, which had long remained stifled under colonial rule, in forging a foreign policy that, according to one such critic, could "provide satisfying answers to the political and psychological needs of the society."[83]

The Limits of Resistance Under Dependence

A number of observations on the actual policy implications of the psychological dimension of dependency can be made. But at this point, one confronts a practical problem. How does one ascertain, through a "nonclinical" examination of the Nigerian policymakers, whether their policy reactions derived from subjective, traumatic experiences or were based on other calculations? The plausible answer rests ultimately on the objective fact of Nigeria's greater need for U.S. ties than the reverse and the perceived lack of a viable alternative to those ties by the leadership. Nigeria possessed no vital material leverage with which to induce an alternative U.S. policy or to resist unfavorable U.S. demands. Incidents of successful resistance can only be deemed to have derived either from a combination of forceful domestic opposition and the leadership's "counterdependence" power, from U.S. deference based on a calculation of its own self-interest, or from a combination of all three factors.

In the bilateral sphere, the first prominent exhibition of defiant behavior toward the United States occurred in relation to the escalating number of requests submitted to the Nigerian government for the expansion of U.S. communications and NASA satellite-tracking and scientific facilities in Nigeria. No attempt is made here to document the full range of such U.S. facilities in the country. An indication of their rapid expansion since 1961 was the fact that in one year, 1962, and within only one of the categories listed above, more than five project requests were presented to the Nigerian authorities.[84] As such requests multiplied in the first half of 1963, and coincidental with the baffling experience at the aid level, Nigerian cabinet officials became less compromising in processing the requests, in sharp contrast to their attitude during the 1960–1962 period.

Whereas the NPC as the senior government party (and indeed the government coalition as a whole) continued to regard the general ties to the United States as its best security insurance, individual members of that party were now showing open paranoia over the security aspect of those ties and urging the government to be more discriminatory in approving nondevelopment-related U.S. projects. As one NPC member, M. A. Ibrahim, stated, "the volume of the American installations of the so-called rocket and satellite detection depots . . . in this country is getting dangerous and suspicious."[85] Because Ibrahim's view, cited above, must have reflected his party's uneasiness (and hence that of the government), its more complete version is worth quoting:

> Let us not be carried off our vital track of nation-building by the power of foreign aid. . . . Our nation would rather remain poor, but free, safe, peaceful . . . than rich and bound. . . . This country is gradually but surely being made a target of destruction and that is because of the already existing number of satellite and rocket projects. A dangerous limit of installations has already been reached, and it is understood many more are coming shortly. These enterprises constitute two major dangers to Nigeria, the danger of being spied by America and the danger of being destroyed by Russia.[86]

In July 1963, Palmer reported to Washington that the Nigerian cabinet "seems to be taking a harder [and longer] look at the requests for U.S. projects to be located in the country."[87] Without desiring to reject U.S. project requests outright, Nigerian officials now demanded that such projects, in order to be approved, must possess tangible development advantages for Nigeria (for example, in the scientific field). That is, the projects had to be such that they would enable the government to convince domestic critics that approval was in the national interest. The government also demanded participation (or initiative) in the conduct of publicity dealing with such U.S. projects as a means of controlling their political cost. Military-related projects were, especially, to undergo close scrutiny. In actual fact, these measures were only a temporizing technique used to reduce the number of U.S. installations. The Nigerian authorities were thereby attempting to cut both the psychological and the political costs of U.S. ties without necessarily depriving themselves of their basic advantages. In the process, they also successfully forced the United States to concede a measure of their decisionmaking freedom.

The operation of the Peace Corps Volunteer Program in Nigeria was another contentious bilateral area in which the Nigerian regime overtly sought to exert its decisional independence. Despite its express development value, this program was, at its inception in 1961, vehemently criticized by domestic opponents as yet another "agency of neo-colonialism" imported into Nigeria. In the wake of such public criticism, the federal cabinet reacted dramatically by insisting on specific conditions before allowing the program to become operative. Among these were the conditions that Nigeria participate fully in the selection of the volunteers in the United States, that Nigeria be responsible for placing the selected volunteers in Nigerian institutions, and that Nigeria share both the cost and the operation of the program. Here was a singular opportunity for the government to convince not just the public, but itself, that it was not a servant, but an independent partner of the United States in development; that the PCVs were in Nigeria's interest and not "a derogation of national sovereignty." The minister of economic development, Waziri Ibrahim, was able to convince Palmer that these arrangements "are as much in the interests and protection of the United States as they are of the government of Nigeria."[88]

In the realm of foreign policy relationships (as shown in Chapter 4), Nigerian policymakers were invariably torn between the objective imperative of cooperating with the United States and the subjective need to maintain their decisional autonomy, especially in the face of a highly critical public, emotionally sensitive about continued ties of colonial dependence. Perhaps Palmer's empathetic observation sums up this conflict:

> Nigeria has just gotten its independence after a long period of colonial domination. While there is no doubt that the basic sympathies of the responsible leaders lie with the West, there is nevertheless both a latent fear that somehow or other Nigeria's newly won sovereignty may . . . be compromised and a concern at the impression which unquestioning cooperation with the West may have on Nigeria's ability to exert a position of leadership in Africa.[89]

The struggle to reconcile these compelling needs would result in a foreign policy generally lacking in clarity of purpose, tepid and haphazard in the implementation of declared objectives.

Summary

The salient forms of direct Nigerian-U.S. economic ties in the period 1960–1966 were foreign aid, technical assistance personnel, and private U.S. investment. The processes involved in establishing these ties, particularly within the framework of the first national development plan and in conjunction with intense domestic competition for political power, created subtle channels of influence allowing U.S. personnel to condition the environment of decisionmaking in Nigeria, especially with regard to regional affairs.

The Nigerian regime could not champion the expansion of economic ties with the Soviet Union for two main reasons: (1) such ties were seen to inhere serious political and security dangers for the state, and (2) encouragement of Soviet ties was considered an impediment to a successful cultivation of the more desired economic relations with the United States, given the existing political context. The Balewa government was convinced that it could not seriously promote Soviet economic programs in Nigeria, even if it was ideologically inclined to do so, because of Nigeria's fundamental ties to the West. Besides, the nature of vital state interests pursued by the government necessarily led to a close alignment between economic and political dependency.

It was also observed that the subjective feelings of dependence experienced by policymakers were aggravated by exceptional sources emanating both from the Nigerian domestic situation and from the channels of bilateral ties with the United States. Thus, the psychological pressure of dependence reinforced the inclination of the government to resist certain damaging bilateral demands by the United States and reinforced its willingness to assert some degree of autonomy in particular areas of policy. But given the concrete interests of the ruling regime, as indicated above, Balewa's government was also compelled to accommodate basic U.S. preferences. One major outcome of this contradiction, in terms of foreign policy, was a regional posture that tended to be reactionary throughout the period.

Notes

1. This tactic was played out rather dramatically before G. Mennen Williams, the U.S. assistant secretary of state for Africa, during a 1963 visit to Nigeria's Western Region. To Williams' amazement, the premier of the region's government publicly asked for more U.S. economic aid by flatly expressing the hope that Williams' "visit would be followed by a rain of American dollars" because, according to the premier, the U.S. "is fabulously wealthy." The premier followed up this unusual protocol by boasting that "Nigerians are defenders of democracy"

and strongly believed in democracy. The whole episode was the more comical because the region had just experienced a serious crisis of democracy due to a clear failure of its leadership to operate the inherited parliamentary system. See Williams (in Lagos) to Wayne Fredericks, February 13, 1963, Telegram no. 1165, G. Mennen Williams Files, General Records of the Department of State, Record Group 59, National Archives, Washington, D.C. (Hereinafter, records in the National Archives building are indicated by the abbreviation NA.)

2. Douglas G. Anglin seems to have adopted just such an approach. See his pioneering article on this subject, "Nigeria: Political Non-alignment and Economic Alignment," *Journal of Modern African Studies* 2 (July 1964): 247–263.

3. Policy Report, "U.S. Policies and Problems in Nigeria," (undated) 1961, Williams Files, NA.

4. Policy Report, "U.S. Policies and Problems in Nigeria," (undated) 1961, Williams Files, NA.

5. See "U.S. Policies and Problems in Nigeria." On official criteria for U.S. development aid, see Joan M. Nelson, *Aid, Influence, and Foreign Policy* (New York: The Macmillan Company, 1968), pp. 31–45.

6. *Business Opportunities in Nigeria*, Report of the U.S. Trade and Investment Mission to Nigeria, September 16 to November 4, 1961 (Washington, D.C.: U.S. Department of Commerce, Bureau of International Business Operations, Trade Missions Division, 1962), p. 3.

7. Ibid., p. 1.

8. Nelson, *Aid, Influence, and Foreign Policy*, p. 36.

9. See "Report of the Special U.S. Economic Mission to Nigeria" (Washington, D.C.: Department of State, 1961) (hereinafter referred to as "The Rivkin Report").

10. Just before independence and again shortly thereafter, the Nigerian federal government defined its foreign policy principle on the East-West conflict very vaguely as "nonalignment." According to the prime minister, this meant that "Nigeria will follow an independent line . . . no matter from where the truth comes, whether it is from the East or from the West." See *House of Representatives Debate* (hereinafter cited HRD), November 24, 1960, p. 196.

11. *Mr. Prime Minister: A Selection of Speeches made by Alhaji the Right Honourable Sir Abubakar Tafawa Balewa* (Apapa, Nigeria: Nigerian National Press Ltd., 1964), p. 65.

12. "U.S. Policies and Problems in Nigeria."

13. The Rivkin Report, pp. 10, 101.

14. Ibid., pp. 100–101.

15. Between 1953 and 1957, only 9 percent of the funds administered by U.S. aid agencies was in the form of loans. In the period 1962–1968, this proportion increased to 53 percent. Robert S. Walters, *American and Soviet Aid: A Comparative Analysis* (Pittsburgh, Pa.: University of Pittsburgh Press, 1970), p. 150.

16. Ibid.

17. Alan Carlin, "Project Versus Program Aid: From the Donor's Viewpoint," in Gustav Ranis, ed., *The United States and the Developing Economies*, rev. ed. (New York: W. W. Norton & Co., Inc., 1973), pp. 158–171.

18. Angus Maddison, *Foreign Skills and Technical Assistance in Economic Development* (Paris: Development Centre of the Organization for Economic Cooperation and Development, 1965), p. 21, and, "Report on Trip to Nigeria: W. Trimble to Williams," January 15, 1963, Williams Files, NA.

19. *U.S. Overseas Loans and Grants and Assistance from International Organizations, July 1, 1945–September 30, 1977* (Washington, D.C.: USAID, 1977), p. 233.

20. For a detailed review of the development projects undertaken by USAID and their location in Nigeria, refer to *U.S. Technical and Capital Assistance in Support of Economic Development in Nigeria, Report as of January 1, 1967* (Lagos: USAID, 1967).

21. One revealing example occurred in the same research period with respect to The Republic of the Sudan. Here the United States pointedly sought to tie U.S. readiness to finance an important Sudanese road project to a willingness by the Sudanese government to nullify a proposed civil air agreement with the Soviet Union. See Ambassador McEl-hiney to Department of State, May 9, 1962, Telegram no. NIACT 20m, Williams Files, NA.

22. *HRD*, September 25, 1964, p. 83.

23. Ibid.

24. Gordon J. Idang, *Nigeria: Internal Politics and Foreign Policy (1960–1966)* (Ibadan, Nigeria: University Press, 1973), p. 139.

25. For one critique of Dr. Stolper's approach to the plan, see Sayre P. Shartz, "Nigeria's First National Development Plan (1962–1968): An Appraisal," *Nigerian Journal of Economic and Social Studies* 4 (July 1963): 221–235.

26. *West Africa*, April 6, 1963, p. 375.

27. See discussion below in subsection "Politics of Aid Implementation."

28. See Okotie-Eboh's statement as quoted in a letter from Ambassador Palmer to Williams in Washington, May 21, 1963, Williams Files, NA; also *West Africa*, April 13, 1963, p. 408.

29. Letter from Palmer to Williams, May 21, 1963, Williams Files, NA.

30. This comprised the prime minister's secretary; high-level representatives from the ministries of finance, economic development and external affairs; the prime minister's personal economic adviser; the governor of the Central Bank; and representatives from the regional governments.

31. *West Africa*, June 29, 1963, p. 339.

32. Members of the consultative group and their contributions were as follows: IBRD, £28 million; U.S., £5 million; U.K., £3 million; Italy, £9 million; and the Netherlands, £2 million. *HRD*, March 23, 1964, p. 328. (Note: 1 pound = $2.80 in 1963.)

33. *Federal Government Development Program, 1962–1968: First Progress Report*, Sessional Paper No. 3 of 1964 (Apapa, Nigeria: National Press, 1964), p. 405; also Edwin R. Dean, "Factors Impeding the Implementation of Nigeria's Six-Year Plan," *The Nigerian Journal of Economic and Social Studies* 8 (March 1966): 113–125.

34. Gerald K. Helleiner, *Peasant Agriculture, Government, and Economic Growth in Nigeria* (Homewood, Ill.: Richard D. Unwin Inc., 1966), p. 342.

35. *First Progress Report*, pp. 4–5.

36. G. Mennen Williams to Dean Rusk, February 13, 1963, Telegram no. 1168 (Section 1 of 2), Williams Files, NA.

37. G. Mennen Williams to Dean Rusk, February 13, 1963, Telegram no. 1168 (Section 2 of 2), Williams Files, NA.

38. G. Mennen Williams to Wayne Fredericks, February 13, 1963, Telegram no. 1172 (Section 1 of 2), Williams Files, NA.

39. Ibid.

40. G. Mennen Williams to Wayne Fredericks, February 13, 1963, Telegram no. 1169, Williams Files, NA.

41. *HRD*, March 23, 1964, pp. 329–330.

42. W. I. Jones, "The Search for an Aid Policy," in Helen Kitchen, ed., *Africa: From Mystery to Maze* (Boston, Mass.: Lexington Books, D. C. Heath and Company, 1976), pp. 341–396.

43. Ibid., pp. 349–350.

44. The U.S. Battle Act of 1951 bars all forms of American assistance to a country that exports columbite and other strategic materials to Communist-bloc nations.

45. Jones, "The Search for an Aid Policy," pp. 348–349.

46. *Review of External Trade, 1966* (Lagos, Nigeria: Federal Office of Statistics, 1966), p. 11.

47. Arthur D. Little Inc., *Energy in Nigeria and Attendant Opportunity for Industrial Development*, Report prepared for the Federal Ministry of Commerce and Industry under the Program of USAID (Washington, D.C.: Arthur D. Little Inc., 1963), p. 1.

48. *U.S. Technical and Capital Assistance in Support of Economic Development in Nigeria, Report as of January 1, 1967* (Lagos: USAID, 1967), pp. 82–83.

49. Ibid., pp. 85–86.

50. David R. Mummery, *The Protection of International Private Investment* (New York: Praeger Publishers, 1968), p. 4.

51. See R. I. Flemming to Joseph Palmer II, December 7, 1962, Williams Files, NA.

52. William J. Crockett to G. Mennen Williams, September 10, 1963, Memorandum, "Utilizing Services of the Special Assistant for International Business and the Advisory Committee on International Business Problems," Williams Files, NA.

53. Ibid.

54. Olatunde Ojo, "Nigerian-Soviet Relations," *African Studies Review* 19(3) (1967): 43–44; Robert Legvold, *Soviet Policy in West Africa* (Cambridge: Harvard University Press, 1970), pp. 93–97.

55. E. A. Ajayi, "Nigeria-Soviet Aid Relations," *Nigeria: Bulletin on Foreign Affairs* 1 (January 1972): 3.

56. Ibid.; also Legvold, *Soviet Policy*, p. 94.

57. Legvold, *Soviet Policy*, p. 94; and *Daily Service* (Nigeria), September 13, 1959.

58. Ajayi, "Nigeria-Soviet Aid Relations," p. 3.

59. *Pravda*, October 1, 1969, quoted in Legvold, *Soviet Policy*, pp. 93–94.

60. *HRD*, November 20, 1961, p. 144.

61. These were located in Washington, D.C., New York (at the UN), London, and Bonn.

62. Also, it was said, the Soviet Union was allocated five diplomatic car plate numbers while the United States and United Kingdom were allotted one hundred each. Clause Phillips, Jr., *The Development of Nigerian Foreign Policy* (Evanston, Ill.: Northwestern University Press, 1964), p. 58.

63. Ajayi, "Nigeria-Soviet Aid Relations," p. 4.

64. Interview with Chief S. O. Adebo (Nigeria's Permanent Delegate to the United Nations, 1961–1967), Lagos, Nigeria, June 18, 1978.

65. U.S. officials were unsatisfactorily conscious of this inherent distinction in the attitude of some friendly African states toward the Soviet Union (and China), and on appropriate occasions they took forthright initiative in an effort to correct what Williams once termed the "hazy" picture of "communism by African leaders." See further elaboration on this point in Chapter 4.

66. Walters, *American and Soviet Aid*, pp. 160–162.

67. Quoted in Ajayi, "Nigerian-Soviet Aid Relations," p. 4.

68. Ibid.

69. Phillips, *Development of Nigerian Foreign Policy*, pp. 77–78.

70. *Africa Diary*, October 5–11, 1963, cited in Ojo, "Nigerian-Soviet Relations," p. 53.

71. Ironically, as such projects multiplied in numbers, some members of the governing coalition came to regard them as a source of national insecurity. See *HRD*, Janury 1, 1963, pp. 144–145; also Palmer to Williams, July 10, 1963, Williams Files, NA.

72. Confirmed in interview with Chief S. O. Adebo, June 18, 1978; see also, "The Addis Ababa Conference, May 22–25," (undated) 1963, Williams Files, NA.

73. Phillips, *Development of Nigerian Foreign Policy*, pp. 54–62.

74. Ibid., pp. 57–58; and Joseph N. Greene, Jr., (Lagos) to the Secretary of State, July 10, 1961, Telegram no. 31, Williams Files, NA.

75. Ajayi, "Nigeria-Soviet Aid Relations," p. 4.

76. Ojo, "Nigerian-Soviet Relations," p. 52.

77. The basic theoretical question in this aspect is addressed in Chapter 1. Refer to Marshall R. Singer, *Weak States in a World of Power* (New York: The Free Press, 1972), pp. 40–51.

78. On the notion of cost-reduction in relations involving power asymmetry, see Richard M. Emerson, "Power-Dependence Relations," *American Sociological Review* 27 (February 1962): 33–35.

79. W. Trimble to Williams, January 15, 1963 (report of trip to Nigeria), Williams Files, NA.

80. Kenneth J. Gergen, *The Psychology of Behaviour Exchange* (Reading, Mass.: Addison-Wesley Publishing Company, 1969), pp. 72–80; Neil R. Richardson, *Foreign Policy and Economic Dependence* (Austin: University of Texas Press, 1978), pp. 63–64.

81. See, for example, Idang, *Nigeria: Internal Politics*, p. 24. The nature of Nigeria's foreign policy is discussed more fully in Chapter 4.

82. As an example, see comment by Chief Awolowo, *HRD*, November 29, 1961, p. 23; and a supporting reference by M. Ibrahim Gusau (a government MP), *HRD*, April 14, 1962, p. 852.

83. Idang, *Nigeria: Internal Politics*, p. 15.

84. See Palmer to Williams, December 28, 1962, Telegram no. 867, and Palmer to Williams, July 10, 1963, both in Williams Files, NA.

85. M. Abubakar Ibrahim, *HRD*, April 1, 1963, p. 144.

86. Ibid.

87. See Palmer to Williams, December 28, 1962, Telegram no. 867, Williams Files, NA.

88. Palmer to Sargent Shriver, October 12, 1961, Williams Files, NA.

89. Ibid.

4

Regional Policy Relationship: The Necessity for Moderation and Cooperation

Nigerian policymakers in the Balewa regime developed a basic disposition for moderation in the formulation of their Africa (regional) policy objectives because of a compelling need to cooperate with the United States in order to successfully prosecute those objectives. The necessity for moderation and cooperation was reinforced by the regime's perception that these "virtues" in the realm of regional policy were also vital in safeguarding its domestic interests. The focus of concern here is not only the question of whether such a basic external disposition on the part of the ruling regime was capable of ensuring success for the regime's regional policies, but also the issue of the limits and opportunities inherent in a relationship of foreign policy dependence. The conceptual question is, how does such a relationship affect the decisionmaking autonomy of the dependent elite? These issues are highlighted in two case studies: (1) the Congo crisis, 1960–1964, and (2) the challenge of Ghana and the assassination of Sylvanus Olympio.

THE CONGO CRISIS, 1960–1964

The First Foreign Policy Test

The Congo crisis, which started on July 8, 1960, with mutiny by units of the Force Publique against the Belgian officers just eight days after the Congo's formal independence, led to a split in the central government early in September of that year.[1] On September 5, Patrice Lumumba, the country's first prime minister, and Joseph Kasavubu, the president, mutually dismissed each other from their respective posts. Before this constitutional impasse, other chaotic events had occurred.

112

Among them, Moise Tshombe declared the secession of the mineral-rich province of Katanga, and Albert Kalonji similarly announced his independent state in South Kasai. Lumumba and Kasavubu had jointly requested, on July 12, military assistance from the United Nations to repulse Belgian intervention, after having failed to gain direct aid from the United States.[2]

Nigeria's independence and its admission to the United Nations coincided with the effort of the world body to resolve the constitutional problem confronting the government in Leopoldville. Generally, the UN Operation des Nations Unies au Congo (ONUC) was grappling with grave difficulties in its effort to discharge its presumed mandate in the country. In November 1963, Nigeria had been an independent state for just one month. Its own institutional structures, though carefully nurtured by Great Britain before 1960, were not yet really tested. Its ethnic make-up was nearly as fragmented as the Congo's and was certainly more complex. Its national leadership badly needed time to devote to domestic political consolidation before plunging into the whirlpool of world politics. This opportunity was not be forthcoming, however; Nigeria was too important an African entity to be insulated from an African crisis that was becoming intensely internationalized under cold war conditions. Within this context lies the aptness of Gray Cowan's remark: "Nigeria's introduction to the battles of world politics has been sudden and rude."[3]

The innocence of the official Nigerian view regarding the highly partisan situation in the Congo at this juncture was revealed by some of Prime Minister Balewa's compromise proposals for ending the crisis. Addressing the UN General Assembly on October 7, 1960 (his first speech to the assembly), the Nigerian leader proposed that the UN supervise new elections and appoint a fact-finding mission "to look into the causes of the crisis." He also talked about the need for African states to be primarily responsible for settling the crisis "at the political level."[4] These were all sensible proposals; what was lacking was a grasp of the political determinants of their implementation. For instance, the reluctance to hold new elections or to allow Parliament to reconvene since early September was based on the realization by the Belgians, the anti-Lumumba Congolese faction, and indeed U.S. officials in Leopoldville that the former prime minister was still the most popular political figure in the country and, as such, would readily return to power—an outcome these groups sought to prevent (see below).

Until November 25, Balewa and his cabinet were not certain that Nigeria had any interest "at all in the Congo." "All that we want," Balewa told Parliament, "is that the people of The Congo Republic should find a solution to their present confused situation."[5] All the same, Nigeria, like some Afro-Asian members of the UN, had dispatched troops, police contingents, constitutional experts, and administrators to participate in ONUC. Jaja Wachuku, then Nigeria's UN representative (as well as federal minister of economic development), was elected to chair the Conciliation Commission on November 17, giving Nigeria the appearance of a neutral arbiter within the feuding African Group at the UN. (To maintain its position of impartiality in this capacity Nigeria did not participate in the acrimonious General Assembly voting of November 22, the result of which favored seating the Kasavubu delegation over that of Lumumba.) By the beginning of 1961, however, and coinciding with the beginning of the Kennedy administration, the Nigerian leaders began to change their earlier posture of complacence. They became greatly aroused by the interests at stake and showed sudden awareness of the real politics underlying the operations of ONUC in the Congo. A number of factors—some had been in the making before then— engendered this awakening.

First, through reports of overseas news agencies picked up by the local press and by comments of both MPs in the ranks of the opposition party and government back-benchers, the government became pressed to adopt a more forceful position on the crisis. Reports by Reuters and the Associated Press concentrated on the roles Ghana, Guinea, and the UAR, and their pro-Lumumba activities. From the earlier discussion of the tense relationship of Nigeria and Ghana, it is not hard to see why Nigerian leaders would want to wrest the major African role in the Congo from Ghana.[6] As the confrontation between Dag Hammarskjold, the UN secretary general, and the Lumumba-Kasavubu government escalated over the purpose of the UN presence in the Congo, the *West African Pilot* urged the Nigerian government to put Nigerian troops directly in the service of the Leopoldville authorities, not ONUC, which now was widely thought in the country to act in collaboration with Belgium over Tshombe's secession.[7] During a debate in Parliament on November 24, Chief Awolowo charged that events in the Congo seemed "mystifying" to Balewa because the government lacked a "correct ideological orientation"[8] by which to understand the threat posed by UN inaction against the Belgians to the independence of the Congo— a situation that, he forewarned, could someday confront Nigeria.

Second, the government was feeling pressure directly from the United States and indirectly from Great Britain. For the last two weeks in December 1960, U.S. envoys in Lagos made a sustained effort to stimulate official Nigerian interest in the Congo in favor of the U.S. position while the Nigerian authorities argued that it was inadvisable for the West to take a lead in the crisis instead of the African states. Maitama Sule, a cabinet member and close confidante of Balewa's, warned Ambassador Palmer that any Congolese leader associated with the West is bound to be "mistrusted as a stooge."[9] On January 20, 1961, Ambassador Claire Timberlake visited Lagos from Leopoldville to "expound the U.S. point of view." His mission was specifically to impress on Nigerian officials the grave political problems caused in the Congo by the unilateral actions of the Soviet-bloc states and some African governments and the likely "repercussions in the rest of Africa."[10] The British government and its conservative constituents, through expression of pro-Katanga sentiments, served as an additional catalyst. The concerned public in Nigeria regarded the ouster of Lumumba as a "Western plot" and they were greatly incensed by the knowledge that British officers were in command of Nigerian-UN troops in the Congo (two of three Nigerian military commanders in the Congo were British nationals). These Nigerians wished the government to adopt a policy stance that was independent of the West.

It was President Kennedy's new policy, approved on February 2, 1961, that provided the real momentum for a more dynamic Nigerian policy in the Congo crisis. Due to the uncompromising draft resolutions sponsored, respectively, by the Afro-Asian states on December 16 and by the United States-United Kingdom on the following day, the work of ONUC in the Congo, in the words of Catherine Hoskyns, "had reached a point of maximum crisis."[11] The bitterness felt by those African entities and others most committed to Lumumba (Ghana, for example) upon the admission of the Kasavubu government to the UN and the arrest of Lumumba thereafter made compromise between the Western position, led by the United States, and that of the Afro-Asian group extremely difficult. African states of the Casablanca camp who had already threatened to withdraw their troops from ONUC also decided to recognize the Gizenga regime in Stanleyville. Ominously, a deep concern was now being expressed by Hammarskjold, who, as related by Kennedy staff members charged with evolving the new policy, feared that the UN might be losing its impartial status in the crisis.[12] The UN secretary-general was critical, in a conversation with Ambassador Adlai Stevenson in New York, that the United States "did not seem to discourage Belgian adventures," and that Ambassador Timberlake in Leopoldville was pushing the UN hard "to play the Kasavubu line."[13] There is no doubt that the rationale for this U.S. action under President Eisenhower, as with the subsequent Kennedy administration, was the necessity to resist the Soviet Union from establishing itself in the Congo through Lumumba and his supporters, and hence in Central Africa. The prevailing view was that the Western strategic stake in Central Africa—not to mention the specific economic interests of close allies such as Belgium and Great Britain—was quite high. Thus, the United States felt compelled to help break the deadlock at the UN and within the Congo.

The Kennedy policy had one principal objective: unequivocal support for a stable and unified Congo (which involved an end to Katanga's secession), with adequate insurance against a Communist "takeover." This required the strengthening of ONUC's mandate to enable it to neutralize all military forces in the Congo and maintain law and order, the formation of a "middle-of-the-road" central government in Leopoldville, and above all the enlistment of the support of important Afro-Asian states to assume formal initiative in advancing the new policy under UN auspices, thus according the policy maximum legitimacy in Africa and Asia.[14] Nigeria was considered the critical African link between the U.S. policy and its successful UN implementation. The problem for U.S. officials became how to mobilize Nigeria's active cooperation in this enterprise. The first formal step to this effect was taken shortly after Kennedy gave his assent to the new policy as recommended by Secretary Rusk. Ambassador Palmer was instructed to meet with Prime Minister Balewa and to stress the point that the U.S. program was formulated at the direction of the president and had his personal commitment.[15] The purpose might have been to create an impact and so secure the prompt approval of Nigeria. But this task was made more complicated by the news that Lumumba had been murdered.

By the time the Security Council resolution of February 21, 1961, went into effect, Nigeria was actively pursuing three main objectives in the Congo. In descending order of significance, the first was the termination of Katanga's secession and the attainment of unification in the Congo. The basis of this objective seems self-evident. Political competition in Nigeria operated essentially along regional-ethnic lines, just as it did in the Congo. This was vividly demonstrated by the results of the 1959 elections. The threat of regional secession, perhaps resulting in civil war, was very real. If the secession of Katanga were allowed to succeed in the Congo, a cancerous precedent would have been set not just for Nigeria but for Africa in general. The Nigerian leadership, while it did not approve of the therapy advocated by Kwame Nkrumah's Ghana to deal with the potentiality of secession movements in the region, was equally concerned about the disease itself. Hence, ending Tshombe's secession bid became a consistent objective of Nigeria in the crisis.[16]

The second objective derived from the brewing conflict with Ghana. Ghana had quite early (since 1958, when Nigeria was still a colonial territory) built a relationship of cooperation with Patrice Lumumba; their identity of views on decolonization was crystalized by the secret agreement signed between them on August 5, 1960, whereby the Congo was expected to join the Ghana-Guinea-Mali Union. Among the African states, Ghana's military contribution to ONUC was the largest, and its support for Lumumba's leadership, the most consistent. Just before the independence of the Congo, Nkrumah exercised his personal influence to secure an agreement between Kasavubu and Lumumba leading to the formation of the Lumumba-Kasavubu government.[17] Nigerian leaders wanted to reverse all these acts. Thus, one main object of Nigeria's activist role in the crisis was to subvert Ghana's influence and assert Nigeria's leadership both within the African Group at the UN and within the Congo. The chairmanship of the Conciliation Commission provided a vehicle for this purpose. In March 1961, Wachuku was pleased to discover through his commission's investigations that "Ghana's interference" had contributed to the rift between Lumumba and Kasavubu.

The third objective, impelled partly by the second objective, was the evolution of an African country in "Nigeria's image," as Teslim Elias, Nigeria's minister of justice and attorney general, put it. This meant a basically pro-Western Congo, with whom Nigeria could align in advancing its own conception of decolonization and African unity in regional politics. To further justify this desire, as though it were a natural necessity, Congolese leaders under Adoula's government and Nigeria's Jaja Wachuku often aphorized in public: "If Congo is the heart of Africa, Nigeria is the head."[18] The strategic location of the Congo, with its abundance of natural resources, made the prospect of future cooperation with a nonradical Leopoldville government most attractive to the Nigerian leadership.

If in general these three objectives did not conflict with the broad goals sought by the Kennedy administration as per the policy framework adopted on February 2, still the tactical methods preferred by policymakers of the two countries toward the attainment of the objectives were not always compatible. Both countries were sensitive to different sets of extraneous pressures. However, Nigerian authorities needed U.S. assets and, hence, close cooperation with the United States in the crisis in order to achieve their aims.

The Pattern of Nigerian-U.S. Cooperation in the Crisis

The Issue of Katanga and Unity of the Congo

No aspect of the Congo tragedy was as emotive for concerned Nigerians (and other Africans) as the issue of Katanga's secession. However, Nigerians also expressed profuse passion over the murder of Patrice Lumumba, though their passion was not due to the personality of the man. Nigerians shared, by and large, the same ambivalence toward Lumumba's character as most Westerners did. He was mourned intensely in death because, as many Nigerian press commentators summed up, he was regarded as a victim of UN unwillingness to act against the forces sustaining Katanga's secession, a purpose for which he had appealed to the world organization.[19] The news of Lumumba's death provoked in Nigeria an uncustomary "anti-white" violence. Demonstrators organized by the NTUC, NYC, and NUNS attacked the U.S. and Belgian embassies as well as British commercial buildings and Europeans in the streets. The same groups, along with many members of Parliament, blamed Hammarskjold personally for Lumumba's death and called on the government to withdraw Nigerian contingents from the Congo.[20] Taken by surprise at the level of physical violence against Europeans, Balewa reacted by banning all public demonstrations. The federal minister of finance, Okotie-Eboh, preparing to undertake one of his many overseas trips to solicit foreign aid, warned that such hostile exhibition of anti-Western sentiments would have a prohibitive effect on prospective investors and aid donors.

As for Katanga's secession, the general belief was that Moise Tshombe acted merely as a front for Belgian-British financial interests whose purpose was to frustrate African independence. This popular belief was strengthened immeasurably by the worldwide knowledge that Tshombe's administration was backed economically by such powerful groups as Union Miniere and was backed militarily by mercenaries from an assortment of Western nations as well as South Africa, the Rhodesias, and the Portuguese colonies. With regard to Great Britain, Nigeria's immediate political interest in the Katanga problem was linked to the necessity of stabilizing the unpopular (i.e., to the African majority) Federation of Rhodesia and Nyasaland under Roy Welensky. According to Ernest Lefever, Welensky and the British wished to strengthen economic cooperation between the federation and the mineral-rich Katanga as an independent entity.[21]

The constructive, though qualified, support given by the United States to the Security Council resolution of February 21 was welcomed in Nigeria. The U.S. action produced a somewhat pacifying effect on Nigerian public opinion, especially because the resolution included provisions calling for the withdrawal of Belgian and other foreign military and paramilitary personnel as well as political advisers (not under UN command) and mercenaries; the provisions also called for "immediate and impartial investigation" into the circumstances of Lumumba's death.[22] The implication of the former provisions in weakening the support base for the Katanga regime is clear.

On the day before the Security Council debate, the Nigerian government had rallied to the defense of the United States and Hammarskjold in particular. During the debate Wachuku asserted, "The Nigerian delegation recognized and appreciated the very difficult and trying circumstances under which the Secretary-General and his aides had been attempting to execute a limited and controversial mandate."[23] He went on to express "total satisfaction" with Hammarskjold's actions. Nigeria, it seemed, was set to assume in the UN the kind of responsibility requested earlier by the United States, for Wachuku's decision to defend the secretary-general in this particular manner at this juncture was a very unpopular one among the majority of the Afro-Asian states, not to mention the Soviet Union.

From February to July, Nigeria continued to support fully the reconciliation effort of the Congolese factions; unlike the Casablanca states, it recognized Kasavubu as the legitimate leader of the central government.[24] The Nigerian government's attitude toward Kasavubu was still at extreme odds with how the critical public viewed him (i.e., as a man who had collaborated with the Belgians and Tshombe in murdering Lumumba). Thus when Kasavubu was invited in August to visit Lagos, this segment of the public raised such loud opposition that the visit was promptly called off.[25]

During the same period, Nigerian authorities cooperated closely with the United States against the opposing efforts of Ghanaian and Soviet agents in the appointment of Adoula as the Congo's third prime minister. After Adoula was sworn in, U.S. officials in Lagos exhorted Nigeria to make a public statement at the UN endorsing Adoula's government, perhaps to strengthen Adoula's authority against Tshombe in future negotiations. (Tshombe and his deputies had just frustrated a U.S. attempt to have Katanga participate in the new central government.) In September 1961, Nigeria's UN representative, Wachuku, seemed to have taken precisely such a step in a General Assembly address.[26] For a similar effect, Nigeria invited Adoula to attend the Lagos Summit Conference of Monrovia States in January 1962. In mid-October 1961, two U.S. senators, Albert Gore and Richard Neuberger, visited Lagos with the specific mission of reaffirming to the Nigerian leadership and public the U.S. government's commitment to a unified Congo, thereby reinforcing Nigeria-U.S. cooperation in the crisis.[27]

Despite the effort at policy coordination, developments in the Congo and within the United States after Adoula's government was installed renewed doubts in Nigeria about the strength of the U.S. determination to work for the end of secession in Katanga. A question raised privately by officials and publicly in the press concerned the resolve of the United States to withstand pressures from its allies—Great Britain, Belgium, and France—against ONUC's use of force in Katanga. This concern was engendered by protests raised by the three Western countries following two limited UN military actions against Katanga in late August and in

September—operations "Rumpunch" and "Morthon."[28] The British government, having reluctantly agreed with the United States on the principle of a united Congo, still insisted on "peaceful re-integration" even though Tshombe continued to frustrate such an approach. Worse, the British government under Prime Minister Harold Macmillan, seeking to satisfy the desires of its conservative and business constituents, persisted, until later in September, in pressing the United States to support a sort of confederal status for Katanga, an idea the Congolese politicians themselves (excluding Tshombe and his foreign backers) had long since rejected.[29] British pressures, Nigerians noted, were largely responsible for forcing ONUC troops into a nonproductive ceasefire arrangement with Katanga in the middle of the November campaign.

Within the United States, it became increasingly evident that President Kennedy was meeting opposition from private organizations and congressional figures sympathetic to Tshombe and the autonomy of Katanga. In the State Department, there seemed to have been some polarization between the UN and the Africa Bureau, on one side, and the European Bureau on the other.[30] Both State Department and White House officials, mindful of a costly split with U.S. allies and concerned about an unnecessary loss of domestic support for the president, began cautiously to move the U.S. position closer to that of Great Britain. Between December 1961 (marked by the Kitona Agreement) and mid-1962, the United States pressed the Adoula-Kasavubu leadership to seek peaceful negotiations with Tshombe and at the same time sought to restrain ONUC's desire to use unlimited force against Katanga.

As usual, this restraint on drastic action by the UN was interpreted by the Nigerian public as an indication of Western collusion to allow Tshombe time to consolidate the military position and independence of the secessionist province. The Nigerian government, nonetheless, continued to support the U.S. policy, even as it expressed apprehension that the United States "might feel obliged to defer to the British."[31] In one encounter with Ambassador Palmer, Wachuku appealed to the United States to stand firm on its basic commitment to the Congo. He was particularly concerned that a weakening of the Adoula regime (due to the persistence of Katanga's secession) might lead to its replacement by a pro–Lumumba-Gizenga central government; the implication, he feared, would be a resurgence of Ghanaian and Soviet influences in the Congo. This prospect "he deplored."[32]

Nigeria also asked for U.S. backing of its request that the ANC (Congolese National Army) be included in any future UN military action in Katanga, something the Nigerians argued would legitimize the authority of the Leopoldville government in that province and deprive the mercenaries of their influence and control over Katangese police (gendarmerie). This position was also strongly advocated by Adoula and Mobutu, but the United States showed no enthusiasm for the idea. One major reason was that Belgium had threatened to withdraw all of its nationals if "one ANC entered Katanga."[33] The ANC had a reputation for indiscipline and disorderly conduct.

Katanga's secession was formally ended when UN forces entered Kolwezi on January 21, 1963. The ONUC victory could be traced to the decision of the U.S. National Security Council (NSC) on December 17, 1962, "to give the U.N. whatever equipment was necessary to re-integrate Katanga by force."[34] According to Stephen Weissman, the most important factor in the NSC decision was "the fear that unless Katanga was re-integrated swiftly, Adoula would fall and Lumumbist and Communist influence would rise dangerously."[35] ONUC had solved the Katanga issue, at least for now, but with overwhelming U.S. military, financial, and diplomatic support.

Technical and Security Assistance to Leopoldville
Under the Adoula and Tshombe Regimes

Until the end of 1964, Nigeria had offered various forms of technical, administrative, and security assistance, most of these through the UN, others by direct agreements, to whatever government was in control in Leopoldville.[36] Among these, two forms of assistance and their timing deserve closer scrutiny for the specific purpose of this study. These consisted of aid in the legal and security areas. The point of interest is not that Nigeria extended such aid; since 1961, as indicated earlier, Nigerian policymakers had shown a keen desire to cooperate with the central Congolese authorities. Rather, the more revealing issue is how and under what circumstances the assistance was offered.

Legal Aid. The most outstanding role played by Nigeria in the Congo, within the legal field, was to help evolve a new constitution for the embattled country. The man who contributed most to this effort was Teslim O. Elias, the Nigerian minister of justice and attorney-general (now vice-president of the World Court at the Hague). Elias, a constitution expert, was part of the four-person UN constitutional committee assigned the task of producing a quasi-federal constitution for the Congo, a project that lasted from August 1961 to about August 1962. The agreement for a new constitution to replace the one drafted by the Belgians was reached at the Lovanium Meeting from which the Adoula government emerged. Nigeria's association with this particular UN action in the Congo was encouraged by the United States, and its experience with managing a federal structure within a multiethnic society commended itself highly to U.S. officials—at least in 1961. "We know of no African state better able [to] give constructive advice [on] this subject on [the] basis [of] experience than Nigeria," Palmer had assessed with confidence.[37]

In addition to the formal UN effort, the U.S. government believed it was important to directly expose a number of high Congolese officials to Nigeria's "success" in operating a federal constitution and multiparty parliamentary system. The practical way to achieve this objective, as Secretary Rusk earlier suggested to Palmer, was to facilitate personal contacts between Congolese and "outstanding" Nigerian leaders.[38] Although Wachuku and other Nigerian officials might have seemed enthusiastic about the idea, they nevertheless expressed concern that they did not wish to magnify an impression of interfering in internal Congolese affairs.

The attendance of Adoula and his delegation at the Lagos Summit of Monrovia States, held January 25–30, 1962, provided an initial opportunity for making such contacts. Elias, who has already been appointed a member of the constitutional committee and who was part of the Nigerian delegation to the Congress, was naturally the most prominent figure in this endeavor.[39] Within the UN committee, he played the leading role in coordinating the various proposals and was instrumental in including a nonsecession clause in the final draft of the constitution, an act that reflected his sensitivity about secessionist tendencies in Nigeria.[40]

What exactly the Congolese leaders learned from Nigeria's federal experience is unclear because factional and political cleavages continued to plague the Congo even after the Katanga secession. Perhaps, as in Nigeria in this period, instability within the society proved incurable because it transcended, in a fundamental sense, a diagnostic approach based on a formal constitutional framework. Recurrent rebellions and secessions in the 1963–1965 period lent support to this view.

Security Assistance. In about February 1963, U.S. and Nigerian officials began to express a desire for Nigeria's involvement in three aspects of security work in the Congo. Now that the Katanga phase of the crisis seemed to be under control, the governments of the United States and Nigeria agreed that there was a pressing need for a comprehensive program in the security field that would facilitate the restoration of order and the consolidation of the political authority of the Congolese central government. The most important consideration was given to a project for retraining the ANC and gendarmerie and for modernizing the military. This idea, which came to be known as the Greene Plan[41] and which was also discussed privately with UN and Congo officials, was to be coordinated by the UN as well as through bilateral technical agreements with the Congolese government. Other countries to be involved in its implementation were Canada, Italy, Belgium, Norway, and Israel.

Another aspect of Nigeria's security assistance, which seemed to be a strictly tripartite arrangement between the United States, Nigeria, and the Adoula government, concerned the need to retain the four hundred member Nigerian police contingent in the Congo through 1965. The United States thought, correctly as it transpired, that it was necessary for a disciplined outside force to remain and ensure internal order until the Greene Plan materialized. The political situation in the Congo was still tenuous, and ONUC was due to withdraw its forces in June 1964.

As always, Nigeria was considered the most important pro-America African country to be entrusted with participation in this program; and an African presence, as in previous cases, was thought vital for its legitimation.[42] The United States felt so strongly about Nigeria becoming associated with this project that it overruled Mobutu's consistent "disinterest" in receiving military assistance from African or Asian countries. The colonel, who as late as February 1963 had repeated this position to Ambassador Edmund Gullion, visited Nigeria in late March and thereafter announced publicly that Nigeria "comes first in a list of African countries from which the Congo expects more military aid."[43] But the matter of Nigerian involvement, and indeed of the Greene Plan in general, would not be a simple one for the United States.

The Greene Plan ran into difficulties at the UN. In early March 1963, UN Secretary-General U Thant became reluctant to proceed with the idea because Afro-Asian members of the Congo Advisory Committee (CAC) were unreceptive to its structure.[44] It is true that on December 27, 1962, Adoula had written to Thant requesting that the UN coordinate the retraining of the ANC, and the secretary-general had replied in the affirmative. But once it became clear that the UN would need to approve the strictly bilateral aspect of the project, and as it became known that the major participating states in the scheme were all NATO members plus Israel, it was obvious that Thant would face immense opposition from the more "neutralist" Afro-Asian troop contributors to ONUC as well as from the Soviet Union. Although the United States still pressed, in private, for the adoption of the plan in its original form, which Secretary Rusk strongly argued was in the "national interests and [those of the] free world," the concept never came to fruition.[45]

And what about Nigeria? As soon as the identity of the participants in the Greene Plan was made public, the Nigerian government, rightly anticipating domestic opposition, raised its own objection in discussions with U.S. personnel. On June 12, Ambassador Palmer indicated to the State Department that Nigeria would be reluctant to serve in any "formal co-ordinating mechanism with NATO powers and Israel."[46] The regional atmosphere for such a formal Nigerian participation was essentially inauspicious. Nigeria had recently, at the formation of the OAU, reaffirmed its "nonalignment" cold war policy orientation. The Nigerian government decided that it was best for the Congolese authorities to invite individual countries to provide specific types of assistance. In the end, this was the approach that seemed to have been agreed upon. On May 20, Nigeria and the Congo signed a technical assistance agreement that, among other things, provided for the training of Congolese police in Nigeria.[47] Israel and Italy also entered into direct agreements to train Congolese paratroopers and air force personnel, respectively.

The United Nations was preparing to phase out its operations in the Congo by the end of 1963. However, at that same period, a rebellion broke out in the Kwilu Province, continuing into 1964. In the second half of 1964 rebellions and widespread disorders occurred in other parts of the Congo, including Kivu, Katanga, and Leopoldville.[48] In the face of these conflicts, ONUC was due to end its mandate. That the whole picture looked very bleak and disheartening from the viewpoint in Washington is an understatement. The entire U.S. investment in the crisis from 1960 to 1963 was on the verge of being wasted.

This was the situation when the United States urged Nigeria (1) not to withdraw its four hundred member police contingent from the Congo and (2) to return one battalion of its army to the Congo to assist the ANC. The first request was raised with Nigerian leaders by Ambassador-at-Large Averell W. Harriman during a visit to Lagos in early 1964. But in a memorandum Wachuku asked Harriman if the United States was "prepared to help defray the cost to Nigeria" if the Nigerian police were left in the Congo after ONUC's withdrawal.[49] The arrangement was not new or peculiar to the Congo. Indeed, at that particular juncture, Nigerian troops were engaged in suppressing an army mutiny in Tanganyika (presently Tanzania), but the government of that country was responsible for almost all expenses incurred by the Nigerian forces—a fact that Williams mentioned in his memorandum. Besides, the presence of the Nigerian police in the Congo until then was financed substantially by the United States through a special allotment to the UN Civilian Operations.[50] Nigeria, of course, had been paying its own assessment toward ONUC's work, but that was another matter. This information emphasizes both the extent of the Nigerian-U.S. interaction and the U.S. commitment to seek a solution to the Congo crisis.[51]

An impediment to the realization of the second U.S. request—that Nigeria return one army battalion to the Congo to assist the ANC—turned out to be the Congolese leadership itself. Apparently embarrassed by the renewed chaos after such a monumental sacrifice by outsiders, it repeatedly stalled on U.S. advice that it allow the last Nigerian army battalion to assist the ANC in suppressing the revolt in Kivu before June 30 (the date ONUC was due to end its mandate). Ambassador McMurtie G. Godley (who had taken over from Gullion early in 1963) characterized this Congolese reluctance in terms of amour propre.[52] Even Nigerian officials with close ties to Adoula, such as Wachuku and Ambassador Osakwe in Leopoldville, evidently failed to persuade Adoula on this issue. Meanwhile, the Nigerian battalion had been withdrawn, revolts had spread to other parts of the Congo, including, ominously for the United States, Lumumba's former stronghold, Stanleyville, and Adoula's government had been replaced by, ironically, Moise Tshombe.

With Tshombe, the number one enemy of nationalist Africa, in power in Leopoldville and with the immediate public interest this aroused in Nigeria, the flow of demand and influence was suddenly reversed. The Nigerian government was torn between private U.S. pressures to return its troops to the Congo and the storm of protest this would create at home and in the OAU.[53] It seemed that from July to August 1964 the United States was bent on ensuring a positive response by Nigeria toward Tshombe's request for military assistance. For instance, on August 6, Secretary Rusk cabled the new envoy in Lagos, Elbert Mathews, and asked, somewhat sternly, that he approach the Nigerian leadership "at appropriate level" to urge its "support of any Congolese government request for military or other assistance in the present crisis."[54]

Whether or not the Nigerian government privately provided military assistance, as expected by the United States, to the Tshombe regime, its public actions in vigorously defending Tshombe's status as the legal prime minister of the Congo displayed a continuation of Nigeria's basic alignment with the United States in the crisis. U.S. officials were taking every step to have Tshombe and his new government recognized by OAU members.[55]

The trouble for Nigeria and the United States was that Tshombe's return to, and leadership of, the Congo was an explosive as well as a traumatic issue in Nigeria and the rest of Africa, not viewed in neat legal terms. Tshombe's very name was linked to every ugly episode Africans found degrading about the Congo experience: foreign mercenaries, the murder of Lumumba, the power of the giant multinational corporations in sustaining Katanga's secession, and so forth.[56]

The finale, and certainly the most illustrative act, of Nigerian-U.S. collaboration in the Congo as 1964 ended occurred in late November. At that time, the Nigerian government took the lead at the UN and in the OAU in a strenuous defense of the U.S.-Belgian paratroop rescue operation in Stanleyville on November 24. Defying a chorus of domestic criticism, the Nigerian policymakers easily advanced the U.S. position, justifying the operation on humanitarian grounds. There was nothing wrong with this explanation except that it was not complete. In any case, it was the zeal with which Nigerian spokesmen assumed responsibility for defending an unpopular event that diverted attention from the merit of their argument. Chief Adebo, a faithful executor of Nigeria's policy at the UN since 1961, described the negative effect created by his government's position at the Security Council debate of December 15:

> The Nigerian delegation was greatly embarrassed. We were indicted by a majority in the Africa group, while our position damaged Nigeria's leadership status within the group. That was really how we got the bad name in the Congo. It took a long time before we could wash our clothes clean of this stain.[57]

What conclusions can be drawn from the foregoing? One outstanding fact was that the process of Nigerian-U.S. policy coordination in the Congo corresponded quite closely with that of their bilateral relations in the same period. The objectives of the two countries coincided roughly, thus reinforcing a general tendency of cooperation. Even if this were not the case, Nigerian policymakers would still, quite probably, have sought cooperation with the United States if they hoped to realize some of their projected objectives in the crisis or to sustain the framework of their bilateral ties. During the Congo crisis, Nigeria's policy alignment with the United States, as such, seemed to have proved successful in achieving its objectives up to the end of 1963; thereafter, the policy alignment became more of a liability to the ruling regime relative to its domestic position and its leadership status in Africa.

THE CHALLENGE OF GHANA
AND THE ASSASSINATION OF SYLVANUS OLYMPIO

We may face a greater threat from Ghana, Guinea, and the U.A.R. than the Soviet Union. The African imperialists are much better equipped than the Soviets to appeal to the aspirations of the African masses.

—Ambassador Elbert Mathews
U.S. Regional African Conference
Lagos, July 25, 1961

There is not only the question of Western imperialism, but also one of African imperialism.

—Jaja Wachuku
Nigeria's foreign minister
August 31, 1961

The Conflict with Ghana: Domestic
and Regional Factors

The basic factors that coalesced to sustain a state of conflict in Nigerian-Ghana relations have already been alluded to. What will be stressed here is the linkage of these factors in determining the form of interaction between the two nations with regard to the regional politics of decolonization. Ultimately, of course, the essential focus of analysis remains the assessment of the effect of U.S. ties on Nigeria's side of this conflict.

To most Nigerian and Ghanaian citizens, the persistent, official hostility between their two countries in the period 1960–1966 was both puzzling and regrettable. To judge by the early colonial contacts of the countries, the later sourness in their relations was something quite unexpected. Indeed, within the vortex of their modern existence as colonial possessions of a common imperial power, the two territories shared numerous essential ties (until 1957, the year Ghana attained independence). Reinforcing this closeness was the fact that as the two most important[58] anglophone West African colonies, they were each surrounded by many French-administered territories—a historical accident that engendered their sense of distinctiveness.

In more concrete ways, the two colonies were linked to each other through a network of interterritorial institutions and services, covering such areas as communication, currency, education, the judiciary, produce marketing, and so forth.[59] Although, just as in British East Africa, the official purpose for creating these joint networks was to increase economy and efficiency in colonial administration, the unintended effects included an immense flow in transterritorial migration and a heightened cultural awareness. Outside the official sphere, cooperation at the private level in social, economic, and nationalist matters blossomed among the emergent Western-educated elites in both territories. Significantly, it was a notable Nigerian nationalist—later to become Nigeria's first president—Nnamdi Azikiwe, who contributed to radicalizing the Ghanaian nationalist movement during his domicile in Accra as a journalist between 1934 and 1937. It was also Azikiwe who inspired Ghana's future leader Kwame Nkrumah with the idea of undertaking his historic journey to the United States for advanced education.[60]

But the attainment of independence first by Ghana in 1957 and then by Nigeria in 1960 effectively reversed the expected hope of a postcolonial collaboration between the two nations in the emergent African interstate system. Instead, the state of relations until 1966 was marked by extreme competition and polarization of their ruling regimes.[61] At the root of this unhappy experience, and fatefully reinforcing one another, were (1) the evolution and consolidation of incompatible ideologies of African decolonization; (2) the domestic political and security dilemma confronting the Nigerian national leadership since 1960; and (3) what was usually regarded as the struggle for regional leadership between Nigeria and Ghana.

Incompatible Ideologies of Decolonization

The conflict in ideology assumed concrete form over a set of fundamental issues faced by the decolonizing continent. Perhaps, the most substantive of these issues was the question of what to do about colonially imposed territorial boundaries. The views of the Nigerian and Ghanaian leaderships on this perplexing problem naturally reflected their contrasting conceptions of decolonization. The Nigerian authorities regarded such boundaries to be inviolable once independence was gained, even if the original act of division had arbitrarily split many previously homogeneous peoples. As they saw the matter, the best that could be done, given the new reality, was to build a loose regional framework within which the emergent sovereign entities could collaborate on various fronts, thus ameliorating potential harmful effects of territorial fragmentation (e.g., irredentism and interstate conflict). According to Mallam Y. Maitama Sule, the Nigerian chief spokesman at the Second Conference of Independent African States, held in Addis Ababa in 1960, the way to break down the "artificial barriers" was "to build international roads, promote exchanges of information [and lift] any ban on the movement of free trade and people between the various African countries."[62] This solution to the problem of colonial boundaries was part and parcel the official Nigerian approach to Pan-Africanism in general. Throughout this period, Nigerian policymakers held to the position that the realization of African unity hinged on the recognition of inherited boundaries.

For Ghana, the boundary problem in Africa was one that could be resolved effectively only by an immediate continental political union. From this perspective, political union would in addition bring about real unity by submerging the fragmented jurisdictions under one supreme political authority and eliminate the root of political and material weakness by creating a powerful federal entity. Kwame Nkrumah, the foremost opponent of existing colonial boundaries, unflinchingly regarded the boundary problem as an inherent dimension of the general process of decolonization, and he regarded its rectification (through political unification) as an essential insurance of African independence. Thus, for Ghana, colonial boundaries, decolonization, and African unity were problems that issued from a single historical source—colonialism. Their solution would thus require, logically, a comprehensive approach, not a piecemeal effort.[63]

The Issue of Subversion

An extension of the conflict of views between the two countries on the boundary question and a problem that remained a constant source of open confrontation between the ruling regimes was the issue of unsolicited "interference" in the domestic affairs of one African state by another. One element in Nigeria's defense of its conservative orientation to decolonization (indeed, a vital force behind this orientation) was an aversion to any form of outside intrusion in internal politics. Nigeria's leaders were so consumed with the threat of Ghana's destructive intrusion in national politics that they fought tirelessly to entrench what would become the principle of noninterference first in the Monrovia Charter and later more indelibly in the OAU Charter.

Ghana's subversive image, nurtured particularly in the conservative states (including the French-speaking Union Africaine et Malgache UAM, later called the Organisation Commune d'Afrique et Malgach, OCAM), marked Ghana as the black sheep of African politics until the end of 1965. No other factor contributed so critically to the adverse relations between Nigeria and Ghana as the issue of subversion. The reason for this lay in its incendiary effect on an already volatile state of internal political struggle in Nigeria. In a very stark sense, the power-wielders in the Nigerian federal system believed that Ghana's aim was to transform the sociopolitical structure in Nigeria (which Ghanaian spokesmen incessantly taunted as neocolonialist) and thereby reverse the Nigerian power balance. (As will be discussed, the desperate attempt by some Nigerians to transform the national power balance in the form bequeathed by Great Britain, through a military coup d'etat, was the immediate cause of the country's civil war.) The Nigerian regime's almost paranoiac belief in Ghana's capacity to negatively affect domestic politics in their country was no doubt strengthened by the extreme vigor with which the Ghanaian leadership (Nkrumah especially) strove to propagate its view of decolonization and by the open link between Ghana and the Soviet Union in this endeavor, beginning in 1961. The Soviet Union, it should be recalled, had publicly extolled the Casablanca group as the only anti-imperialist, genuinely revolutionary force in the continent. But the crowning evidence for the Nigerian regime of Ghana's subversive intent in Nigeria (and the Soviet role in it) came to light in connection with the treason trials of 1962–1963.[64]

The Nigerian federal government's public identification of Ghana with the aspirations of dissident groups within Nigeria sharpened after mid-July 1961. The leader of the opposition party in the national assembly (and the regime's foremost enemy), Chief Awolowo, had just returned from a political "pilgrimage" to Ghana, after which he abandoned his earlier hostile attitude to that country's domestic and regional policies. He now recommended Ghana's brand of socialism for Nigeria and urged Nigeria to join the Ghana-Guinea-Mali Union. Likewise, his party's official foreign policy spokesman, Anthony Enahoro, condemned the government's functionalist approach to African unity "at a time when the climate of progressive opinion throughout Africa is for organic union.[65] Ghana's initial association with the Action Group–inspired plot to overthrow the federal government in Nigeria was alleged to have occurred during Awolowo's visit to Accra.[66]

Foreign Minister Jaja Wachuku, in a press conference on June 9, 1962, pointedly accused top Ghanaian officials, including Nkrumah and Ghana's chief envoy in Lagos, G.E.K. Doe, of plotting the overthrow of his government. He followed up this charge by claiming that Ghanaian agents had infiltrated Nigerian organizations such as the Nigerian Co-operative Movement, the Nigerian Trade Union Congress, the Nigerian Farmer's Council, and the Local Government Council Association of Nigeria. The Ghanaian government, Wachuku threatened, should either cease its "black" imperialistic activities or risk being toppled in "twelve months" by Nigeria.[67] The significance of Wachuku's statement lies not in its virulence nor in the credibility of the challenge to Ghana. (In terms of existing military capacity, Ghana, with less than six times Nigeria's population of 55 million, possessed a qualitatively superior standing force of 9,000 men to Nigeria's 8,000. Moreover, Ghana's defense budget in 1964 was 2.2 percent of its GDP; Nigeria's was 1.1 percent.) The significance of the minister's statement was that it high-lighted the centrality of the issue of subversion in the Nigerian-Ghana conflict relationship. And this effectively shaped the perception of Nigeria's policymakers toward Nkrumah's Ghana and was also most crucial in defining the basic interest of the Nigerian regime in the decolonization process.[68]

The Struggle for Regional Leadership

As a third factor underlying the competition and polarization between Nigeria and Ghana one cannot underestimate the dynamic quest of Ghana under Nkrumah to remain the inspirational source of African nationalism and independence. Why was this so? Was it, as Scott Thompson seems to believe, a result of Nkrumah's sheer vanity and personal ambition for power? Was the reason submerged in the rigid conviction of the Ghanaian leader that his was the only redeeming approach to African emancipation? Or, was it merely because of the historical fact that Ghana was the first black African state to gain independence from foreign rule? Whatever the proper explanation (and it could well have been a combination of all of the above), one fact emerged: Ghana's desire to retain the leading role in the decolonization movement clashed head-on, after 1960, with Nigeria's self-image as the more natural spokesperson for Africa south of the Sahara.

Having said this, two points of clarification should be stressed. First, the mere flexing of African leadership impulses in the two nations did not account for the level of discord that existed between the ruling regimes. Leadership at any level is, after all, not simply claimed but earned through concrete performance. What was loosely called the leadership struggle became such a bone of contention (from the Nigerian standpoint) because of its linkage to the subversion issue and hence the security of the Nigerian state. The very nature of Nigeria's "leadership" performance in regional diplomacy demonstrates this interconnection.

One marked feature of Nigeria's policy was its reactiveness, for it was primarily aimed at either matching Ghana's more populistic initiatives or containing that country's threatening influence in every African crisis situation as well as in diplomatic councils. Thus what one might very liberally call Nigeria's leadership strategy was narrowly determined by the interest of the ruling regime to deal with the domestic security concerns perceived to issue from Ghana and by the regime's related desire to legitimize its own conception of decolonization (as opposed to Ghana's) and have it institutionalized as a collective norm in regional diplomacy. What actually prevailed then was more a strategy of "enlightened" self-preservation of a regime than any ambitious inclination to assume regional leadership by virtue of the nation's acclaimed status or by any consuming interest in decolonization per se.

Illustrative of this reactive strategy were Nigeria's actions, for example, in the Congo crisis and the conflict in Togo after the assassination of President Sylvanus Olympio (see below). Likewise, the regime's perceived need to isolate Ghana and weaken its influence fueled Nigeria's promotion of countervailing regional groupings and conferences such as the Monrovia group and the Lagos conference of 1962.[69] It was, however, at Addis Ababa in May 1963, during the formation of the OAU, that Nigeria succeeded in neutralizing most effectively Ghana's approach to decolonization (and thus regional unity). Admittedly, this could not have been as easy for the Nigerians without support gained through U.S. diplomatic leverage. Notice, for instance, the mediating role of Manuel Trucco, the secretary-general of the Organization of American States (OAS) and U.S. ambassador to Chile, with Nigeria, Liberia, and Ethiopia in working out the compromise draft charter for the OAU.[70] The final chapter of the organization embodied essentially the principles advocated at Monrovia and reaffirmed at Lagos in 1962. (Ghana's failure to influence these activities became even more glaring by its exclusion from, and

Nigeria's domination of, the nine-member Liberation Committee, which was charged with the coordination of policy on regional decolonization, of which Ghana had been the most vocal advocate). Nigeria's open satisfaction with the outcome of the Addis Ababa proceedings is indicated in the prime minister's sanguine statement, on returning home, that: "The Addis Ababa charter is ninety-nine percent what I hoped for. I would not have signed it if it did not satisfy me."[71] The foreign minister made even more vaunting remarks, saying that the exclusion of Ghana from the Liberation Committee was a defeat for its "brand of anti-colonial policy" and that the original idea of setting up the committee was "a result of one of Nigeria's proposals.[72]

The second point worth emphasizing follows from the first, and that was the lack of consonance between the operative strategy of the Nigerian policymakers and the wider public expectation about Nigeria's regional leadership. The lesson embedded in this experience for policymakers is that they stand the risk of popular disenchantment when their public pronouncements on vital policy issues persistently fail to match actual government performance. Recall that before independence and shortly thereafter, Nigerian political leaders and intellectuals were unrelenting in articulating the view that Nigeria bore a natural obligation to assume an energetic leadership to ensure a rapid decolonization of the continent. In fact, the government's performance was judged by the enlightened public to be too narrowly focused and excessively circumspect. The inability of the ruling government to adopt a broader regional policy strategy more reflective of the wider aspirations of the nation deprived it of sustained domestic support in its effort to contain Ghana's threats. By 1966, the absence of mass support for Nigeria's regional policy became even more accentuated by the public's widespread disaffection with the regime's internal policies.

The U.S. Reaction to the Nigeria-Ghana Conflict Relationship: The Effect on Nigeria's Response

One could readily deduce that the U.S. government had energetically abetted Nigeria's policy of counterconfrontation with the regime of President Nkrumah. Such a position could be based on prima facie considerations linked to the strongly held U.S. impression of Ghana, from late 1960, as a radical anticolonialist state, a Communist sympathizer, and an African imperialist. Conversely, U.S. officials would have been expected to provide unrestricted support to the Nigerian government because of the contrasting image of Nigeria as a "moderate" on colonialism and an anti-Soviet, pro-Western state. However, to properly understand the actual U.S. behavior in the Nigeria-Ghana conflict, it is necessary to recall the relevant U.S. objectives in Nigeria and to relate them to developments in direct U.S.-Ghana relations, especially in the period from 1961 to 1963, as well as to maintain a coherent perspective on overall U.S. aims in the West African subregion.

Ghana as a Problem to U.S. Objectives in West Africa

In Chapter 3, it was noted that one immediate objective of U.S. policy in Nigeria was to strengthen, in collaboration with Great Britain, Nigeria's fledgling parliamentary experiment. In the medium term at least, the goal was to sustain Nigeria's ability to serve as a vital and continuous link between the West and the subregion of West Africa. A specific U.S. political objective was to bolster the domestic security of the Nigerian regime for the sake of enhancing its capacity both to resist direct Soviet pressures and to assume "responsibile" leadership, aimed at countering radical forces in the regional political process. Clearly, on both grounds, the Nigerian-Ghana conflict and in particular Ghana's attempts to destabilize the Nigerian polity by subversion constituted obstacles for the United States because they conflicted with the stated U.S. objectives.

U.S. officials under the Kennedy administration had become aware of the serious nature of the problem of Ghana's subversion in late 1962. Before that time, the issue was interpreted in less ideological terms merely as part of Ghana's effort to generate African mass support for its regional "leadership ambition." But in December 1962, Kofi Busia, a leading Ghanaian dissident who in 1972 became Ghana's second civilian prime minister, painted for the U.S. administration a dire picture of Ghana's subversion plans. In a testimony before the U.S. Senate Subcommittee on Internal Security, chaired by Senator Thomas E. Dodd of Connecticut, Busia charged that Nkrumah was a "long-standing member of international communism and that Ghana was . . . being used by him as a base for Communist subversive activities throughout Africa." Further, he accused Nkrumah of "supporting [the] underground subversion movement in Nigeria."[73]

Was the Nkrumah regime subverting Nigeria and other West African states for the interest of international communism, as Busia alleged? That possibility was discounted a year earlier by President Kennedy and the Africa Bureau of the State Department, backed by the respected opinion of Great Britain's Sir Robert Jackson (a one-time chairman of Ghana's development commission), Lady Barbara Ward Jackson, and Prime Minister Harold Macmillan.[74] At any rate, the view already stressed in this study is that subversion, as a tool in Ghana's Africa diplomacy, was linked fundamentally to the regional decolonization process and the struggle for preeminence of the contending conceptions,[75] and not to communism. (The left-wing faction of Ghana's ruling Convention People's party (CPP) might have pressed Nkrumah, especially after Ghana's diplomatic defeats in the Congo crisis, to enlist greater support of the Soviet Union in this regional political contest, but that hardly turned Nkrumah into a Communist agent.

Early in 1963, the United States was confronted with more concrete evidence of Ghana's subversive activities in Nigeria. Ambassador Palmer was receiving regular reports from Nigerian officials to the effect that the Nigerian government was "fully aware of Ghanaian plotting," of the training of Nigerian insurgents in Ghana, and of Ghana's active support of the Action Group (witness the evidence obtained in the treason trials). Palmer was also told of a Ghanaian military aircraft that had landed unauthorized in Lagos in November 1962 and of two "Soviet submarines recently acquired by Ghana." Furthermore, Nigeria expressed grave concern that as a result of radical changes within the country, Ghana "could develop . . . into an African Cuba."[76] As will become clearer later, the Nigerian government was probing, attempting to impress on U.S. officials the seriousness of the threat it perceived from Ghana, which it presumed should naturally be of equal concern to the United States. The government's aim was to dramatize its security difficulties in a manner that would elicit more drastic and proportionate U.S. assistance—such as military aid—with which they could challenge Ghana more effectively. But although the State Department and President Kennedy personally empathized with Nigeria's view of Ghana's subversion and its effect on the country's stability, the U.S. view differed from Nigeria's with regard to the specific measures to engage in resolving the problem.

True, the United States had, as previously noted, taken actions earlier that resulted in strengthening the position of the Nigerian regime in the context of the Nigerian-Ghana conflict relationship. For example, the United States offered vital diplomatic support for Nigeria's bid to isolate Ghana in the Congo as well as in important regional councils. Within Nigeria, U.S. personnel had rendered direct and indirect encouragement to that faction of the Nigerian Trade Union movement with a pro-government orientation—the Trade Union Congress of Nigeria (TUCN) led by H. P. Adebola—against the Nigerian Trade Union Congress (NTUC), which was alleged to receive covert assistance from Communist sources.[77]

It was a different matter, however, to expect the United States to actively abet an intensification of the Nigerian-Ghana conflict to the extent of actual military confrontation, a risk inherent in the Nigerian expectation of its alignment with the Americans. The Nigerian leadership, it appeared, was no longer content with the old type of support from its dominant partner. The regime now faced physical threats to its survival, linked to the opposition "coup plot" and the uprising in neighboring Togo, both of which Ghana was believed to have instigated. It was beginning to contemplate military means for containing Ghana or at least for deterring its insidious designs. Surely, this was to be the supreme test of the regime's dependency relationship with the United States in the context of its regional policy. But in Washington, this was considered a dangerous development. The United States had to weigh other important interests, some of which could obviate a disposition to respond favorably to Nigeria's expectation. The direct U.S.-Ghana relationship contained one such interest.

It was stressed earlier that Ghana's ardent propagation of a transformative approach to decolonization in Africa was bound to alienate the United States and complicate U.S.-Ghana direct relations. And so it did.[78] At the start of the Kennedy administration, U.S.-Ghana differences were cast in sharp relief by the clash of policy over the emergence of the Casablanca and Monrovia groups, the recognition of the Algerian FLN provisional government and, most fatefully, the Congo crisis. But it was especially after the murder of Lumumba in February 1961, which Ghana linked to a "CIA-Belgian conspiracy," and the subsequent failure of Nkrumah's diplomacy in that crisis that relations between the two countries turned precipitously downhill. The Ghanaian leadership henceforth put aside its earlier proclaimed policy of nonalignment and openly but cautiously coveted an alignment with the Soviet Union. Domestically, it also adopted a number of authoritarian political and economic measures necessary, according to Nkrumah, to rid the country of neocolonial influences and set it on a socialist course. Concurrently, the Ghanaian press attacked the United States, claiming that it was an "imperialist, neo-colonialist power preying on Africa." Such attacks, becoming especially vehement after the Kulungugu assassination attempt on Nkrumah in August 1962, induced U.S. Ambassador to Ghana William P. Mahoney, Jr., to lodge numerous protests with the Ghana government, pointing out the harm that could come to bilateral U.S.-Ghana relations by such anti-American sentiments.[79]

Despite the strongly conflicting positions of the two governments on bilateral and international issues, President Kennedy considered it in the interest of the United States to approve, in December 1961, Ghana's aid request for the building of the Volta dam. For Ghana, that gesture was significant because the Volta dam, in Nkrumah's words, "was the greatest of all our development projects," designed to "provide the electrical power for our great social, agricultural and industrialization programme."[80] For the United States, the decision to provide $40 million (in loans) for the Volta project and to assist in other aspects of Ghana's development program, was justified on three specific grounds: the desire to ingratiate the people of Ghana (especially, the civil servants) whom U.S. officials believed to be basically Western-oriented in their values and sympathy—a sort of "holding action," pending the end of Nkrumah's leadership tenure; the desire to pull the Ghanaian government away from a pro-Soviet orientation on East-West issues; and the need to not give evidence to other African countries that U.S. economic aid was contingent on political allegiance.[81] Viewed in the context of the 1961–1963 period, the interest of the United States in salvaging its ties with Ghana constituted a restraining factor in the U.S. government's support of Nigeria's regional interests.

Yet another significant consideration for the United States was related to its overall political interest in the subregion of West Africa. Above all, U.S. interest vis-à-vis the necessity of preventing a Soviet intrusion dictated a policy approach that would discourage a local arms race between the two most important states in the area. As Assistant Secretary Williams recognized, a condition that fueled an arms race in the subregion would only heighten interstate conflicts, intensify instability by diverting scarce resources and efforts from socioeconomic development, and create openings for the penetration of Soviet-Chinese influences. In fact, in one basic sense, the U.S. identification with Nigeria's position concerning the inviolability of colonial boundaries rested on the conviction (on the part of the United States) that an attempt to readjust those boundaries according to Ghana's prescription would, given the reality of separate independence and sovereignties, engender tensions and hence subsystemic instability. Following this logic, it was not in the U.S. interest to contribute to a situation in which the boiling relations between Nigeria and Ghana could actually explode into armed conflict.

There was also, for the United States, the no less important consideration of direct British interests in both Nigeria and Ghana. Both states were leading African members of the British-led commonwealth. Despite the stridency of the British press in its condemnation of "repressive developments" within Ghana, the U.K. government could not but worry about the prospect of a full-blown crisis involving two commonwealth partners that in turn might further crack an already strained association. In addition, there were large British firms still operating in Ghana, despite the ostensible stirrings of a "new socialist order." For both its political and economic stakes, Great Britain was not yet prepared to adopt a precipitous bilateral stance toward Nkrumah's regime. Witness the government's enthusiastic promotion of Queen Elizabeth's visit to Ghana in the fall of 1961 at the height of the British-Ghanaian media hostility and Macmillan's advice to Kennedy not to renege on funding the Volta dam project.

The extent to which the United States could support Nigeria against Ghana was also tempered by this critical British connection. And, in any event, any serious U.S. role had to be coordinated with Great Britain, in the latter's capacity as America's chief ally and because of Nigeria's military ties to Great Britain.

The Togo Insurrection and Nigeria's Insecurity

The Togolese military revolt of January 13, 1963, involving the assassination of President Olympio and the overthrow of his government, put in a clearer focus the problematic link between issues of colonial boundaries and subversion in the regional politics of decolonization.[82] For Nigeria, the dramatic event in Togo showed even more clearly how the security interest of the ruling regime defined its leadership role in the decolonization process. The Togolese conflict can also be studied as a situation through which the U.S. attitude and role in the Nigerian-Ghana conflict relationship can be evaluated, particularly the impact of the conflict on Nigeria's attempt to deal with the underlying security threat posed by Ghana.

Nigeria Charges Ghana With Complicity

On January 16, three days after the insurrection, the *Nigerian Citizen* (a pro-NPC party newspaper) publicly indicated Ghana's complicity. Its editorial clearly stated this position:

> The causes leading to the coup d'etat are yet to unfold . . ., but recent events left us no doubt that a *more powerful* [emphasis added] country has been interfering in the internal affairs of Togo. It is a well-documented fact that Togo's neighbour is seriously planning the downfall of many lawfully constituted Governments of independent African nations in their crazy—though unrealisable—bid to make their leader a Napoleon.[83]

On February 12, Balewa, speaking for his cabinet, told U.S. Assistant Secretary Williams that he had evidence "that Ghanaians [were] behind Olympio's assassination."[84] Balewa expressed anxiety about the prospect of Idrissou Meatchi (a Togolese politician who had been imprisoned by Olympio but had escaped and taken refuge in Ghana) coming to power and of Togo becoming integrated as a region of Ghana. To understand the significance of the diplomatic offensive mounted by Nigeria after January 13, it is necessary to comment briefly on the link between Ghana and the event in Togo.

Despite the *Citizen's* editorial and Balewa's "evidence," the problem of establishing Ghana's culpability was to become a thorny one for the

Nigerian government. Indeed, the accusation in the form presented appeared to have been largely deductive. The general premise from which opinion was drawn about Ghana's involvement was the popularized image of Nkrumah's regime as the bastion for subversive forces against "nonprogressive" states. However, a more specific reason why Ghana might have wished to overthrow the Olympio government was the smoldering dispute between the two states regarding their unification.

During and before the April 1958 preindependence election in Togo, the Ghanaian government had championed the presidential candidacy of Sylvanus Olympio against the French-supported Nicholas Grunitzky. Ghana had staked its support on Olympio because of his strong resistance to the idea of joining a French union. (Grunitzky had campaigned as a pro-union candidate, thus gaining the bad name in Togo and Ghana of a French puppet.) Furthermore, there was an expectation—which turned out to be illusory—that an independent Togo under Olympio would willingly integrate with its Western neighbor, Ghana, in a political union. Olympio, it is said, had created the impression of sharing Nkrumah's ideological conception of colonial boundaries by accepting financial assistance from Ghana for his election campaigns and through his anti-French stance at the Independent African States (IAS) meeting in Accra just before the Togo election.[85] In actual fact, Olympio merely capitalized on Nkrumah's zeal for political union in order to rid Togo of French influence. His real preference was an association with Ghana based on practical economic cooperation that precluded sacrificing Togolese sovereignty. This disposition might have been strengthened during Olympio's meeting with Balewa in Lagos in 1961.

On its part, Ghana had wistfully envisaged political integration with Togo in 1958 to enlarge its territorial domain, precisely in keeping with its philosophy of decolonization. Notice that in about the same year the Ghanaian government was making "union" deals with other nationalist leaders in colonial territories soon to gain independence: Patrice Lumumba in 1958; Sekou Toure in 1958; and Modibo Keita in 1960. But there was also a cultural-irredentist factor in Ghana's agitation for a union with Togo: the need to reunite the splintered Ewe ethnic populations on the southeastern and southern borders, respectively, of the territories. Indeed, the boundary problem of the "French" and "British" Ewes was used by Nkrumah to dramatize his case for revising colonial boundaries and for a regional political union.[86] The reluctance of Togo to become politically integrated with Ghana, preferring instead to retain an independent identity, was perceived in Ghana as a case of "backing out" of a well understood commitment. Consequently, from 1959 to 1962 each regime envisaged the other as a security hazard. The Togolese suspected Ghana of resorting to subversion to assure realization of its long-standing object; the Ghanaian leadership, beyond a sense of feeling betrayed by Olympio, viewed Togo as a dangerous haven for dissidents seeking to assassinate Nkrumah.[87] This, approximately, was the state of Ghana-Togo relations when the Togolese military decided to settle their own score with the Olympio government.

The Nigerian national press, just after January 13, in its initial reaction to the Togo insurrection, took a position appreciative of the government's express security concerns. True, the public as a whole was visibly shocked by the spectre of an African ruler being eliminated through such a violent means. Only two years after Nigeria's independence, assassination of a head of state was still a novelty in African politics; the only other assassination was that of Lumumba in the Congo. But Togo, unlike the Congo, is a short distance from Nigeria's western border, separated only by a weak Dahomey (Republic of Benin). The *Citizen*, it has already been noted, made no sober effort to address the ground forces in Togo relating to the uprising except to paint Ghana as the villain. Two other papers, the *West African Pilot* and the *Daily Express*, went a little further, defining the nature of Olympio's domestic rule as dictatorial, but they then drew contrasting conclusions as to the source of the uprising. The *Pilot* exonerated Olympio's repression of opposition elements because they had been subversive of his government; the *Express*, echoing the sentiments of the opposition groups to the ruling government in Nigeria, explained the assassination as the only avenue open to the Togolese to eliminate a dictatorial regime.[88]

Nigerian Diplomacy in the Togo Affair via the IAMO

From January 24 to 26, a meeting of the foreign ministers of states belonging to the Inter-African and Malagasy States Organization (IAMO) was held in Lagos, having been summoned by the Nigerian government. The subjects of the meeting were the Olympio assassination and subversion in Africa. To underscore his government's extreme concern over developments in Togo and its conviction that Ghana had to be the instigator, Wachuku, in announcing the proposed conference, revealed a crude diplomatic style, prejudging in public what should have been determined through collective discussion among the council of foreign ministers two days later. He warned that Nigeria would view recognition of the new regime in Togo as an "unfriendly act" and stated that henceforth the western border of Nigeria would become, for security reasons, the Togo-Ghana boundary. He also stated that the Olympio assassination was a "cold-blooded murder, financed and carried out by somebody" (an inference to Nkrumah) and that Ghana should withdraw its forces from the border with Togo.[89]

At the opening of the conference, Wachuku, in his capacity as the chairman, outlined the essential tasks before the conferees. These, it should be noted, embodied the Nigerian government's immediate objectives in the developing conflict. Primarily there were three tasks. First, the conferees were urged to adopt resolutions barring the recognition of the provisional civilian government set up by the insurrectionary committee following the coup and to repudiate, as a "principle," the change of governments by means other than "recognized constitutional" ones. Second, Wachuku proposed that the conferees set up an investigative commission to uncover the circumstances leading to Olympio's murder. Third, Wachuku proposed that a defense arrangement embracing IAMO members be created to deal with future occurrences of the type in Togo. Further, he called on member states to declare the presence of Ghanaian troops along the Togo-Ghana border an action that constituted "a threat to the independence and territorial integrity of Togo."[90]

Interestingly, Wachuku's proposals to the assembled ministers, viewed properly, presented the IAMO states with an opportunity to give practical meaning to the principles they had earlier espoused at Monrovia and reaffirmed at Lagos, namely noninterference and inviolability of national borders. Yet most of these states could give only weak support to Nigeria's tough position, and the final resolutions adopted by the conference failed to mention the centerpiece of Nigeria's strategy in the conflict—nonrecognition. Individual members, instead, retained the option of granting or withholding recognition according to their particular interests. Even as the conference was being proposed by Nigeria on January 22, Senegal had already joined Ghana in extending recognition to the Togolese provisional regime under Grunitzky, who, during the Olympio rule, had lived in exile in Dahomey.[91] On the opening day of the conference, Dahomey, whose president, Hubert Maga, according to Helen Kitchen, "played a major role in getting the Provisional government set up in Lome," gave de facto recognition to the regime "while awaiting the outcome of the conference"; at the same time, both Gabon and Cameroon were strenuously arguing in favor of recognition.[92]

Significantly, all of these countries belonged to the French-backed UAM (and states in this group were to be partially responsible for the failure of Nigeria's diplomacy in this conflict); all were firmly tied to France economically, politically, and militarily. Could the French have played a part in Olympio's assassination? The Nigerian authorities were convinced that although the coup was mainly the handwork of Ghana, it had been executed with France's collaboration. The suspicion of French involvement appeared to have been strengthened by evidence supplied to the conference by M. Theophile Mally, one of the ministers in the ousted Olympio government. Later, Wachuku was to elaborate to U.S.

Ambassador Palmer and Assistant Secretary Williams that the French ambassador in Lome "had known of the coup at 9 P.M., January 12, but had failed to warn Togolese authorities."[93] The French behavior, Wachuku said, was based on a desire to pull Togo into the UAM and hence into its own orbit (a step Olympio had resisted) and to isolate Nigeria from former French colonies in West Africa. Olympio, it is true, had attempted to use Nigeria's influence to neutralize the UAM bond; he often complained that UAM members were unable to exercise "their full freedom" because they were "too heavily" influenced by France.[94] If Wachuku needed any confirmation of his suspicion, the coup organizers in Lome promptly made known that they favored an early association of Togo with the twelve-member UAM.

Of the seven resolutions adopted by the IAMO conference, two were of particular consequence from Nigeria's standpoint, that is, given the country's failure to secure formal agreement on "nonrecognition," which was for Nigeria merely a holding action. These resolutions were (1) the call for a commission of inquiry, which would comprise the Ivory Coast, Niger, Dahomey, Upper Volta, and Nigeria, to investigate Olympio's assassination in order to expose any external forces that had been involved; and (2) the holding of free elections before May 1963 and the reinstatement of the constitution as well as the prompt release of all political detainees (this referred to members of the Olympio government placed under arrest during the coup). Behind those two resolutions, verbal allusions to constitutionalism notwithstanding, lay Nigeria's real objectives in the conflict. The Nigerian government, enlivened by its conviction of Ghana's prime responsibility for the Togo insurrection (a conclusion now bolstered by the knowledge of Ghanaian involvement in the attempted coup in Nigeria, the legal consideration of which was progressing concurrently with the events in Togo), hoped to use the commission of inquiry to expose Nkrumah's imperialistic designs before Africa and the world at large. Beyond this, Nigeria saw in Togo an appropriate opportunity to stop Ghana in its tracks; the cancer of Ghana as a regional source of regime insecurity could be eliminated once and for all.

The Failure of Diplomacy

Thus, between February and early May 1963, Nigeria's diplomacy was, blindly, directed toward restoring the status quo in Togo, regardless of the popular wish of the Togolese. According to Nigerian officials, the post-Olympio regime, being a creature of Ghana, would be dominated by Nkrumah, and Togo would only become a closer base of Ghanaian subversion against Nigeria. Making this prospect not so implausible was the observation that Dahomey, the only buffer state between Togo and Nigeria, seemed outwardly to approve the course of events in Togo and even to strike a friendly relationship with the Ghanaian leadership immediately following the coup.[95] Given this self-imposed reality, Nigerian officials contemplated a policy onslaught comprising crude political leverage and/or outright military force. Clearly, Nigeria's policymakers were setting out on a diplomatic limp, being incapable of exercising a more dispassionate assessment of the political forces at work in the Togo conflict and at the same time possessing no independent resources to back up the tough policy they projected.

Nigeria's diplomatic setbacks commenced with the difficulties confronted by the commission in discharging its central mandate, that of visiting Togo to investigate the circumstances surrounding the conflict and calling both internal and external culprits to account. This, as it turned out, was never to be accomplished. The reasons for the failure were apparent from the start, although Nigerian policymakers envisioned otherwise. First, during the conference itself, the delegation sent by the military council in Togo succeeded, with the aid of the UAM members, in defeating a Nigerian move to have the conference approve the participation of a pro-Olympio delegation led by Mally. Instead, both delegations were denied formal seating but given the opportunity to present their respective positions. Second, once the exact purpose of the commission of inquiry was understood in Togo by the soldiers who had carried out the coup and who, indeed, were the real power behind the Grunitzky government, the proposed visit by the commission was cast in doubt. On January 28, Grunitzky spoke on radio in Lome, saying that he regretted the fact that the "Monrovia Group Foreign Minister's meeting did not give *de facto* recognition to his Provisional Government."[96] This was not completely accurate, for a number of the countries had, as shown above, already accorded de facto recognition (and even countries like Nigeria, by agreeing to go to Lome to work with the ruling government on the commission's task, had in fact accepted its existence). What the Grunitzky government had expected from the IAMO Conference was recognition *de jure*. But if Grunitzky expressed his "disappointment" mildly, the military council was not as conciliatory. It refused any cooperation with the commission; beyond this, it failed to guarantee the physical safety of the commission's members should they, nevertheless, choose to go to Togo.[97] Using this open exhibition of hostility as justification, two members of the commission—the Ivory Coast and Upper Volta—dropped out of further participation. The rest of the commission, with Nigeria's lead, did visit Lome once, but seeing no prospect of cooperation from the government, they suspended their work "indefinitely" on February 4.

At this juncture Nigeria's diplomacy in the conflict seemed to have reached a dead end. Such was the verdict of the Nigerian public. The ire of the nation for the humiliation it felt was given vent by a generally nonpartisan press commentary and by the views of important members of the governing parties. The villain was none other than the foreign minister. The pacesetter was the NCNC's *Pilot,* which on January 31 accused Wachuku of "opening his mouth too wide" with "boasts" and "threats" (referring to the minister's public statement on the extension of Nigeria's security border to Togo), saying that he only succeeded in alienating other delegates, including the Togolese, during the last conference. The paper concluded that Wachuku was becoming a "liability to the people of Nigeria."[98] The *Express* questioned Wachuku's objectivity in the Togo situation, reporting that he was "allowing his anti-Ghana sentiments" to dictate policy (which was true).[99] The Kano branch of the senior party in government, the NPC, in a similar vein, considered Wachuku's January 22 speech to have been "uncalled for" and repudiated the Nigerian government for "interfering" in the domestic affairs of other states (thereby breaking a cardinal principle of Nigeria's foreign policy). According to this group, African states "should allow the Grunitzky government and the Togolese [people] to solve their own problems."[100] However, as will be seen later, whatever Wachuku's personal default, the basic line of policy he pursued was that of his government and was shared very much by his prime minister.

Wachuku's Military Option and U.S. Ambivalence

The angry reaction of the public notwithstanding, the government's policy on Togo had not yet run its full course. Because of the opposition of the Togolese authorities to the IAMO mission, the Nigerian government had, in private, assured U.S. officials that it was willing to drop its investigation into Olympio's assassination. But in practice, its efforts were now directed toward using alternative means to achieve the same objectives noted above. Whereas previously Nigeria gave the appearance—certainly through Wachuku's rambunctious pronouncements and actions—that it could, by its independent diplomatic clout, manage the goings-on within IAMO to its advantage, it was now apparent to the policymakers that success of policy required the invocation of the dependency alignment with the United States. Recall that in the more calamitous Congo crisis, the dependency alignment had served Nigeria's policy very well. By the end of January 1963, Nigeria had exhausted its merely symbolic regional influence just when the need to achieve the desired objectives in Togo had become ever more compelling.

The new tactic Nigeria employed was two-pronged, and both efforts indicated sheer desperation. The first was to influence, by every means, the projected national elections in Togo in a manner that would assure victory of the Union Togolaise (UT), the party of the late President Olympio. (Grunitzky, though having Nigeria's ideological sympathy, could not win because he was said to have no popular following; besides, he was under the influence of the insurgents, Ghana and France, a bizarre combination indeed.) The second and simultaneous effort was to display military strength on Togo's eastern border in order to warn Ghana of the consequences of any preemptive interference. Nigerian officials attempted to convince the United States (or rather, themselves) that under this latter circumstance the victory of the UT in the elections would definitely be assured.[101]

This situation generated an intensity in U.S.-Nigerian policy coordination. Immediately after the Togo insurrection, Nigerian leaders had solicited from the U.S. government only a simple cost-free act, namely, to withhold recognition of the provisional government and to persuade its NATO allies to follow suit pending the completion of the work of the IAMO Commission. That request was not difficult to effect because, indeed, the United States preferred to work behind the scenes to induce a collective African initiative to strictly African problems. And here was an opportunity for the IAMO Commission to assume responsibility for bringing about a settlement to the conflict in Togo. In February 1963, Assistant Secretary Williams, addressing the press in Lagos, stressed the initial convergence of policies between Washington and Lagos: "I would say our relationship to events in Togo and our reactions to [the events] and our future plans are just about exactly [the] same as Nigeria['s]."[102] That consensus of purpose was, however, rapidly breaking down.

Given the paralysis of the IAMO mission from late January to early February, the United States was already coming under pressure from both its ambassador in Lome, Leon Poullada, and, apparently, French authorities to grant recognition to the provisional government. Poullada argued that the existence of the new regime was a fact and that the United States should extend recognition. The same view was pressed by the French, who were by no means unsympathetic toward the military insurgents and President Grunitzky personally. (Note that the real military instigators of the January 13 revolt were ex-Togolese soldiers in the French national army.) However, Wachuku and his ministerial permanent secretary, Francis Nwokedi, still denied the obvious failure of the IAMO mission, regarding its stalled operation as merely a "suspension." Moreover, Nigerian officials informed the United States that they were "violently opposed" to Ambassador Poullada's recommendation for recognition of the provisional government.[103] Not wishing to precipitate a total breakdown of the IAMO diplomatic effort, and indeed still very much willing to work with Nigeria within that framework in order to minimize Ghana's influence on a postelection Togolese regime, the United States continued to defer to Nigeria on the recognition issue, that is, until the situation became irrelevant in May.

For Nigeria and the United States, the issue came to a head when both sides finally acknowledged, on February 13, the death of the IAMO mission under its existing terms of reference, which could not be tolerated by Lome. For both partners, the question became what to do next? Somewhat like the U.S. vis-à-vis United Nations "action" against North Korea during the Korean crisis, the conflict in Togo was developing into a costly problem to be borne mainly by Nigeria. The two remaining members of the commission showed scant interest in the continuation of its work. To no avail Nigeria and the United States sought a remedy through changing the wording of the commission's purpose to read, simply, "a goodwill mission sent [by IAMO] to the Togo provisional government [to help] restore constitutional democracy."[104] U.S. officials went further, urging the French to work conjointly (and discreetly) with them to persuade the Lome government to receive the mission, given its modified agenda. But even so, the new solution meant different things to the two sides, simply because their basic goals in the conflict were at variance.

The Nigerian government wished to act under the guise of such an arrangement—helping in a friendly manner to organize free elections—for the prime purpose of determining the outcome of those elections. It was to help this prospect that Wachuku recommended the presence of Nigerian troops at the Dahomey-Togo border; such a measure would help centralize the Togolese military and deter Ghana from intervention.[105]

However, the hollowness of this scheme was revealed, first, by the fact that President Maga of Dahomey—bolstered by the French—would not allow Nigerian troops to cross into his territory, and, second, by the fact that the United States was in fact pushing for a resumed effort by the IAMO mission under the new terms of reference as a device for "saving Nigeria's face" as well as that of the African Council, and not as a military device. In short, the United States was still talking the language of a political solution (a solution, no doubt, still aimed at Ghana) while Nigeria was heading in a militaristic direction by choosing to misinterpret U.S. intentions. After meeting with Wachuku in Lagos, Assistant Secretary Williams and ambassadors McCilvaine in Dahomey, Poullada in Togo, Mahoney in Ghana, and Palmer in Nigeria arrived at the conclusion that the Nigerian government "now appears to believe

[that] political solution is unpromising. . . . Hence, matters will be resolved by [a] show of strength. [But] there is serious doubt that the [Nigerian] military solution is shared by [other UAM] members."[106]

What made the Nigerian stance even more alarming for the United States was the fact that the Nigerian leaders were counting on its supportive assistance if the military option were to be exercised. The sense of urgency was heightened when the normally restrained Prime Minister Balewa made a passionate "plea for United States arms assistance" both as a result of the situation in Togo and for the longer range purpose of protecting the Nigerian political system against Ghana. Balewa compared Nigeria's light arms against superior "weapons acquired by Ghana from [the] communist bloc."[107]

In a report to Washington, Williams captured the full impact of the predicament in which the Nigerian policymakers, through spasmodic reactions to a phantom threat, placed themselves. The assistant secretary saw Balewa as suffering from "severe shock":

> He [Balewa] said several times over that he had never thought Nigeria would need arms to protect itself against another African country. With evident sorrow and not without trauma he now realizes that Nigeria must arm to protect itself and to support its leadership position. More ominously he sees behind Ghana's [thrust against Nigeria] Communist strength and influence.[108]

Nigerian officials had formulated a policy that succeeded in placing the cart before the horse. They had adopted a policy decision favoring military confrontation before adequately considering the means for backing up that policy. The underlying restraints limiting the extent of support the United States could offer Nigeria against Ghana have already been clarified; those restraints applied with greater urgency in this particular case. In response to Balewa's request for large-scale build-up of Nigeria's military force, the best the United States was willing to discuss was the possibility of backing a collective arms (and political) agreement among the IAMO states. This hardly served Nigeria's vital and urgent purpose nor did it attract the interest of the UAM subgroup within IAMO, whose security was safely underwritten by France.

The Nigerian leaders simply had underestimated the effect that extreme dependence could impose on a country's foreign policy actions especially in a policy area in which there existed a divergence of basic goals between the dependent and dominant elites. More fundamentally, the Nigerian government had failed to realize its main objectives in Togo because of a dearth of concrete sources of influence with which it could affect the conflict situation directly and induce a more favorable outcome.

Summary

The Congo crisis was a policy area in which the United States had cogent interests, direct and indirect, that were worthy of defending. Directly, U.S. interest consisted, above all, of resisting Soviet (read Communist) control of a part of Africa rich in strategic economic resources. Indirectly, U.S. interest revolved around the need to protect important financial, economic, and political interests of its NATO allies—particularly Great Britain, Belgium, and France—in the Congo and adjacent territories. These compelling interests made it desirable for the Kennedy administration to mobilize its bilateral influence in Nigeria for the purpose of inducing the latter's collaboration throughout the crisis. Nigeria was an important African entity whose alignment the United States considered crucial in galvanizing the support of a majority of independent African states behind U.S. policy.

There was strong public and some official opposition in Nigeria to what was widely viewed as the exhortative role of Great Britain and Belgium in the rebellion of Katanga. Moreover, the initial U.S. hesitation on the utilization of UN military forces to end the secession was interpreted by Nigerians as a NATO scheme to frustrate Congolese independence. Further, specific Nigerian government positions in the crisis—such as its uncritical defense of the Stanleyville rescue operation— were highly unpopular to a large segment of the foreign policy public.

In the Congo crisis, the Balewa government was to a considerable degree successful in achieving its stated objectives, at least until the end of 1963; but this was because those objectives corresponded essentially with those pursued by its dominant partner, the United States, which possessed the superior resources for their execution.

On the other hand, Nigerian-U.S. diplomacy concerning Ghana in general and the Togo problem in particular leads to the following conclusions about the effect of a dependent foreign policy. Mutual interest with a dominant partner cannot be assumed, nor can identity of goals on specific policy problems be presumed, without prior efforts to harmonize those goals, including the employment of acceptable instruments to that end. The chances of success of policy for a dependent elite (or at least the opportunity for respectable retreat should previously unforeseen obstacles arise) rest crucially on the convergence of its objectives with those of the dominant partner. The odd thing about Nigeria's leadership performance in the Togolese conflict was that it had a priori defined for itself a very tough course of action, without a realistic appraisal of the U.S. attitude and degree of commitment toward the situation (unlike in the crisis of the Congo). What made this even more odd was that Nigeria, it seemed, was counting on the commitment of the United States to carry through its own preferences. As events transpired, the only noticeable gesture of solidarity from the United States was its decision to withhold official recognition of the Lome government until almost all African states had formally recognized the government (the United States and Great Britain announced recognition in early June; Nigeria and Guinea did so on June 13).

The logic of the Balewa regime's security dilemma and its conservative orientation on decolonization effectively defined the structure of the conflict relationship with Ghana. Ghana's policy on decolonization was comparatively more populistic, intensely transformative, and aggressively "power-oriented," and thus the conduct of its diplomacy in regional councils tended always to provoke tension against Nigeria's conservative positions. It is, however, incorrect to conclude, as Balewa's government did, that Nkrumah's Ghana was behind every conceivable threat to the stability of the Nigerian state. Ultimately, the real sources of threat were located in the entrenched domestic power structure. Moreover, the Nigerian federal government's feelings of insecurity were bred in rigidly unpopular national and regional policies, poorly defended by the policy-makers. In the end, the regime was consumed in the flames of this latter reality.

Notes

1. This is not a history of that epochal chapter in the African decolonization movement. Although relevant side aspects will be introduced in the analysis, the focal concern remains the conjuncture between Nigerian and U.S. policies. For some informative texts on the crisis itself, see the following: Ernest W. Lefever, *Uncertain Mandate: Politics of the U.N. Congo Operation* (Baltimore, Md.: The Johns Hopkins Press, 1967); Crawford Young, *Politics in the Congo* (Princeton, N.J.: Princeton University Press, 1965); Stephen R. Weissman, *American Foreign Policy in the Congo, 1960–1964* (Ithaca: Cornell University Press, 1974); Catherine Hoskyns, *The Congo Since Independence, January 1960–December 1961* (London: Oxford University Press, 1965); Kwame Nkrumah, *Challenge of the Congo* (New York: International Publishers, 1967).

2. The request of the Congolese leaders immediately resulted in two Security Council resolutions: that of July 14, which formally sanctioned the dispatch of UN forces to the Congo; and that of July 22, which reaffirmed the UN mission and renewed the call for withdrawal of Belgian troops. Later, a controversy arose regarding the interpretation of the UN task in the Congo. Was it primarily to help the government "restore law and order," as Hammarskjold held? Or was it to repulse "Belgian aggression" as Lumumba and Kasavubu had expressed in their original telegram to the secretary-general? See Hoskyns, *The Congo Since Independence*, pp. 484–485.

3. L. Gray Cowan, "Nigerian Foreign Policy," in R. O. Tilman and T. Cole, eds., *The Nigerian Political Scene* (Durham, N.C.: Duke University Press, 1962), p. 116.

4. Tunde Adeniran, "A Developing Country in the United Nations System: A Study of Nigeria's Participation in the United Nations, 1960–1975" (Ph.D. Dissertation, Columbia University, 1978), p. 92; and *General Assembly Official Records* (hereinafter, GAOR), 893rd Meeting, October 7, 1960.

5. *House of Representatives Debate* (hereinafter, *HRD*), November 25, 1960, p. 251. Chief S. O. Adebo, Nigeria's chief delegate at the UN from 1961 to 1967, explained that one of the real problems facing the government at this time was "how to reconcile its pro-Western disposition with the general pro-African sentiments of the country." This accounted in part for Balewa's initial constitutionalist approach to the crisis as a compromise. Interview, June 18, 1978, Lagos.

6. For commentary on Ghana's early role in the Congo, see O. Aluko, *Ghana and Nigeria, 1957–1970* (London: Rex Collings Ltd., 1976), pp. 147–148, and Nkrumah, *Challenge of the Congo*, pp. 21–66, passim.

7. *West African Pilot* (editorial), September 16, 1960, quoted in A. B. Akinyemi, *Foreign Policy and Federalism* (Ibadan: University Press, 1974), p. 42.

8. *HRD*, November 24, 1960, pp. 100–101.

9. Palmer to Rusk, February 1, 1961, Telegram no. 583, G. Mennen Williams Files, Record Group 59, National Archives, Washington, D.C. (hereinafter, NA).

10. Joseph N. Greene, Jr., (Lagos), January 20, 1961, Memorandum, Department of State Files. (Hereinafter all documents retrieved directly from the State Department are designated by the abbreviation DSF.)

11. Hoskyns, *The Congo Since Independence*, p. 300.

12. Confidential source. The Soviet Union had petulantly attacked Hammarskjold of partiality and demanded the termination of the UN operation in the Congo. See Walter Honson, ed., *The Papers of Adlai E. Stevenson*, Vol. 8 (Boston: Little, Brown and Company, 1979), 3:35.

13. Confidential source; also see Weissman, *American Foreign Policy*, pp. 100–111.

14. Rusk to Kennedy, February 1, 1961, Memorandum, Williams Files, NA; Lefever, *Uncertain Mandate*, pp. 80–81.

15. Rusk to Palmer, February 2, 1961, Telegram no. 712, National Security Council Files, John F. Kennedy Presidential Library, Waltham, Massachusetts (hereinafter, Kennedy Library).

16. Interview with T. O. Elias, former Nigerian minister of justice and attorney general, and member of the UN Constitutional Commission on the Congo, Lagos, August 29, 1978; Interview with Victor Adegoroye, former director of the African Department, Ministry of External Affairs, Lagos, September 5, 1978. According to Adegoroye, it was also considered important to sustain the independence of a unified Congo in order to deflate opposition to African decolonization made by European populations in South Africa, the Rhodesias, and Portuguese colonies.

17. Aluko, *Ghana and Nigeria*, p. 147.

18. *Daily Times* (Lagos), February 19, 1962; also interview with Adegoroye.

19. See, for example, an editorial of the *West African Pilot* written to mark the first anniversary of the Congo's independence, June 29, 1961; see other comments in Akinyemi, *Foreign Policy and Federalism*, pp. 52–53; for comments about what may be termed mass reaction to Lumumba's death, refer to K.W.J. Post, "Nigerian Pamphleteers and the Congo," *Journal of Modern African Studies* 2(3) (1964): 405–418.

20. Adeniran, "A Developing Country in the United Nations Systems," p. 99.

21. Lefever, *Uncertain Mandate*, pp. 124–125. Great Britain's role in restraining a more forceful UN action against Katanga met with strong condemnation in Nigeria by both the press and other pressure groups. *Morning Post* (editorial), December 11, 1961; *Daily Express* (editorial), December 11, 1961; *West African Pilot* (editorial), December 14, 1961.

22. Hoskyns, *The Congo Since Independence*, Appendix II, p. 489.

23. Adeniran, "A Developing Country in the United Nations Systems," p. 99.

24. Interview with T. O. Elias; Interview with V. Adegoroye, Lagos, September 5, 1978. According to Adegoroye, one main reason why Nigeria supported Kasavubu against the claims of Lumumba's successor, Antoine Gizenga (i.e., before the Lovanium Conference in August), was the fact that the United States and the UN secretariat favored Kasavubu. "It was the U.S. which provided the political and financial backing for the Kasavubu government. This measure, of course, did not conflict with the Nigerian objective."

25. *Daily Times* (editorial), August 10, 1961; also Akinyemi, *Foreign Policy*, pp. 58–59.

26. Palmer to Williams, October 23, 1961, Kennedy Library.

27. Ibid.

28. Weissman, *American Foreign Policy*, pp. 153–161; Hoskyns, *The Congo Since Independence*, pp. 404–428.

29. Samuel E. Belk to M. Bundy and W. W. Rostow, Memorandum, September 26, 1961; Hoskyns, *The Congo Since Independence*, pp. 343–347.

30. Weissman, *American Foreign Policy*, pp. 166–176; Interview with G. Mennen Williams, conducted by W. W. Moss, January 27, 1970, Oral History Programme, Kennedy Library.

31. Palmer to Rusk, December 24, 1961, Telegram no. 619, Williams Files, NA. A little earlier, Adoula presented, on a number of occasions, the same basic argument to the State Department. See Gullion to Rusk, December 13, 1961, Telegram no. 1480, Kennedy Library.

32. Telegram no. 619, cited in no. 31, supra.

33. Ibid., and Gullion (in Leopoldville) to Rusk, February 15, 1963, Telegram no. 2109, Section 1 of 2, Kennedy Library.

34. Weissman, *American Foreign Policy*, p. 184; Roger Hilsman, *To Move a Nation* (New York: Doubleday and Company Inc., 1967), p. 267.

35. Weissman, *American Foreign Policy*, p. 184.

36. Aluko, *Ghana and Nigeria*, pp. 149–150; *Morning Post* (Lagos), February 17, 1962.

37. Palmer to Rusk, January 22, 1962, Telegram no. 697, DSF; also interview with Elias.

38. Telegram no. 697 (cited in note 37, *supra*); also Rusk to Palmer, January 17, 1962, Telegram no. 853, DSF.

39. Interview with Elias; and Palmer to Rusk, January 20, 1962, Telegram no. 691, DSF.

40. Dr. Elias asserted that the Leopoldville leadership was particularly grateful for this act. This, according to him, accounted for Mobutu's support of the federal Nigerian government in its bid to suppress the Biafran secession five years later. Interview with Elias.

41. The project was named after U.S. Colonel Michael J.L. Greene whom the U.S. government had sent to the Congo in July to assess the security situation. Lefever, *Uncertain Mandate*, pp. 68–70; also *Daily Times* (Lagos), February 16, 1963.

42. See J. O'Sullivan (Leopoldville) to Rusk, March 22, 1963, Telegram no. 2433, and Ball to Palmer, June 25, 1963, Telegram no. 2235, both in the DSF.

43. Press release, March 28, 1963, Federal Ministry of Information, Lagos; see also Gullion to Rusk, February 16, 1963, Telegram no. 2113, and O'Sullivan to Rusk, March 22, 1963, Telegram no. 2433, both in the DSF.

44. Rusk to Stephenson (New York), March 26, 1963, Telegram no. 2439, DSF; Lefever, *Uncertain Mandate*, p. 69.

45. See Telegram no. 2439 (cited in note 44, supra). Canada, Norway, and Italy also showed disinclination to be associated at this point.

46. Palmer to Rusk, June 12, 1963, Telegram no. 1875, and Rusk to Palmer, June 17, 1963, Telegram no. 2159, both in the DSF.

47. Aluko, in *Ghana and Nigeria*, p. 150, reports that by the "end of 1964, two sets of Congolese policemen had undergone training" in Nigeria; see also Gullion to Rusk, May 22, 1963, Telegram no. 2859, DSF.

48. See the list of events in this period (chronologically arranged) in Hoskyns, *The Organization of African Unity and the Congo Crisis, 1964–65* (Dar es Salaam, Tanzania: Oxford University Press, 1969), pp. xii–xv.

49. G. Mennen Williams to A. W. Harriman, April 9, 1964, Memorandum, DSF.

50. Ibid., and Ball to Palmer, April 13, 1964, Telegram no. 1961, DSF. On the extent of the U.S. financial contribution to ONUC, see Lefever, *Uncertain Mandate*, pp. 199–206.

51. When ONUC forces pulled out at the end of June, the only Nigerian army battalion still in the Congo at that time was also recalled home. But the police contingent remained until the end of the year, under the financial arrangement referred to above.

52. Godley to Rusk, May 23, 1964, Telegram no. 156, DSF.

53. Recall that in 1964–1965 Nigeria was confronted by a new political (indeed, constitutional) crisis markedly linked to the controversial outcome of the federal and regional elections, an event that set the stage for the first military coup in January 1966. But recall also that 1964 was marked by an intensification in USAID activities in Nigeria. Hence, domestic imperatives and external obligation resulted in contradictory pressures on the government.

54. Rusk to Mathews, August 6, 1964, Telegram no. 285. There is no clear-cut evidence that Nigeria had complied with this request. The whole sensitive

matter was handled with the utmost secrecy. There are two circumstantial indications that compliance might have taken place: On August 7, Osakwe, in Leopoldville, without any notice, took a night flight to Lagos. This caused U.S. and British ambassadors to speculate optimistically that he had gone to Nigeria to be briefed on the government's "affirmative response." On the August 8, Mathews was cabled by Harriman from Brussels to confirm this speculation, and, in any case, to "do everything possible . . . to assure affirmative response." See Godley to Rusk, August 7, 1964, Telegram no. 402, and Harriman to Mathews, August 8, 1964, Telegram no. 207, both in the DSF. The Ghanaian government believed that Nigeria had returned a nine hundred member battalion to Leopoldville after June. See Nkrumah, *Challenge of the Congo*, p. 248.

55. Evidence provided above shows that Tshombe had the full backing of the United States. Tshombe now proclaimed himself a true nationalist of one Congo, and the U.S. government thought his leadership could somehow bring an end to the endemic fragmentation of the country. As additional evidence of measures taken by the United States to assist Tshombe's government, see Williams to Rusk, October 17, 1964, Memorandum, Kennedy Library.

56. How Nigerians and other Africans reacted to Tshombe's prime ministership is related, respectively, in Akinyemi, *Federalism and Foreign Policy*, pp. 64–68, and in Hoskyns, *The Organization of African Unity*.

57. Interview with Chief Adebo.

58. Their importance in this specific sense was based on these facts: Both territories provided, in combination, for over 95 percent of the total population of British West Africa; they constituted, in size, about 97 percent of this imperial domain; and in agricultural and mineral resources, they possessed the predominant share. Olajide Aluko, *Ghana and Nigeria, 1957–1970* (London: Rex Collins Ltd., 1976), p. 1.

59. Ibid., pp. 40–62.

60. Nkrumah, in *Ghana: The Autobiography of Kwame Nkrumah* (New York: International Publishers, 1957), pp. 22–23, relates his early contact with Dr. Azikiwe.

61. The first real sign of incompatible national objectives occurred shortly after Ghana's independence, with the unilateral dissolution of almost all the colonial-interterritorial functional organs. By 1966, only one institution survived— the West African Examinations Council, which still embraces Nigeria, Ghana, Sierra Leone, and The Gambia (with later association by Liberia). Aluko, *Ghana and Nigeria*.

62. Colin Legum, *Pan-Africanism: A Short Political Guide*, appendix, p. 191. Contrast this with the speech by Ako Adjei, the foreign minister of Ghana, at the same forum, ibid., pp. 288–289. On the interlink between colonial boundaries and African politics, see Saadia Touval, *The Boundary Politics of Independent Africa* (Cambridge: Harvard University Press, 1972).

63. Whether out of true conviction or propaganda reasons, or, as the Nigerian prime minister scornfully thought, because of the personal ambition of its president, Ghana took certain unilateral and multilateral steps to underscore its philosophical approach to decolonization (with clear implication for the boundary

question): the surrender of its sovereignty to a union of African states, the attempted union with Guinea in 1958, and the Ghana-Guinea-Mali Union declared in August 1960.

64. For a balanced assessment of the role of Chief Obafemi Awolowo, the central culprit in the treason trials, see Richard Sklar, "Nigerian Politics: The Ordeal of Chief Awolowo, 1960–1965," in M. Carter, ed., *Politics in Africa* (New York: Harcourt, Brace and World, 1966). And for what is essentially a cold war perspective on this event in the Nigerian-Ghana conflict, see W. Scott Thompson, *Ghana's Foreign Policy, 1957–66* (Princeton, N.J.: University Press, 1969), pp. 237–244.

65. *HRD*, September 4, 1961, p. 345; and Aluko, *Ghana and Nigeria*, p. 83.

66. Thompson, in *Ghana's Foreign Policy*, p. 242, makes this connection based on an interview with Philip Asiodu, a high-level Nigerian civil servant; see also accounts in the Ghanaian military government's publication, *Nkrumah's Subversion in Africa* (Accra: Ministry of Information, 1967).

67. *Sunday Times* (Lagos), June 10, 1962; *West African Pilot* (Lagos), June 11, 1962.

68. Another illustration of the link between domestic security politics and the conflict with Ghana was the alternating partisanship displayed in commentaries by party-controlled newspapers. A typical case, though by no means the only case, was the attitude of the *West African Pilot*, owned by the NCNC party. Before the post-independence federal coalition government was formed (with the NCNC as partner), the *Pilot* exhibited the African nationalistic sentiments of its party through supportive appraisal of Ghana's decolonization activities in the continent; thereafter, the paper became the most virulent critic of Nkrumah personally. By supporting internal dissidents in Nigeria, Ghana was now seen as a threat to the NCNC's stake in national power. See Akinyemi, *Foreign Policy and Federalism*, pp. 75–99, 149–173, passim, for a comprehensive review.

69. The Monrovia group emerged from a meeting that was arranged, in its final form, principally by the Nigerian prime minister and President William Tubman of Liberia and was held in Monrovia (Liberia), May 8–12, 1961. Although the original intent of the conveners of this meeting might have been to attract all the independent states and attempt to resolve their differences on such ongoing regional conflicts as those in the Congo, Algeria, Mauritania, and Morocco, the majority of states that actually attended constituted the conservative conceptionists. It is then correct to say that the meeting was in effect designed to counter, as revealed by most of the adopted resolutions (such as those for noninterference), radical positions on vital political principles that had been espoused earlier in the deliberations of the All-Africa Peoples Conferences (1958 and 1960), the declarations of the Ghana-Guinea-Mali Union (1960), and the charter of the Casablanca group (January 1961).

Similarly, the Nigerian government convened a meeting of the Monrovia states in January 1962. Ostensibly, all twenty-eight independent African states were invited, but no one with an acute understanding of the basic cleavage between Ghana and Nigeria expected Ghana to attend that Nigeria-sponsored conference. With Ghana's persuasion, the Casablanca states declined attendance.

What emerged from this conference was an informal structure called the Inter-African and Malagasy States Organization (IAMO).

70. Publicly and privately, U.S. government leaders expressed "satisfaction" with the positive outcomes of both the Monrovia Conference (whose conferees later formed the IAMO in Lagos) and the OAU formation in 1963. See, for example, the statement by President Kennedy congratulating Prime Minister Tafawa Balewa on the success of his role at Monrovia, *Public Papers of Presidents of the United States, John F. Kennedy, January 20 to December 31, 1961* (Washington: United States Government Printing Office, 1962), p. 541; see also Mahoney to Rusk, May 29, 1963, Telegram no. 1323, NSC Files, Kennedy Presidential Library.

71. Aluko, *Ghana and Nigeria*, p. 123; *HRD*, August 1, 1963, p. 52.

72. Aluko, *Ghana and Nigeria*, p. 123.

73. Busia's testimony, as evaluated in Rusk to Mahoney (Accra), December 12, 1962, Telegram no. 603, Williams Files.

74. Schlessinger, *A Thousand Days*, pp. 3570–3573; Thompson, *Ghana's Foreign Policy*, pp. 191–193.

75. However, this position needs some qualification: After 1961, with increasing incidents of threats on the life of President Nkrumah allegedly hatched by dissidents based both inside his country and in neighboring states, it is possible to explain Ghana's "subversive" efforts also in terms of preemptive security actions. See below for further prognosis along this line in relation to the Togo affair.

76. Report of Trimble (Lagos) to Williams, January 15, 1963, Williams Files, NA; also Rusk to Mahoney (Accra), January 29, 1963, Telegram no. 730.

77. Plausible indications to this effect are contained in two available sources: Palmer to Rusk, April 10, 1962, Telegram no. 987, and George P. Delaney, "Recommendations on Labour Problems Observed During Assistant Secretary of State G. Mennen Williams' African Mission (February 15–March 18, 1961)," (undated), both in Williams Files, NA.

78. For part of the account, see Thompson, *Ghana's Foreign Policy*, especially pp. 162–186, 190–194; also see Nkrumah's viewpoint in *Neo-colonialism*, passim. Note: Although Ghana's independence in 1957 was enthusiastically welcomed by President Eisenhower (who sent his deputy, Richard M. Nixon, to represent the United States at the new nation's inauguration), with high expectations of cordial relations, the seed of future discord between the United States and Ghana was sown in the divergence of interests regarding the consuming issue of African decolonization. Before the end of the Eisenhower administration, this conflict was demonstrated in Ghana's voting pattern at the UN and in its aggressive anticolonial activities within Africa.

79. Problems in U.S.-Ghana relations in the period 1961–1963 are indicated in the following: Mahoney to Rusk, September 23, 1962, Telegram no. 508 (Sections 1 of 2 and 2 of 2); Rusk to Mahoney, January 29, 1963, Telegram no. 730; *Ghanaian Times*, September 24, 1962, quoted in Thompson, *Ghana's Foreign Policy*, p. 272.

80. Kwame Nkrumah, *Dark Days in Ghana* (New York: International Publishers, 1968), pp. 77, 82.

81. Except for very brief intervals in early 1963 and mid-1964, the fundamental discord in U.S.-Ghana domestic and foreign preferences persisted until the end of Nkrumah's rule in February 1966. See Thompson, *Ghana's Foreign Policy*, pp. 190–193, for information on the intra-administration debate leading to Kennedy's decision on Ghanaian aid.

82. The insurgents, led by a Major Dooze, former adjutant to the French infantry, justified their action ostensibly on the following grounds: the governments' insensitivity to escalating unemployment; the "pervasive atmosphere of authoritarian paternalism"; the "sterile isolation" of Togo's external policy; and Olympio's "profound contempt for the army." They thus emphasized that the coup was an entirely national affair, with no external instigation. See Helen Kitchen, "Filling the Togo Vacuum," *Africa Report* 8(2) (February 1963): 7–10; and *Africa Diary* 3(6) (February 2–8, 1963): 985–987.

83. "The Evil That Men Do," *Nigerian Citizen*, February 16, 1963, quoted in Akinyemi, *Foreign Policy and Federalism*, p. 181.

84. The alleged evidence consisted of information, perhaps furnished by the Nigerian mission in Lome, to the effect that two Ghanaian "undercover" teams had entered Togo "by water" before the coup. According to the evidence, one team murdered Olympio while the second contacted the military. See Williams (in Lagos) to Fredericks, February 13, 1963, Telegram no. 1167, Williams Files, NA. Ghana publicly justified Nigeria's conclusion by, on January 21, becoming the first nation to recognize the provisional government formed by the military insurgents in Togo.

85. Thompson, *Ghana's Foreign Policy*, pp. 81–86, 229–237; and *West Africa*, May 3, 1958, p. 413; ibid., May 10, 1958, p. 449.

86. The Ewes were split after World War I, when the former German-administered Togo Protectorate was divided between the British and French sectors as Trust territories by the UN under the Trusteeship system. The British sector later joined the Gold Coast, following a UN-held plebicite in 1957, as present Ghana. But the plight of the Ewes within French Togoland was not resolved.

87. For an indication of security "incidents" between the two neighbors, see *West Africa*, January 19, 1963, p. 57, and Thompson, *Ghana's Foreign Policy*, pp. 231–234.

88. These views are contained in the relevant editorials of both papers, cited in Akinyemi, *Foreign Policy and Federalism*, pp. 180–181.

89. *Daily Times* (Lagos), January 22, 1963, quoted in Akinyemi, *Foreign Policy and Federalism*, p. 181. Much of the information on the proceedings of the IAMO meeting in Lagos is based, with appreciation, on Akinyemi's book.

90. Akinyemi, *Foreign Policy and Federalism*, p. 183.

91. In the confusing aftermath of the coup, both Grunitzky and Meatchi were invited simultaneously from their separate exiles to head a provisional government, pending new elections. Grunitzky was ultimately appointed the president; Meatchi assumed a number of ministerial portfolios, including finance.

92. In a joint statement, Houphuet-Boigny of the Ivory Coast and M. Yameogo of Upper Volta expressed their "friendly feeling" for Grunitzky but refrained

from recognizing his government "under the known conditions." Kitchen, "Filling the Togo Vacuum," p. 8; *Africa Diary* 3(6) (February 2–8, 1963): 985–987. On the other hand, not only did Sekou Toure of Guinea strongly condemn the assassination of Olympio, he relentlessly denied recognition to the succeeding regime. Sekou Toure had developed a personal bond with Olympio; they were the only prominent nationalist leaders to oppose France on the union proposal.

93. Williams (in Lagos) to Fredericks, February 13, 1963, Telegram no. 1177, Williams Files; also Akinyemi, *Foreign Policy and Federalism*, p. 182.

94. During their brief encounter with Olympio, U.S. officials were impressed by his determination to be independent of France. While visiting President Kennedy in March 1962, Olympio had requested U.S. assistance for building a second Togolese army. Olympio made this request with an immediate eye on the ongoing border threats by Ghana, but the real significance of the request was that Olympio approached the United States for this purpose even though it had a standing "military understanding" with France. On the same visit, Olympio also discussed with George Ball the prospect of U.S. subvention for the purpose of establishing a Custom Union embracing Nigeria, Dahomey, Niger, and Togo. See the following: "Customs Union: Niger, Nigeria, Dahomey, Togo," Williams to Henry Tasca, March 20, 1962, Memorandum, and "Togo Second Army Company," Williams to Tasca, March 20, 1962, Memorandum, both in Williams Files, NA.

95. *Africa Diary* 3(8) (February 16–23, 1963): 1008.

96. Ibid., p. 1007.

97. Akinyemi, *Foreign Policy and Federalism*, p. 184.

98. *West African Pilot*, January 31, 1963; and *Africa Diary* 3(8) (February 16–22, 1963): 1008–1009.

99. *Daily Express*, January 24 and 29, 1963, as cited in Akinyemi, *Foreign Policy and Federalism*, p. 187.

100. *Africa Diary* 3(8) (February 16–22, 1963): 1015.

101. Williams (in Lagos) to Rusk, February 13, 1963, Telegram no. 1181, Williams Files, NA; and confidential interview with a former official in the Nigerian Ministry of External Affairs and Commonwealth Relations, Lagos.

102. Quoted by Ambassador Palmer in Telegram no. 1209, February 19, 1963, to Secretary Rusk.

103. Palmer to Williams, February 6, 1963, Telegram no. 1120 (Section I of II), Williams Files, NA.

104. See Telegram no. 1177, cited earlier.

105. See Telegram no. 1181, cited earlier.

106. Ibid. The proposed change in the commission's task was never put into effect. Hence, the work of the commission remained unresumed. Nigeria's militaristic option was stalled as a result of obstacles cited in the text, while the regime's sense of insecurity persisted. On April 10, 1963, Togo's President Grunitzky accused Nigeria, in a press conference, of engineering an attempted coup against his government. Although a statement issued by the Foreign Office in Lagos formally denied this, the charge was not entirely baseless, for Wachuku, in his characteristic fashion, had alluded to this as a tenet of his "military"

option. See document cited above; and *Africa Diary* 3(18) (April 27–May 3, 1963): 1130. On May 6, Grunitzky was formally elected president in a popular election conducted without African observers.

107. Williams (in Lagos) to Rusk, February 13, 1963, Telegram no. 1167, Williams Files, NA.

108. Ibid.

5

The Changing Bilateral Structure, 1967–1976: Political Economy of War and Oil

The Significance of the Nigerian Civil War, 1967–1970

The military coups that preceded the Nigerian civil war and the war itself represented, conjointly, the high-water mark of the decolonization process within Nigeria in the first decade of independence.[1] These historical developments pointedly attested to the abject failure of the post-independence political leadership to adequately manage elite interests and related conflicts—a central problem of nation-building and economic development, both of which are subsumed in the domestic process of decolonization. The crisis also confirmed what critics had always claimed: that the pattern of international alignment pursued by the previous Balewa government was highly at variance with the purposes of Nigeria's emergence as an independent state, especially one with regional leadership ambition. Indeed, the structure of the Balewa regime's foreign alignment, which was untenably neocolonial, clearly contributed in generating domestic sociopolitical conflicts at the elite level that eventually consumed the rest of the society.

Further, the civil war arrested what might have been an orderly development of Nigerian-U.S. relations, both economically and politically. Economically, there was a sudden contraction in the three primary areas of bilateral ties: trade, private investment, and foreign aid. At the end of 1965, there was great expectation on both sides of a substantial expansion of relations in these areas, as indicated for instance by the dramatic increase in USAID activities. Whereas in 1966 the U.S. share of Nigeria's total imports was 16.2 percent, this share dropped to 12.8 percent in the first quarter of 1968. There were naturally no new investments by U.S. companies during the war. Indeed, except for Gulf

Oil, which continued to exploit its offshore oil wells, existing U.S. investments in the war zones of eastern Nigeria were severely threatened. Also, the operations of USAID in the country came to a virtual standstill after 1966. Although the United States and Nigeria signed about seven development-related small-loan agreements between 1966 and 1969, only in two cases had the authorized amount, worth a total of only $2,955, actually been disbursed. But it was not because of the noted contractions in bilateral ties that the civil war period was a watershed in the development of Nigeria-U.S. relations; such ties were, after all, still very much in their formative stages. Rather, the postwar relationship became markedly different from the prewar relationship primarily because of crucial changes in the economic characteristics of Nigeria and because of the unexpected experience of political hostility between the two countries, borne of America's policy in the war.

Official U.S. policy throughout the Nigerian civil war had been one of direct noninvolvement, politically and militarily.[2] Based on this policy, the State Department announced on July 10, 1967, four days after the start of conflict, an arms embargo against the two sides in the war. A parallel dimension to this policy of neutrality was America's participation in the international relief effort to provide food, medical supplies, and other forms of emergency assistance to the civilian victims of the war especially inside the secessionist enclave of Biafra.

The July 10 arms embargo announcement was made in response to the Nigerian federal government's request to purchase arms from the United States for use in suppressing the rebellion. Federalists in Nigeria interpreted the U.S. decision as constituting support for the secessionists' cause of seeking to create a separate political entity, and the sense of bitterness and disappointment evoked in Lagos by this singular act was not minimized by the fact that the United States consistently recognized the federal military government, following Great Britain's lead, as "the legal government of Nigeria"[3] or by the fact that the State Department played an outstanding role in combating a grossly hostile anti-Nigeria public opinion throughout the war. The policy of neutrality was, moreover, suspect in Lagos because U.S. authorities insisted on providing relief assistance directly to the rebels, in defiance of the Nigerian federal government, which sought to exercise control over the flow of international relief materials into the country. To the federalists, there was really no clear distinction between the humanitarian and political aspects in the civil war—a distinction the Americans wished to make—for both the federalists and the Biafrans were well aware of the fact that the humanitarian question could be manipulated in various ways to determine the political outcome of the war.

The successful prosecution of the war, largely a result of mobilizing internal resources, leading to the restoration of territorial unity, had a tremendous effect in arousing a new sense of national awareness among most Nigerians, which was quite low in the 1960s. The wartime experience, moreover, seemed to reaffirm the old sentiment about Nigeria's leadership destiny in sub-Saharan Africa; national self-confidence was at its peak, and this naturally entered into direct relations with the United States after 1970. As related by John Foley, a U.S. diplomat in Africa, in the immediate postwar period Nigerian officials displayed a degree of independence in their bilateral contacts with their U.S. counterparts that was unimaginable during the Balewa era.[4] General Yakubu Gowon (Nigeria's new head of state), for example, refused, until September 1971, to meet with any U.S. embassy official in Lagos, including Ambassador William Trueheart.[5] Repeated U.S. requests to provide bilateral humanitarian aid were rejected by the federal authorities even after the goodwill visit of Secretary of State William Rogers to Lagos in February 1970. Mobil Oil nearly lost its offshore production rights early in 1970 as a result of a highly "punitive" decision: According to Trueheart, Mobil had allegedly wavered during the war in its confidence about the capacity of federal forces to protect its oil installations from Biafran attacks and had moreover postponed resumption of production even after the area in question was secured by federal troops.

Based on his personal role in these circumstances, Foley concluded: "If Nigeria had achieved sovereignty in the 1960s, she gained independence only after 1970." By this he meant, as he elaborated, that the U.S. government henceforth regarded Nigeria as "coming of age," ready to exert its maturity, demanding to base its bilateral relationship with the larger power on a more equal and reciprocal footing. "The old patron-client relationship, in which the U.S. expected to receive special treatment and maintain special interests over the Soviet-bloc nations and other Western countries [except Great Britain] was being challenged by the Nigerians."[6]

However, Nigeria's new self-assertion and greater disposition to project independent behavior in dealings with the United States rested on a firmer base than the emotional reaction to the U.S. position in the war, as will be illustrated shortly. The fact was that oil was beginning to gain new significance worldwide just when the Nigerian civil war was drawing to a close at the end of 1969—a fortunate coincidence of history. By this time, the scale of oil production and the total income accrued by the Nigerian government from this source was already more than double the prewar level. Moreover the Nigerian policy of state involvement in the operation of foreign oil companies originated at this time when a law was passed providing for 51 percent compulsory state participation in all future concessions to be granted these firms.

From this, one can infer that federal officials were confident, by the end of 1969, in their estimation of the important role that oil resources would play in financing postwar reconstruction and development. If their estimation proved correct, Nigeria might no longer rely so heavily on direct U.S. financing for future develoment with the attendant risk of reincurring costly handicaps. U.S. personnel in Nigeria also seemed to have shared this expectation. In March 1972, Ambassador John E. Rheinhardt (who took over from Trueheart after September 1971) reported, "With oil exports now providing ample funds, financing is no longer a bottleneck to carrying out the construction projects in the development [1970–1974] plan."[7] Ironically, the federal military government spent in one year (1972) about $225 million on road construction alone—the equivalent of the total U.S. government aid offer for the 1962–1968 plan.

Without the assurance furnished by oil, it is highly probable that responsible authorities in Nigeria would have sought promptly, irrespective of public sentiments, to restore the mode of prewar ties with the United States for the practical reason that the United States alone was in a position to offer (or pledge) the level of capital aid Nigeria required for postwar reconstruction. Indeed, this line of action would have been inevitable for the additional reason that the civil war did not engender any basic changes in the traditional socioeconomic structure of Nigeria. Further, the Soviet Union would not have been in a position to fulfill that need. Having played a critical role in ensuring federal victory in the war, the Soviets were handicapped to offer what was most needed for reconstruction and future development.

The State of the Economy and Ties with the United States, 1970–1976

In the period 1970–1976 Nigeria's economy remained, in basic terms, externally dependent, just as it was in the 1960s. The following are some pertinent indicators to this effect.

The country's foreign export sector was now dominated by one primary commodity—crude petroleum. Revenues from this and related sources constituted, respectively, about 58 percent of total export income in 1970, 82 percent in 1973, and 93 percent in 1976. (See Table 5.1 for a comparison of the export value of petroleum and that of other traditional primary commodities for the years 1966 and 1970–1973; see Table 5.2 for the comparative value of import items.) The importance of crude petroleum to the rest of the economy is revealed by its contribution to

TABLE 5.1

Total Exports by Value from Nigeria, 1966 and 1969–1973 (in million naira)[a]

Principal Commodity	1966	1969	1970	1971	1972	1973
Petroleum	184	272	510	953	1,156	1,893
Groundnuts	82	72	43	24	19	45
Palm produce	67	20	23	29	16	19
Cocoa	57	105	133	143	101	112
Tin	31	28	33	25	19	15
Rubber	23	20	18	12	7	19
Others	122	112	117	95	97	158
Total	566	629	877	1,281	1,415	2,261

[a]In 1973, 1 naira (Nigerian new currency unit) = $1.63.

Source: Geography 60 (November 1975): 308; Federal Office of Statistics, *Review of External Trade* (1976): 27–29.

TABLE 5.2

Total Imports by Value into Nigeria, 1966 and 1969–1973 (in million naira)[a]

Principal Commodity	1966	1969	1970	1971	1972	1973
Machinery and transport	191	147	283	429	393	491
Equipment and machinery	159	146	226	319	268	324
Food and live animals	56	42	59	88	95	126
Chemicals	42	61	88	122	103	133
Miscellaneous manufactures	38	27	40	71	83	94
Crude inedible material	14	12	17	21	21	27
Mineral fuels, etc.	8	31	22	9	10	13
Others	5	31	21	20	18	17
Total	513	497	756	1,079	991	1,225

[a]In 1973, 1 naira (Nigerian new currency unit) = $1.63.

Source: Geography 60 (November 1975): 308; Federal Office of Statistics, *Review of External Trade* (1976): 27–29.

the nation's overall GDP: It was 45 percent of GDP in 1973–1974, 44.7 percent in 1974–1975, and 43.8 in 1975–1976. Oil revenues accounted for 43.3 percent of total foreign exchange reserves available to the federal government in 1971 and 86.3 percent available in 1974.[8] The proportions of all government revenues derived from the oil sector were 44 percent, 60 percent, and 82 percent for 1971, 1973, and 1974, respectively.[9]

A further index of an externally structured economy was the continued low level of industrial activities during this period. Manufacturing constituted a paltry 8 percent of GDP by 1975 (it was about 5 percent in 1960), despite the dramatic growth in the levels of national income and other aggregate economic indicators since 1970.[10] (The nation's GDP rose from $8.6 billion in 1970 to $24.4 billion in 1974—a four-year growth jump of 285 percent.)[11]

TABLE 5.3
Direction of Nigerian Foreign Trade with Five Top Partners, 1971–1973, 1976 (in million naira)

Country	Exports				Imports			
	1971	1972	1973	1976	1971	1972	1973	1976
United States	228	292	549	2,353	151	103	126	560
United Kingdom	279	302	424	702	344	292	332	1,195
West Germany	70	63	81	444	131	135	182	826
Netherlands	176	194	299	695	37	45	49	234
France	191	199	286	582	44	58	87	383

Source: Geography 60 (November 1975): 309; Federal Office of Statistics (Lagos), *Review of External Trade* (1976): 32.

Also, although the federal government had moved energetically during this period to assume "majority participation" in the exploitation of the oil industry—the backbone of the nation's economy and development—and revenues from petroleum had climbed steeply from \$1.4 billion in 1970 to \$9 billion in 1974, still the vast capital, technology, and management personnel needed in the actual exploration and operation of the industry remained effectively under the control of the foreign oil concessionaires. As stated in an article in the March 1974 issue of *West Africa*, transformation of the opulent oil resources into "permanent economic assets"—i.e., viable domestic industry, adequately trained manpower, improved agriculture, efficient public services, equitable spread of incomes—remained to be accomplished by the Nigerian leadership. Truly, the possession of abundant oil wealth had provided a powerful weapon with which the leadership could tackle, by means of enlightened public policies, the constraints of external dependence in this period; but it did not as yet change the basic reality.

On the bilateral plane, the United States and Great Britain retained their relative position as leading foreign economic partners for Nigeria. By 1973, the United States had surpassed Great Britain as the major market for Nigerian exports (see Table 5.3 for the direction of Nigeria's foreign trade with five top partners). In 1974, for instance, the United States received about 30 percent of all Nigerian exports; in 1976 this proportion was 38 percent. But more crucially, the U.S. share of total Nigerian crude oil production in the period 1973–1976 shifted between 30 and 56 percent, constituting 18–26 percent of the overall U.S. crude imports.[12] The implication is clear: U.S. market demand for oil provided the major source of the accumulation of the unprecedented amount of Nigerian government revenues and foreign reserves already noted and was, consequently, a crucial contributor to the other impressive aggregate features of the national economy.

In the same time period, Great Britain remained Nigeria's largest import market, although it was rapidly declining in significance. In 1974, 1975, and 1976, the British share of Nigerian total imports averaged about 23 percent. The United States and Great Britain, moreover, supplied the bulk of Nigeria's private direct investment in this period. The cumulative value of the U.S. investment in 1971 was $549 million, representing 25 percent of the total; Great Britain's investment accounted for 44 percent. By 1974, U.S. investment had reached approximately $1 billion and was set to overtake that of Great Britain, whose investment value was $1.2 billion.[13] Almost two-thirds of the U.S. investment in this period, it should be stressed, was concentrated in the pivotal mining industry, although diversification had grown, since 1971, into other sectors such as construction, pharmaceutical, telecommunication, insurance, and petrochemical. It should also be mentioned that British and U.S. oil firms held the majority foreign interest in the Nigerian oil industry and were effectively responsible for its operation (Shell-B.P.— with 50 percent British government interest in B.P.—Gulf Oil, Mobil, and Phillips together controlled about 90 percent of all production in 1974; there were also nine other U.S. oil groups operating in Nigeria— see Appendix B). Thus, both in general and bilateral terms, the crucial elements of Nigeria's economy were basically determined by nonindigenous forces, even though the growth rate in general had accelerated rapidly, averaging about 10 percent per year.

Alterations in the Form of External Dependence

At certain epochs in history, developments occur in the international system that provide great opportunities for alterations in forms of dependence with far-reaching sociopolitical outcomes, both internally and externally. The period in question seemed to have witnessed one such historical phenomenon.

Between 1970 and 1974 forces were injected into the world political economy that, in turn, affected qualitatively the texture of Nigeria's socioeconomic relations with the great Western industrial nations for much of the decade. Crude petroleum, vital as a source of fuel for industrial development and as a strategic resource, had assumed greater economic and political importance. OPEC (the Organization of Petroleum Exporting Countries) had wrested the power to regulate both production and price levels for non–socialist world oil supplies from its erstwhile preponderant international oil corporations.[14] Nigeria had joined OPEC in 1971 as the sixth largest world producer of crude oil outside the socialist system, and its government had acquired vast revenues due to high oil prices (increasing rapidly with the OAPEC [the Organization of Arab Petroleum Exporting Countries] embargo against the West and the quadrupling of prices in 1973–1974) and to large royalties, rents, taxes, etc., extracted from the foreign oil firms. Moreover, buoyed by the new economic leverage of OPEC, the Nigerian federal government took over 55 percent majority equity interests in all operating companies, as was done by most of the other OPEC producers, and formed in 1971 the Nigerian National Oil Corporation as the vehicle of public participation in the exploitation of the nation's oil resources.[15]

But majority joint-participation with foreign firms in the oil industry (as in the banking and other high-capital sectors) was only an aspect of a more general surge in economic nationalism, stimulated by the oil situation, the psychology of past dependence, and the self-confidence generated by the successful execution of the thirty-month civil war. Whereas under the previous Balewa regime state economic philosophy militated against direct government interference in the operation of foreign enterprise, preferring instead the relatively liberal policy of Nigerianization, after 1970 state attitude toward this sector became, in the words of one observer, "blatantly populist."[16] High-level state officials now championed and sought translation into public policy the theme song of radical opposition elements in the first republic, namely that a truly independent nation cannot allow its objectives and priorities to be distorted or frustrated by the manipulations of powerful foreign investors.

The new populist economic ethos found concrete expression in the indigenization program of 1972. This program involved the reservation of certain enterprises for Nigerian citizens exclusively and stipulated that in enterprises with alien interests "Nigerians must henceforth have an equity participation of not less than 40 percent."[17] Indigenization of the economy, of course, is not the same thing as nationalization. One major object of the indigenization program was to strengthen local capitalism through state intervention on behalf of the fledgling Nigerian business class. Nor was indigenization aimed, as might appear in the revised program (see note 17), at a general exclusion of foreign enterprises from the domestic economy. In actual fact, most of the businesses that were taken over were simply transformed by their local benefactors into joint operations with foreign partners. Under the program, the state also claimed the right to enter directly into joint business ventures with foreign governments and private firms. All said, the policy of indigenization constituted a bold attempt to redefine the relationship of foreign and domestic Nigerian capital. But whether this program would be successful in nurturing a more independent national development and an egalitarian society is another matter.

TABLE 5.4
The Financing of Public Sector Investments Under Three National
Development Plans, 1962–1980 (in million naira)

	1962–1968		1970–1974		1975–1980	
	Total	Percentage	Total	Percentage	Total	Percentage
Effective public						
sector investment	1,307.8	100.0	1,156	100.0	20,000	100.0
Sources of finance						
Domestic	526.0	40.2	1,258	80.6	26,739	133.7
External	654.2	50.0	302	19.4	–	–
Uncovered gap	127.6	9.8	–	–	–6,739[a]	–33.7[a]

[a]Net surplus, i.e., excess of domestic resources over planned public sector investment.

Source: Federal Ministry of Economic Development, First National Development Plan, 1962–1968, Second National Development Plan, 1970–1974, and Third National Development Plan, 1975–1980.

Alterations in the form of external dependence were demonstrated in other respects as well. For example, Nigerian policy officials, having control over an immense source of capital accumulation, were able to initiate large-scale development programs without traditional inhibition about how to finance implementation—a concern that had plagued development policies of the Balewa administration. The Second National Development Plan, 1970–1974, launched shortly after the civil war, was designed for the purpose of reconstructing the economy as well as laying the groundwork for a greater "mass-welfare" oriented development in the 1970s. Both the scope of the plan and the scale of domestically derived financial resources envisaged for its implementation (considering that this was a period of national emergency) reflected a basic confidence on the part of the leadership about the dominant role that oil would play in the economic destiny of the country.

The nominal (as opposed to effective) public sector investment in the second plan was projected at 2.1 billion naira. Significantly, 80.6 percent of the effective investment was to be derived from domestic sources; only 19.4 percent was sought in the form of foreign aid (recall that in the first plan 50 percent of total public expenditure was to be externally financed—see Table 5.4).[18] This contrast is even more glaring in the context of the Third Development Plan, 1975–1980, introduced on March 29, 1975. In the third plan, the nominal public investment was estimated at 32 billion naira (this sum was revised upward in 1977 to 43 billion naira as a result of the high inflation rate in the intervening period); for the first time since 1960 Nigeria sought no external capital in financing its public development programs. To government officials and the intellectual community alike, the internal sources of wealth were perceived to be so stable by 1974 that the nation could assume complete financial responsibility for the public investments called for in the plan.[19] Thus, an erroneous creed became implanted in the public mind that Nigeria at last had broken through the poverty trap, now to become a wealthy country. Never mind that the average yearly personal income remained less than four hundred dollars.

These alterations in the external features of the Nigerian economy generated certain effects, albeit by interacting with emerging internal trends, on the distribution of political power among various domestic strata.[20] These also tended to produce greater strains within the channels of the Nigerian-U.S. relationship.

After 1969, effective power (i.e., in the sense of a disproportionate influence on economic development and foreign policies) became noticeably concentrated within two main sectors of the Nigerian society: the central government in Lagos vis-à-vis the constituent states (which had been created to replace the old largely autonomous regions), and senior federal bureaucrats as well as top military officers relative to other social groups, such as labor unions, the press, university intellectuals, and students. The point, though, is not that the latter groups were without any influence on national policies. To the contrary, they played a crucial role, as will be seen with regard to foreign policy, in constantly pressing the top federal bureaucrats and their military advisers to live up to the nationalist-populist promise of the ruling administrations. Federal power over the states was strengthened in proportion to the growth in national income under its disposal, for its was the federal government that exercised legal jurisdiction over the petroleum sector. Moreover, the gradual irrelevance of the principle of "derivation" as a statutory basis for revenue allocation to the states had the result of further enlarging the "distributable pool" of funds under federal control. True, the shift in political power to the center had begun with the centralization of decisionmaking authority in Lagos in the course of prosecuting the civil war; however, it was the postwar changes in the national economic situation that consolidated this trend.

It is also indisputable that senior civil servants in both federal and state bureaucracies enjoyed wide decisionmaking authority and political influence in the country following the proscription of organized politics after the military takeover in January 1966. The so-called military administration in Nigeria, as a number of observers recognized, was actually a coalition between top military personnel and civil servants.[21] The political influence of senior federal civil servants such as Allison Ayida, Abdul Atta, Phillip Asiodu, Joseph Iyalla, and Ime Ebong was a direct function of their indispensability to the military rulers in providing technical advice vital for making complex policy decisions. Between 1970 and 1975, especially, these civilian advisers acquired unbounded power. They constituted, for instance, the crucial negotiatory link between the government and the prospecting foreign oil subsidiaries. Their status and material advantage over other segments of society also benefited from the authority they exercised in recommending highly profitable contracts eagerly sought by foreign and local business groups in connection with the large development projects budgeted for in the two plans.[22]

The altered form of dependence within the political economy of oil is central to an understanding of the mode of Nigerian-U.S. overall relations in the second period. In attempting to trace the interrelationship between their bilateral ties and Nigeria's regional policy orientation, the broad approach adopted for assessing the Balewa period will be followed. That is, the processes underlying core issues within the altered bilateral structure are examined in order to deduce the manner of their impact on the Nigerian decisionmaking environment in the realm of regional policy. Two policy cases are examined in Chapter 6 to help generate some conclusions about the resultant regional relationship between the two countries in this period.

Oil: The Linchpin of Economic "Interdependence"

"The United States needs Nigeria's oil and its market, and hence has to accommodate the country's views on Africa," asserted a deputy economic adviser in the Nigerian Ministry of External Affairs.[23] Between June and December 1971, the *New Nigerian*, an influential daily publication, ran feature articles and editorials castigating the U.S. aid program in Nigeria as an unmitigated mechanism of political control. In its December 9, 1971, edition, the paper recommended that Teresa Hayter's book, *Aid as Imperialism*, be read by "all those responsible for making policy in this country."[24] Obviously, these views are too uncomplicated and as such do not capture the subleties of Nigerian-U.S. ties in this period. They are cited because they do, however, underscore in a general sense the psychological setting within Nigeria that would impinge on the processes of both economic and political relations with the United States.

A crucial offshoot of the new psychological profile was that economic ties with the United States (and the United Kingdom) were now articulated, at official and private levels, in terms of "interdependence" rather than dependence. No doubt, this popular image of interdependence as merely a situation of mutual dependence is at variance with the more complex, more historically based, conception of that phenomenon provided by academicians Robert Keohane and Joseph Nye. To these experts what determines a state of interdependence is the possibility of incurring "reciprocally costly effects" arising from such a relationship.[25] As further explained by Kenneth Waltz, "If domestic substitutions or adjustments cannot be made, or can be made only at high cost, trade becomes of higher value to a country and of first importance to those who conduct its foreign policy."[26]

Given the fact that the Nigerian policy elite placed a very high value on the relative stability of the U.S. oil market and in view of the associated technological and political advantages they envisaged to obtain in doing business with the United States, how disruptive would it be for the national economy should the dominant U.S. market become unintentionally shut off as a result perhaps of a drastically diminished demand? There are many interesting facets to this question with a number of built-in implications, but this should not delay the discussion. The significant thing to remember is that in group relations just as in interstate affairs what is perceived to be real is sometimes as important a determinant of behavior as the concrete reality. A combination of both is an even more potent factor. Simply put, Nigeria's image of its importance to the United States derived in general from its being the second largest supplier of crude oil (Canada was the largest) to the U.S. market since 1973-1974. (Nigerian crude is of top quality, with light gravity and very low sulphur content; this was one reason for its high demand by U.S. refineries.) Nigerian policymakers often regarded Nigeria's capacity to satisfy the U.S. oil demand by itself as a priceless collateral for obtaining desired economic assets from the United States, such as high-technology and joint-venture investments, on terms the policymakers determined. Augmenting this sense of self-value was the shrewd awareness by responsible officials that a prolonged petroleum shortage in the U.S. market would present an unacceptable political problem for the Nixon-Ford administration and, hence, that Washington would continue to cultivate the Nigerian oil source for some time. However, the sense of economic interdependence also strained the political sphere of Nigerian-U.S. ties; oil wealth, which provided an unexpected magnitude of financial self-reliance, was seen as conferring a new power on state officials, allowing them to make tough demands on their U.S. counterparts and to adopt domestic as well as external policies usually at odds with U.S. preferences.

The Politicization of Economic Issues

The Indigenization of the Oil Industry

An initial irritant to Nigerian-U.S. oil ties pertained to the changing relationship between the Nigerian government and the multinational oil companies, including those of U.S. origin—notably Gulf, Mobil, Phillips, Texaco, and Ashland. The real issue was the decision of the Nigerian federal government, first hinted by the 1969 Petroleum Decree and reaffirmed in 1974, to acquire participation rights in all facets of the oil industry.[27]

Beginning in early 1970, multifarious pressures were brought to bear on the federal government by the public, the Soviet Union, and, through nationalistic policies, OPEC-African members such as Libya and Algeria regarding the necessity of nationalizing the Nigerian oil-gas industry or at the least acquiring majority state ownership in the concessions of the operating foreign companies.[28] The local business community (as represented by the chambers of commerce) urged the government to indigenize the industry but vigorously opposed state participation, insisting instead that private individuals be allowed to enter freely into partnerships with foreign firms. As in the past, federal officials adopted a more realistic attitude than outright nationalization. Because of the unavailability of sufficiently experienced Nigerians with the technical capacity to operate such a pivotal industry efficiently, nationalization could lead to a drastic reduction in production, adversely affecting the economy. On July 9, 1970, General Gowon tactfully sought to assure worried Gulf Oil officials, telling them that the government was uninterested in nationalization and would only demand its "fair share of the royalty" from the oil companies.[29]

Ambassador Trueheart, perhaps due to minimal contact with high-level state officials, took at face value Gowon's statement about the government only demanding its fair share of royalty and thus failed to foresee the impending clash between the Nigerian government and the major oil producing companies on oil-related issues apart from nationalization. He had naively reassured Secretary Rogers in Washington that public pressures had little effect on the Nigerian government's oil policy, which he said was "essentially conservative." As for joint participation, he reported that the government was only interested in new concessions, not existing ones.[30] Indeed, Gowon's assurance to the oil companies had no factual basis. Back in May, the federal government had given clear indication that Nigeria was interested in more than an increase in royalties. The major companies had been told then to expect a revision in all existing agreements. The government had formally revealed its intention, via the second development plan, to get involved in three specific branches of the oil industry, namely, exploration-mining, refining, and distribution-marketing. Nigeria had already adopted OPEC's new tax system, based on posted prices instead of on the realized market value of oil, and there had been strong speculations in the local oil community that the existing level of posted prices might be boosted, following the examples of Libya and Algeria.[31] Substantial change was looming ahead while Trueheart saw relative calm.

By February 1971, U.S. officials in Washington began to exhibit concern over Nigerian oil policy in general and its pricing and marketing aspects in particular. These concerns, along with the prospect of Nigeria extending its indigenization policy to affect assets of major U.S. companies, worried members of the State Department, especially in view of the deteriorating relations between oil-producing companies and a number of oil-exporting countries in the Gulf and North Africa.[32] Consequently, with direct instructions from the State Department, embassy personnel in Lagos attempted on many occasions to express their concern to responsible officials in both the Ministry of External Affairs and the Nigerian National Oil Corporation (NNOC).

The Nigerian federal government, however, reacted promptly by accusing the United States of direct interference in Nigeria's oil policy. More than that, Nigeria formally barred U.S. personnel from making further contacts with Nigerian oil functionaries. Nigerian oil policy, according to Gowon, was to be the sole responsibility of the federal government.[33] U.S. officials at the embassy and the State Department, it is said, were puzzled and shocked by the hostile manner of the Nigerian action. Since the end of the war, the United States had undertaken extensive measures (which need not be specified here) of goodwill toward the victorious federal government, seeking to rectify the poor state of relations during the war period. By such gestures, U.S. officials actually hoped to restore a good degree of their prewar position of influence in Lagos. But instead of reciprocating, the Nigerian government, it seemed, was stiffening its attitude. U.S. personnel exhibited an inability to understand that the emerging oil situation would make postwar ties with Nigeria significantly different from what they were before, whether the regime in power was military or civilian. Hence, U.S. personnel continued to interpret the persistent Nigerian acts of intransigence mainly in terms of the war experience regarding the U.S. policy of neutrality.

June 11, 1973, can be said to mark a milestone in the state's relationship with the oil firms in Nigeria. On that date the government acquired, after a lengthy and what was described by the central participants as a very difficult negotiation process, 35 percent "of all the assets" of Shell-B.P. Company in Nigeria.[34] (Shell-B.P. was the pioneer of the international majors, and was the dominant oil corporation in the country.) Phillip Asiodu, the key decisionmaker behind the government's participation policy, expressed the general public and official feeling regarding the oil firms and why participation was desirable:

It all adds up to the fact that left on their own the oil companies have been organized and will continue to be organized in this country purely as an extractive industry, investing locally the barest minimum necessary to find oil and take it out. They and their associates have been content to contract out all the services they can to overseas companies and to make their purchases from America and Western Europe, and have not tried in any way to encourage ancillary industrial development in this country.[35]

Asiodu offered an illustration of his contention, stating that in 1970 about $182 million was spent locally by the oil industry, but only 10 percent of that amount was actually expended on services provided by Nigerian-controlled enterprises or on materials manufactured in Nigeria with a high local content.

A few months later, the government began negotiations with Gulf, Mobil, and Texaco. But these U.S. companies were presented with more stringent terms than those Shell-B.P. had managed to obtain. The government demanded 40 percent state ownership and higher prices for "buy back" crude. Indications about the tough demands on the companies filtered to Ambassador Rheinhardt on August 19 through Nigeria's director of petroleum resources, Chief M. O. Feyide. However, U.S. embassy personnel were, unusually, kept in the dark about the content of the negotiations through most of the process, until a stalemate ensued.[36] When the U.S. companies, which were negotiated with separately, declined to accept what they regarded as discriminatory terms, the federal government confronted them with what amounted to an ultimatum. September 30 was given as the deadline for reaching an agreement, with the implied threat that they stood to lose their existing concessions thereafter.[37]

The point of interest here is not what the government did but what underlay its action. What specifically encouraged Nigerian officials to adopt a get-tough stance with all the oil firms after the June agreement with Shell-B.P. was something external to the country's borders. The Middle East conflict had erupted, and worldwide demand for crude oil was starting to escalate. In fact, the Nigerian government might have had wind of the impending OAPEC oil embargo should the tide of war turn against the Arabs. Because of these circumstances, the relatively favorable concessions earlier granted Shell-B.P. were overturned, and by early 1974, Nigeria entered into new agreements with all the major companies, including Gulf, Mobil, and Texaco. The state now sought and obtained a majority interest of 55 percent, plus other substantial rights. Equities so acquired were compensated for within two years.

The Issue of the Second
Investment-Guarantee Agreement

The second investment-guarantee agreement between Nigeria and the United States was signed on August 3, 1974, and came into effect after ratification in March 1975.[38] By that agreement, direct U.S. investments in Nigeria became eligible for insurance by the U.S. Overseas Private Investment Corporation (OPIC). The process of reaching this agreement, begun in 1971, was "arduous and extremely protracted" and presents an illustration of the independent attitude exhibited by Nigerian authorities toward U.S. initiatives to participate in Nigeria's economic development. It was not that Nigeria had become suddenly so economically self-reliant that it wished to forgo valuable private U.S. contributions to its national development effort. To the contrary, public and private statements made by responsible officials continually indicated a desire for U.S. investments as well as admiration for U.S. enterprise in general. For example, while addressing representatives of major U.S. banks and government agencies in January 1975, Nigeria's ambassador in Washington, Olu Sanu, exhorted private investors to demonstrate greater commitment to the country's development because Nigerians needed "access to sophisticated American technology and mangement" skills.[39] Later in the same year, Joseph Iyalla, the permanent secretary of the Ministry of External Affairs, articulated the same basic interest to the U.S. chief envoy, Donald B. Easum: "What Nigeria needed . . . was the responsible American concern that could bring needed technology and expertise into long-term partnership with Nigerian counterparts."[40]

Why then did the Nigerians deliberately impede U.S. requests for renewal of the OPIC agreement? Underlying the problem was the strong interconnection between economics, politics, and psychology in Nigerian-U.S. relations of this period. For instance, Dr. Eyitayo Adetoro, the Nigerian commissioner for industries, alluded to the disappointment Nigerian decisionmakers might have felt in the process of past investment ties with the United States as a possible reason for the delay. Adetoro's remarks at the formal signing of the agreement are revealing in this regard:

This agreement replaces the former one signed in 1962. At that time this country was on the verge of launching its first National Development Plan. The agreement was welcomed as a positive move to ensure effective American participation in our industrial development. It may not be too much to say that our earnest expectations on that agreement were not fully met.[41]

There were still other pertinent factors. For example, although Nigerians by and large still craved U.S. private investments, decisionmakers now demanded, rigidly, to determine the types and terms of such investments. In the course of a conversation with Ambassador Easum, Joseph Iyalla, a senior federal civil servant, noted rather comically that Nigeria "was [no longer] interested in the fly-by-night operator who thought he could make a quick sale or promote a short-term lucrative deal." Direct foreign investment was sought almost entirely in the form of joint ventures. Sectoral priorities for such joint enterprises were listed as agro-based industry, manufacture of basic and intermediate industrial chemicals, automotive parts, and technical services.

The general climate of opinion about foreign aid was similar to that for foreign investment. As indicated in the editorial writings of the *New Nigerian*, earlier cited, the government was "frustratingly selective" with regard to external aid. From 1972 to 1974, Ambassador Rheinhardt reported at length to Washington about the changed aid environment encountered by potential foreign donors. For example, in a cable of July 19, 1974, he made the following observations:

> Although many Nigerians recognize the potential contribution of outside help in the development process, the kinds of assistance which would be most useful are in many cases also the most politically sensitive—and thus pose the greatest problems in terms of their acceptability to the Federal Military Government. . . . By making the [government] far less dependent on external financial resources for its development effort, these new oil revenues have accentuated the sense of self-sufficiency and insistence on uncompromising sovereignty long characteristic of Nigerian behaviour. In consequence, any suggestion that a potential donor seeks to alter basic [government] development priorities or to take over key decision-making positions would risk a sharply negative reaction. Even in 1972, . . . multilateral donors like IBRD and IMF were troubled by the [government's] "dogmatic insistence on near-absolute freedom to determine its own economic policies without outside advice," and bilateral donors often stirred even greater suspicions when they sought to proffer advice.[42]

The indigenization program was the institutional mechanism for deciding what type of foreign investment was acceptable and the price to pay for it. The program thus became a concrete factor obstructing the signing of the OPIC agreement. Some potential U.S. investors, who had already expressed concern that indigenization would ultimately lead to outright expropriation of foreign assets, became even more reluctant to establish companies in Nigeria without the redeeming assurance provided by the OPIC agreement.[43] Nigerian officials, on the other hand, were unwilling to legally commit themselves to the restraining terms of the proposed agreement because the public was agitating for a more comprehensive indigenization policy. (As noted earlier, the program initiated in 1972 was revised in 1977 to affect all categories of foreign enterprise.) Caught in the middle was the State Department, and especially the Africa Bureau, whose immediate interest was twofold: to help U.S. investors compete successfully with the Western Europeans in a very lucrative African market and to establish a commanding U.S. presence in the Nigerian economy as a means of eroding whatever advantage the Soviet Union might have gained during the civil war.

Perhaps the most ostentatious display of financial self-confidence on the part of the Nigerian federal government was the argument that Nigeria could obtain private investments elsewhere if the United States insisted on the OPIC agreement as a price for U.S. investment. In sharp contrast to the official perception in 1962, the government now viewed the agreement as an imposition on national integrity and independence. The agreement was said to constitute a lack of U.S. confidence in Nigeria[44]—a "fact" that no longer needed any proof. So reluctant was the Nigerian government to become bonded by the agreement, despite the conciliatory views of such officials as Ayida, Atta, and Asiodu, that it employed various delaying tactics, including insistence on specific choice of words and numerous redraftings, in an attempt to frustrate the Americans. Even after the final draft had been agreed upon, the government stalled on signing, "excusing its behaviour on public critics which regarded the agreement as a way of institutionalizing dependency."[45]

Thus, the acquisition of financial self-reliance (or at least its perception) by Nigeria was a fundamental source of political strain in its bilateral economic relations with the United States. Additionally, the keen realization within Nigeria of the mutual dependence by both countries on the valuable resource of oil reinforced a disposition toward independent action by groups in Nigeria vis-à-vis the United States. This does not mean that the two countries did not share a common stake in strengthening their basic economic ties. Indeed, the underlying source of Nigerian wealth was the continued value of oil imports to the U.S. economy. Paradoxically, though, this mutual dependence led not to harmony but to divergence in oil policy.

Another example of such disharmony related to the more inclusive conflict between the United States and OPEC in the period 1973–1975 and was due to the cartel's price policy. The unhappy reaction of the United States to the steep rise in posted oil prices and to the embargo imposed by OAPEC in 1973–1974, marked particularly by Henry Kissinger's threat to employ military force and invoke the U.S. Trade Act of 1974, generated hostile responses in Nigeria both at the official and public levels. An extreme but not unrepresentative press comment was made by the *Nigerian Tide*, which, in an editorial, blandly termed as "blackmail" President Ford's "Executive Order placing Nigeria and 12 other members . . . of OPEC on a trade black list unless they formally agree to supply oil at reasonable prices."[46] Perhaps representing the highpoint of the Nigerian-U.S. conflict on oil policy was the U.S. effort in 1974 to block an IBRD loan package worth $107 million for agricultural development in Nigeria, even though Nigeria had concurrently extended a loan of $240 million to the World Bank. All other executive directors of the bank, including the United Kingdom, France, and Italy, had supported offering the loan to Nigeria.[47]

Summary

From 1970 to 1976, the second period of research, the Nigerian economy remained basically dependent relative to the dominant world economy. The central indicator of this continued dependence was the over-reliance of the domestic economy on one pivotal export commodity— crude petroleum. One potential danger in this situation was that any significant reduction in production and export prices of oil would in turn have deprived Nigeria of its major source of capital formation, foreign reserves, government revenues, as well as personal incomes to strategic social groups.

There were substantial alterations in the forms of Nigeria's foreign economic relations, which affected, in consequence, the country's direct links to the United States and Great Britain. These two countries retained their relative position as Nigeria's dominant economic partners in the areas of trade and private investment; but being largely self-reliant financially, Nigeria did not depend, in this period, on external sources for its development capital—a drastic change from its experience in the former period. However, the United States was clearly a more vital partner than Great Britain in Nigeria's international economic relations: It provided the predominant market for Nigerian oil and, hence, a large proportion of Nigeria's development finance.

At the official and public levels in Nigeria, there was a deep change in the psychological perception of ties with the two Anglo-Saxon powers. With the United States, especially, economic relations were now viewed in terms of interdependence—by which Nigerians meant mutual dependence. A sense of financial self-reliance by government and crucial strata engendered a rigid disposition toward independent behavior in the country's overall economic and political dealings with U.S. officials and private groups. Thus, as will be shown in the next chapter, the mode of the Nigerian-U.S. regional policy relationship, quite unlike the experience of the earlier period, was more conflictual than cooperative.

Notes

1. This study is not about the Nigerian civil war—a subject that requires a full-scale study of its own. For background information, refer to S. K. Panter-Brick, ed., *Nigerian Politics and Military Rule: Prelude to the Civil War* (London: The Anthlone Press, 1970); Gavin Williams, ed., *Nigeria: Economy and Society* (London: Rex Collins, 1976).

2. The decision by the Johnson and Nixon administrations to maintain a position of neutrality in the conflict was influenced by various factors, the most important ones being presidential politics of 1968, the restraints of the Vietnam War, specific group pressures, and the preference of the British government. For a detailed analysis of the U.S. policy, see Francis C. Ogene, "Group Interests and United States Foreign Policy on African Issues" (Ph.D. dissertation, Case Western Reserve University, Cleveland, Ohio, 1974), pp. 97–176. On external influences in the war generally, see John J. Stremlau, *The International Politics of the Nigerian Civil War, 1967–70* (Princeton, N.J.: Princeton University Press, 1977).

3. Faced with the U.S. arms embargo and Great Britain's refusal to sell military aircraft, bombs, and offensive weapons more sophisticated than small arms, the federal government turned to the Soviet Union, which was only too willing to provide these materials.

4. Interview with John Foley, former desk officer for Nigeria, Department of State, and political counselor, U.S. embassy, Lagos), Washington, D.C., May 30, 1979.

5. Ambassador Trueheart was recalled to Washington after September in large part because of this problem of "inaccessibility" to the Nigerian government. Interview with William Trueheart (U.S. ambassador in Lagos, October 1969 to September 1971), Washington, D.C., January 13, 1979.

6. Interview with John Foley, May 30, 1979.

7. Rheinhardt to Department of State, March 18, 1972, Airgram no. A-75, Department of State Files, Washington, D.C. (Hereinafter all documents retrieved directly from the State Department are designated by the abbreviation DSF.)

8. S. A. Madujibeya, "Oil and Nigeria's Economic Development," *African Affairs* 75 (July 1976): 286–290, 314.

9. Central Bank of Nigeria, *Economic and Financial Review*, June 1975; Madujibeya, "Oil and Nigeria's Economic Development," p. 287.

10. Federal Republic of Nigeria, *Third National Development Plan, 1975–80*, Vol. 1, p. 147; Richard A. Joseph, "Affluence and Underdevelopment: The Nigerian Experience," *Journal of Modern African Studies* 16(2) (1978): 224–227.

11. *Nigeria: A Survey of U.S. Business Opportunities* (Washington, D.C.: U.S. Department of Commerce, May 1976), p. 4.

12. In a single month, November 1974, Nigeria, according to the U.S. Bureau of Mines, exported 30,373,000 barrels of crude oil to the United States. This

prompted a U.S. embassy official in Lagos to report, "It was [the] first month in history that any country except Canada exported more than one million barrels per day to [the] U.S. At this rate, [the] U.S. would be paying . . . $5 billion per year for Nigerian oil." Crosby ([Lagos] to Secretary of State, April 7, 1975, and Telegram no. 3155, and Robinson [Washington] to Easum [Lagos], October 9, 1976, Telegram no. 252076, DSF.

13. Central Bank of Nigeria, *Economic and Financial Review* 14(1) (March 1976): 15–16; *Background Notes: Nigeria* (Washington, D.C.: Department of State, September 1977), p. 7. As will be assessed later, the Nigerian government relied very little on (official) external capital aid for national economic development in this period.

14. Luis Vallenilla, *Oil: The Making of a New Economic Order, Venezuelan Oil and OPEC* (New York: McGraw-Hill Book Company, 1975), especially Chapter 9; also Raymond Vernon, ed., *The Oil Crisis* (New York: W. W. Norton and Company, 1976).

15. Kola Adeniji, "State Participation in the Nigerian Petroleum Industry," *Journal of World Trade* 11 (March-April): 156–179; Eno J. Usoro, "Foreign Oil Companies and Recent Nigerian Petroleum Oil Policies," *The Nigerian Journal of Economic and Social Studies* 14(3) (November 1972): 301–314.

16. Douglas Rimmer, "Elements of the Political Economy" in Keith Panter-Brick, ed., *Soldiers and Oil: The Political Transformation of Nigeria* (London: Frank Cass and Company Ltd., 1978), p. 156.

17. "Nigerian Enterprises Promotion Decree, 1972," *Supplement to Official Gazette Extraordinary* 58 (February 28, 1970): Part A. In 1977, this decree was revised: A third category was added in which Nigerians were to own 40 percent interests, and indigenous participation in the second category was increased to 60 percent. Thus, through the revised program, the government opened up all enterprises with foreign equity interests to Nigerian participation. The first phase of the program was widely critiqued in Nigeria. See *The Quarterly Journal of Administration* 9(2) (January 1975).

18. Federal Republic of Nigeria, *Second National Development Plan, 1970–74* (Lagos: Ministry of Information, 1970).

19. Even when in 1978 the need arose for external loans as a consequence of low oil production, diminishing foreign reserves, and a high inflation rate, government officials preferred to seek such loans in the private Eurodollar market rather than enter into official deals with foreign governments. See "Marketing in Nigeria," *Overseas Business Report* (Washington, D.C.: U.S. Department of Commerce, April 1979), p. 5; *West Africa*, October 30, 1978, p. 2151.

20. Paul Collins has assessed how the indigenization program, also, might have intensified patterns of social-ethnic conflict. "The Political Economy of Indigenization: The Case of the Nigerian Enterprises Promotion Decree," *The African Review* (Dar es Salaam) 4(4) (1974): especially 501–508.

21. From about the start of the civil war in mid-1967, a number of civilians, notably former politicians, had been co-opted into the military administration to provide a form of local representation. Generally, they were accorded titular responsibilities over government ministries as commissioners. However, policy

decisionmaking authority remained very much the prerogative of high-level bureaucrats and senior military leaders. Henry Bienen and Martin Pitton, "Soldiers, Politicians, and Civil Servants," in Keith Panter-Brick, ed., *Soldiers and Oil: The Political Transformation of Nigeria* (London: Frank Cass and Company Ltd., 1978), pp. 25–53.

22. The processes by which such officials might have used their public positions, sometimes in collaboration with local business intermediaries, for self-enrichment through illegal conduct have evoked critical analysis in and outside Nigeria. See, for example, Terisa Turner, "Multinational Corporations and the Instability of the Nigerian State," *Review of African Political Economy* 5 (January-April 1976): 63–79; and P. C. Asiodu, responding to Turner's article, in "Aspects of Nigerian Oil Policy," *Lagoon Echo* (Lagos), March-April 1977.

23. Confidential interview, Lagos, August 22, 1978.

24. *New Nigerian* (Kaduna), June 10, 1971, December 7, 1971, and December 9, 1971. It is significant that this publication represented the basic interest of the powerful political forces in the old Northern Region—i.e., those that most consistently defended the pro-U.S. (Western) foreign orientation in the first republic.

25. Robert Keohane, *Power and Interdependence: World Politics in Transition* (Boston: Little, Brown and Company, 1977), pp. 8–19.

26. Kenneth N. Waltz, *Theory of International Politics* (Reading, Mass.: Addison-Wesley Publishing Company, 1979), p. 142.

27. Kola Adeniji, "State Participation in the Nigerian Petroleum Industry," p. 161; *African Development* 6 (June 1972): 10–11.

28. Soviet commentators between 1967 and 1970 unrelentingly urged complete nationalization of the industry to avoid what they saw as foreign domination of the Nigerian economy. See, for example, article by V. Solodovinikor, *Daily Times* (Lagos), September 30, 1970.

29. Trueheart to Rogers, July 23, 1970, Airgram no. A-265, DSF.

30. Ibid.

31. *Second National Development Plan, 1970–74*, p. 164; Airgram no. A-265.

32. The secretary of state, Rogers, was not as optimistic about the direction of events in Nigeria as his ambassador was. On the other hand, the U.S. and British governments were sufficiently disturbed by the OPEC price policy to send representatives to negotiate with the cartel in February 1971. See Rogers to Trueheart, September 25, 1970, Airgram no. A-49, DSF; and *The Observer* (London), February 1971.

33. Information obtained through confidential interview.

34. *Nigeria: Bulletin of Foreign Affairs* 3(1-4) (January-December 1973): 155–158; *African Development* 6 (June 1972): 10–12.

35. *African Development*, p. 11. To Asiodu's charges, the managing director of Shell-B.P., L. C. Van Wacheam, defended the record of his company in meeting "the aspirations of Nigerians" since 1958. *Nigeria: Bulletin of Foreign Affairs* 2 (June 1972): 157.

36. Rheinhardt to Kissinger, August 30, 1973, Telegram no. 7110, DSF. That the Nigerian government refused to involve the embassy, unlike the experiences

in the first period, in such an important transaction was itself evidence of increasing autonomy in its bilateral dealings with the United States.

37. Rheinhardt to Kissinger, September 10, 1973, Telegram no. 7382, DSF; *Petroleum Economist* 43(1) (January 1976).

38. By that agreement, direct U.S. investments in Nigeria became eligible for insurance by the U.S. Overseas Private Investment Corporation (OPIC). See *Nigeria: A Survey of U.S. Business Opportunities* (Washington, D.C.: Department of Commerce, May 1976), p. 11. The Nigerian government was clearly responsible for the long delay in signing the agreement. Confidential interview.

39. News release no. 30, January 9, 1975, Federal Ministry of Information, Lagos.

40. Easum to Kissinger, June 11, 1975, Telegram no. 5464, DSF.

41. *Nigeria: Bulletin on Foreign Affairs* 4(1-4) (January-December 1974): 170; also *Africa Research Bulletin*, August 14, 1974.

42. Rheinhardt to Department of State, July 29, 1974, Airgram no. A-171, DSF. Compared to the first period, U.S. aid in 1970–1976 played a very insigifnicant role in bilateral diplomacy with Nigeria. Since 1971, although the United States continued to offer technical assistance to Nigeria, this became essentially a business transaction in which the Nigerian government paid for "support" services rendered. In 1974, the Nigerian and U.S. governments decided mutually that USAID should scale down its activities in the country.

43. Interview with Edward Lollis, desk officer for Nigeria (1975–1977), State Department, Washington, D.C., November 16, 1978; also unpublished paper presented by Emmanuel Obe of the Nigerian embassy, Washington, D.C., at a seminar on investment in Nigeria, American Management Association, New York City, Winter 1976.

44. Confidential interview.

45. Ibid. The specific argument that the agreement, in the view of the government, represented a lack of U.S. confidence in Nigeria is confirmed by Joseph Iyalla. See note 40 above.

46. *Nigerian Tide*, March 30, 1975. The Nigerian government presented a diplomatic note to the U.S. Embassy formally defending the OPEC price policy. See Note no. G1637/75, September 30, 1975, Ministry of External Affairs, Lagos. The United States was opposed to IBRD lending to OPEC in general.

47. After a period of objection, the United States finally abstained when the IBRD Board of Management voted on the loan request for Nigeria. Interview with Edward Lollis; and Kissinger to Easum, December 1, 1974, Telegram no. 27744, 1974, DSF.

6

Regional Policy Relationship: Straining for Independent Leadership

The Essence of the New Pattern

The central proposition of this chapter is that there was greater tendency toward conflict than cooperation in the pattern of Nigeria-U.S. regional policy relations in the 1970–1976 period. It is not thereby asserted that relations in this sphere had, invariably, been replaced by complete polarization and hostility. Clearly, that could not have occurred without seriously damaging the bilateral (economic) ties between the countries. As shown in Chapter 5, both countries, even without so verbalizing, placed a high value on sustaining this aspect in their respective national interests. From the Nigerian perspective, what distinguished the mode of regional relationships in this period from that in the earlier period were the incessant disagreements over attempts to reconcile policy objectives and a strong inclination, on Nigeria's part, to assert regional leadership independent of U.S. resources.

Apart from Nigeria's relative financial self-reliance, two additional conditions helped to reinforce the noted tendency in regional relationships during this period. The first was that Nigeria, under the regimes of General Yakubu Gowon and Brigadier Murtala Mohammed, adopted an ardently nationalistic (not to be confused with irrational radicalism) policy on regional decolonization, which was the core of an evolving general policy precept that emphasized the country's strong identification with the rest of Africa.[1] This redefinition of national interest in decolonization was a by-product of the civil war. The most compelling factor in recasting official thinking on this continental issue was the role played by South Africa, Southern Rhodesia, and Portugal in actively assisting the secession of Biafra against the authority of the Nigerian federal government. After the Nigerian civil war, federal policymakers drew the firm conclusion on what had previously been speculation, that the three colonialist states wished to see Nigeria dismembered; obviously, a united and powerful Nigeria was thought to pose a serious danger to the continuation of their colonialist objectives in Africa. Henceforth, Nigeria's interest in the regional decolonization process was defined more concretely in terms of the survival of the national entity, linked to a quest for expanding the country's political influence southward to the rest of the continent.[2] Ambassador Easum, testifying before the Senate Sub-Committee on Africa in 1976, described Nigeria as a "country that has . . . taken a very deep interest in Southern African issues for years, a country that has viewed its own role as important in Southern Africa and a country, therefore, that has been more concerned with [its] approach to Southern Africa than perhaps some others."[3]

The second condition that reinforced Nigeria's new tendency in regional relationships was the U.S. policy preference on African decolonization adopted by President Richard M. Nixon and maintained by his successor, Gerald Ford. This policy was the brainchild of Henry Kissinger, formerly national security adviser and later U.S. secretary of state. The essence of the Kissinger prescription on the colonial situation in southern Africa was the acceptance of the existing status of forces in that region; at the time it seemed comfortable to assume that change was impossible through armed pressures. Much has been written about the National Security Council's Interdepartmental-Group Study on Southern Africa commissioned by Kissinger in April of 1969, a great deal of it normatively condemnatory, much less addressed to the original purpose of the study. Option 2 of that study, advocated by the NSC, which in essence proposed that the United States accept the power reality in southern Africa and "tilt" its policy in favor of the white authorities who held that power, became the opium of the more liberal critics in the United States, who argued that U.S. policy was in fact based on this option and was thus conclusively against decolonization.[4] But the real question should be whether the choice was adequate for safeguarding the desired U.S. interests not only in the immediate area but in the rest of the subcontinent.

The adoption of Option 2 could hardly have been based on an in-depth understanding of the decolonization momentum in southern Africa nor on an appreciation of its interconnection with other U.S. concerns in the rest of sub-Saharan Africa. The policy choice, as it was, did not represent the most rational approach to ensuring U.S. interests although that was said to be its object. At the very least, its implementation meant a flagrant disregard of what Easum, in 1974 (then assistant secretary for Africa), reminded Kissinger was still the most consuming issue in inter-African politics. In turn, it constituted a signal to concerned Africans that their aspiration for independence in southern Africa was to be placed on the back burners of U.S. foreign policy, not even to receive the modest support it was given by the past two administrations.

There is, of course, an alternative explanation for the choice of Option 2, which was probably closer to the mark, i.e., that Kissinger's southern Africa policy was an aspect of his general strategy for sustaining a stable global order. In addition, the preference may also have been a casualty of the strain placed on U.S. foreign policy machinery by the Vietnam War.

In Nigeria, the reported shift in policy was interpreted as indicative of U.S. accommodation for, or worse, collaboration with, the white minority governments against the aspirations of the black majority in southern Africa for self-determination. For the United States (and its relations with Nigeria), the timing of Kissinger's policy could not have occurred at a worse juncture, one marked by a perceptible decline in U.S. leverage within the medium of its bilateral ties with Nigeria and by the latter's adoption of an ardently nationalistic approach to decolonization. The contradiction in these conditions assured the noncooperative orientation in their regional relationship noted above.

Did Nigeria evolve a new policy on decolonization between 1970 and 1976? This question has already been touched upon but needs further clarification in view of the prevailing experience before the civil war. Almost imperceptibly, the postwar Nigerian military leadership appeared to have projected a new approach to regional problems in general and decolonization in particular. This development (which was far from fully advanced) reached its relative apogee during the policy performance over the Angola crisis, but it had been evolving since 1971. It was characterized by an independent (one might say unilateral, i.e., outside the institutional confines of the OAU) disposition to assert leadership in the region, whether it was under the guise of Gowon's "low profile" or Mohammed's "dynamism."[5]

This quest, ironically, took as its conceptual premise Nkrumah's position on the need for developing a credible regional power center through which to bargain with extraregional forces on economic, technological, and political issues. Nkrumah's methodology was still prudently rejected, but the old "conservative" recipe that mandated undivided OAU consensus in order to initiate functionalist enterprises was quietly discarded. Independent leadership now required not disregard for OAU opinion but proposing imaginative and bold ideas about regional problems and then mobilizing the majority of OAU members toward their implementation. Further, Nigerian regional leadership on decolonization now involved the use of both multilateral channels (e.g., the Liberation Committee of the OAU and the UN Committee of 24) and bilateral media to implement national policies. In sum, during this period, Nigeria sought to project its leadership position and augment regional capability not through the costly route of politically uniting the diverse national entities, but rather by advancing its own growth as a potential center of power in the region.

Illustrations of this orientation are not hard to find. Two examples of a mobilizing leadership as conceived above are Nigeria's role in the negotiations for and subsequent formation of the Economic Community of West African States (ECOWAS) in May 1975 and its role in the signing of the Lome Agreement earlier that year between African, Caribbean, and Pacific countries and the European Economic Community (the ACP-EEC Agreement). On decolonization, Nigeria contributed about $5 million per year to the special fund of the Liberation Committee; it also provided direct financial and military assistance comprising small arms and ammunition and the use of two C-130 transport planes.[6] Clearly, the change in the national economic situation and its political concomitant proved to be the crucial elements in this new thrust.

Postwar Ties with the Soviet Union: Their Meaning and Extent

That the critical diplomatic and military support rendered by the USSR to the Nigerian federal government during the civil war did not, after 1970, turn Nigeria into a Soviet outpost in West Africa is a statement that is by now outdated.[7] The acquisition of Soviet arms had been in the form of a commercial transaction, involving the payment of hard cash in most cases, thereby limiting the extent of dependence and hence of influence possibilities for the Soviets. It is not, however, incorrect to say that Nigerians were likely to feel a psychological indebtedness to the USSR for some time, especially because Soviet military assistance was a decisive factor in reviving the sunken morale of the Federalists, both soldiers and civilians. This was especially so given the timing of the assistance; it came at a time when the federal government felt handicapped due to the arms embargo imposed by the United States and the exceedingly pro-Biafran propaganda activities of private groups in both the United States and Great Britain. However, what ultimately served as the effective guarantee of Nigeria's independence in its dealings with the USSR after 1970 consisted of the same basic conditions that affected the Nigerian-U.S. bilateral relations in this period.

In June 1973, the federal government took action to impress Nigeria's independent stance upon the Soviets. Gowon's first official visit to Europe after the civil war was to Great Britain (despite strained relations with the British during the war) and not to the USSR. (He traveled there the following year.) Many informed Nigerians were critical of Gowon's visit to Great Britain and felt it was a signal of ingratitude to the Soviet government, but the point was made.[8]

In a larger sense, Nigerian decisionmakers seemed to have derived from the experience of alignment with the Soviet Union during the civil war a more profound understanding of the nature of international politics and the limits of a dependent foreign policy. The director of the American Department of the Ministry of External Affairs, H. Bello Musa, reflected,

> The unexpected pro-Federal role by the Soviets provided a learning experience about the realities of world politics, potential constraints on foreign policy and the imperative of certain actions, the value of pursuing a relatively independent policy orientation in relations with the super-powers; and above all, about the necessity of developing independent sources of powers.[9]

The thinking subsumed in this observation has since 1970 formed a substantial basis of Nigeria's ties to the Soviet Union in the military and technological fields. For the first time since independence, the Nigerian government officially sanctioned the need to strengthen seriously relations with the Soviets in those areas in which it was ideologically feasible to do so. But priority was accorded military and technological links. Militarily, Nigeria, for instance, continued to purchase almost all of its jets from the Soviet Union, an arrangement that began during the civil war. The Nigerian government also financed a program for the training of air force pilots and related personnel, which was conducted both in Nigeria and in the Soviet Union.[10]

In the technical sphere, Soviet assistance was prominent in two strategic areas. First, Soviet experts have been associated with the construction of the massive iron and steel complex at Ajaokuta, in the central part of Nigeria. This has been an ongoing activity since 1970. Second, and equally significant, Soviet technical aid has been linked to the growth of the Nigerian oil industry. In May 1973, Nigerian authorities signed an agreement with the Soviet Union in which the latter pledged to assist the NNOC in conducting offshore seismic work as well as to furnish all the needed equipment. During the previous year, another bilateral agreement had provided for the establishment of a petroleum training institute in Warri to be run by Technoexport, a Soviet state enterprise.[11] By April 1975, about thirty Soviet instructors and lecturers were said to be working at the institute, which was to train about five hundred technicians at a time.[12] Another Soviet enterprise was a 900-kilometer oil pipeline linking Warri to Ilorin via Lagos.[13]

The promotion of Soviet ties in these two fields was justified as a hedge against possible future constraints that might be imposed on Nigeria's freedom of action (including actions in foreign affairs) as a result of its still overwhelming social, economic, and technological links with the West. (An element of the "once burned" syndrome dictated this strategy.) In theoretic terms, Nigeria's modest effort to involve Soviet technical and scientific expertise in the development of the strategic sectors of petroleum and iron and steel signaled an awareness of the risk of overdependence on the West as well as the necessity of advancing an independent technological capability.

Overall, the pattern of external relationship that emerged appeared to be the rudiment of what may be called the "Indian Model": maintaining basic economic, ideological, and intellectual ties with the United States while simultaneously involving the Soviet Union in key areas of national development, such as defense and the acquisition of technology. The government's long-range purpose, among the other goals, was to strengthen Nigeria's capacity as an evolving regional power to act more independently in African affairs.[14]

The Rhodesian Conflict: UN Sanctions
and the Byrd Amendment, 1971–1973

Although the constitutional impasse in Southern Rhodesia (now Zimbabwe) caused by Prime Minister Ian D. Smith's unilateral declaration of independence (UDI) in 1965 was in theory a British problem, the conflict it engendered became an irksome element in Nigerian-U.S. regional relations after 1971. The specific aspect of that problem examined here is the issue of the implementation of UN-mandated sanctions by the United States. To Nigeria, the continued observance of UN-mandated sanctions by the United States against the Smith regime was a concrete test of U.S. commitment to majority rule in Rhodesia—the prime Nigerian objective in the crisis.

After the announcement of UDI in Rhodesia on November 11, 1965, the UN Security Council, at Great Britain's request, met and passed Resolution 232, which called for mandatory economic sanctions (on selected items) against the illegal regime in Salisbury. The declaration of independence by Ian Smith on behalf of the minority European population constituted a rebellion against the British Crown and was an affront to Africans, within and outside Rhodesia, who had expected majority rule before the colonial territory became independent of Great Britain. In May 1968, these sanctions were made comprehensive by Security Council Resolution 253.[15] On both occasions the United States joined Great Britain in working, and voting, for the council measures. To make the sanctions operative in the United States, Lyndon Johnson issued Executive Orders 11322 of January 1967 and 11417 of July 1968.[16] And by all accounts, the U.S. government was meticulous in its enforcement of these comprehensive UN-mandated economic actions against the recalcitrant state.

One of the trade items embargoed by the Security Council resolutions and the two U.S. executive orders was chrome. Yet, by 1970, demand for lifting the ban against importation of Rhodesian chrome and indeed the desirability of continuing the observance of the UN sanctions became a controversial political issue in the U.S. Congress. Why? And what effect did this have on Nigerian-U.S. relations concerning decolonization in Southern Rhodesia?[17]

The Issue of Chrome and UN Sanctions

The U.S. government was put in the uncomfortable position of contravening UN sanctions against Rhodesia when President Nixon signed into law on November 17, 1971, the Byrd Amendment.[18] The amendment authorized the importation from Rhodesia of seventy-two "strategic and critical material[s]" into the United States. The most important of these were chrome, ferrochrome, and nickel. In early 1972, the first shipment of Rhodesian chrome arrived at a port in Louisiana.[19] The formal argument of supporters of the amendment was that chrome was a strategic and critical material and that the United States should not have to rely on its importation from the Soviet Union when an alternative and more dependable source existed in a "free world" country. Thus, the issue became couched in terms of national security needs and anticommunism—a proposition that most members of Congress found inconvenient to challenge even in 1971—rather than in terms of opposition to participation in the UN sanctions. Still more significant, Senator Byrd had managed to attach his amendment to a military procurement act already approved by the House and under consideration by the Senate Armed Services Committee.[20]

News of the amendment seemed to receive its first public airing in Nigeria the day before President Nixon signed it into law. On November 16, a commentator on the National Broadcasting Corporation (NBC) radio program "Newstalk" declared that the United States was about to import chrome from Rhodesia.[21] This report did not immediately arouse public passion, but the news soon would because of a separate development also linked to Rhodesia. In the same month, Great Britain's new Tory government under Prime Minister Edward Heath was making another effort at ending the Rhodesian rebellion peacefully. The result was the Home-Smith Agreement, which received almost worldwide condemnation because its implementation would have indefinitely postponed majority African control of the Rhodesian government.[22] Given the timing and nature of the agreement, already regarded as a sellout

by Africans, Nigerians quickly linked it to the Byrd Amendment, establishing an Anglo-American collusion in Rhodesia. The Nigerian
government, meanwhile, took time to study the development before
confronting U.S. officials.

Criticism of the amendment in the Nigerian press increased toward
the end of November and reached a crescendo after the first shipment
of chrome arrived in the United States. An editorial in the November
25 *New Nigerian* attributed both the Home-Smith Agreement and the
Byrd Amendment to "white racial and commercial solidarity." The
editorial concluded that Africans in Rhodesia should "now rise and
regain their independence."[23] A less emotional appraisal and one of
particular concern to the U.S. embassy was an article written in *The
Daily Times* by Dr. O. Ojedokun, then acting director-general of the
Institute of International Affairs. Ojedokun explained the amendment
in terms of U.S. "malignant unconcern" for Africa. He noted that the
U.S. stockpile of chrome was in excess of its emergency needs and that
prior to the UN sanctions the United States was importing a sizeable
proportion of its chrome from the Soviet Union. After this essentially
accurate argument, Ojedokun continued by seeking to match the public
mood; he too hinted at the possibility of a "conspiracy" between the
United States and Great Britain.[24] U.S. embassy officials in Lagos were
worried about these public comments because Ojedokun was said to
be a "respected commentator on foreign affairs . . . and influential
among [Nigerian] intellectuals."[25] Moreover, given his formal position,
his views could influence the government.

By focusing single-mindedly on the immediate damage done by the
Byrd Amendment, Nigerian commentators failed to trace the amendment
to its original source—Option 2 of the Kissinger study. This also accounted
for the unnecessary attempt to relate the U.S. action to the Home-Smith
Agreement.[26] In a sense, this was unavoidable since the existence of the
Kissinger study (National Security Study Memorandum 39, NSSM 39)
and its recommended option was not known (even to most U.S. writers)
until 1974. But the basic outlines of the Nixon administration's policy
on southern Africa had been apparent since the end of 1970. For example,
the new policy was clearly the underlying rationale for the granting of
exceptional right to Union Carbide to import chrome from Rhodesia
that allegedly had been paid for prior to the executive order of 1967.[27]
The administration had in 1970 already decided to slacken sanctions
against Rhodesia, before the amendment became an issue. Senator Byrd,
who was provided tangible information by Union Carbide with which
to defend his bill, was merely taking his cue from a sympathetic White
House.

Nigeria Protests Officially

In late March, Nigeria's commissioner for external affairs, Dr. Okoi Arikpo, lodged the first government protest against the Byrd Amendment and the resumption of chrome import from Rhodesia. This was to be the first stage in an unusually coordinated effort by the Nigerian federal government to put pressure on the United States to stop further importation of the offending material if the amendment itself could not be repealed. The protest note that Arikpo presented, in his characteristically gentle manner, to Ambassador Rheinhardt came directly from General Gowon. Rheinhardt was asked, in a language reflecting the self-assuredness described in the last chapter, to convey "to the highest level of your government" official Nigerian dissatisfaction with "any American policy" that permits importation of Rhodesian chrome.[28] Gowon believed that the U.S. action would encourage other nations to publicly violate sanctions and that Ian Smith would read more into the U.S. action than America's good intentions. According to Gowon, Smith would only become more obdurate, believing that he now had the support of the United States. Arikpo then added extemporaneously, "Please convey to your government [Nigeria's] urgent request that the U.S. government not permit another ship to dock at American ports with Rhodesian chrome."[29]

To Rheinhardt, the tone of this message was quite unsettling. In fact, he sounded rather despondent in attempting to transmit to Washington a message whose content he was convinced represented "official and unofficial Nigerian sentiment on an issue destined to give [the United States] more and more trouble."[30] What made the experience more confounding to U.S. envoys in Lagos was the fact that they had already used up all the "background" information suggested by the State Department to explain the meaning of the amendment to Nigerian officials at a time when the latter were still merely studying the unfolding problem. Besides, UN ambassador George Bush had recently traveled to Lagos from New York to explain the chrome situation in great detail to influential Nigerians.[31] In the end, Rheinhardt could only ask Washington for a new set of facts with which to defend his position in Nigeria.

On the day after Arikpo's meeting with Rheinhardt, Edwin Ogbu, Nigeria's permanent envoy to the UN, presented yet another letter of protest to Bush. The latter responded on March 17, essentially emphasizing his and Rheinhardt's previous arguments.[32] The extent of the strain caused by the importation of chrome was indicated by the fact that the Nigerian Ministry of External Affairs decided to release to the press the texts of the two confidential diplomatic exchanges between

Ogbu and Bush. By this act, the ruling government won high credit with the public on its decolonization policy.

The Second Chrome Shipment and Failure of the McGee Amendment

In early April, another shipment of Rhodesian chrome entered the United States for Union Carbide. Nigerian newspapers quickly carried the news. This time, their editorials reflected frustration more than anger, which had been well spent following the initial chrome development. The *Morning Post*, in its editorial of April 10, conveyed this somber mood, claiming that the United States had displayed a "nonchalant" attitude toward African protests and that the UN secretary-general should take action against the United States for defying the United Nations.[33]

Meanwhile, on May 31, the U.S. Senate voted to delete from a major authorization bill an amendment that had earlier been attached thereto by Senator Gale W. McGee, chairman of the Senate Sub-Committee on Africa. The object of McGee's effort was the repeal of the Byrd Amendment.[34] Senator McGee, a strong believer in U.S. leadership at the United Nations on the issue of Rhodesian sanctions, asserted that he had received an unfulfilled pledge of support from the White House before initiating his action in the Senate. The failure of McGee's effort led to a more severe reaction by the Nigerian government following the second chrome shipment. This time Gowon personally confronted Ambassador Rheinhardt. The chief U.S. envoy, who had gone to see Gowon to discuss "our China breakthrough," instead received a harsh lecture from the normally mild general on U.S. relations with the regime of Ian Smith in Rhodesia. With full passion, Gowon stated that southern Africa, "is just as important to Nigeria . . . as Vietnam and China are to the U.S. For some reason, Americans never seem to be able to appreciate this fact. By importing chrome [from Rhodesia], the U.S. has cast its lot with the U.K. in creating legalities out of illegalities [a reference to the Home-Smith Agreement]."[35]

When the first attempt to repeal the Byrd Amendment ended in failure, the Nigerian ambassador in Washington, acting in concert with a number of other African diplomats as well as with the Congressional Black Caucus, Senate liberals, and the State Department mounted a major lobbying campaign in Congress aimed at overturning the legislation. In late 1973, the Senate voted to repeal the amendment, but on September 25, 1975, the House of Representatives refused to follow suit, voting against a repeal. However, with the lobbying campaign in Congress, Nigeria demonstrated its willingness to carry the chrome fight directly to the center of the people's power in the United States. This was a self-confident action and the first by a Nigerian government.[36] It symbolized, quite apart from its visible impact, an urge to portray Nigeria's economic self-importance to the American public. But it was also an alternative to adopting drastic measures of reprisals, such as economic boycotts, that might have damaged Nigeria's relationship with the United States in oil.

The Angola Crisis, 1975–1976

The preceding account of Nigerian-U.S. diplomacy regarding the chrome issue clarifies an important point about the nature of the political relations between these countries in the post-1970 period, especially over the problem of decolonization. It is now clear that the difficulties experienced by the two countries in this sphere did not start with the much-publicized confrontation during the Angola crisis.[37] Rather, the difficulty was built into the altered structure of their bilateral economic ties, and its origin could be traced to 1970. The eruption in relations over Angola could be regarded as the climax of that trend. This is why emphasis is given in this section of the analysis to the Rhodesian chrome case and not the Angola crisis, though both are important in illustrating the thesis.

One minor qualification should be made to the point raised above. To say that the strain in political relations was a function of changes in the bilateral dimension might not mean that this outcome was inevitable through an organic logic. Incessant conflicts became inevitable because U.S. officials were naturally not yet willing to concede, as explained in Chapter 5, the new bilateral reality in their relationship with Nigeria—especially since it deprived them of a traditional leverage for modifying Nigerian policy behavior—and because Nigerian decisionmakers tended to be highly compulsive in demonstrating their new sense of independence.

The Alvor Accord and Nigeria's Position:
January–November 1975

From the signing of the abortive Alvor Accord[38] in January 1975 to Portugal's hurried granting of independence to the territory of Angola in November 1975, Nigeria's policy aimed clearly at unifying the three competing nationalist groups—the Popular Movement for the Liberation of Angola (MPLA), the National Front for the Independence of Angola (FNLA), and the National Union for the Total Independence of Angola (UNITA)—toward the objective of forming an Angolan government of national unity. In hindsight, it is possible to fault this policy, for it was apparently based on an assumption that failed to account for the deep political, ideological, and ethnic schisms between the three movements.[39] However, the policy was generally in accordance with the new leadership profile described earlier and also reflected Nigeria's experience with multiethnic political coexistence. Moreover, it conformed with the consensus of OAU opinion in this period, as revealed most clearly at the Kampala Summit in August 1975.[40]

The Murtala Mohammed government, which replaced the Gowon government pursued even more vigorously the policy of reconciliation among the feuding Angolan nationalists. Three days before Angola's independence on November 11, the new commissioner for external affairs, Colonel Joseph Garba, undertook a tour of the Congo (Brazzaville), Zaire, Zambia, Tanzania, and Uganda. His mission was to convince the leaders of those countries to support Nigeria's proposal for a postponement of Angola's independence for three weeks until the three liberation groups could be reconciled and a government of national unity formed.[41] The commissioner publicly chastised the Soviet Union for assisting the MPLA—an action he thought would make reconciliation more difficult. In fact, even after Portugal had withdrawn, as planned, by offering independence to Angola, Garba was still, on November 21, cautioning the OAU against recognizing only one of the movements.[42]

Garba was, of course, toeing the line prescribed by the traditionalist bureaucrats in his Ministry of External Affairs who, apart from being ideologically pro-West in their policy orientation, had sympathy for the FNLA with whom they had established contact since the early 1960s. They probably also were convinced that an all-party government would prevent a civil war and an escalation of foreign intervention in Angola. But this position did not receive unanimous approval within the Nigerian government.[43] For example, within the Supreme Military Council, Mohammed (the head of state), Brigadier Olusegun Obasanjo (his deputy), and M. D. Yusuf (the inspector-general of police) were known to favor an alternative policy requiring immediate recognition of the MPLA and an end to the OAU mediation effort. By this time, news of South African military assistance and of CIA activities on behalf of the two opposing movements was gaining ground in the country. Given this information, the articulate public became less disturbed by simultaneous reports of a Soviet-Cuban role in favor of the MPLA. The South African intervention, along with speculations in the foreign and domestic press about a possible U.S. collaboration, was henceforth the central focus of public attention. The stage was thus set for the government to change course in Angola.

November–January 1976: Confrontation
with the United States

The Nigerian government had been well aware of the South African problem but had hoped to circumvent it by rallying the fractious Angolans together. On the day of Angola's independence, a Nigerian fact-finding delegation arrived in Luanda to verify South African activities. On returning to Lagos, it confirmed that South Africa had in fact intervened militarily. Still, the Nigerian leadership tried to avoid any drastic change of policy that might cause dissension in the OAU. Rather, it approached the U.S. government sometime in mid-November and asked the United States to use its influence to effect South Africa's military withdrawal.[44]

Since Ambassador Easum's arrival in Nigeria in mid-1975, his paramount task had been to work for normalization in Nigerian-U.S. relations, especially in the political sphere. He had just begun to make some headway (and might personally have played a restraining role on Nigeria's Angola policy before November), but the issues surrounding the Angola crisis would set that process back. Secretary of State Kissinger responded to Nigeria's request by treating Angola as a U.S.-Soviet concern rather than an African problem in which Nigeria had a legitimate interest. This position was contrary to the embassy's recommendation, which stressed consultation with Nigeria.[45] On November 26, Nigeria reacted by recognizing the MPLA administration in Luanda as the only legal authority in Angola. On December 2, Mohammed, the Nigerian leader, sent a personal message "to the people of Angola," pledging material and moral support until "your struggle succeeds."[46] Thereafter, Nigeria offered the MPLA government, among other support, $20 million in nonrefundable financial aid and pledged, in addition, $100 million credit in foreign reserves[47] for the purchase of military arms.

As part of these developments, the Nigerian government declared publicly its support for Soviet-Cuban military assistance to the MPLA and rejected Kissinger's suggestion that withdrawal of South African troops from Angola be linked to the withdrawal of other foreign (Soviet-Cuban) troops.[48] Nigeria also embarked on a diplomatic offensive to persuade other OAU members to adopt its new policy. In an unprecedented manner, envoys were dispatched to many African states to explain Nigeria's change of policy. This pro-MPLA diplomatic campaign was promoted both before and after the extraordinary summit of the OAU, held January 11–13, 1976, to consider the Angola situation. (The result of the conference was that twenty-two members voted for recognition of the MPLA government, twenty-two withheld recognition, and zero recognized the rival government formed by the coalition of the FNLA and UNITA—an outcome that the Nigerian government claimed as victory for its policy.)

The nadir of the conflict over Angola between Nigeria and the United States occurred with respect to a confidential letter sent by President Gerald Ford to most OAU members, including Nigeria, about one week before the OAU meeting.[49] It was in this letter that the United States proposed the linkage of Soviet-Cuban troop withdrawal to that of South Africa. The reaction in Lagos was sharp. Relations between the two countries had never sunk so low. Mohammed saw the Ford letter as an "attempt . . . to insult the intelligence of the African nations and the dignity of the black man."[50] He charged that Ford "has not only dispatched an envoy on an arm-twisting mission to Africa but has also addressed an over-bearing circular letter to all Heads of State of African countries."[51] And so, as the Angolan civil war raged, Nigeria's political relations with the United States slipped precipitously to a point of utter hostility.

It is important to place the Nigerian reaction to the South African military intervention in Angola in the general perspective of this chapter. First, whether South Africa had intervened with U.S. knowledge or not, the action was seen in Lagos as flowing from the prescribed policy of the United States toward southern Africa (refer to the Kissinger study). Second, South Africa's involvement in Angola contravened a critical interest of Nigeria in the decolonization process of southern Africa. The occupation of southern Angola by South African troops was regarded in Lagos as an initial step toward a planned design to establish a pliant state in Angola under South Africa's tutelage. Such an advance northward by South Africa would not only thwart the decolonization effort in the subregion, but would also pose a physical threat to Nigeria in the long run, given the deep antagonism between the two countries. Third, the Angola experience once again confirms what has been said about the pattern of Nigerian-U.S. regional relations in the period 1970–1976, i.e., that it tended toward greater conflict than cooperation in contrast to the immediate post-independence period.

Summary

Nigeria-U.S. relations with regard to regional policy in this period were marked by a greater tendency toward discord than cooperation. Above all, the source of this conflictive relationship was the profound determination on the part of Nigeria to exert its leadership responsibility in the movement of regional decolonization independent of U.S. resources and prescription.

Nigeria's policy on decolonization became more intimately interwoven, during the Mohammed-Obasanjo regime, with a new conception of national security interest and with a rejuvenated desire to extend national influence and prestige throughout sub-Saharan Africa. The postwar activist orientation in the decolonization process was most graphically demonstrated in Nigeria's diplomacy during Angola's civil war and transition to independence. But the difficulty earlier encountered by Nigeria and the United States over the issue of chrome and UN sanctions against Rhodesia significantly heightened the discordant trend in their regional policies after 1970. This pattern of Nigeria-U.S. political relations did not, however, commence with the much-publicized confrontation in the Angolan conflict; rather, it was an outcome of the altered structure of bilateral ties that was traced to 1970. The violent clash over Angola clearly represented the highest point of that trend.

Despite the decisive military assistance offered to the Nigerian federal government by the USSR during the civil war, Nigeria did not become, consequently, a Soviet outpost in West Africa. The Soviet assistance had no impact whatsoever on, for instance, the basic capitalist structures in the Nigerian society. The autonomy of Nigerian leaders in their dealings with Soviet officials in this period was guaranteed by the postwar conditions of financial opulence and political self-confidence, although most Nigerians felt a psychological indebtedness to the USSR for its all-round defense of Nigerian territorial unity during the conflict.

Soviet involvement in the Nigerian civil war, moreover, left a permanent imprint: It engendered a new conceptual awareness among the Nigerian public and policymakers regarding the inherent danger to sovereign Nigeria in maintaining exclusive ties of dependence to the United States and the West in general. The decision to seek Soviet technical assistance in the metallurgical and oil industries, as well as in the military field, emanated from this new consciousness.

Notes

1. It was not that the Balewa regime did not identify with the independence aspiration of Africa, although that identification might have been circumscribed ideologically and by the nature of external alignment. Neither can it be said that the Balewa leadership did not appreciate the region as one in which its primary interests were located—its decolonization policy, as illustrated previously, was guided by the need to safeguard such interests.

The contrast lies in the fact that the postwar regimes sought to adopt less of a cold war approach to decolonization, recognizing decolonization intrinsically as a regional problem. One particular reason for the change was that Nigerians on the federal side during the civil war were shocked to realize that none of the four African states that accorded recognition to Biafra belonged to the group conventionally referred to as radical.

2. It seems to this writer that much of the intellectual discussion by local and foreign commentators about Nigeria's role in Africa in the latter period is still mired in the pre-1966 paradigm of pro-West, pro-East. There is a lack of

serious effort to assess, more perceptively, the forces (internal and regional) that shape Nigeria's interest in this process, especially in light of objective developments since 1970. An analysis that reflects this awareness is A. B. Akinyemi, "Nigerian Foreign Policy 1975: A Nation Reborn, National Interest Re-defined" (unpublished), Nigerian Institute of International Affairs, Victoria Island, Lagos.

3. "U.S. Policy Towards Africa," *Hearings Before the Sub-Committee on African Affairs*, 94th Congress, Second Session, March and May 1976 (Washington, D.C.: U.S. Government Printing Office, 1976), p. 168.

4. On the text of National Security Study Memorandum 39 (NSSM 39) and its complete list of recommendations, see M. A. El-Khawas and Barry Cohen, eds., *The Kissinger Study of Southern Africa* (Westport, Conn.: Lawrence Hill & Company, 1976) (hereinafter, *The Kissinger Study*); Anthony Lake, *The "Tar Baby" Option: American Policy Toward Southern Rhodesia* (New York: Columbia University Press, 1976), especially Chapters 4–7. Various views on U.S. southern Africa policy in this period are contained in "U.S. Policy Toward Southern Africa," *Hearings Before the Sub-Committee on Foreign Relations, United States Senate*, 94th Congress, First Session, June–July, 1975.

5. True, Nigeria still espoused the principles instituted in the OAU Charter, such as noninterference in domestic affairs of other members and equality of member states. And some Nigerians have argued that since those principles served Nigeria well during the civil war, by deterring African recognition of Biafra, a proposition that is debatable, the Nigerian government should adhere to them even more strictly. Paradoxically, forces released by the civil war in the country coupled with the accelerated development of Nigeria's material resources relative to many of the weaker members of the OAU did not enhance undilated conformity with rules that have become sterile in a very dynamic regional environment. See Olajide Aluko, "Nigeria's Role in Inter-African Relations with Special Reference to the Organization of African Unity," *African Affairs* 72 (287) (April 1973): 160–162; and Okoi Arikpo, "Nigeria and the Organization of African Unity," *Nigerian Journal of International Affairs* 1(1) (July 1965): 1–11.

6. O. Aluko, "Nigeria, the United States and Southern Africa," *African Affairs* 78(310) (January 1979): 94; Arikpo, "Nigeria and the Organization of African Unity," p. 7.

7. The Soviet Union supplied the federal government with a number of jet aircraft including MIGs 17 and 21, with heavy 122-mm artillery guns, and with a team of military technical advisers. Confidential source, Department of State, Washington, D.C.; also *Africa Diary*, February 19–25, 1970, p. 4842.

8. *Nigeria: Bulletin on Foreign Affairs* 3 (1-4) (January-December 1973): 158–159; *New Nigerian*, June 21, 1973, pp. 5–6.

9. Interview, August 22, 1978, Lagos.

10. Nigeria also financed an officer-training program in the United States. See "U.S. Policy Toward Africa," *Hearings*, March and May 1976, pp. 175–176; Interview with John Foley, former desk officer, Nigeria, Department of State, May 30, 1979, Washington, D.C.

11. United Nations Conference on Trade and Development, *Prospects for Trade and Economic Cooperation Between Nigeria and the Socialist Countries of*

Eastern Europe (New York: UNCTAD Secretariat, United Nations, 1979), pp. 15–17.

12. Ibid., p. 17.

13. Ibid., and *African Development* 7 (August 1973): 11.

14. *New York Times*, May 29, 1980, p. A10; and Bhabani Sen Gupta, "Waiting for India: India's Role as a Regional Power," *Journal of International Affairs* 29(2) (Fall 1975): 171–184.

15. Cited in *The Kissinger Study*, p. 144.

16. Lake, *The "Tar Baby" Option*, Appendices 2 and 3, pp. 295–300.

17. The "chrome" story as related by Anthony Lake (note 16) is another intriguing exposition of interagency as well as intragovernmental politicking over an aspect of U.S. foreign policy. Much of the circumstances concerning the subject at hand has been well covered in the Lake book. (Lake was a privileged insider.) Wherever it was necessary in the following discussion to refer to specific aspects of the controversy ensuing in the United States, the accounts in the *The "Tar Baby" Option* were relied upon. The central interest, however, is to review the Nigerian-U.S. diplomacy concerning this episode.

18. The Byrd Amendment (hereinafter referred to as the amendment), named after its main author, Senator Harry F. Byrd, Independent from Virginia, was passed by Congress on November 11.

19. Lake, *The "Tar Baby" Option*, pp. 198–238.

20. Ibid., pp. 204–205.

21. Discussions on this program, as U.S. envoys in Lagos realized, were usually a fair indicator of the government's thinking on an important issue.

22. The agreement reached between British foreign minister Sir Alec Douglas-Home and Ian Smith was rejected overwhelmingly by the African majority. This was the finding of the Pearce Commission, formed to seek the view of the Africans. The commission also reported that Africans strongly preferred a continuation of UN sanctions. See Lake, *The "Tar Baby" Option*, p. 45; A. B. Akinyemi, "The Home-Smith Rhodesian Proposals: A Sell-Out," *Nigeria: Bulletin on Foreign Affairs* 1 (January 1972): 9–15.

23. *New Nigerian* (editorial), November 25, 1971.

24. *The Daily Times*, March 15, 1972.

25. Rheinhardt to Rogers, March 15, 1972, Telegram no. 2200, Department of State Files (hereinafter, DSF), Washington, D.C.

26. The point is that it was not necessary to link the two developments in order to establish the change in U.S. policy. But, in fact, President Nixon and his aides had been discussing Rhodesia with the Tory leadership, especially Mr. Heath and Lord Home, before the British elections of June 1970. See Lake, *The "Tar Baby" Option*, pp. 140–141.

27. Ibid., pp. 148–157.

28. Rheinhardt to Rogers, March 23, 1972, Telegram no. 2466, DSF; Confidential interview.

29. Telegram no. 2466 (note 28, supra).

30. Ibid.

31. Ambassador Bush had met with top state personnel, representatives of the press, and the academic elite. But his explanation—essentially, that the

amendment was a law passed by Congress and as such the executive branch could not interfere with it—was not convincing, in view of what his audience already knew about the position of the president on sanctions and southern Africa in general. Bush's visit had been made before the first shipment of chrome arrived in the United States. Somehow, the Nigerian government still could not imagine, at this time, the U.S. president actually permitting Rhodesian chrome to be imported, despite the amendment. Hence, the news of the first shipment came as a shock, as reflected in Gowon's message.

32. Bush to Rogers, March 24, 1972, Telegram no. 1092, and Bush to Rogers, March 28, 1972, Telegram no. 1118, both in DSF. See also *The New Nigerian,* April 6, 1972.

33. *The Morning Post* (editorial), April 10, 1972; *Nigerian Observer* (editorial), April 10, 1972.

34. Lake, *The "Tar Baby" Option,* pp. 215–216; and G. W. McGee, "The U.S. Congress and the Rhodesian Chrome Issue," *Issues* 2(2) (Summer 1972): 2–7.

35. Rheinhardt to Rogers, April 7, 1972, Telgram no. 2917, DSF; Interview with Foley.

36. Interview with Foley.

37. Some commentators in the aftermath of that crisis sought to give that impression. See, for example, commentary by Colin Legum, *New York Times,* January 11, 1976, p. 3.

38. The Alvor Accord, signed on January 15, 1975, between Portugal and the three opposing nationalist movements bound the latter to participate with the Portuguese in a transitional government pending independence in November and to compete peacefully in elections to the held in October. *Africa Contemporary Record, 1974–75,* pp. C221–226.

Useful commentary on the Angola crisis can be found in John A. Marcum, *The Angolan Revolution,* Vol. 2 (Cambridge, Mass.: The MIT Press, 1978); Nathaniel Davies, "The Angola Decision: A Personal Memoir," *Foreign Affairs* (Fall 1978): 109–125; John Stockwell, *In Search of Enemies: A CIA Story* (New York: W. W. Norton & Company Inc., 1978); "U.S. Involvement in Civil War in Angola," *Hearings Before the Sub-Committee on African Affairs, Committee on Foreign Relations, United States Senate,* 94th Congress, 2nd Session, January–February, 1976.

39. Under the Gowon regime, which ended in a bloodless coup on July 29, 1975, it was asserted that Nigeria showed early inclination toward UNITA, perhaps because that party had the widest mass following in Angola. *Africa Contemporary Record, 1975–1976,* p. A7.

40. Colin Legum and Tony Hodges, *Africa and Angola: The War over Southern Africa* (New York: African Publishing Company, 1978), p. 67.

41. Federal Ministry of Information, Lagos, New Release no. 1359, November 8, 1975.

42. Federal Ministry of Information, Lagos, New Release no. 1428, November 21, 1975; *Daily Times* (editorial), November 11, 1975.

43. Alaba Ogunsanwo, "The Nigerian Military and Foreign Policy, 1975-76" (Unpublished manuscript, University of Lagos, Political Science Department), p. 25; *New Nigerian,* November 17, 1975.

44. Confidential interview. Before this action the Nigerian government had confronted the U.S. ambassador, Donald Easum, with evidence of South African troops' penetration deep into Angola's territory.

45. *Hearings, Sub-Committee on African Affairs*, March and May 1976, pp. 170–171; and Easum to Kissinger, January 19, 1976, Telegram no. 00683, DSF.

46. *Nigeria: Bulletin on Foreign Affairs* 5(3,4) (August-December 1975): 89; *African Contemporary Record*, 1975–1976, pp. B798–800.

47. *African Contemporary Record*, 1975–1976, p. B799; Ogunsanwo, "The Nigerian Military," p. 28.

48. Interview with Robert Bruce, political counselor, American embassy (1975–1976), November 17, 1978, Washington, D.C.

49. Federal Ministry of Information, Lagos, News Release no. 16, January 6, 1976.

50. Ibid.; *Hearings, Sub-Committee on African Affairs*, March and May 1976, p. 171.

51. *Hearings, Sub-Committee on African Affairs*, March and May 1976.

7

The Promise of a Partnership: Obasanjo and Carter, 1977–1979

The distinguishing feature of the Nigerian-U.S. experience in the 1977–1979 period was the mutual confidence, shared particularly by the two ruling governments, in the possibility of a genuine interdependent relationship not only bilaterally but also in the regional sphere. As 1977 progressed, the belief became strengthened that both countries, while acting as independent entities, could forge a partnership that would result in their mutual benefit as well as that of Africa. The United States was willing to concede to Nigeria the position of preeminence in African affairs, and the Nigerian leaders in turn endowed the U.S. claim to Western leadership in Africa with a moral legitimacy. This change in attitude by Nigeria, unlike that exhibited toward the Nixon-Ford administration, can, essentially, be traced to President Carter's avowed commitment to human rights—which applied specifically to racial justice in South Africa as well as majority rule in Rhodesia—and his nonmilitary approach to foreign policy.

Early in 1977, Andrew Young, the chief U.S. envoy to the United Nations and the principal exponent of U.S. policy in Africa during Carter's administration, visited Nigeria several times as part of the process of confidence-building and, specifically, to discuss the framework of the ensuing relationship. Young's task, considering the rigidity of relations in the previous period, was not simplified merely by the fact that he is an Afro-American but rather because he was actually effective at this early stage in convincing the Nigerian leadership that Carter's commitments to human rights and his diplomatic approach to foreign policy ran parallel to Nigeria's interests both in securing majority rule in white-ruled southern Africa and in upholding Africa's independence relative to superpower interventions in regional conflicts.[1] In Washington, White House and State Department officials worked successfully to repeal the Byrd Amendment, which had been a serious irritant in U.S.-

African relations during the previous administration. This was followed by Obasanjo's state visit to the United States in October and President Carter's celebrated return visit in early 1978—the first official visit by a U.S. president to black Africa. These events, among others, nurtured the climate of confidence that made it possible for the two countries to work jointly on such regional problems as the Rhodesian and Namibian independence negotiations, the Ogaden conflict, and Shaba I and II (the military incursions into Zaire's Shaba province by Angolan-based Katangese insurgents in 1977 and 1978) and also in resolving outstanding bilateral difficulties that had previously obstructed the expansion of their economic relations.

The burst of interest and activities that attended Nigerian-U.S. relations on both sides during President Carter's administration certainly presented a remarkable contrast to the situation of suspicion and hostility that existed before 1977. As demonstrated in Chapters 5 and 6, the Nigeria-U.S. relationship, which since the end of Nigeria's civil war had been defined, paradoxically, by a basic pattern of economic coexistence and political conflict, came to a head under the brief leadership of Murtala Mohammed. It reached a definite climax during the Angola crisis and the violent mass reaction in Nigeria to the allegation of U.S. complicity in Mohammed's assassination in February 1976.[2] Additional evidence of the incompatible political objectives of Nigeria and the United States (and an unprecedented determination on the part of Nigeria to pursue its independent objectives) during that period was the fact that Kissinger was denied entry into Nigeria on three separate occasions. To Nigerians, the U.S. secretary of state personified, because he was its principal formulator, the highly detested U.S. policy on Africa during that period.[3]

The Philosophical Premise of Carter's Policy

From the outset of his administration, Jimmy Carter's thinking and policy course on Africa were influenced by the conflicting pressures of two broad philosophical approaches to U.S. foreign policy: the global-strategic and the regional-diplomatic. The first claims, in application to Africa, to derive from a "realistic" appreciation of what constitutes U.S. interests in the continent, the pertinent obstacles to the realization of those interests, and the most effective protective measures to adopt. Proponents tend to view African (regional) problems in light of the "larger" East-West strategic and ideological competition. In the formulation of U.S. policy, they habitually understress local roots of regional conflicts as well as the autonomous interests of regional entities. This characteristic stems from an inherent colonialist disposition on the part of U.S. policymakers to impose a Western perception of regional security on Third World countries—a disposition that in turn has influenced the postwar preoccupation of U.S. policymakers with constructing a Western-directed security order in Third World regions. The material basis of this tenacious concern is, no doubt, as noted in Chapter 1, the fact that vital Western interests are in the direct assault path of the movement of decolonization. Furthermore, proponents of this approach attach a profound importance to demonstrating U.S. power and influence, especially in the Third World, through the regular application of military forces; they, in fact, pay little regard to what are considered moral and "idealistic" concerns in conceptualizing U.S. global interests and in the execution of policy.

The second approach, by contrast, takes as its conceptual starting point the fact that most African conflicts can be explained in the context of the African decolonization experience. Local conflicts, therefore, have mainly local roots and are not merely traceable to the "evil conduct" of the Soviet Union and its allies. To ensure U.S. strategic and Western interests, "the most effective policies toward Africa," according to Carter's secretary of state, Cyrus Vance, "are affirmative policies. . . . A negative, reactive American policy that seeks only to oppose Soviet or Cuban involvement in Africa would be both dangerous and futile. Our best course is to help resolve the problems which create opportunities for external intervention."[4] To advocates of this approach, of which Vance was undoubtedly the leading voice within the administration, the essential instruments of policy are diplomacy and a reliance on internal African nationalism to resist the imposition of Soviet will and influence that does not conform to the regional desire for independence. They contend that military force should only be employed, if it must, indeed, be used, strictly as an adjunct of a "diplomatic" policy strategy and not as an end in itself. An Africa policy (and, indeed, policy toward the Third World in general), they argue, must be infused with a strong commitment to human rights and racial justice based on U.S. norms and ideals.[5]

The regional-diplomatic approach was strongly favored and recommended to Carter by Africanists mainly in the State Department and academia. However, there were also advocates of the global-strategic approach firmly lodged in the National Security Council (NSC). The tension that marked the relationship between Zbigniew Brzezinski, the president's national adviser, and Vance (until his resignation in 1980) was at base a conflict between the two contending policy approaches, which repeatedly pressed on Carter for resolution. The first serious occasion of such conflict occurred in early 1978 and concerned the way the United States should interpret the dramatic intervention of the USSR and Cuba in the Ogaden war and the manner in which the U.S.

government should respond. Characteristically, Brzezinski's viewpoint was that Soviet action was "part of a larger, well-defined strategy" and that such behavior was at variance with the U.S. policy of "balancing competition with cooperation." Consequently, he urged the United States and its allies to take measures to make Soviet "adventurism" more expensive. Vance, on the other hand, was not convinced that Soviet actions (in the horn or elsewhere in Africa) constituted a "grand Soviet plan, but rather attempts to exploit targets of opportunity." He did not believe that Soviet actions were "unimportant" but felt that realism required the United States "to deal with these problems in the local context in which they had their roots." He continued, "This was in keeping with the President's intention, which I shared, that we will not allow ourselves to become so preoccupied with the Soviets that we lose sight of our basic policy objectives in Africa."[6]

From 1977 to 1979, the Africanists successfully asserted control over the direction of U.S. policy in Africa. But this success was buttressed in large measure by the personal stance of the president. From the beginning of his presidency, Carter shared the philosophical premise of the regional-diplomatic proponents with regard to Africa; their moral purpose was in tune with both his human-rights concerns and political sensitivity to black American interests at home and in Africa. Carter's selection of Andrew Young as the U.S. ambassador to the United Nations and key spokesperson for the administration on Africa was a direct result of his basic orientation to U.S.–Third World relations.

The Carter administration's interest in forging a special relationship with Nigeria stemmed from its choice of a regional-diplomatic policy strategy toward the Third World. According to Brzezinski, one of the ten foreign policy goals of the administration (throughout its four-year tenure) was "to weave a worldwide web of bilateral, political, and, where appropriate, economic relations with the new emerging regional 'influential,' thereby widening . . . our earlier reliance on the Atlantic Community."[7] The NSC adviser specified that the goal was to consult "on critical issues with such countries as Venezuela, Brazil, Nigeria, Saudi Arabia, Iran, India, and Indonesia."[8]

For Carter and most of his team, Nigeria eminently qualified as a regional "influential" in Africa. They made this assessment not only on the basis of the traditionally cited attributes of population and economic and human resources potentiality. In addition to these, they attached far greater significance, economically and politically, than the Ford administration had, to Nigeria's position as a leading supplier of crude oil to the United States and to the phenomenal U.S. trade deficit with Nigeria. (This deficit, $10 billion in 1980, was the largest in U.S. experience with any country.) They recalled, in exaggerated terms, the burst of activism that characterized Nigeria's regional policy under Mohammed, specifically the country's historic defiance of President Ford over Angola in 1975. They acclaimed (and indeed valued) the quality of Nigeria's diplomatic assets, including its skilled personnel and material resources as compared to other African states. These assets, backed by Nigeria's "fanatical" commitment to decolonization in southern Africa, transformed Nigeria, in Young's words, into a "virtual partner with the Frontline States at various stages of the negotiations for a settlement [in Zimbabwe]."[9] In their view, moreover, Nigeria had provided "considerable leadership" in the OAU and "dominates the Economic Community of West African States." For these reasons and others, Young concluded, "For the foreseeable future, the achievement of U.S. aims in Africa will require close cooperation with this African giant."[10] Consequently, he called for a durable political and economic partnership between Nigeria and the United States. Carter's historic visit to Nigeria in 1978 was designed to give impetus to the construction of such a partnership.

There is a particular significance, from the point of view of the methodological approach of this study, to the changed U.S. attitude toward Nigeria. The U.S. government, by this change of attitude, had given a clear indication of a readiness to accept Nigeria as an independent political entity—i.e., as an autonomous actor, not an adjunct of Great Britain, with whom it could deal directly on crucial policy matters. (Recall that the U.S. practice in the first decade of Nigeria's sovereignty was to deal with Nigeria indirectly through London.) Brzezinski's statement about the need to widen, "in keeping with historical circumstances, *our earlier* [emphasis added] reliance on the Atlantic Community"[11] referred precisely to this readiness by the United States. Indeed, Carter's perspective about Nigeria's special status in Africa was strengthened when, in 1979, the Obasanjo government unilaterally "vetoed" British policy on Zimbabwe's independence settlement by nationalizing the assets of British Petroleum, "dumping" 500 million pounds sterling on the European currency market, and rejecting "a bid from a British firm for a $200 million port-development project."[12]

John F. Kennedy had made a symbolic start in the early 1960s to steer the United States into a direct relationship, not bound entirely by British consent, with the newly independent Nigeria because he was morally opposed to European colonialism in Africa. Jimmy Carter sought to develop this orientation of direct association with Nigeria, in substance because he was impressed by the country's power potentiality and its utility for U.S. Africa policy. Mainly for this reason, this period was an important one in the development process of Nigerian-U.S. relations.

Resilience of the Bilateral Structure

The U.S. political perception of Nigeria during the Carter period flowed, unambiguously, from a keen appreciation of the changes that took place since 1970 in both the structure of the Nigerian economy and the context of bilateral relations with the United States. When Carter assumed office in 1977, the prevailing assessment in Washington was that Nigeria's economy was basically buoyant and sufficiently resilient to weather short-term problems that might be linked to fluctuations in the price of oil in the world market. This benevolent assessment persisted even though, by 1978, Nigeria had begun to experience serious economic difficulties (for example, a persisting marginal growth in the food sector, increasing balance-of-payment and budget deficits, and higher inflation and unemployment) that led the government to impose a set of highly restrictive economic and monetary measures.[13]

Far more revealing of the severity of the economic situation was the fact that as a result of a relative decline in oil revenues the federal government was forced in 1977–1979, for the first time since the end of Nigeria's civil war, to resort to large-scale foreign borrowing in order to support its capital development projects. Examples of such borrowing include a $1 billion Eurodollar loan signed in 1977; a second loan agreement worth $750 million signed in 1978; and a third loan agreement of about $425 million obtained from West German banks early in 1979. Further, Nigeria was fast changing from a net exporter of agricultural products to a food-dependent nation. Its rapidly rising food import bill clearly indicated this trend. In 1975, the value of U.S. agricultural exports alone to Nigeria was $97 million; in 1976, it was $149 million; in 1977, $230 million; and in 1978—out of a total food import bill of 1.5 billion dollars—it was $300 million.[14] To U.S. policymakers, however, the pertinent economic facts, which appear to have negated, for them, the implications of the harsh conditions noted above were that Nigeria's GDP of $30 billion had surpassed that of South Africa, that Nigeria continued to supply 16 percent of total U.S. oil imports (accounting for over 50 percent of total Nigerian production), and that its large population presented a vast market for U.S. private investors as well as an opportunity for expanded export ties, with the immediate objective being to redress the large U.S. trade deficit. Though Nigeria was turning once again to international lending to supplement its development finance, it had no serious outstanding bilateral loan obligations to the United States or its institutions. In fact, the Nigerian government continued to pay cash for U.S. technical assistance to Nigeria, for example, in the field of education.

The primary challenge of Nigerian-U.S. bilateral diplomacy in this period was determining how to harness the emerging political entente between the two countries for the purpose of expanding the frontiers of their economic ties. Carter's closest advisers on Africa, including Vance, Young, and Easum, were convinced that a political partnership with Nigeria would open up (for U.S. penetration) the ECOWAS subregion, "which is really . . . a 150-million-person market, 90 million of whom are in Nigeria."[15] However, in order to push U.S. exports (with a value of about $700 million) and private investment (over $1 billion) beyond their modest levels, these officials believed that U.S. companies would have to make a "major" entry into Nigeria, a market "long dominated by Europeans." This, in turn, would require the pursuit of "aggressive U.S. [government] export development policies."

Nigerian officials shared the optimistic sentiment that extended cordiality in political relations would inevitably result in intensive economic ties. Major-General Musa Ya'ardua (the second-in-command to the head of state), for instance, was strongly motivated by this logic when he decided to appeal directly to the Carter White House to put pressure on Phillips Petroleum Company in order to ensure the prompt implementation of its agreement on the Bonny liquified natural gas (LNG) project.[16] There were initially some concrete signs that seemed, indeed, to confirm this expectation. Four instances stand out. First, during the Lagos International Trade Fair held at the end of 1977, the thirty-five firms in the U.S. pavillion made direct sales of $41 million. This was an all-time record: four times the highest sales ever recorded by the U.S. Commerce Department for participation at a trade fair.[17] Because this event occurred shortly after Obasanjo's visit to Washington, U.S. observers saw it as an outcome of very good political relations with Nigeria. Second, in the first six months of 1977 the United States was one of the two major trading partners to have increased its percentage share of the Nigerian market.[18] Italy was the other. Third, between September 1977 and January 1978, Nigeria sent a thousand of its students to the United States on a crash program in mid-level technical manpower training. Fourth, U.S. firms were becoming successful in winning large (Nigerian) government contracts in competition with European and Japanese firms. For instance, Phillips Petroleum was selected as the government's technical partner in the construction of the $5 billion LNG project.

The distinction between the conduct of U.S. policy in Nigeria during the Carter presidency and that during the Ford years needs to be stressed. During the Ford administration, policy was aimed at undermining Nigeria's economic assets in order to weaken its political capability in regional affairs. During the Carter years, Nigerian economic "power" was taken as a fact and even cherished. Consequently, the aim of U.S. policy under Carter was to capitalize on that power for political and economic ends. The concrete bilateral task for Nigeria and the United States was to design appropriate instruments for both resolving past obstacles in economic cooperation and charting future opportunities beyond the traditional exchange pattern dictated by oil.

"Bilateral talks" (at high levels) and joint economic commissions have become essential features of U.S. bilateral economic diplomacy with key Third World countries. In the wake of Obasanjo's visit to Washington, a joint Nigeria-U.S. Study Commission was instituted to assess the areas and modalities of effecting technical and economic cooperation. Four committees were set up, covering the areas of agriculture, education, economic development-business investments, and technical assistance.[19] Under Carter, Nigeria and the United States held five bilateral talks. The talks, in general, were designed to develop a sustained dialogue, especially on trade and investment issues, but one particular area of interest and focus was agriculture.

Apart from oil, agriculture presented the central focus of official Nigerian-U.S. economic cooperation during this period. Both countries expected to derive immediate and long-term advantages from the exploitation of agriculture. The Nigerian federal government needed U.S. assistance, in conjunction with its Operation Feed the Nation program, in reversing the decline of the country's agricultural sector. Further, Nigeria was faced with the immediate necessity to import basic food items such as rice, corn, and wheat to meet the escalating domestic demand, and the United States became a major supplier of these foods. The United States, on the other hand, would benefit from the "protective" investment opportunities that would be provided by the Nigerian federal government, and, in the short and medium terms, the United States stood to gain especially by serving as the primary import source of agricultural products for Nigeria. This benefit was in addition to the payments that would result from the sale of U.S. farm machinery, technology, and management expertise. Overall, agriculture—particularly farming and food processing—was an attractive sector for U.S. private investors in Nigeria's economy for the fundamental reason that domestic production in this sector was not colonially determined; it had not been "dominated" by European firms as were other sectors of the economy. Agriculture was practically a virgin area for foreign investors and, therefore, one in which superior U.S. technology and experience could be applied to maximum advantage in terms of profit and expanded trade while still contributing to the long-term goal of Nigerians, which was to achieve self-reliance in food production.

The common interest of the two governments in developing cooperation in the field of agriculture led to the signing, in July 1980, of a memorandum of understanding. The memorandum envisaged a framework of cooperation that consisted of the following major objectives:

1. To provide technical support in the implementation of agricultural programs
2. To cooperate in training personnel in all fields of agricultural planning, development, and research
3. To cooperate in developing and expanding commercial agricultural relations
4. To foster private sector involvement in projects and activities consistent with the agricultural development policies and objectives of the two governments[20]

The memorandum recommended the establishment of a joint agricultural consultative committee (JACC) to engineer the cooperation of the U.S. private sector in Nigeria's agricultural development. More will be said about this in the next chapter.

By the end of the Carter administration, Nigeria's food problem had truly intensified. Whether private U.S. investment and technical expertise would ever contribute seriously in boosting domestic production, as contemplated in the memorandum of understanding, was a matter of conjecture. True, for Young and Obasanjo, the model of such partnership with the U.S. private sector was the award of contracts to the M. W. Kellogg consortium for the construction of an 80 million naira nitrogenous fertilizer complex and the Nigerian government's joint venture participation with M. W. Kellogg in the proposed National Fertilizer Company.[21] However, for the moment, the reality of cooperation in agriculture was demonstrated by the continually expanding level of U.S. export to Nigeria of surplus agricultural products. Between 1979 and 1981, U.S. agricultural sales to Nigeria increased by 150 percent. This situation revealed to the Nigerian foreign policy public the possibility of a long period of food dependence on the United States involving the expenditure of huge sums of foreign exchange, a prospect they regarded as highly abhorrent because of its foreign policy ramifications.

It should be stressed that the issue of dependence—resulting either from renewed financial borrowing in the capitalist market or from increased importation of U.S. food grains—was not a direct constraint on Nigeria's foreign policy orientation during this period. Just as in the second period of this study, Nigerian policymakers and bureaucrats were operating substantially within a psychological milieu of relative financial independence and self-assuredness. Consequently, throughout this period Nigeria maintained its relative policy autonomy, even as it cooperated closely with the United States in resolving contentious regional conflicts. Witness Nigerian-U.S. diplomacy in Zimbabwe and other areas.

U.S.-Nigerian Partnership in Regional Affairs

Of all recent U.S. governments (including that of Ronald Reagan), Jimmy Carter's was most outstanding in its readiness to involve African states, through consultations, in the practical execution of its regional policy. This sensitivity for local participation evolved, as already explained, from the presumption that the best policy strategy for assuring the interest of the United States in the African continent was one that allied squarely with African interests and aspirations as embodied in the quest for decolonization. In terms of both public articulation of policy and policy implementation, the Carter government showed exceeding inclination to, as its domestic conservative critics charged, "permit African aspirations to determine the content of U.S. policy."[22] This was a significant development from an African perspective, for an environment was nurtured in which the United States did not, by conscious design, allow the pressure of East-West confrontation to thwart solutions to regional problems (a characteristic of the Reagan administration's bellicose performance in the continent). The outcomes of the Ogaden war (in which the OAU principle of territorial integrity was upheld) and Zimbabwe's crisis (where authentic majority rule under the Patriotic Front was eventually established) showed that some major regional conflicts were resolved largely according to African specifications. In fact, in the second Shaba incident, where East-West considerations impinged on U.S. reaction, the outcome was the retrogressive Pan-African Security Force, which was directed by NATO and condemned by a great majority of Africans.

The basic U.S. strategy relied to a considerable extent on the role of Nigeria as a core mobilizer of its regional input. In this context, U.S. officials consulted Lagos routinely on regional issues that required some tactical alignment of policies.

The Shaba Incident

An example was during the first Shaba incident early in 1977. The approach that Vance, characteristically, recommended at the onset and that Carter approved was to consider the Katangese rebels' attack on Zaire's territory an "African problem" requiring African mediation, even as the United States gave limited assistance to Zaire. The United States was anxious to bring about a stable accord between Mobutu's Zaire (its African proxy) and Angola. Because of the Angolan government's ties to the South-West African People's Organization (SWAPO), Vance wished to secure its cooperation in resolving the Namibian conflict. Besides, the Carter government hoped to move toward establishing normal bilateral relations with Angola. But the primary reason for Vance's concern with the problem was linked to the prospect of Cuban-Soviet intervention in Zaire should the conflict escalate. "I wanted the crisis resolved before it provided an opportunity for Soviet or Cuban meddling in Zaire, which could turn into an East-West test of strength. The Soviets and Cubans present in Angola would hold most of the cards in that case."[23] Although the United States supported Nigeria's mediatory initiative in the conflict, the motivations and perceptions of the two countries were different.

Nigeria's willingness to mediate between Zaire and Angola was strengthened by the stated U.S. approach to the problem. On a visit to Washington, Joseph Garba, Nigeria's commissioner for external affairs, was assured by officials that the United States did not intend to intervene "massively" in Shaba and would send only military spare parts to Zaire. Garba cautioned that a massive military intervention by the West would encourage the socialist countries to escalate their own support for the Angolan government and that under this cold war condition Nigeria's mediation would not be forthcoming.

The Obasanjo regime had a strong interest in seeking, directly, to reconcile the Zaireans and Angolans. Nigeria's preoccupation with the success of the decolonization process in southern Africa was a paramount factor. The two countries had to be reconciled in order to refocus their attention, in concert with other OAU members, on the more compelling struggle for majority rule in Zimbabwe, Namibia, and South Africa. Incidents like Shaba constituted irritating diversions from this central concern, especially because they provoked foreign military interventions and created disarray in the ranks of the OAU. These were exactly the results of Shaba II. In May 1978, France and Belgium staged a "rescue mission" in Kolwezi making use of U.S. military transport planes, and NATO decided to set up its so-called Pan-African Security Force on behalf of sovereign African states.

The Shaba incident revealed the precariousness of a Nigerian-U.S. partnership in regional (political) affairs. It emphasized the underlying constraint that the two entities do not share a common strategic perception about most of the central issues in the decolonizing continent, such as NATO military interventions in local conflicts, the role of armed struggle in the quest for independence, and the contributive role of Cuban military forces in that process. Although Nigeria and the United States may try tactically to rationalize policy actions to achieve specific objectives, such an effort cannot easily endure because of the inherent contradiction in their strategic concerns. Following the NATO paratroop drop in Kolwezi and the constitution of the abortive Pan-African force, the Nigerian government made a formal protest to the United States, and, later, Obasanjo strongly condemned the action of "certain ex-colonial European powers" for their "naked and unashamed attempt to determine what Africa's true collective interests should be."

> We reject the notion that Africa's interests or collective security needs can be discussed or determined by the Western nations or anybody else for that matter without our consent. . . . A new Berlin type conference is not the appropriate response to the kind of issues thrown by the recent Kolwezi episode. Paratroop drops in the twentieth century are no more acceptable to us than the gunboats of the last century were to our ancestors.[24]

But the Carter administration for its part had not endorsed these two NATO actions without reservation. Its decision to play a limited role in the rescue mission was, in fact, intended to appease hardliners in the administration, such as Brzezinski, and mollify other domestic critics who alleged that the president was too "soft" toward the Soviet Union. The endorsement of the idea of a Pan-African force was, for the administration, an acceptable alternative (because of the African composition of the force) to an earlier recommendation by Belgium that the United States participate in a Western international force designed "to provide internal and external security for Mobutu," which Carter rejected outright.[25]

Nigerian-U.S. Diplomacy on Zimbabwe

The determination of the Nigerian and U.S. governments to build a partnership in regional affairs was most strenuously demonstrated in the diplomacy over Zimbabwe. The focus of close consultations between the two countries was the Anglo-American plan formally presented in October 1977, which embraced proposals for ending the long military conflict in Southern Rhodesia and bringing into being an internationally accepted majority rule in an independent Zimbabwe.[26] For a number of reasons, the Obasanjo regime decided to endorse the proposals provisionally despite misgivings about certain aspects, the most vexing being the idea of guaranteed representation for the white minority in the Parliament, entrenchment of land rights for whites, and white control of the civil service and the judiciary.

The Patriotic Front of Zimbabwe (sponsored by the Zimbabwe African National Union, led by Robert Mugabe, and the Zimbabwe African People's Union, led by Joshua Nkomo) also gave provisional support to the Anglo-American proposals, as did the presidents of the five Frontline States (the states that bordered the zone of conflict with the white minority regimes). President Julius Nyerere of Tanzania, the highly regarded chairman of the Frontline States, had privately given Carter a personal commitment of support during his visit to Washington in August 1977 after receiving an assurance that the military formation of independent Zimbabwe would be based on the liberation forces of the Patriotic Front. Moreover, Carter had informed Nyerere and, subsequently, other Frontline leaders that the United States would support UN economic sanctions against South Africa as a means of pressuring Rhodesia in the event that the Patriotic Front accepted the Anglo-American proposals but Smith rejected them.[27]

It would have been awkward for Nigeria to be seen working at cross-purposes with the very elements whose immediate interest it claimed to be advancing in southern Africa. Furthermore, although Nigeria "has always maintained that it is only through the armed struggle that the Zimbabwe impasse can be speedily resolved," its governments had never been averse to the possibility of a political settlement, which the proposals represented. These considerations, in addition to the Obasanjo regime's genuinely warm disposition toward the United States, led Nigeria to "become the most ardent African advocate of the Anglo-American proposals."[28]

To the Nigerian public, however, the government was far from justified in sponsoring with such vigor the Anglo-American peace plan. At the root of the public dissatisfaction was a basic distrust of U.S. and British motives in southern Africa and a general uneasiness about the pattern of Nigerian-U.S. collaboration in Africa that was emerging under the Carter presidency. They were especially apprehensive of the exclusive privileges to be entrenched in the new constitution for the whites. According to B. Akinyemi, the proposals "were seen as an attempt by Britain and the United States to rob the Patriotic Front of the fruits of their labour. [Furthermore] Nigerians, remembering the anti-Lumumba role of the United Nations in the Congo in the 1960s, were skeptical about whether to entrust the United Nations with another role in Zimbabwe."[29] Particularly offensive to the Nigerian public was the fact that the government seemed to be exerting overbearing pressure on the Patriotic Front to accept the peace formula in view of the above deficiencies. It was not so much that the government did not share the general skepticism of its critics but that it felt, nonetheless, that the proposals were a helpful basis for further negotiations. In any case, adopting such a stance was diplomatically tactical while contingency options were being refined for implementation under changed circumstances.

One element of the unfolding diplomacy on Zimbabwe's independence, as indicated above, was the supportive, but in fact dominant, role of the United States after 1977. Although the Rhodesian conflict was nominally still a British affair and although the Anglo-American proposals had been worked out jointly by British and U.S. officials, the United Kingdom lacked the requisite political and diplomatic assets to sustain the momentum toward a successful settlement. After twelve years of a very embarrassing record at resolving the Rhodesian rebellion, Great Britain had lost the self-confidence to proceed unilaterally even under the favorable circumstances that prevailed in 1976–1977. From the outset David Owen, the British foreign minister under labor prime minister James Callaghan, pleaded for full U.S. partnership with Great Britain in a new bid to effect a settlement—including, unprecedently, U.S. direct participation in a constitutional conference on colonial Rhodesia. Owen, the principal U.K. official in the numerous consultations with the various actors during the ensuing process, was convinced that only the United States "could influence the South Africans and the frontline states to persuade Smith and the guerrilla groups [respectively] to resume negotiations."[30]

The United States, as earlier indicated, consulted closely with Nigeria in both the process of formulating the Zimbabwe proposals and the execution of those proposals. The immediate rationale, as Easum explained, was linked to the expectation that Nigeria would help the United States and Great Britain "define the positions of the Frontline states as well as the Patriotic Front so as to promote compromise and success over [Ian] Smith." The understanding underlying these consultations was that Nigeria and the Frontline governments would "deliver" the Patrotic Front while the United States and Great Britain on their part would "deliver" Smith to facilitate the process. Moreover, the United States hoped that Nigerian involvement would dilute the Zimbabwean nationalists' distrust of Great Britain.

On March 3, 1978, Ian Smith announced his "internal settlement" with Bishop Abel Muzorewa, Ndabaningi Sithole, and Chief Jeremiah Chirau (home-based black political leaders)—a development that for all practical purposes torpedoed the more comprehensive Anglo-American plan. In response, and in keeping with the U.S. role as a bridge between the African actors and the Anglo-Americans, Garba proposed, during Carter's visit to Lagos, the Dar es Salaam meeting between U.S. and British officials and foreign ministers of the Frontline States, preparatory to an "all-parties" conference. The proposed all-parties conference, which Carter announced publicly before leaving Lagos, was intended to revive and intensify the original effort. Nigeria and the United States agreed during Carter's visit that the internal settlement of March 30 was illegal and unacceptable because it did "not guarantee a genuine transfer of power to the majority."[31]

The Road to Lancaster House

Nigeria's central involvement in the diplomatic process placed it in an advantageous position to apply pressure not only on the Patriotic Front but also on the Americans and the British. U.S. officials understood quite clearly that the Nigerian disposition to bolster the Anglo-American efforts rested basically on continued U.S. commitment to genuine majority rule and, moreover, on the determination of the United States to prevent the British from subverting that objective. Between the signing of March 3, 1978, agreement and the subsequent internal elections in April 1979, Nigerian authorities constantly pressed the United States "to keep the British feet burning" so that Great Britain might not jeopardize the interest of the Patriotic Front in the negotiations or, worse, abandon once again its responsibility for Rhodesia by recognizing the internal settlement. At the same time, Nigeria mounted direct pressure on the U.S. government so that it would not succumb to domestic opposition, spearheaded by Senators Jesse Helms and S. I. Hayakawa, by either suspending the UN sanctions or recognizing the illegal Muzorewa government in Salisbury or both. Here, President Carter was hemmed in by an unpleasant reality with consequences for U.S. interest in Africa and for his personal political standing domestically: Recognition of the Muzorewa government would be interpreted in Africa as U.S. identification with the minority white regimes in the region, but failure to recognize the government would be regarded by many domestic observers as "appeasement of Soviet-backed forces" and refusal to support a "moderate" solution.

Nigeria utilized various channels to maintain pressure on the United States to stay on course. For example, Nigerian officials directly appealed to decisionmaking organs in Washington using the easy access they had to the White House, the State Department, and the relevant sections of the Congress (such as the House Africa Affairs Committee headed by Representative Stephen Solarz and the Congressional Black Caucus) for lobbying purposes. Nigeria also used its membership in the Security Council and its chairmanship of the UN Anti-Apartheid Committee in its attempt to help influence the wider American public about the general situation in southern Africa and the implication of U.S. actions on Rhodesia particularly. For example, from his presidential chair of the Security Council in January 1978, Foreign Affairs Commissioner Garba rebuked (in his capacity as Nigeria's chief delegate) the United States and Great Britain for deliberately stalling the implementation of their joint Rhodesian proposals in order to allow Ian Smith sufficient time to effect an internal solution, "so that the international community is faced with a fait accompli."[32] Another channel of influence was, as always, the perception of "a Nigerian oil weapon." Although the Nigerian government never seriously contemplated invoking this weapon, at least not against the United States, many influential Americans regarded the possibility as a hanging threat. While urging Carter in May 1978 not to end sanctions or recognize Muzorewa's government, Anthony Lewis of the *New York Times* wrote,

> The reaction would be . . . strong from the most important country in Africa, Nigeria. Its leaders have acted before now against Western firms that did business with Rhodesia. Nigeria's oil is important to the West. So are its financial deposits, especially in Britain.[33]

Within Africa, Nigeria engaged its extensive diplomatic influence to keep the African states in line against any unilateral decision to recognize the internal settlement. Nigerian emissaries regularly visited many African capitals for this purpose. Further, Nigeria offered direct material assistance, including military assistance, to the guerrilla fighters of the Patriotic Front and to some Frontline States to help strengthen their resistance against the military forces of the Rhodesian regime. For example, "Nigerian airforce planes were moved to Dar es Salaam in Tanzania where they carried supplies to the Patriotic Front forces based in Zambia and Mozambique."[34] Nigeria also provided substantial financial aid to Zambia and Tanzania, designed to alleviate the economic hardship they had borne as a result of the UN sanctions against Rhodesia.

Ultimately, the greatest leverage was brought to bear on the United Kingdom because of its de facto responsibility for the calamity in Rhodesia and because of the inclination of its recently elected conservative government to accept the status quo in Salisbury. Nigeria's actions in this respect contributed immeasurably in changing British attitude toward the internal arrangement, in convening the all-parties Lancaster House Conference at the end of 1979, and in the final, favorable outcome for Zimbabwe's independence.

The election of the Conservative Party and of Margaret Thatcher as prime minister in May 1979 had given cause for expectation in Salisbury that British policy would change radically in favor of recognition of the Muzorewa government. Thatcher had promised that much in her preelection rhetoric. But Nigeria had also earlier demonstrated the type of punitive/economic measure it was willing to inflict against Great Britain in the event of a contemptuous policy against black African interests in southern Africa. Multinational corporations with operations in Nigeria had been warned that they would have to reappraise their interests in the Republic of South Africa if they were to qualify for government contract awards. When Barclays Bank Nigeria Limited fell foul of this new rule, all government transactions with that bank were promptly terminated, and the government took over 80 percent of the company's shares and changed the bank's name to Union Bank Nigeria Limited.[35] This action was followed in August 1979, just before the Lusaka Commonwealth Conference, with the nationalization of all the assets of British Petroleum Company in Nigeria and the implied threat of a similar action against any of the many other British companies in the country. Mrs. Thatcher had made a threatening statement promising to supply South Africa with North Sea oil, but worse than that, British Petroleum had on two occasions secretly lifted Nigerian oil to South Africa, thus violating the terms of its concession agreement with the Nigerian government.

Much earlier in this chapter it was stated that Nigeria also withdrew part of its large sterling reserves from London and transferred it to other currencies, causing a run on the British pound in the European market, and subtly denied British firms opportunities to bid on profitable contracts. These measures, in addition to the perception of an impending threat to the survival of the Commonwealth, which involved unfavorable consequences for British interests in black Africa, led to a change of attitude in London. (The threat was real enough to prompt the Australian prime minister, Malcolm Fraser, to send an urgent appeal to Vance and to Lord Carrington, the new foreign secretary of the United Kingdom, urging the remedy of negotiations between the Salisbury group and the Patriotic Front.) Certainly, Nigeria played a crucial role in conditioning the outcome of the Lusaka Commonwealth Conference, which paved the way for the final fulfillment of the goals of the Zimbabwean nationalists.

Summary

The distinctive feature of Nigerian-U.S. relations in this period was the high degree of mutual expectation shared by the two ruling governments concerning the possibility of achieving a genuine partnership both bilaterally and in the regional sphere. The historic exchange of state visits by General Obasanjo and President Carter in 1977 and 1978, respectively, symbolized that expectation. This development, which started within one year of Jimmy Carter's election as the thirty-eighth president of the United States, was, to a considerable extent, remarkable in view of the conflictive atmosphere that permeated Nigeria-U.S. relations especially during the period of the Ford administration.

More than any other factors, Carter's avowed commitment to ensuring majority-ruled independence in the white minority-administered territories of southern Africa and his expressed preference for a regionalist strategy of U.S. Africa policy appealed to Nigerians in general and to the federal military government in particular. His strategy converged, in its practical application, with desired African interests and aspirations.

Paradoxically, the traditionalist foreign policy establishment in the United States strongly opposed Carter's progressive foreign policy strategy with its avid human rights content. His opponents advocated a return to the global-strategic approach of the Ford-Kissinger era, an approach they felt would better guarantee U.S. and Western interests in the overriding competition with the Soviet Union. The anti-Carter opposition was manifested very boldly in the election of Ronald Reagan as the next president in November 1980.

Some Nigerian observers were skeptical about the durability, if not the wisdom, of a Nigerian-U.S. partnership as nurtured by Obasanjo and Carter. To the more perceptive segment of the foreign policy public, the idea of partnership with the United States in regional affairs bordered on illusion, considering the lack of basic consensus between the two countries on fundamental African issues. In regard to the particular issue of majority rule in Zimbabwe and Namibia this group remained, almost to the end, keenly suspicious of the probability of collusion between the United States and Great Britain to impose white-influenced "internal settlements" on the black majority.

Notes

1. During his first official meeting with General Olusegun Obasanjo, Nigeria's head of state, at Dodan Barracks in February, Young outlined what would be the basic tenets of U.S. Southern Africa policy: equality, true majority rule, and self-determination. Thereafter, Obasanjo reportedly told the U.S. envoy, "I like what I hear from you; if Carter acts on the basis of these precepts then you should expect Nigeria's full support." Interview with Ambassador Donald Easum, Washington, D.C., May 24, 1983. What transpired in private was later confirmed in public when Obasanjo and Young held a joint press conference. *The Guardian* (London), February 11, 1977.

2. By the end of 1975, even before the open conflict over Angola, U.S. government officials had in fact begun to accept the inevitability of this pattern in the relationship with Nigeria. For instance, in a December 1975 "confidential assessment" of Mohammed's five months in power, embassy personnel in Lagos stressed, in ebullient terms, the "new atmosphere" that "bodes well" for U.S. business in the economic and commercial fields, but at the same time, they acknowledged that "the United States and Nigeria will more often find themselves on opposite sides of the fence in international fora, particularly . . . on those issues which involve Southern African questions." See American Embassy Lagos to State Department, December 21, 1975, Airgram A-185, Dept. of State Files, Washington, D.C.

3. Recall that in April 1976, two years after the collapse of the Portuguese colonial empire in Africa and sensing impending defeat of the white supremacist regimes in Zimbabwe and Namibia, Kissinger was forced to reassess his previous strategy in southern Africa. Refer to his Lusaka speech, *New York Times*, April 28, 1976, p. 16.

4. *Department of State Bulletin*, August 8, 1977, p. 166, Washington, D.C. At a later contentious juncture, Vance vehemently expressed his conviction, in opposition to the proponents of the first approach, that "the heart of our strategy [in Africa] must be to combine diplomacy, negotiations, concerted Western actions, and the powerful forces of African nationalism to resolve local disputes and to remove ostensible justification for Soviet involvement." See Cyrus Vance, *Hard Choices: Critical Years in American Foreign Policy* (New York: Simon and Schuster, 1983), p. 85.

5. For a critique of these two approaches see the following: W. Scott Thompson, "U.S. Policy Toward Africa," *Orbis* (Winter 1982): 1011–1024; Peter Jay, "Regionalism as Geopolitics," *Foreign Affairs* 58(3) (1979): 485–514; and C. Coker, "Neo-conservation and Africa: Some Common American Fallacies," *Third World Quarterly* 5(2) (April 1983): 282–299.

6. Vance, *Hard Choices*, pp. 84–85.

7. Zbigniew Brzezinski, *Power and Principle* (New York: Farrar, Straus, Giroux, 1983), p. 53.

8. Ibid., p. 53–54.

9. Andrew Young, "The United States and Africa: Victory for Diplomacy," *Foreign Affairs* 59(3) (1981): 656. This perception of the Carter government about Nigeria was also stressed by Ambassador Easum during an interview in New York City, May 31, 1983.

10. Young, "The United States and Africa," p. 656; also Donald B. Easum, "Nigerian-American Relations," *Africa Report* (July-August 1981): 52–53.

11. Brzezinski, *Power and Principle*, p. 53.

12. Young, "The United States and Africa," p. 653.

13. Such measures included cuts in public spending, a six-month embargo on all new contracts, extensive import controls, suspension of the states' development plans, and a tight monetary policy by the Central Bank.

14. *Foreign Economic Trends and Their Implications for the United States (Nigeria)*, April 1979, U.S. Department of Commerce, p. 6.

15. "U.S. Policy Toward Africa," *Hearings, Sub-Committee on African Affairs*, 95th Congress, Second Session, U.S. Government Printing Office, 1978), pp. 12–13.

16. Ya'ardua was dismayed by the oil company's vacillation in implementing the agreement on the LNG project. More important, he thought that the existing political atmosphere imposed an obligation on the U.S. government to ensure implementation of the project. Interview with Easum.

17. *Foreign Economic Trends*, March 1978, p. 10.

18. Ibid., p. 3.

19. One noteworthy development of this period was the intensification of cooperation at a high level between Nigerian and U.S. universities, with the

Nigerian Universities Commission serving as the liaison organ on the Nigerian side. See Alaba Ogunsanwo, "Nigerian Military and Foreign Policy 1975–1979" (Unpublished manuscript, University of Lagos, Political Science Department, 1980), note 55, p. 101.

20. *Foreign Agriculture* (Washington, D.C.: Department of Agriculture, June 1981), pp. 12–13.

21. This project, which was initiated by the Carter and Obasanjo governments, was finally launched in 1983 under the civilian regime of President Shehu Shagari with credit facilities provided by the U.S. and Japanese export-import banks. At the time of the award of the contracts to M. W. Kellogg, it was said that although the U.S. company was chosen on "the basis of sound economic" recommendation by a European consulting firm, both Young and Obasanjo were "determined to produce one showpiece of Nigeria-U.S. economic ties to justify their political investment" in the partnership. This explanation was prompted by allegations of impropriety in the award of the contracts. Confidential interview.

22. Thompson, "U.S. Policy Toward Africa."

23. Vance, *Hard Choices*, p. 70.

24. From General Obasanjo's address at the OAU Summit, Khartoum, July 27, 1978.

25. Vance, *Hard Choices*, pp. 89–90; also *Washington Post*, June 1978, and *New York Times*, May 28, 1978, p. E15.

26. For the full text of the proposals, see *Department of State Bulletin*, October 3, 1977, Washington, D.C. In December 1976, Henry Kissinger had managed to arrange a meeting in Geneva involving Ian Smith and the Rhodesian nationalist groups, hoping to achieve a settlement of the conflict. This had predictably broken down because of irreconcilable demands by both sides.

27. Vance, *Hard Choices*, p. 271. This information, which must have been communicated to Nigeria as well, definitely encouraged the government to publicly support the proposals. When Carter later failed to live up to this commitment, Nigeria openly condemned the U.S. duplicity and proceeded to apply direct pressures on Great Britain and the United States not to recognize Smith's internal settlement.

28. B. Akinyemi, "Nigerian-American Relations Re-examined," in O. Oyediran, ed., *Survey of Nigerian Affairs 1976–77* (Macmillan Nigeria Publishers Ltd., 1981), p. 107.

29. Ibid., p. 108.

30. Vance, *Hard Choices*, p. 261.

31. *New York Times*, April 3, 1978, front page. Another occasion in which Nigeria acted as a bridge between the Anglo-American side and the Patriotic Front–Frontline States was during the secret but ill-advised Smith-Nkomo meeting in Lusaka in August 1978. With Garba and President Kenneth Kaunda also in attendance, part of the "agreement" at this meeting was that Obasanjo would subsequently arrange an expanded meeting in which the co-leader of the Patriotic Front, Robert Mugabe, would be persuaded to participate in addition to Smith and Nkomo in order to seek a compromise solution to the internal settlement. When news of the meeting leaked, many Nigerians saw this as proof that the

Anglo-Americans were attempting to split the Patriotic Front with Nigerian and Zambian connivance. See Vance, *Hard Choices*, pp. 291–292; *Daily Times* (Lagos), September 8, 1978, p. 3.

32. *West Africa*, February 6, 1978, p. 263.

33. *New York Times*.

34. Ogunsanwo, "Nigerian Military and Foreign Policy," pp. 39, 42; *West Africa*, October 9, 1978, p. 2016.

35. Ogunsanwo, p. 45; refer also to note 12; also Olajide Aluko, *Essays in Nigerian Foreign Policy* (London: George Allen to Urwin, 1981), pp. 55–72.

8

Retrogression: Shehu Shagari and Ronald Reagan, 1980–1983

The Return of Cynicism

Midway through Shehu Shagari's first government in Nigeria, following the restoration of civilian rule, observers both foreign and national had already come to the conclusion that Nigerian-U.S. relations had indeed turned full circle and were exhibiting basic features of the seminal experience of the 1960s.[1] In reaction to this reversal, Professor Ali Mazrui cautioned in a published article against the "dangers of growing intimacy" between Nigeria and the United States. Although the eminent Africanist was impressed that the two countries seemed at the time to be evolving what he regarded as a worthwhile form of interdependence based on commerce and federalism, he nonetheless was concerned that such a relationship should not "become too close an embrace," for this, according to him, would seriously "compromise Nigeria's credentials for leadership in Africa. . . ."[2] Even before this juncture, at the start of Ronald Reagan's presidency in 1981, Nigeria's restless intellectuals were already voicing apprehension about the uncertain drift of the relationship under Reaganite conservatism in Washington and Shagari's National Party of Nigeria (NPN) regime in Lagos. There was a compulsive suspicion in that circle that U.S. Africa policy under Reagan would strive to undermine Nigeria's political assertiveness in the regional decolonization movement by manipulating the processes of Nigerian-U.S. bilateral economic relations.

Nigerians in general lamented what they saw in the four years of the NPN rule as both a painful return to the placid tradition of Nigerian foreign policy in the first republic and a loss of the gains achieved in the "good old days" of the 1970s, especially during the country's exploits in Angola and Zimbabwe. A commentator in the *New Nigerian* recalled,

"Nigeria in the past four years had little or no influence over events in our neighbouring states, nor in Africa or on the globe. . . . Our foreign policy under Shagari reversed . . . the achievements of the military administrations and took us back to our early days of independence, when Nigeria could not take its stand on international issues. . . . We were indecisive. We lost our will. We lost our voice."[3]

Yet another commentator expressed nostalgic sentiments in the *Sunday Guardian*, wishing for the "glorious times" when "this nation . . . took on a superpower and won,"[4] as during the Angola crisis. On his part, the former commissioner for foreign affairs in the Mohammed-Obasanjo regime, General Joseph Garba, admitted, when Shagari was finally forced out of power by a military coup at the end of 1983, that the Shagari government had "pampered the United States to a dangerous degree." According to Garba, Nigeria under Shagari behaved as if "its foreign policy was being dictated by the United States."[5]

Put in the perspective of the last two periods examined, 1970–1976 and 1977–1979, the all-round verdict on the Shagari regime at the end of its tenure was that through it Nigeria had lost its momentum in asserting a regional leadership that was relatively independent of U.S. resources and tutelage. Whether in respect to its performance over Namibia, Angola and South Africa, Libya, Chad, the OAU, or the western Sahara, the NPN government, as seen by the foreign policy public was, at best, helping to implement U.S.-fashioned policy guidelines rather than formulating its own policies that could advance independent Nigerian and African objectives. This public perception of a subservient status and inept conduct in regional affairs contributed in undermining the regime's domestic legitimacy and security self-interest. However, the crisis of legitimacy and security suffered by President Shagari and his government throughout their rule was more substantially compounded by their abysmal performance in domestic affairs.[6]

Reverses in the Bilateral Structure

The setbacks experienced by Nigeria in its relationship with the United States in regional affairs during this period of study were associated with adverse, unexpected changes in the structure of its bilateral ties with the United States, which were also related to changes in Nigeria's domestic political economy. This was aggravated by the reinstitution of the dynamics of competitive party politics within the old dysfunctional structure of political practice in the country. These factors and their implications for Shagari's regional policy are analyzed in this chapter.

It was earlier contended that Shagari's attitude toward the United States and the concomitant orientation of his regime in regional affairs represented, in the opinion of this writer and other observers, a veritable return to the seedy experience of the 1960s. Similarities between the two periods included the absence of a material base of leverage in Nigeria's overall diplomacy with the United States and the regimes' assessments as to the nature of their vital state interests—paramount of which were financial viability and domestic political security—and the way those interests might be ensured through a deferential alignment with the United States, given a domestic environment of high-stake competitive politics.

The Erosion of Material Leverage

Under Shagari, Nigeria, almost self-consciously, depleted the existing stock of its economic resources, which had provided the backbone of a relatively autonomous policy toward the United States. As one concrete indicator of a depleted material base for policy, Nigeria, since 1982, has ceased to be the second most important supplier of crude oil to the U.S. market, partly as a result of escalated competition by Mexico and Great Britain and partly because of a drastic decline in the demand for imported oil in the United States. Nigeria fell into seventh place behind Mexico, Canada, Venezuela, Great Britain, Indonesia, and Saudi Arabia as a U.S. oil supplier. As another indicator, the trade balance between the two countries, which in the past had progressively favored Nigeria, declined noticeably: from $9 billion in 1980 to $7 billion in 1981, down to $5 billion in 1982. Yet another indicator was the fact that the national stock of external reserves was nearly depleted in the tenure of Shagari's first government; although it increased from 5.6 billion naira in 1980 to 6.4 billion naira in 1981, it then declined precipitously to 1.1 billion naira in 1982. In the first six months of 1983, the available foreign exchange at the disposal of the government was barely enough to sustain the country's import bill for one month. This was indeed ironic, for it was in the four short years of the Shagari regime that Nigeria disposed of 55.2 percent of its total oil sales since 1958, providing the federal government with a total revenue of 43.6 billion naira.[7]

When the Shagari regime became pressed by its economic straits to appeal to the IMF (with expected U.S. mediation) and to Saudi Arabia for financial rescue, the U.S. government was graphically notified that Nigeria was henceforth effectively devoid of a tangible leverage on U.S. diplomacy in Africa. A report in the *New York Times* had already (in 1981) informed the U.S. public that pressures emanating from oversupply in the world oil market would most likely force "Africa's economic giant" to slow down its development projects and seek overseas borrowing.[8] Gone were the days when any serious observer could claim that the U.S. Congress was influenced by the threat of a Nigerian oil sanction when considering legislation on a contentious Africa problem, as was the case in 1978 when under the Carter administration the Senate voted against recognition of Muzorewa's illegitimate government in Zimbabwe, conceivably in deference to Nigeria's diplomacy.[9]

The experience with the United States in the Shagari period was not new for Nigeria. Recall that in the period from 1960–1966 the fledgling Balewa regime could not contemplate an aggressive policy toward the United States and the West especially with regard to regional affairs for the fundamental reason that Nigeria lacked the requisite material resources for backing up such a posture. To the contrary, Prime Minister Balewa and his government deferred to the United States largely because, as was demonstrated, they strongly believed that the United States and its major Western allies were the only viable sources of financial support for Nigeria's economic growth within the framework of the first national development plan. Recall specifically that in 1961 the Nigerian government expected that 80 percent of the total expenditure in that plan would be financed through external (Western) sources.

The condition of bilateral impotence for Nigeria under Shagari was almost guaranteed from 1982 by the accelerated decline in the objective base of the country's economy. Between 1982 and 1983, a combination of persistently falling demand for oil in the world market, aggressive competition by non-OPEC producers, and the inability of OPEC to agree on a common base price or on production quotas resulted in a critical depression of the Nigerian oil industry, deeply affecting production, exports, and foreign exchange earnings. For instance, crude output for January 1983 averaged 840,000 barrels per day (b/d) as opposed to 1.2 million b/d in December 1982. In fact, Nigeria could sell only a negligible amount of its oil in the first six months of 1983. The gloomy prospects for oil production and exports were truly alarming for the government given the country's dependence on the oil sector for over 95 percent of its foreign exchange receipts.

Moreover, since the economic well-being of the majority of Nigerians had, for over a decade, been tied exclusively to oil production and earnings, any precipitous decline, as was then being experienced, spelled imminent danger for national economic and social development with attendant political instability.[10] And this indeed was the bleak outlook that forced the government, early in 1983, to take the drastic unilateral action of cutting the price of Nigeria's high-grade crude by $5.50 below OPEC's $35 reference prices. It used as an immediate justification for this action the earlier British National Oil Corporation's decision to cut the price of its similar North Sea brand to $30.50 per barrel, which made Nigerian oil grossly overpriced in an already glutted market. The economic predicament for Nigeria was in no way resolved by the unilateral price cut against OPEC solidarity. When OPEC acted to finally stabilize its share of the world market, Nigeria was saddled with a mandatory production quota of 1.3 million barrels per day while its oil sold for about $30 per barrel, compared to the 1980 production level of 2.1 million barrels per day of oil selling at $40 per barrel.

An additional factor that influenced the structure of bilateral ties with the United States and had potentially serious consequences considering Nigeria's rapid population growth was the deterioration of the food situation since 1979. Scarcity of basic food items was, at base, a direct consequence of a short-sighted neglect of the agricultural sector of the economy since the inception of the "oil boom" era, worsened by the experience of drought in the northern regions. Stagnation in domestic food production and the prohibitive cost of the food that was available created an unprecedented social phenomenon in Nigeria's modern experience: Many citizens were faced with the actual prospect of starvation, and malnutrition among the rural population and urban poor was especially severe despite the government's overpublicized Green Revolution program. And the prediction for the future promised further deterioration. According to the International Food Policy Research Institute, "Nigeria's food deficit in 1990 may represent 35–39 percent of the country's food needs."[11] The implication was clear: If no drastic solution was effected, such a situation would place Nigeria in a weakened position vis-à-vis food-exporting states.

Nigeria relied mainly on the United States for the bulk of its imported foods, agricultural equipment, and technical services and for guarantee of World Bank credits.[12] The United States, for example, was its leading supplier of wheat grain and also accounted for 60 percent of its total import of rice. From 1979 to 1983, Nigeria's bill for food importation from the United States alone increased dramatically in direct response to the abject decline in domestic production. The political significance of this development rested on the coincidence that Nigeria was becoming increasingly dependent on U.S. food supplies in the same period that its oil lost its significance to the U.S. market.

Domestic Policies as a Catalyst to Deferential Alignment

The restoration of competitive party politics in 1979 facilitated an accommodative relationship (in both bilateral and regional spheres) with the United States. This is the second aspect of similarity with the experience of the 1960–1966 period.

What was striking about this development in Nigeria's political history was not the abandonment of British parliamentary democracy in preference for the U.S. presidential model but rather the reinstitution of the politics of the Balewa period (referred to by Nigerians as the first republic) within its traditional framework of regional and ethnic divisiveness. The 1979 constitutional guidelines on the operation of politics had, through historical miscalculation, predetermined the calamity that afflicted the second republic. The guidelines ensured the reactivation of the contending political forces of the first period, with their political bases intact in the erstwhile three regions, and with former key actors, imbued with old-time prejudices, playing essentially their previous leadership roles. The organ of the new emergence was the old regional party reincarnated under new names, with minor national groups aligning with the major parties.

As in the past, the object of political competition was the absolute control of state power or, alternatively, a substantial share of it. This time, though, the contest was even more fierce because the state presided over the distribution of the proverbial oil wealth of the country, which the emergent politicians and their allied groups fervently appropriated in the name of development but mostly for private ends.[13] This provided the political framework for the colossal mismanagement of the national economy and rampant corruption that characterized the tenure of the Shagari federal government. Clearly, the trend, which the military intervention arrested, was toward a resurgence of politics of national polarization, as witnessed by the scale of violence and fraud unleashed in the conduct of the elections that preceded the coup and by a bankrupt economy.

Within this setting, the ruling national party was overburdened by three preeminent interests in the conduct of domestic affairs, especially in the second half of its life: salvaging the economy from the brink of bankruptcy; securing its political power and authority, which seemed to be constantly threatened by opposition elements; and restraining the avarice for financial acquisition (via corruption) exhibited by its leadership ranks. Thus, the Shagari regime was hard put to pursue a policy of radicalism toward the Reagan administration. Rather, like the Balewa coalition government in the first period, it became thoroughly captivated by a paralyzing sense of the strategic role of the United States in the world economy. The regime, for example, was convinced that the United States had strong influence over decisions of the IMF, which was why Shagari expected to engage Reagan's mediation with that body in securing a bailout loan for Nigeria. Government officials in Lagos also knew that the U.S. decision to switch to non-OPEC suppliers in the Western hemisphere and Great Britain's North Sea oil, a decision that adversely affected Nigerian exports to the U.S. market, was based in large part on political and geo-strategic motives. The British, for instance, had been a catalyst in the critical price fall of early 1983—a role the Americans welcomed.[14]

Thus, in the political sphere, Nigeria regarded the United States as a superpower "ally" in the grim domestic struggle to control the Nigerian state and economy—an ally that should only be courted not challenged. Consequently, the policy process in Lagos, relative to U.S.-Nigeria relations, was once again (as in the first period) permeated by a crude psychology of dependence. The pervasive feeling seemed to be that expressed privately by a top government functionary: "We are critically dependent on the United States economically, therefore we should not act counter to American political preferences in African affairs."[15]

The return to competitive party politics also enhanced an accommodative relationship with the United States through a predictably more direct approach than the rather indirect manner already suggested. By the adoption of presidential federalism as a system of governance, an ideological medium became instituted in Nigerian-U.S. bilateral relations with the potential of rendering the existing relationship more amenable to U.S. influences. Nigeria's then presidential federal system was believed, by Nigerians and Americans alike, to be modeled on the pattern of the United States. This constitutional development raised the possibility of confirming the post-independence trend whereby Nigeria has progressively sought to establish greater affinity with the United States, first in the area of higher education, then in the economic sphere, and now in the realm of constitutional practice, all at the expense of Great Britain.

The beginning of this political experiment opened up, sometimes in a bewildering fashion, many channels of interaction between Nigeria's three arms of government and their U.S. counterparts. For example, Nigerian legislators, on numerous instances, visited Washington and many U.S. state capitals for the purpose of learning about American legislative practice or to participate in State Department–sponsored symposia on the U.S. political process. Nigerian legislative personnel routinely attended short courses in the United States aimed at familiarizing them with U.S. congressional procedures. Also, many U.S. Congressmen and other U.S. government as well as private functionaries regularly visited Nigeria in a crusade to provide support for the country's new gamble in presidential democracy.

Naturally, one would expect the United States to have a strong motive in fully assisting the most populous country in Africa to succeed in its apparent effort to build a democratic society in the U.S. image. If this were the noble desire at the State Department, the same enthusiasm for Nigeria's success was not demonstrated by the behavior of the president and his staff at the White House.[16] To them, the overriding concern seemed to be restricted to the short-term question of whether the ruling government in Nigeria would be willing to sustain Reagan's policy initiatives in Africa, most especially with respect to Libya, Chad, and southern Africa, in exchange for concerted economic assistance. "The foreign policy of a nation," said Kissinger, "should be directed toward affecting the foreign policy of other societies; it should not be the principal goal of American foreign policy to transform the domestic structures of societies with which we deal."[17] The Reagan administration, acting in accordance with the Kissinger prescription, saw the ensuing linkages in the process of the democratic experiment in Nigeria as advantageous mostly for the purpose of further influencing the Nigerian decisionmaking framework on behalf of immediate U.S. policy goals in the region.

Thus, the following factors contributed to weakening the bilateral advantage for Nigeria in the Shagari period: (1) the deteriorating prospects both in the oil-based economy in general and in the production of basic food requirements; (2) extensive mismanagement of the national economy by the government and the outright theft of public funds on a monumental scale by public officers and their collaborators in the private sector, which greatly aggravated the first factor; and (3) the reinstitution of party politics within the fundamental framework of political rivalry of the first republic, thus enhancing national polarization and foreign penetration of the decisionmaking process in the area of foreign affairs.

Regional Leadership Under Siege

That the bilateral structure provides, potentially, for the United States a critical medium of influence upon Nigeria's policy options in regional affairs has been one of the unifying themes throughout this study. More generally, this medium has always served, when stripped of details, as a locus of leverage for successive U.S. administrations from Kennedy to Reagan in their foreign policy dealings with key African states. In Nigeria, this linkage was sometimes illustrated very graphically in the Shagari period,[18] as in 1981 when President Reagan demonstrated, in his pungent style, the connection, from the U.S. perspective, between the bilateral and regional dimensions of Nigeria-U.S. relations.

During their first meeting, at Cancun in Mexico in 1981, Reagan confronted Shagari with a demand that Nigeria oppose Muammar Gaddafi's impending chairmanship of the OAU in 1982, a task the Nigerian president said his country could not undertake. Reagan was, of course, not persuaded, and he charged, "You mean that mad man is going to become the next OAU Chairman?"[19] Innocuously, Shagari replied that he really saw nothing wrong with that, since "we have had madder people like Idi Amin become OAU Chairman." According to

Abba Dabo, Shagari's chief press secretary, who reported this exchange, one result of the encounter was that the United States reneged on an earlier "promise" to assume the cost of the OAU peacekeeping forces in Chad. Even more ominously, the exchange at Cancun made it very difficult for Shagari to later approach the U.S. government (Reagan's subsequent attitude toward Nigeria was "cold and distant") for economic aid with which to rescue Nigeria's battered economy, including assistance in convincing the IMF to approve its outstanding loan request without its stringent conditionalities. The Shagari government had regarded the anticipated $2 billion loan from the fund as a necessary antidote in salvaging the country's worsening international credit position. However, Reagan made agreement with the IMF a precondition for U.S. offers of badly needed import credits to Nigeria. When, for example, the Nigerian government requested from the United States a $128 million commodity credit guarantee for importation of wheat and other food items—a request the State Department approved—Reagan, siding with the Treasury Department, released only $30 million. Thereafter, he "personally ruled out further guarantees until an IMF stand-by agreement was in place."[20]

The outcome of the Cancun encounter helps explain Shagari's ambivalent behavior on the occasion of the first abortive OAU Summit in Tripoli. Whereas the foreign policy public had expected Shehu Shagari, as the president of the Federal Republic of Nigeria, to rally the other OAU leaders to attend and form a quorum for the nineteenth summit in order to safeguard the integrity of the organization, Shagari not only failed to perform this necessary leadership duty but, worse, he remained in Lagos one day after the meeting was to have begun in the Libyan capital.[21] His reason for not traveling to Tripoli in time for the opening of the conference, strangely, was that he wanted to make sure that a quorum was formed before he left Lagos. Colonel Gaddafi, the leader of Libya, was expected to be elected the next OAU chairman at that summit. By acting as he did, Shagari actually contributed to the failure of the summit to take place, and, moreover, fueled the general suspicion held in the region that the Reagan administration used Nigeria in its design to thwart the summit and deny Gaddafi—its implacable foe—the OAU chairmanship.[22]

The more inclusive significance of Nigeria's behavior, especially when seen in light of the country's parallel action in the Chadian conflict, was that 1982 marked the beginning of the effort toward Nigeria-U.S. policy collaboration in the Shagari period. Henceforth, the Shagari regime and the Reagan administration appeared to coordinate their policy approaches to outstanding regional issues such as the Libyan role in Africa, the Chad conflict, and even the dominant process of liberation in southern Africa. From 1982 onward there was no real evidence, apart from platitudinous public statements of discord, of any real conflict in the policy objectives and strategy of the two countries. But before pursuing this development further it is worth stepping back to reappraise the events of 1980–1981 in their correct perspective.

Shagari and Reagan, 1980–1981

It is, indeed, discernible from Shagari's posture of apparent defiance of Reagan at their first meeting that there was an initial phase of chilliness in the contact between the two governments. Shagari, as well as many other Nigerians, had shown outward disappointment over Reagan's defeat of former president Jimmy Carter in the U.S. presidential election of 1980. The Nigerian leader had publicly expressed support for Carter's candidacy and had, during his visit to the UN General Assembly, paid Carter a visit in the White House just prior to the election to show his solidarity. The action was against the better judgment of his advisers, who argued that it would undercut relations with Reagan should he win, but Carter showed his appreciation by giving Shagari a "red-carpet welcome" on the South lawn of the White House estate.[23] In fact, after Reagan's victory, Shagari vacillated for some months before finally sending a congratulatory message to the new president.

Another element contributing to the chill in relations between Nigeria and the United States in this period was Reagan's cold war pronouncements, particularly in relation to southern Africa, throughout the election campaign. Everything Reagan said about U.S. intentions in Africa under his presidency directly challenged Nigeria's aspirations and policy objectives in the continent as pursued in the Mohammed-Obasanjo periods. All this had generated an atmosphere of suspicion and unfriendliness in the months following Reagan's inauguration. In addition, recall that when Shagari came into power at the end of the military era Nigerian policymaking in foreign affairs was still substantially characterized by a psychological milieu of relative financial independence and national self-confidence. Specifically, the issue of dependence did not act as a direct constraint on Nigeria's regional policy initiatives at that time. In the subperiod from 1980 to 1981, the Shagari government was basking in the residual glow of this environment.

This accounted, to a great degree, for the Shagari government's tough statements on regional issues. For example, addressing the General Assembly in November 1980, President Shagari warned that

> Nigeria will no longer tolerate the provocation of South Africa or the
> dilatory tactics of its allies in the self-determination and majority rule for

Namibia. . . . We shall continue to assist, encourage and support [the liberation] struggle with all our might and resources until ultimate victory is won.[24]

And when talking to U.S. reporters about the Namibia conflict, Shagari even, subtly, threatened the use of Nigeria's "petrol power" against the U.S. government when he said, "When it comes to fighting for freedom one can use any weapon available and we will use it against them if we have to."[25] Again in July 1981, Shagari launched what a reporter termed a "blistering attack" on the United States, this time for "concluding a military pact" with South Africa: "Those who align themselves with the apartheid system against the rest of Africa as well as a substantial body of world opinion must, therefore, accept blame for the inevitable escalation of the rift between Pretoria and the rest of Africa."[26]

In the same vein, Nigeria's foreign minister, Ishaya Audu, a man who was to become one of the most unpopular foreign ministers in Nigeria, condemned Reagan's anti-Soviet policy in the continent as well as the emerging Pretoria-Washington alliance, which he claimed was bound "to clash with the real concerns of Africa, with respect particularly to decolonization and elimination of racial discrimination from the continent." He also indicated that Nigeria would use its oil against the United States "if there was extreme provocation by the Reagan administration."[27] This posture persisted until late 1981. But thereafter, the combined impacts of recession in the oil industry, fear of an impending economic collapse, and the consuming chaos of domestic politics set in, calling for an orientation of prudent accommodation with the directing forces of the capitalist world economy, which centered around the United States.

It is often stated with reference to the domestic arena that politics is the art of the possible; the same holds in the realm of interstate politics when tangible interests have to be secured through bilateral interaction in the absence of a material base of bargaining. This was the reality of the Nigeria-U.S. connection for the Shagari regime after 1981, so much so that when, in July 1983, the Speaker of the House of Representatives, Edwin Ume-Ezeoke, daringly told Thomas Pickering, the U.S. Ambassador in Lagos, that the "U.S. government should be condemned by all lovers of peace in the world for her continued relationship with the racist regime in South Africa," a perceptive Nigerian commentator dismissed the unusual "radicalism" of the Speaker as the difference between bark and bite. In a tone of self-resignation, he captured the prevalent reality as recognized by the Nigerian government:

It is self-deception to pretend that Nigeria can have a foreign policy independent of her relationship with the U.S. and the West in general. As long as we remain dependent on the West and cultivate this dependency, all statements condemning or threatening the U.S. will be meaningless.[28]

In the final analysis, the Shagari regime, by its very nature as well as circumstances of its existence, was not disposed to pay the material price that was almost inevitable for pursuing a bolder regional policy that ran against U.S. interests in Nigeria and in Africa generally.

Policy Convergence on Libya, Chad, and Southern Africa

Nigeria's policy (or, more accurately, Nigeria's lack of policy) with respect to Libya, Chad, and southern Africa illustrates the dependent and nebulous role the country played in regional affairs during this period. Reference has already been made to Shagari's contribution to the failure of the nineteenth summit of the OAU in Tripoli, an action that exposed unmistakably the essential contradictory forces operating on Nigeria's regional policy process at the time. These forces included (1) the preferences of the United States—in this instance, the U.S. prejudice against Libya and Gaddafi personally; (2) Nigeria's national aspiration in the African arena, which dictated a more or less autonomous role for Nigeria in the OAU; and (3) the concrete interests of the ruling government, which required, in its considerations, accommodation with the United States. Even under these circumstances, a resourceful, purposeful, and determined leadership might have been able to harness other attributes at Nigeria's disposal (both domestic and regional) to perform creditably well. But this was beyond the capacity of Shehu Shagari and his government; plainly, they did not demonstrate these qualities.

From its inauguration, the Reagan administration had developed a fixation with Libya, which in a certain manner was out of step with what one would expect of a superpower, considering the size of Libya. In March 1981 an article in the *Washington Post* reported that Secretary of State Alexander Haig was "obsessed with knocking Libya's Colonel Muammar Gaddafi from power" because he viewed the Libyan leader "as an agent of International Soviet-backed terrorist conspiracy."[29] The United States under Reagan regards Libya's actions in Africa as subversive, acting against pro-Western governments in the Sudan, Egypt, Ghana, Tunisia, Senegal, The Gambia, and other countries. Underlying this passionate objection to Gaddafi's conduct, however, is a more profound concern in Washington—a concern shared more widely by the foreign policy establishment in the United States—that the Gaddafi regime is a serious obstacle to the construction of a U.S. regional security design in North Africa, West-Central Africa, and the Middle East. Libya is, in short, considered to be a major destabilizer of the type of security order the United States would like to see prevail in the African continent despite the attainment of formal independence. For the United States in its experience with African leaders since 1952, perhaps only the late Gamal Abdel Nasser of Egypt and Kwame Nkrumah of Ghana rank as the historical equivalents of Gaddafi. From the perspective of this study, the conflict between Gaddafi and the United States and the West with regard to Africa is an embodiment of the struggle for fundamental decolonization of the regional system, which is why the Libyan leader attracts the sympathy of radical African nationalists.

The Reagan administration's objection to Libya's chairmanship of the OAU can be understood in this context. However, the objection also stemmed, relatedly, from the larger configuration of concern mentioned above: The OAU, just as other Third World regional organizations, is regarded by the two global alliances (NATO and the Warsaw Pact) essentially as a multilateral instrument for managing their security interest in Africa.[30] In the thinking of Reagan and his advisers, Gaddafi, as chairman of the OAU, would have been detrimental, because of his "madness," to U.S. influence and security considerations in the continent; he therefore had to be stopped by every possible means.

Could Nigeria share Reagan's assessment of Gaddafi in the context of Africa? From an objective position, the answer is obviously, no, for given the generally accepted conception of Nigeria's vanguard role in the decolonization movement, Libya's anticolonial policy enhances the prospects of African autonomy and self-respect. Further, Nigerians do not consider themselves threatened by Libya in any fundamental sense. A well-organized and productive Nigeria, with an estimated population of 100 million nationals compared to Libya's 3.5 million people, has nothing to fear from Libya, apart from episodic provocations. In terms of regional influence, Nigerians also feel that the power attributes of their country put it in a position of natural superiority over Libya.[31] As former head of state, General Obasanjo, put it, "Libyan diplomacy in Africa and beyond has not yet attained and may never attain its objectives of Arab unity, liberation of Palestine, enthronement of the People's Congress, and placement in power all over Africa of leaders sympathetic to Gaddafi."[32] What all this means for concerned Nigerians is that the issue of a Libya "phenomenon" in Africa should be addressed primarily on the basis of a determination of how it would affect the legitimate interests of Nigeria, particularly in the West-Central subregion.

For the Shagari government this was not clear-cut. To a substantial extent, the government shared what may be called the nationalist perception of the Libyan foreign posture toward the major Western powers, as witnessed, for example, by Shagari's defensive response to Reagan at Cancun. But as a conservative ruling group, it naturally abhored Libya's radical brand of Arab socialism and vice versa. Thus, in 1980 when the Libyan government unilaterally changed the conventional designation of its embassy in Nigeria to the Bureau of the Socialist Popular Libyan Arab Jamahiriya, the Nigerian foreign minister promptly issued a statement asking the Libyans to either revert to the name by which they were granted accreditation or close down their mission. For the same reason, the Shagari government and Libya were on opposite sides over the OAU's recognition of the government-in-exile of the Polisario Front of West Sahara (Saharawi Arab Democratic Republic, the SADR) as the fifty-first member of the OAU. Similarly, the Nigerian government condemned alleged Libyan subversive activities in independent African states and vehemently opposed the abortive Libya-Chad political union announced in early 1982.

But, more than any other factor, it was pressure from the United States that led to the emergence of a strategic consensus between the Nigerian and U.S. governments with regard to Libya's role in Africa. Libya became a common regional security problem for both countries, requiring a coordinated policy approach. In fact, Nigeria's actions in relation to Chad, to the Libyan OAU chairmanship, and to the OAU recognition of SADR ultimately coincided with the U.S. preferred line of action. For example, when the OAU "peacekeeping" force intervened in Chad in 1982, the general expectation was that the force would play a pacifying role by neutralizing the two opposing forces of Goukouni Queddei and Hissene Habre in order to create a conducive environment for the implementation of the Lagos Accord in a unified Chad.[33] Nigeria, along with Zaire, as contributors to the peacekeeping force, appeared to have maneuvered Habre into power at the expense of the former Chadian leader, Queddei. The United States had backed Habre's ambition for national leadership of Chad with financial, military, and diplomatic assistance, and the Sudan, a local U.S. ally, provided Habre's forces with a base of operation against President Queddei.

The coincidence of a Nigeria-U.S. strategic consensus on regional security was not, however, necessarily translated into a coherent and consistent policy by President Shagari. The actual policy behavior of the Shagari regime was clouded by ambiguity and characterized by an uncertain commitment to any definite goals. Whenever action was taken, it was with great hesitancy as an afterthought and often in a reactionary fashion. Two noteworthy examples follow.

At the end of 1981, when Nigeria finally decided to do something about the conflict next door in Chad, it was because of Libya's military intervention and announcement of a merger with Chad. But worse than that, the Nigerian government became involved, through a haphazard calculation, in the unpopular OAU military mission in Chad while counting on a vague U.S. promise to underwrite the expenditure of the mission. In the end, the United States disputed any such undertaking, and Nigeria was forced, embarrassingly, to bear the financial burden of the operation, amounting to the sum of 80 million naira.[34]

In the second example, President Shagari belatedly announced in 1983, while on a foreign visit, that Nigeria would support the replacement of Cuban troops in Angola with an all-Africa military force, apparently without clearance by the Angolan government. However, he quickly repudiated this position on his return to Nigeria as a result of public outcry against his proposal. The proposal, according to Nigerian critics, was, with regard to Namibia's independence, tantamount to an endorsement of the hated concept of linkage, which Shagari had previously denounced. Besides, the critics feared, correctly, that an OAU military presence in Angola would have been manipulated by the Reagan administration and South Africa to install Jonas Savimbi's UNITA forces in power, while yet undermining the capacity of SWAPO to prevail in Namibia. These aims, Nigerians knew, were not incompatible with the intrinsic purpose of Reagan's policy of constructive engagement in southern Africa. With such a record in ineptness and undynamism in regional affairs, Shagari's government, not surprisingly, failed to earn the support and respect of the Reagan administration, given the latter's action-oriented and militaristic foreign policy. Top U.S. officials were contemptuous of that government, just as Nigerians villified its regional policy performance.

Reagan's Approach Versus Carter's Approach

A final note to this chapter is a brief comment on the contrast between the Carter and Reagan approaches to U.S.-Africa policy and a discussion of the relevance Reagan's approach had on the failure of Nigeria's leadership in the regional sphere. Many U.S. experts on foreign affairs have criticized the Reagan administration for failing to formulate an explicit foreign policy. The record shows instead that the administration has tended to subsume foreign policy within a bolder thrust of defense (military) policy, rather than the other way around.[35] With respect to Africa, other critics have charged that the United States under Reagan has reinvigorated the Kissingerian cold war (globalist) framework as a basis of U.S. actions in the continent. For example, the experienced analyst Helen Kitchen noted that "the Reagan administration is more categorical than its predecessor in linking aid to Africa to the U.S.

national interest. Moreover, calculations of the U.S. national interest in Africa place heavier emphasis on countering Soviet influence [now] than on the concept of helping Africa construct the building blocks of economic and political self-reliance."[36]

A more pertinent observation, for our purpose, is not that Reagan's government placed greater emphasis on the satisfaction of U.S. national interests in Africa, for this is as it should be, but that Reagan's policy approach in the continent, when compared even to that of the Kissinger era, was too militaristic, thus clashing more conspicuously with Africa's cherished aspirations. "In the almost three decades of U.S.-African relations," remarked General Obasanjo, "there has never been a period as frosty as that of the last few years."[37] Evidence of Reagan's militarism in Africa included a drastic increase in the amount specified for foreign military sales credit (from 1981 to 1982 the amount increased 178 percent, totaling $203 million[38]); air confrontation with Libya in the Gulf of Sidra; repeated joint military exercises with local allies; the apparent military thrust of the policy of constructive engagement under which South African forces regularly violated the territorial boundaries of Frontline States in southern Africa; and the U.S. military involvement in the Chadian conflict. Most observers anticipated that Reagan would have this type of approach to U.S.-Third World relations in general, judging from his firmly held views on how to project U.S. power in the world.

During the long campaign before his election, Reagan continuously stressed the theme that U.S. influence in the Third World had suffered a dangerous decline, a situation he attributed partly to Carter's reluctance to demonstrate U.S. military power in Third World conflicts. The inability of the previous administration to resolve the hostage crisis in Iran without causing severe damage to U.S. prestige helped Reagan fuel this indictment in the public perception. As a corollary, Reagan derided the former president for failing to adopt forceful measures aimed at countering what conservative Republicans conceived as the growth of Soviet military and political involvement in the developing regions at the expense of the West. He pointed to Soviet military intervention in Afghanistan in 1980 as a recent example of a pattern that started in Angola in 1975–1976.

Reagan's militarism, exhibited apparently as an end of U.S. foreign policy, invites a definite contrast with the foreign policy approach of the two previous administrations. In the Ford-Kissinger period, U.S. foreign policy was based on a Machiavellian manipulation of power, broadly conceived, toward the attainment of identifiable ends; moral concerns had no place in the Kissingerian policy strategy. Under Carter, U.S. policy sought, essentially, to transmit American power and influence to the world on the platform of American ideals and moral principles. In Reagan's first term as president, the United States was determined to impose its will on others—especially in the Third World—largely by military force.

Reference has already been made to some of the manifestations of the Reagan militaristic approach in Africa. Clearly, Reagan's focus on bilateral support, as opposed to multilateral assistance, together with his augmentation in the level of arms transfer to subregions experiencing intense conflicts (e.g., Western Sahara and the Horn) led to a new phenomenon of local arms races (as between Libya, Sudan, and Egypt and between Morocco and Algeria) as well as fragmentation in the solidarity of the OAU. (The most serious consequence of the latter was the failure of the member countries, in two attempts, to hold the nineteenth annual summit in 1982.) Thus the general thrust of U.S.-Africa policy under Reagan contributed, specifically, in undermining Nigeria's leadership capacity to resolve regional problems. This was unlike the Carter era when U.S. policy propensity did not, in relative terms, challenge Africa's interests and integrity. During Carter's presidency, the U.S. policy framework actually buttressed the capacity of Nigeria to provide the desired leadership in Africa's collective interest.

Summary

During the Shagari period, Nigerian-U.S. relations seemed to have turned full circle in the sense that the relationship experienced many of the basic features that prevailed in the earliest period of the Balewa regime. Of central significance was the noticeable absence of a material base of leverage with which Nigeria could bargain with the United States in the realm of regional affairs. Rather, there was a return to the lopsided dependency in bilateral and regional ties characteristic of the 1960s.

Three main factors largely accounted for this deficiency. The first was related to the crisis experienced by the Nigerian economy as a result of the worldwide depression of the oil market, financial mismanagement and extensive corruption by the Shagari ruling group, and the high cost of food importation due to stagnation in agricultural production. The second factor was linked to the restoration of competitive party politics on the fundamentally divisive model of the first republic, which reactivated the old spectre of national polarization and a weak leadership in regional affairs. The third factor, which aggravated the regional policy consequences of the first two, was the militaristic Africa policy of the Reagan administration. This tended to heighten African conflicts such as in southern Africa and Chad, while at the same time encouraging fragmentation in the ranks of the OAU.

On the whole, we can conclude that the state of the relationship in this period was retrogressive for two broad reasons. First, Nigeria suffered an absolute breakdown in its quest for national economic and political development. The relationship with the United States in this period failed to engender positive long-term sustenance of the democratic experiment begun in 1979 or of self-reliant economic growth. Second, there was a loss in the momentum, previously attained in the Mohammed-Obasanjo regime, toward an achievement-oriented national leadership in regional affairs.

Notes

1. October 1979 marked the end of the first period of military rule in Nigeria. Thereafter, competitive party democracy was restored on the basis of a presidential constitutional system that shared a number of common features with the U.S. model. Alhaji Shehu Shagari of the National Party of Nigeria (NPN) served as the first (and only) executive president under the new system.

2. "Nigeria and the United States: The Need for Civility, the Dangers of Intimacy," *Orbis* (Winter 1982): 858–864.

3. Emmanuel Yawe, *Sunday New Nigerian,* February 19, 1984, p. 3.

4. Sully Abu, *Sunday Guardian,* November 20, 1983, p. 9.

5. Yawe, *Sunday New Nigerian,* p. 3; *New Nigerian,* January 27, 1984, p. 11.

6. The second experiment in Nigeria's short history with a liberal democratic government failed at the end of December 1983. President Shagari's government was ousted from power by the military on December 31, 1983, primarily as a result of its colossal mismanagement of the national economy and of unprecedented corruption by politicians and other privileged elites. See below.

7. Total oil sales for the country from 1958 to 1983 amounted to 78.9 billion naira. See *Sunday Concord,* February 5, 1984, p. 1, which cites sources from the International Monetary Fund and the Nigerian National Petroleum Corporation.

8. *New York Times,* July 23, 1981, p. D1.

9. *West Africa,* June 25, 1978, p. 1104.

10. Bassey Ate, "Nigeria Needs a New Oil Strategy," *Nigerian Forum* (March-April 1984): 80–87.

11. See Mark W. Delancey, "Nigeria: Foreign Policy Alternatives, Background Notes at the Beginning of Civilian Rule," Mimeograph, State Department, Washington, D.C., p. 11; also *Nigerian Call,* December 6–12, 1981, p. 6.

12. As indicated in Chapter 7, the Joint Agricultural Consultative Committee (JACC) is the institutional mechanism for coordinating Nigeria-U.S. cooperation in the agricultural field focusing on private sector participation. The JACC comprises representatives of Agro-business groups from both countries. Apart from having responsibility for identifying feasible joint venture projects, its

primary function is to promote the sales of U.S. farm produce, machinery, and services in Nigeria.

13. The startling details of how political stalwarts of the major parties pillaged the national treasury are being compiled by ongoing tribunals and commissions of enquiry (see note 18).

14. Jean Herskovits, "Dateline Nigeria: Democracy Down But Not Out," *Foreign Policy* 54 (Spring 1984): 186.

15. Confidential interview, Lagos.

16. Herskovits, "Dateline Nigeria," p. 187.

17. Quoted in Samuel P. Huntington, "American Ideals Versus American Institutions," *Political Science Quarterly* (Spring 1982): 23, note 25.

18. The impact of bilateral ties on regional policy orientation also manifested itself, rather crudely, in the narrow personal plane. For example, the practice by chieftains of the ruling National party of accepting large financial kickbacks, often in foreign currencies, on commercial deals involving imported rice and fertilizer or exported oil was one that enhanced a docile political relationship with the United States and other Western powers. See the case of Umaru Dikko, the former minister of transport and aviation and chairman of the Presidential Task Force on Rice Importation. *Daily Times,* June 10, 1985, p. 1; *The Punch,* June 10, 1985, p. 1; *Nigerian Herald,* June 10, 1985, p. 1.

19. This was related by Abba Dabo, Shagari's chief press secretary. See *Sunday New Nigerian,* January 22, 1984, p. 3.

20. Herskovits, "Dateline Nigeria," p. 187.

21. *The Punch,* August 13 and 18, 1982, p. 7. The failure of the Tripoli Summit was blamed on a number of factors. The first was the admission to the OAU of the Saharawi Arab Democratic Republic of Western Sahara as the fifty-first member by the secretary-general without general consensus. The second factor was the opposition of some member states to the prospect of Libya assuming the chairmanship of the organization. Third, and most significant, was the campaign of opposition waged by the United States against the hosting of the summit in Tripoli and against the prospective chairmanship of Libya.

22. Special issue of the *Nigerian Forum,* October 1982, on the failed nineteenth summit; also *Africa Now,* September 1982; and *Counter Spy,* September 1982.

23. Confidential interview with a senior official in Shagari's government; also *Africa* 111 (November 1980): 30.

24. *Africa* 111 (November 1980): 32.

25. Ibid.

26. *Daily Times,* July 2, 1981, p. 1.

27. Ibid., p. 10; also *New York Times,* July 27, 1981, p. A3.

28. *National Concord* (Lagos), July 11, 1983, p. 3.

29. Cited in Helen Kitchen, "On Safari—Again," *Orbis* (Winter 1982): 855. As a result of this consideration, the new U.S. administration launched what was reported to be a concerted program to destabilize the Libyan government, including measures of a coordinated anti-Libyan propaganda and assassination of Gaddafi. See the following: *Newsweek,* March 3, 1981, p. 19; *Atlanta Constitution,* January 27, 1981; *Daily News* (New York), May 7, 1981.

30. Bassey Ate, *Nigerian Forum* (October 1982): 789–793; also The Atlantic Council of the United States Security Series, *After Afghanistan—The Long Haul: Safeguarding Security and Independence in the Third World*, Washington, D.C., March, 1980.

31. This viewpoint was supported, for instance, during a national seminar organized by the Nigerian Institute of International Affairs in 1983 on "The Situation in Chad."

32. Olusegun Obasanjo, "Africa's Needs," *Foreign Policy* (Winter 1984): 86.

33. During the Obasanjo regime, Nigeria was the center of diplomatic efforts to end the conflict in Chad. Two famous agreements emerged from those efforts in 1979: the Kano and Lagos Accords.

34. Haroun Adamu, "Nigeria: A Mercenary Nation," *The Punch*, December 11, 1983, p. 6. Of the 80 million naira, which was the total cost of the operation, the United States paid back to Nigeria only 4 million naira.

35. Robert W. Tucker, "The Role of Defense in the Foreign Policy of the Reagan Administration," *The Jerusalem Journal of International Affairs* 7 (1-2) (1984): 47–56.

36. Kitchen, "On Safari," p. 856.

37. Obasanjo, "Africa's Needs," p. 85.

38. Kitchen, "On Safari," p. 856.

9

Conclusion

Recapitulation

One common strand in the development of Nigerian-U.S. relations over the twenty-four year period covered in this study was the close association between the structure of the bilateral ties between the countries and the character of Nigeria's foreign policy, demonstrated especially in its diplomacy with successive U.S. governments on African issues. The central assumption, more concisely, was that to properly understand an existing mode of regional relations between the two countries one must examine closely the medium of their developing bilateral ties, most specifically the interconnection of economics and politics. The dynamics within this setting, it was argued, would provide a clue to that perennial question in politics: Who influences whom, how and why? The interests of the most influential members of a dependent society like Nigeria's are likely to be tied, as Marshall Singer observed, to the material indexes of the bilateral relations—capital aid, private investments, trade in raw materials, contract transactions, and so forth. Additionally, the domestic and regional security needs of the same strategic groups somehow become linked to the bilateral medium. Therein lies the potential political leverage afforded the dominant entity in the relationship.

The peculiarity of the bilateral structure of each period, the study shows, determined the scope of both policy autonomy and leadership dynamism for the Nigerian regime in power in the diplomacy of African decolonization. Thus in the period 1960–1966, Nigeria's regional leadership as well as its policy relationship with the United States was marked, characteristically, by a tendency toward subordination of what can be considered the national will—as distinct from the regime's narrow self-interests—to U.S. initiatives. The experience of the Balewa regime (which was to be repeated in 1980–1983 under Shehu Shagari) illustrates the underlying pressure for this outcome.

In that period, the governing political parties (primarily the NPC and NCNC coalition along with their associated groups) strongly favored the establishment of intimate economic ties with the United States. U.S. authorities responded to this Nigerian desire generally with equal enthusiasm. Each side had its own justification. The Nigerian leadership needed to obtain vital investment capital and high-level technical assistance for the prosecution of the first post-independence national development plan. But that was only part of the explanation. Economic ties with the United States were also intended to generate political assets for ensuring the regime's domestic security concerns and regional interest. For the United States, the evolving bilateral context was of crucial political value: It offered to U.S. personnel a channel of influence to be utilized in moderating the actions of Nigerian policymakers on domestic and regional issues. The basis of a mutual relationship was thus secured. The point that needs to be stressed, though, is that the pattern of Nigerian interests as shaped by those who most influenced its policies and the lack of tangible power resources with which the ruling government could pursue those interests resulted in an alignment with the United States that was necessarily one of dominance and dependence. Apart from the developing direct Nigeria-U.S. relations, Great Britain played a significant role in boosting U.S. political influence on the policy process in Nigeria. The traditional British connection to Nigeria proved to be a definite asset for U.S. policy. Despite periodic charges of "Albionian perfidy in the commercial sphere"[1] by U.S. diplomats and businessmen in Lagos, the United States and United Kingdom maintained intimate cooperation on Nigerian affairs especially in the political and security fields, where their interests clearly coincided.

The debate over nationalization of the economy and external financing of the first national development plan (1962–1968) underscored another facet of the emerging Nigerian-U.S. relationship, namely the recurrent discordance between governmental actions and public expectations in foreign relations. The debate showed, for instance, that groups both within and outside official circles persistently took a different position from that of the Balewa government with regard to the country's post-independence foreign economic policy. Those groups—notably, the official opposition party in the House of Representatives, independent MPs, the Nigerian Youth Congress, the Nigerian Trade Union Congress, and university intellectuals—wished Nigeria to restrict its colonial linkages with Great Britain and to diversify its economic ties away from the West in general and toward the socialist bloc. Exclusive dependence on the West, greatly magnified by the colossal influence of the United States, would, they argued, corrupt the historic leadership role of Nigeria in the regional decolonization movement. The views of these groups, no doubt, were considered irrational by the authoritative leadership, given the objective realities of the time; their pressure, nevertheless, constituted an effective check on the government's conduct with the United States.

The rise of crude petroleum to a position of prominence in international economic relations, which coincided roughly with the end of Nigeria's civil war in 1970, altered the bilateral structure of Nigeria-U.S. relations from 1970 to 1979. With this historic development, Nigerians generally believed that, and indeed acted as if, their country had become economically self-reliant. They were convinced that the terms of their economic relations with the United States could henceforth be dictated from within by those who were in charge of managing the country's fortuitous wealth. It would have been unimaginable in the previous period for a Nigerian decisionmaker to refer to a potential private U.S. investor, in the presence of a U.S. ambassador, as a "fly-by-night operator" for which Nigeria did not care. Such a statement was an indication of a changed perception about Nigerian ties with the United States. For both policy officials and private Nigerian groups, the earlier psychology of total dependence was profoundly transformed into one that regarded economic relations with the United States in terms of interdependence. This development highlights the critical point of distinction between the pattern of Nigeria-U.S. relations in the 1960s and that in the 1970s: The altered conditions in the bilateral economic setting eliminated for the United States the material element it needed to exercise leverage on policy actions of Nigerian decisionmakers. Also, the former British link had become, in this sense, substantially irrelevant.

There were a number of manifestations of the changed bilateral ties after 1970. First, Nigeria terminated its pre-1966 reliance on official capital aid from the United States; as a corollary, the third development plan (1975–1980) called for no external capital for financing its public sector programs, in sharp contrast to the first plan. Second, the state indigenized operations of the foreign oil companies, including those of U.S. ownership, claiming 55 percent ownership in those firms. Third, the program of indigenization itself, first promulgated in 1972, was a response by federal decisionmakers to pressure from the public and the local business community, which clamored for control over the economic and political influence of multinational corporations and the terms of prospective direct investments from abroad. Fourth, Nigeria emerged in this period as the second largest supplier, after Canada, of crude oil to the U.S. economy.

One major outcome of this change in the bilateral structure was the introduction of incessant political strains in the overall Nigerian-U.S. ties, including relations on crucial regional issues. Nigerians had emerged from their civil war exceedingly confident and more convinced than ever before about their preeminent status and special mission in sub-Saharan Africa. The possession of a large pool of financial resources due to oil provided the material substance to this self-image. Concomitantly, Nigerians expressed a disposition to exert an independent policy behavior relative to the United States. As a consequence the prevalent mode of Nigeria-U.S. relations, regionally, tended more toward conflict than cooperation, which had been the hallmark of the 1960–1966 period.

Relative to the apparent gains made from 1970 to 1979, the brief interlude of the Shagari regime (1979–1983) was considered by Nigerians to have engendered retrogression in their country's relationship with the United States. In four short years, all the bilateral advantages they had enjoyed against the Americans abruptly evaporated, routing the relationship full circle to the infant experience of the Balewa era. The Nigerian impression of retrogression was reinforced by the glaring impotence of Nigeria's leadership performance in regional affairs. The intensity of that disappointment helped explain the mass jubilation that accompanied the overthrow of the Shagari government in December 1983 and the promise of the new military government headed by Major-General Mohammadu Buhari to restructure the fabric of national leadership and the domestic economy prerequisites of a more enduring foundation for Nigerian foreign relations.

The Promise of Buhari

Two early undertakings by the Buhari federal military government are significant to the purpose of this study: the program to reorder the national economy, and the pronounced determination to nurture, out of the decadence of the recent past, a national leadership that, in Buhari's words, is "imbued with discipline, public accountability and integrity," since no country, as he further pointed out, "can command the respect and admiration of the international community without a dedicated and purposeful leadership."[2] A resilient domestic economy and purposeful national leadership are conditions that obviously determine Nigeria's relative autonomy in the arduous process of its relationships with the United States and other world powers.

The task of reordering the national economy can be confronted in three stages: short-term, medium-term, and long-term.[3] Prominent among the short-term steps Buhari plans to institute are measures for reducing government expenditures and rescheduling international trade debts accumulated by the Shagari government. The most critical action in reducing government expenditures is to be the reduction of personnel cost in the bloated public service, the creation of opulent oil wealth of the 1970s. But this involves, on the whole, a systematic retrenchment of workers not only in the public service but also in the private sector, since the drastic decline in the level of available foreign exchange affects the fortunes of the (private) manufacturing companies, which rely on foreign sources for over 70 percent of their needed raw materials. In the area of the settlement of external debts, the government is already taking some measures aimed at refinancing trade arrears, including uninsured debts and guaranteed arrears with Western export credit agencies. This is to be a thorny issue for the government, for not only is the Buhari regime determined to negotiate a settlement of the nation's outstanding trade debts on their own merits but the major creditors, including those in the United States, insist, collectively, that Nigeria must enter into agreement with the IMF (i.e., in essence, that Nigeria must accept the IMF loan offer with its conditionalities) before substantial progress can be made on debt rescheduling and before new lines of credit can be arranged. There is, however, no prospect of early agreement with the IMF because of three partricularly controversial conditions attached to the loan offer: devaluation of the naira, trade liberalization, and removal of government subsidies on petroleum and allied products.

In the medium term, the new government aims to achieving self-sufficiency in food production "and in the production of at least 50% of the raw material needs of agro-based industries, if not 100%."[4] It plans to review the existing industrial policy primarily for the purpose of discouraging "import-dependent industries." Another critical step is a serious consideration to "privatize" a number of public-run corporations in order, as the planning minister put it, "to inject private participation and methods into them." There has for some time been a growing concern in Nigeria that many government enterprises are a drain on public resources apart from providing substandard services to the citizens who must pay for their existence. From the available indications, the Buhari government seems bent on reorienting the national economy to attain the following fundamental (long-term) objectives, among others: self-sufficiency in agricultural production (it is even contemplated that Nigeria would become once again a net exporter of food crops), and a restructuring of the manufacturing sector so that the majority of related industries could obtain at least 80 percent of their raw materials from local sources. More than in the past, Nigerians will be expected to contribute to the cost of providing social services in the areas of education, health services, pipe-borne water, transportation, telecommunications, etc.[5] It is difficult to say at this early stage whether the Buhari government will sustain its immediate post-Shagari resolution to wage the economic battle, which is a necessity for national recovery, or whether the measures envisioned can ensure the desired results even with the best of effort. However, it can be said with some certainty that the public appears to accept the reality of the new struggle even though it involves enormous sacrifices.

On the political front, the quest to institutionalize a new ethic of national leadership based on discipline, public accountability, and integrity has focused on the special tribunals set up to investigate former politicians and other public officials and inflict stiff penalties on those found to have engaged in corrupt self-enrichment activities. Long prison sentences are being imposed on guilty officials. In addition they are being required to forfeit the stolen funds in cash and property. "I think this is something new in Nigerian political culture," declared the renowned novelist and social critic Chinua Achebe in assessing the potential impact of these "draconian punishments" on the prospect of accountability in public life in the country. "I don't think Nigeria will ever be the same again no matter what happens to the rest of their [the Buhari's government's] programmes."[6] This assessment is only partially correct. The policy of the Buhari government on this score will indeed help engender the desired leadership ethics in public life, but only if it is in conjunction with radical changes in Nigeria's total political economy such that equal participation and reward are guaranteed to the many parts that constitute the Nigerian entity.

Future Prospects in Nigerian-U.S. Relations

What is the future direction of Nigeria-U.S. relations in both the bilateral and regional realms? To put the question differently, what are the advantages and disadvantages of a future partnership between Nigeria and the United States? This speculation is undertaken at two levels: it centers on the role of the United States in the growth of the Nigerian economy and on the prospect of U.S. power as asset or liability in the advancement of Nigeria's regional potentials.

In arguing for a special relationship between Nigeria and the United States, the first substantive foreign minister of postcolonial Nigeria, Jaja Wachuku, stressed, in a private interview, the existence of certain pull factors that should enhance such a partnership. According to Wachuku, Nigeria is a young country requiring modernization. "Although rich in ancient African culture and tradition, in terms of modern culture of politics, science and technology it is a young country. The USA, also, is relatively a young country, but one which has evolved for 200 years and has developed the tenets of modernization, and is regarded as the most powerful country in the world."[7] Further, Nigeria has the largest concentration of blacks, of any country in the world, and the United States has the largest concentration of blacks outside Africa. Moreover, Wachuku pointed out, both countries share a common aspiration toward liberal democratic ideals, apart from the additional advantage of a common language [English]. "We [Nigeria] are closer to that country [the United States] in all respects than to Western Europe, USSR and China." He concluded, "Nigeria and the United States need to bridge the Atlantic." The current U.S. ambassador in Nigeria, Thomas Smith, similarly observed that Nigeria and the United States are large countries that have found that a federal system of government "is best suited to promote unity in diversity." Federalism as well as other factors of similarity have, in the ambassador's view, enabled the two countries to enjoy "close relations" over the years.[8]

The basic elements of similarity noted above provide the building blocks of a strong Nigeria-U.S. relationship. But the building process itself calls into play other critical forces and realities. In the real world of conflicting perceptions of interests, security, and international aspirations, of great disparities in resources and power attributes, and of dissimilarities in historical experiences, it is pragmatism borne by necessity of self-promotion that determines the forms of bilateral and international associations. On this basis, Nigeria needs the United States bilaterally for the sake of imbibing the dynamic U.S. technological culture and benefiting from the vast experience of its private entrepreneurship as a vehicle for generating self-sustaining economic growth and development. For instance, although Nigerians and Americans may subscribe, fundamentally, to opposing conceptions of regional security in Africa, it is, nevertheless, a matter of urgent self-interest for Nigeria to cultivate private U.S. expertise in expanding its sluggish agricultural productivity; this, in turn, is a factor of immense significance in enhancing its regional power position. On the other hand, an intimate technological and economic relationship with the United States may multiply the prospects of dependent, not autonomous, development for Nigeria. But the historical question that Nigerians must confront in the context of an inevitable relationship with the United States is what short-run price, in terms of erosion of national autonomy, should they consider acceptable in order to attain greater long-term development and regional independence?

An intensification of Nigeria-U.S. bilateral ties in the future may very likely bring into play, more prominently than in the past, the mediating role of particular institutions and groups. In a sense, these bodies will actually stimulate the intensity of linkages between the two entities. One refers to the potential disposition of the Nigerian-U.S. chambers of commerce, a Nigeria-U.S. business council, Nigerian graduates of U.S. educational institutions (about 30,000 Nigerians have been enrolled per annum in U.S. higher education institutions in recent years), and black American–Nigerian business and cultural groups to serve as active transmission belts in an expanding exchange of resources, ideas, and values between the countries. What is anticipated is not that the intensive mediation of these bodies will necessarily result in a conflict-free bilateral experience in the future, but that such mediation is bound to stretch the frontiers of that relationship.

Regionally, the intertwining involvement of Nigeria and the United States in the decolonization movement of Africa is bound to endure. In spite of what Nigerians may wish, the intervention of the United States and other world forces in shaping the dialectics of this movement will persist. Nigeria does not, in the foreseeable future, possess the power resources (or state of national development) to assume a preponderant responsibility for maintaining order in Africa. Put differently, it is beyond the power of Nigeria to assume unilaterally the burden of regional security. But then, the nature of the U.S. role in African political affairs, which has in the past tended to be backward-looking, has been a regular source of conflict in view of Nigeria's deep commitment to fundamental changes in Africa's colonial relationships. The atmosphere of conflict has often been aggravated because U.S. foreign policymakers have habitually failed to appreciate that Nigerians (and Africans generally) are as concerned with problems of economic development, drought, and hunger, to which the United States has provided immense aid, as they are with issues of regional security and positive political change, over which U.S. policy has been detrimental. To be progressive, America's future involvement must relate squarely to Africa's desire for complete emancipation from the deleterious aspects of its colonial legacy. Africa needs the United States to help liberate itself from past limitations in the true spirit of the American revolution, not to be hampered by a narrow preoccupation with the affairs of the Soviet Union. The United States must demonstrate an interest in a patient promotion of its traditional ideals and values in Africa at the expense of pursuing geostrategic benefits that in the short run may seem worthwhile but are totally ephemeral in the sphere of its longer-term interests.

Ideally, what Nigerians desire is complete decolonization of Africa and a positive national economic development that promises less bilateral dependence. Can the United States be relevant in these aspirations?

Notes

1. This phrase was coined by U.S. Ambassador Elbert Mathews in a report to the State Department on the state of U.S.-U.K. relations in Nigeria following the first military coup in January 1966. Mathews to Williams, February 10, 1966, G. Mennen Williams Files, Record Group 59, National Archives, Washington, D.C.

2. Refer to speech by Major-General Buhari on the occasion of the Annual Patron's Dinner of the Nigerian Institute of International Affairs, December 3, 1984.

3. This aspect of discussion is based on information provided in a lecture titled "Reviewing the Nigerian Economy," delivered by Chief Michael S. Adigun, federal minister of national planning, March 19, 1985.

4. Ibid., p. 12.

5. Ibid., p. 11.

6. *New Nigerian*, April 5, 1985, p. 2.

7. Interview with Wachuku in Aba, Imo State.

8. *U.S.I.S. News*, January 8, 1985, p. 4.

Appendix A

Private U.S. Institutions and Firms Working in Nigeria Financed by USAID as of December 1966

Contractor	Activity	Location
The Federal District and throughout Nigeria		
Western Electric Inc.	Telecommunications Urban-rural electrification (technical assistance, T.A.)	Throughout Nigeria
International Telephone and Telegraph	Telecommunication (supply of instruments)	Throughout Nigeria
Daniel, Mann, Johnson & Mendenhall	Lagos water supply (engineering)	Lagos, Federal District
Wilbur Smith & Associates	Federal roads (economics)	Lagos and western Nigeria
Sverdrup and Parcel & Associates Inc.	Federal roads (engineering)	Lagos and western Nigeria
Lockheed Aircraft Corporation	Civil aviation (economics & engineering)	Lagos and Kano
Arthur D. Little	Industrial planning & project appraisal (T.A.)	Throughout Nigeria
Education & World Affairs	Educational planning & advisory services (T.A.)	Throughout Nigeria
J. G. White Inc.	Electricity Corporation of Nigeria (T.A.)	Lagos, Federal District
University of California at Los Angeles	Federal Advanced Teachers College (T.A.)	Lagos, Federal District

Contractor	Activity	Location
New York University	School of Administration, Faculty of Business and Social Studies, University of Lagos (T.A.)	Lagos, Federal District
American Institute for Research	Test development and research (T.A.)	Throughout Nigeria
Franklin Book Programs	Educational book publishing (T.A.)	Throughout Nigeria
Board of Education, Washington County, Md.	Modern aids to education (T.A.)	Throughout Nigeria
Research Triangle Institute	Agricultural statistics (T.A.)	Throughout Nigeria

East

Contractor	Activity	Location
Michigan State University	University of Nigeria, Nsukka (T.A.)	Nsukka
University of California	Comprehensive secondary school (T.A.)	Port Harcourt
Colorado State University	Umudike Agricultural Center (T.A.)	Umuahia
Louis Berger Inc.	Calabar-Ikom Road (engineering)	Calabar-Ikom
	Port-Harcourt Umuezeala Road (engineering)	Port Harcourt
	Igrita-Umuezeala Road (engineering, architecture and economics)	Igrita-Umuezeala
	Umudike Agricultural Center (architecture)	Umuahia
Stanford Research Institute	Rural electrification study	Throughout area
Robert R. Nathan Associates	Port Harcourt-Aba Road	Port Harcourt-Aba

Contractor	Activity	Location
Tippetts-Abbett-McCarthy-Stratton (TAMS)	Port Harcourt-Aba Road	Port Harcourt-Aba
Wilbur Smith & Associates	Port Harcourt arterial streets (economics)	Port Harcourt
Sverdrup and Parcel & Associates Inc.	Port Harcourt arterial streets (engineering)	Port Harcourt
Michigan State University	Rural education program	Throughout area

West

Contractor	Activity	Location
Cooperative League of U.S.A.	Agricultural cooperatives (T.A.)	Throughout area
Western Michigan	Technical College, Ibadan (T.A.)	Ibadan
Ohio University	Advanced Teacher's College of Education (T.A.)	Ibadan
Harvard University	Comprehensive secondary school (T.A.)	Aiyetoro
Pascal & Ludwig	Ibadan water supply mains	Ibadan
	Asejire Dam	Asejire
University of Wisconsin	Faculty of Agriculture, University of Ife (T.A.)	Ibadan
	School of Agriculture (T.A.)	Akure
Gilbert Associates	Ibadan water distribution (construction supervision)	Ibadan
Stanley International	Ibadan water distribution (management services)	Ibadan
Gilbert Associates	Western region water reconnaissance	Throughout area
International Pipe & Ceramics Corps	Western Nigeria water supply	Throughout area

Contractor	Activity	Location
	North	
Ohio University	Advanced Teacher's College (T.A.)	Kano
University of Pittsburgh	Zaria Institute of Administration (T.A.)	Ahmadu Bello University
Kansas State University	Faculties of Agriculture & Veterinary Medicine (T.A.)	Ahmadu Bello University
Stanley International	Urban water supply (engineering)	Gusau, Ilorin Maiduguri
University of Wisconsin	Northern Nigeria Teacher Education Program (T.A.)	Throughout area
Brezina Nigeria Ltd.	Industrial Development Center Workshop (construction)	Zaria

Appendix B

U.S. Companies in the Oil and Gas Industry in Nigeria (owned in whole or part by U.S. citizens or U.S. parent companies) as of 1976

Allied Oilfield Services (Nig.) Ltd. (AOS)
  (Oiltools International Intairdril)
Ashland Oil (Nigeria) Company
Baker Nigeria Ltd.
  (Baker Oil Tools Inc.)
Baroid of Nigeria Ltd.
  (Drilling Chemicals Products Ltd.)
Bonny Oil & Gas Industries (Nig.) Ltd. (BOGI)
  (Williams Companies)
Brown & Root Nigeria Ltd.
  (Haliburton)
Camco Ltd.
Cameron Iron Works (Nigeria) Ltd.
Coastal & Offshore Plant Systems Inc.
Dowell Schlumberger (Nigeria) Ltd.
  (Dow Chemical Company, Schlumberger)
Dresser Nigeria Ltd.
  (Dresser Magcobar Minerals Ltd.)
Foster Wheeler (Nigeria) Ltd.
Gulf Oil Company (Nigeria) Ltd. (GOCON)
Haliburton Nigeria Ltd.
International Drilling Company (Nig.) Ltd. (IDC)
  (The Offshore Company)
Keydril Nigeria Ltd.
McDermott (Nigeria) Ltd.
Mobil Oil Nigeria Ltd. (MONL)
Mobil Producing Nigeria Ltd. (MPNL)
Oceaneering Nigeria Ltd.
  (Oceaneering International)
Otis of Nigeria Ltd.
Pan Ocean Oil Corporation (Nigeria)
  (Marathon Oil)
Petroleum Consultants (Nigeria) Ltd.
  (Cabot Corporation)
Phillips Oil Co. (Nigeria) Ltd.
Raymond International of Delaware Inc.
Santa Fe Nigeria Development Co. Ltd.

Saybolt (Nigeria) Ltd.
  (E. W. Saybolt & Co.)
Schlumberger (Nigeria) Ltd.
Sedco-Bean Constructors & Southeastern Drilling Co. of Nigeria Ltd.
  (SEDCO)
Seismograph Service (Nigeria) Ltd. (SSL)
  (Raytheon Corporation)
Service & Supply Co. of West Africa Ltd. (SASCO)
  (Vetco Offshore Industries)
Solus Schall (Nigeria) Ltd.
  (Solus Schall International-Intairdril Ltd.)
Tenneco Oil Company of Nigeria
Texaco Nigeria Ltd.
Texaco Overseas (Nigeria) Petroleum Co. (TOPCON)
Tidex Nigeria Ltd.
  (Tidewater Marine Service Inc.)
Trans-Africa Engineering Ltd.
  (VETCO Inc.)
Transworld Drilling Company (Nigeria) Ltd.
  (Kerr-McGee Corporation)
United Geophysical (Nigeria) Ltd.
Wayne (West Africa) Ltd.
  (Dresser Industries Inc.)
Whipstock (Nigeria) Ltd.
  (Eastman-Whipstock)
Williams International Group
Zapata Marine Service (Nigeria) Ltd.

Acronyms

AAPC	All-African Peoples Conference
AATUF	All-African Trade Union Federation
AG	Action Group
ANC	Congolese National Army
ANPC	All-Nigerian People's Conference
CPP	Convention People's Party
ECOWAS	Economic Community of West African States
EEC	European Economic Community
FLN	National Liberation Front
FNLA	National Front for the Independence of Angola
FRELIMO	Front for the Liberation of Mozambique
GPRA	Provisoire de la Republique Algerienne
IAMO	Inter-African and Malagasy States Organization
IAS	Independent African States
IBRD	International Bank for Reconstruction and Development—World Bank
IDA	International Development Agency
IFA	International Finance Association
IMF	International Monetary Fund
MP	Member of Nigerian Parliament
MPLA	Popular Movement for the Liberation of Angola
NCNC	National Council of Nigerian Citizens
NNOC	Nigerian National Oil Corporation
NPC	Northern People's Congress
NPN	National Party of Nigeria
NSC	National Security Council
NSSM 39	National Security Study Memorandum 39
NTUC	Nigerian Trade Union Congress
NUNS	National Union of Nigerian Students
NYC	Nigerian Youth Congress
OAPEC	Organization of Arab Petroleum Exporting Countries
OAS	Organization of American States
OAU	Organization of African Unity
OCAM	Organisation Commune d'Afrique et Malgach

ONUC	Operation des Nations Unies au Congo
OPEC	Organization of Petroleum Exporting Countries
OPIC	Overseas Private Investment Corporation
PAIGC	The African Party for the Independence of Guinea and the Cape Verde Islands
PCV	Peace Corps Volunteers
PF	The Patriotic Front
SADR	Saharawi Arab Democratic Republic
SWAPO	South-West African People's Organization
TUCN	Trade Union Congress of Nigeria
UAM	Union Africaine et Malgache
UAR	United Arab Republic
UNITA	National Union for the Total Independence of Angola
USAID or AID	United States Agency for International Development
UT	Union Togolese
WFTU	World Federation of Trade Unions
ZANU	The Zimbabwe African National Union
ZAPU	The Zimbabwe African People's Union

Bibliography

Primary Sources

Records at the National Archives, Washington, D.C. Record Group 59, General Records of the U.S. Department of State. Files of G. Mennen Williams, Assistant Secretary of State for Africa, 1961–1966.
John F. Kennedy Presidential Library. NSC Files, Oral History Program.
Records at the Department of State: Freedom of Information Act (FOI).
Private Interviews.

Government Publications: Nigeria

Central Bank of Nigeria, Lagos. *Economic and Financial Review.* December 1965, 1968, June 1975, March 1976.
Energy in Nigeria and Attendant Opportunity for Industrial Development. Report prepared for the Federal Ministry for Industrial Development, by Arthur D. Little, Inc., under program of USAID. Washington, D.C., 1963.
Federal Ministry of Economic Development, Lagos. National Development Plans. 1962–1968, 1970–1974, 1975–1976.
Federal Ministry of Information, Lagos. Press Release. January–November 1975, January 1976.
Federal Office of Statistics, Lagos. *Review of External Trade.* 1964, 1966, 1972, 1976.
———. *Annual Abstract of Statistics, 1974.*
Federation of Nigeria, Lagos. *Official Gazette Extraordinary, No. 10, Vol. 59.* February 28, 1972, Part A.
House of Representatives Debates. 1958–1965. Lagos: Government Printing Press.
Nigeria: Bulletin of Foreign Affairs. 1971–1976. Lagos: Institute of International Affairs.

Government Publications: United States

Public Papers of the Presidents of the United States, John F. Kennedy, January 20 to December 31, 1961. Washington, D.C.: Government Printing Office, 1962.
USAID. *U.S. Technical and Capital Assistance in Support of Development in Nigeria, 1967.* Lagos, 1967.
———. *U.S. Overseas Loans and Grants and Assistance from International Organizations, July 1, 1945–September 30, 1977.* Washington, D.C., 1977.

U.S. Congress. Senate. Sub-Committee on African Affairs. *U.S. Policy Toward Southern Africa.* 94th Cong. 1st Sess., 1975.

——— . Senate. Sub-Committee on African Affairs. *U.S. Policy Toward Africa.* 94th Cong. 2nd Sess., 1976.

——— . House. Sub-Committee on International Resources, Food, and Energy. *Resources in Rhodesia: Implications for U.S. Policy.* 94th Cong. 2nd Sess., 1976.

——— . Senate. Sub-Committee on African Affairs. *Angola.* 94th Cong. 2nd Sess., 1976.

——— . House. Sub-Committee on Africa and International Organizations. *The Rhodesian Sanction Bill.* 95th Cong. 1st Sess., 1977.

U.S. Department of Commerce. *Business Opportunities in Nigeria: Report of Trade and Investment Mission to Nigeria, September 16–November 4, 1961.* Washington, D.C., 1961

——— . *Foreign Economic Trends and Their Implications for the United States: Nigeria, 1977, 1978, 1979.* Washington, D.C.

——— . *Investment in Nigeria: Basic Information for United States Businessmen, April 1957.* Washington, D.C.: Government Printing Office, 1957.

——— . *Nigeria: A Survey of U.S. Business Opportunities, May 1976.* Washington, D.C.: Government Printing Office, 1976.

——— . *Overseas Business Reports: Marketing in Nigeria, July 1976.* Washington, D.C.: Government Printing Office, 1976.

U.S. Department of State. *Report of the Special U.S. Economic Mission to Nigeria, June 17, 1961.* Washington, D.C., 1961.

United Nations

General Assembly Official Records. 1050th Plenary Meeting (A/PV/1050), November 9, 1961, pp. 607–611.

United Nations Conference on Trade and Development. *Prospects for Trade and Economic Cooperation Between Nigeria and the Socialist Countries of Eastern Europe.* New York: UNCTAD Secretariat, United Nations, 1979.

Secondary Sources

Books

Akinyemi, A. B. *Foreign Policy and Federalism: The Experience of Nigeria.* Ibadan, Nigeria: University Press, 1974.

Aluko, Olajide. *Ghana and Nigeria, 1957–1970: A Study in Inter-African Discord.* London: Rex Collings, Ltd., 1976.

Amin, Samir. *Neo-Colonialism in West Africa.* Harmondsworth, England: Penguin Books, Ltd., 1973.

Arghiri, Emmanuel. *Unequal Exchange: A Study of the Imperialism of Trade.* New York: Monthly Review Press, 1972.

Arkhurst, F. S., ed. *U.S. Policy Toward Africa.* New York: Praeger Publishers, 1975.

Balewa, Abubaker T. *Nigeria Speaks.* London: Longmans Green and Co., Ltd., 1964.

Bergsten, Fred, and Lawrence B. Krause. *World Politics and International Economics.* Washington, D.C.: The Brookings Institution, 1975.

Biersteker, Thomas J. *Distortion or Development: Contending Perspectives on the Multinational Corporation.* Cambridge, Mass.: The MIT Press, 1978.

Bretton, Henry L. *Power and Politics in Africa.* Chicago: Aldine Publishing Company, 1973.

Cardoso, F. H., and E. Faletto. *Dependency and Development in Latin America.* Translated by Marjory Mattingly Urquia. Berkeley: University of California Press, 1979.

Chilcote, Ronald H., and Joel C. Edelstein. *Latin America: The Struggle with Dependency and Beyond.* Cambridge, Mass.: Schenkenman Publishing Company, Inc., 1974.

Cohen, Benjamin J. *The Question of Imperialism: The Political Economy of Dominance and Dependence.* New York: Basic Books, Inc., Publishers, 1973.

Coleman, James S. *Nigeria: Background to Nationalism.* Berkeley: University of California Press, 1958.

Cotler, Julio, and Richard R. Fagen. *Latin America and the United States: The Changing Realities.* Stanford, Calif.: Stanford University Press, 1974.

Cronje, Suzanne. *The Lonrho Connection: A Multinational and Its Politics in Africa.* Encino, Calif.: Bellwether Books, 1976.

Davidson, Basil. *Black Star: A View of the Life and Times of Kwame Nkrumah.* New York: Praeger Publishers, 1974.

———. *Can Africa Survive? Arguments Against Growth Without Development.* Boston: Little, Brown and Company, 1974.

El-Ayouty, Yassin. *The United Nations and Decolonization.* The Hague: Martinus Nijhoff, 1971.

El-Khawas, Mohamed A., and Barry Cohen. *National Security Study Memorandum 39: The Kissinger Study of Southern Africa.* Westport, Conn.: Lawrence and Company, 1976.

Fann, K. T., and Donald C. Hodges, eds. *Readings in U.S. Imperialism.* Boston: Porter Sargent Publisher, 1971.

Fanon, Frantz. *The Wretched of the Earth.* New York: Grove Press, Inc., 1963.

Foster, Philip, and Aristide Zolberg, eds. *Ghana and the Ivory Coast: Perspectives on Modernization.* Chicago: The University of Chicago Press, 1971.

Fox, Annette B. *The Politics of Attraction: Four Middle Powers and the United States.* New York: Columbia University Press, 1977.

Frank, Andre G. *Capitalism and Underdevelopment in Latin America: Historical Studies of Chile and Brazil.* New York: Monthly Review Press, 1967.

———. *Lumpen-Bourgeoisie, Lumpen-Development: Dependence, Class, and Politics in Latin America.* Translated by Marion D. Berdecio. New York: Monthly Review Press, 1972.

Gergen, Kenneth J. *The Psychology of Behavior Exchange.* Reading, Mass.: Addison-Wesley Publishing Company, 1969.

Green, Reginald H., and Ann Seidman. *Unity or Poverty? The Economics of Pan-Africanism.* Baltimore, Md.: Penguin Books, Inc., 1968.

Hayter, Teresa. *Aid as Imperialism*. Harmondsworth, England: Penguin Books, Inc., 1971.

Helleiner, Gerald K. *Peasant Agriculture, Government and Economic Growth in Nigeria*. Homewood, Ill.: Richard D. Irwin, Inc., 1966.

Hilsman, Roger. *To Move a Nation: The Politics of Foreign Policy in the Administration of John F. Kennedy*. New York: Doubleday & Company, Inc., 1967.

Hoskyns, Catherine. *The Congo Since Independence, January 1960 to December 1961*. London: Oxford University Press, 1965.

––––––. *The Organization of African Unity and the Congo Crisis, 1964–65*. Dar es Salaam, Tanzania: Oxford University Press, 1972.

Idang, Gordon J. *Nigeria: Internal Politics and Foreign Policy, 1960–1966*. Ibadan, Nigeria: University Press, 1973.

Keohane, Robert O., and Joseph S. Nye. *Power and Interdependence: World Politics in Transition*. Boston: Little, Brown, and Company, 1977.

Kilby, Peter. *Industrialization in an Open Economy: Nigeria, 1945–1966*. Cambridge: University Press, 1969.

Kitchen, Helen, ed. *Africa: From Mystery to Maze*. Lexington, Mass.: D. C. Heath and Company, 1976.

Knorr, Klaus. *The Power of Nations: The Political Economy of International Relations*. New York: Basic Books, Inc., 1975.

Lake, Anthony. *The "Tar Baby" Option: American Policy Toward Southern Rhodesia*. New York: Columbia University Press, 1976.

Lefever, Ernest W. *Uncertain Mandate: Politics of the U.N. Congo Operations*. Baltimore, Md.: The Johns Hopkins University Press, 1967.

Legum, Colin. *Pan-Africanism: A Short Political Guide*. Revised edition. New York: Praeger Publishers, 1965.

Legum, Colin, and Tony Hodges. *After Angola: The War Over Southern Africa*. New York: Africana Publishing Company, 1976.

Legvold, Robert. *Soviet Policy in West Africa*. Cambridge: Harvard University Press, 1970.

Lenin, V. I. *Imperialism; The Highest Stage of Capitalism*. New York: International Publishers, 1939.

Leys, Colin. *Underdevelopment in Kenya: The Political Economy of Neo-Colonialism*. Berkeley: University of California Press, 1975.

Louis, William R. *Imperialism at Bay: The United States and the Decolonization of the British Empire, 1941–1945*. New York: Oxford University Press, 1978.

McKay, Vernon. *Africa in World Politics*. New York: Macfadden-Bartell Corporation, 1963.

––––––, ed., *African Diplomacy: Studies in the Determinants of Foreign Policy*. New York: Praeger Publishers, 1966.

Maddison, Angus. *Foreign Skills and Technical Assistance in Economic Development*. Paris: Development Center of the Organization for Economic Cooperation and Development, 1965.

Magdoff, Harry. *The Age of Imperialism: The Economics of U.S. Foreign Policy*. New York: Monthly Review Press, 1969.

Marcum, John A. *The Angolan Revolution. Vol. II: Exile Politics and Guerrilla War (1962–1976)*. Cambridge, Mass.: The MIT Press, 1978.

Mazrui, Ali. *Africa's International Relations: The Diplomacy of Dependence and Change.* Boulder, Colo.: Westview Press, 1977.

———. *Towards a Pax Africana: A Study of Ideology and Ambition.* London: The Trinity Press, 1967.

Montgomery, John D. *Foreign Aid in International Politics.* Englewood Cliffs, N.J.: Prentice-Hall, Inc., 1967.

Moran, Theodore H. *Multinational Corporations and the Politics of Dependence.* Princeton, N.J.: Princeton University Press, 1974.

Mummery, David R. *The Protection of International Private Investment: Nigeria and the World Community.* New York: Praeger Publishers, 1968.

Nelson, Joan. *Aid, Influence, and Foreign Policy.* New York: Macmillan Company, 1968.

Nielsen, Waldemar A. *The Great Powers and Africa.* New York: Praeger Publishers, 1969.

Nkrumah, Kwame. *Africa Must Unite.* New York: International Publishers, 1963.

———. *Challenge of the Congo: A Case Study of Foreign Pressures in an Independent State.* New York: International Publishers, 1967.

———. *Neo-Colonialism: The Last Stage of Imperialism.* New York: International Publishers, 1965.

Odell, Peter R. *Oil and World Power: Background to the Oil Crisis.* Third edition. Harmondsworth, England: Penguin Books, Ltd., 1974.

Panter-Brick, S. K., ed. *Nigerian Politics and Military Rule: Prelude to the Civil War.* London: University Press, 1970.

———. *Soldier and Oil: The Political Transformation of Nigeria.* London: Frank Cass and Company, Ltd., 1978.

Phillips, Claude S. *The Development of Nigerian Foreign Policy.* Evanston, Ill.: Northwestern University Press, 1964.

Rhodes, Robert, ed. *Imperialism and Underdevelopment: A Reader.* New York: Monthly Review Press, 1970.

Richardson, Neil R. *Foreign Policy and Economic Dependency.* Austin: University of Texas Press, 1978.

Rosenau, James N., ed. *Linkage Politics: Essays on the Convergence of National and International Systems.* New York: The Free Press, 1969.

Rothchild, Donald, and Robert Curry, Jr. *Scarcity, Choice and Public Policy in Middle Africa.* Berkeley: University of California Press, 1978.

Schlesinger, Arthur M., Jr. *A Thousand Days: John F. Kennedy in the White House.* Boston: Houghton Mifflin Co., 1965.

Schwartz, Walter. *Nigeria.* London: Pall Mall Press, 1968.

Singer, Marshall R. *Weak States in a World of Powers: The Dynamics of International Relations.* New York: The Free Press, 1972.

Sklar, Richard L. *Corporate Power in an African State: The Political Impact of Multinational Mining Companies in Zambia.* Berkeley: University of California Press, 1975.

———. *Nigerian Political Parties: Power in an Emergent African Nation.* Princeton, N.J.: Princeton University Press, 1963.

Spiegel, Steven L. *Dominance and Diversity: The International Hierarchy.* Boston: Little, Brown and Company, 1972.

Stallings, Barbara B. *Economic Dependency in Africa and Latin America.* Sage Professional Papers in Comparative Politics. Beverly Hills, Calif.: Sage Publishers, 1972.

Stockwell, John. *In Search of Enemies: A CIA Story.* New York: W. W. Norton & Company, Inc., 1978.

Stremlau, John J. *The International Politics of the Nigerian Civil War.* Princeton, N.J.: Princeton University Press, 1972.

Tanzer, Michael. *The Political Economy of International Oil and the Underdeveloped Countries.* Boston: Beacon Press, 1969.

Thompson, Scott W. *Ghana's Foreign Policy, 1957–1966: Diplomacy, Ideology and the New State.* Princeton, N.J.: Princeton University Press, 1969.

Touval, Saadia. *The Boundary Politics of Independent Africa.* Cambridge: Harvard University Press, 1972.

Vallenilla, Luis. *Oil: The Making of a New Economic Order, Venezuela and OPEC.* New York: McGraw-Hill Book Company, 1975.

Vernon, Raymond, ed. *The Oil Crisis.* New York: W. W. Norton & Company, Inc., 1976.

Wallerstein, Immanuel. *Africa: Politics of Unity.* New York: Vintage Books, 1967.
_____ . *Africa: The Politics of Independence.* New York: Vintage Books, 1961.

Walters, Robert S. *American and Soviet Aid: A Comparative Analysis.* Pittsburgh: University of Pittsburgh Press, 1970.

Waltz, Kenneth N. *Theory of International Politics.* Reading, Mass.: Addison-Wesley Publishing Company, 1979.

Weissman, Stephen R. *American Foreign Policy in the Congo, 1960–1964.* Ithaca, N.Y.: Cornell University Press, 1974.

Western Massachusetts Association of Concerned African Scholars, eds. *U.S. Military Involvement in Southern Africa.* Boston: South End Press, 1978.

Whitaker, Jennifer S., ed. *Africa and the United States: Vital Interests.* New York: New York University Press, 1978.

Williams, Gavin. *Nigeria: Economy and Society.* London: Rex Collings Ltd., 1976.

Wolfers, Arnold, ed. *Alliance Policy in the Cold War.* Baltimore, Md.: The Johns Hopkins University Press, 1959.

Articles

Ajayi, E. A. "Nigeria-Soviet Aid Relations, 1960–1968." *Nigeria: Bulletin on Foreign Affairs* 1 (January 1972): 1–9.

Ake, Claude. "Explanatory Notes on the Political Economy of Africa." *The Journal of Modern African Studies* 14(1) (March 1976): 1–23.

Amin, Samir. "Underdevelopment and Dependence in Black Africa—Origins and Contemporary Forms." *Journal of Modern African Studies* 10(4) (December 1972): 503–525.

Anglin, Douglas G. "Nigeria: Political Nonalignment and Economic Alignment." *The Journal of Modern African Studies* 2(2) (July 1964).

Cardoso, Fernando H. "Associated-Dependent Development: Theoretical and Practical Implications." In *Authoritarian Brazil: Origins, Policies, and Future,* edited by Alfred Stepan, 142–176. New Haven, Conn.: Yale University Press, 1973.

———. "Dependency and Development in Latin America." *New Left Review* 74 (July-August 1972): 83–95.

Carlin, Alan. "Project Versus Program Aid: From the Donor's Viewpoint." In *The United States and the Developing Economies*, revised edition, edited by Gustav Ranis. New York: W. W. Norton & Company, 1973.

Chase-Dunn, Christopher. "The Effects of International Economic Dependence on Development and Inequality: A Cross-National Study." *American Sociological Review* 40 (December 1975): 720–738.

Churchill, Winston S., Jr. "Africa: The Challenge to the West." *R.U.S.I. and Brassey's Defence Studies*. London: The Royal United Service Institute for Defence Studies, 1977, pp. 62–69.

Coleman, James S. "The Foreign Policy of Nigeria." In *Foreign Policies in a World of Change*, edited by E. Black and Kenneth W. Thompson, 336–338. New York: Harper and Row, 1963.

Davies, Nathaniel. "The Angola Decision of 1975: A Personal Memoir." *Foreign Affairs* 57(1) (Fall 1978): 109–125.

Dean, Edwin R. "Factors Impeding the Implementation of Nigeria's Six-Year Plan." *The Journal of Economic and Social Studies* 8 (March 1966): 113–125.

Ebinger, Charles K. "External Intervention in Internal War: The Politics and Diplomacy of the Angolan War." *Orbis* 20(3) (Fall 1976): 669–699.

Emerson, Richard M. "Power-Dependence Relations." *American Sociological Review* 27 (February 1962): 33–35.

Esseks, John D. "Economic Dependence and Political Development in New States of Africa." *Journal of Politics* 33(4) (November 1971): 1052–1075.

Foltz, William J. "United States Policy Toward Southern Africa: Economic and Strategic Interests." *Political Science Quarterly* 92(1) (April 1977).

Green, Reginald H. "Political Independence and the National Economy: An Essay on the Political Economy of Decolonization." In *African Perspectives: Papers in the History, Politics, and Economics of Africa Presented to Thomas Hodgkin*, edited by C. Allen and R. W. Johnston, 273–324. Cambridge: Cambridge University Press, 1970.

Grundy, Kenneth W. "Intermediary Power and Global Dependency: The Case of South Africa." *International Studies Quarterly* 20(4) (December 1976): 553–580.

Herskovits, Jean. "Dateline Nigeria: A Black Power." *Foreign Policy* 29 (Winter 1977-1978): 167–188.

Kitchen, Helen. "Filling the Togo Vacuum." *Africa Report* 8(2) (February 1963): 7–10.

McGowan, Patrick J., and Smith L. Dale. "Economic Dependency in Black Africa: An Analysis of Competing Theories." *International Organization* 32(1) (Winter 1978): 179–203.

McGowan, Patrick J., and Klaus-Peter Gottwald. "Small State Foreign Policies: A Comparative Study of Participation, Conflict, and Political and Economic Dependency in Black Africa." *International Studies Quarterly* 19(4) (December 1975): 469–497.

Marcum, John A. "Lessons of Angola." *Foreign Affairs* 54(3) (April 1976): 407–425.

Mayal, James. "Oil and Nigerian Foreign Policy." *African Affairs* 75 (July 1976): 317–330.

Mittelman, James H. "Collective Decolonization and the U.N. Committee of 24." *The Journal of Modern African Studies* 14(1) (1976): 41–64.

Moran, Theodore H. "Multinational Corporations and Dependency: A Dialogue for Dependentistas and Non-dependentistas." *International Organization* 32(1) (1978): 79–100.

Ojedokun, Olasupo. "The Anglo-Nigerian Entente and Its Demise, 1960–1962." *Journal of Commonwealth and Political Studies* 19 (November 1971): 229.

————. "The Changing Pattern of Nigeria's International Economic Relations: The Decline of the Colonial Nexus, 1960–1966." *Journal of Developing Nations* (July 1972): 535–554.

Ojo, Olatunde. "Nigerian-Soviet Relations." *African Studies Review* 19(3) (1967): 43–52.

Osoba, Segun. "The Deepening Crisis of the Nigerian National Bourgeoisie." *Review of African Political Economy* 13 (May-August 1978): 63–77.

Palmer, Bruce, Jr. "U.S. Security Interests and Africa South of the Sahara." *American Enterprise Institute Defence Review* 2(6) (1978): 2.

Richardson, Neil R., and Charles W. Kegley, Jr. "Trade Dependence and Foreign Policy Compliance: A Longitudinal Analysis." *International Studies Quarterly* 24(2) (June 1980): 197–222.

Santos, Dos Theotonio. "The Structure of Dependence." In *Readings in U.S. Imperialism*, edited by K. T. Fann and D. C. Hodges, 225–236. Boston: Porter Sargent Publishers, 1971.

Shaw, Timothy, and Malcolm Grieve. "Dependence or Development: International and Internal Inequalities in Africa." *Development and Change* 8 (1977): 377–408.

Sunkel, Osvaldo. "Big Business and 'Dependencia.' A Latin American View." *Foreign Affairs* 50(3) (April 1972): 517–531.

Turner, Terisa. "Multinational Corporations and the Instability of the Nigerian State." *Review of African Political Economy* 5 (January-April 1976): 63–79.

Vengroff, Richard. "Dependency and Underdevelopment in Black Africa: An Empirical Test." *The Journal of Modern African Studies* 15(4) (1977): 613–630.

Wallerstein, Immanuel. "Africa in a Capitalist World." *Issue* 3(3) (Fall 1973): 1–11.

————. "Dependence in an Interdependent World: The Limited Possibilities of Transformation Within the Capitalist World Economy." *African Studies Review* 17(1) (April 1974): 1–23.

Warren, Bill. "Imperialism and Capitalist Industrialization." *New Left Review* 81 (September-October 1973): 3–44.

Wasserman, Gary. "The Independence Bargain: Kenya Europeans and the Land Question." *Journal of Commonwealth and Political Studies* 11(2) (1973).

Zartman, I. William. "Africa as a Subordinate State System in International Relations." *International Organization* 31 (Summer 1967): 545–564.

———. "Europe and Africa: Dependence or Decolonization." *Foreign Affairs* 54 (1976): 325–343.

Unpublished Papers

Adeniran, Babatunde. "A Developing Country in the United Nations System: A Study of Nigeria's Participation in the United Nations, 1960–1975." Unpublished dissertation, Columbia University, 1978.

Akinyemi, Bolaji. "Nigeria and the Superpowers: Equality Not Uniformity of Relations." Unpublished lecture, Institute of International Relations, Lagos, 1978.

Obiozor, George. "The Development of Nigeria–United States Diplomacy— 1960–1975." Unpublished dissertation, Columbia University, 1976.

Ogene, Francis C. "Group Interests and United States Foreign Policy on African Issues." Unpublished dissertation, Case Western Reserve University, Cleveland, Ohio, 1974.

Ogunsanwo, Alaba. "The Nigerian Military and Foreign Policy, 1975–1979: Processes, Principles, Performance and Contradictions." Unpublished manuscript, Department of Political Science, University of Lagos, Nigeria, 1980.

Okolo, Adolph A. "International Political Economy and Nigeria's Development: 1945–1975." Unpublished dissertation, Purdue University, 1978.

Quarterlies and Periodicals

Africa Diary, 1963.
African Development, 1972–1974.
Foreign Policy, 1972, 1977, 1979, 1984.
Geography 60 (November 1975): 307–308.
International Studies Quarterly, 1970, 1975–1976.
Journal of Modern African Studies, 1964–1965, 1976–1978.
Latin American Perspective, 1974, 1976.
New Left Review, 1972–1973.
Nigerian Journal of Economic and Social Studies, 1962–1966, 1972.
Petroleum Economist, 1971–1976.
West Africa.

Newspapers

Daily Express (Lagos), 1959–1963.
Daily Service (Lagos), 1960–1963.
Daily Times (Lagos), 1959–1964, 1970–1976, 1977–1978.
Morning Post (Lagos), 1961–1965.
New Nigerian (Kaduna), 1970–1976, 1978–1984.
New York Times, 1960–1963, 1971–1976, 1977–1978.
Nigerian Tide (Port Harcourt), 1974–1975, 1978.
The Observer (London), 1971, 1976, 1977–1978.
West African Pilot (Lagos), 1959–1964.

SUPPLEMENT TO BIBLIOGRAPHY

Primary Sources

Government Publications: Nigeria

Federal Ministry of Information, Lagos. News Release No. 1830, October 13, 1977; Release No. 183, February 11, 1978.

Government Publications: United States

U.S. Congress. Senate. Sub-Committee on African Affairs. *U.S. Policy Toward Africa.* 95th Cong. 2nd Sess. 1978.

U.S. Congress. House. Sub-Committee on Africa. *United States Policy Toward Rhodesia: A Report on the New Anglo-American Initiative.* 95th Cong., 1st Sess., 1977.

U.S. Congress. House. Sub-Committee on Africa. *Nigeria Returns to Civilian Rule.* 96th Cong., 1st Sess., 1979.

Secondary Sources

Books

Brzezinski, Zbigniew. *Power and Principle.* New York: Farrar, Straus, Giroux, 1983.

Cabral, Amilcar. *Revolution in Guinea.* Translated and edited by Richard Handyside. New York: Monthly Review Press, 1969.

Carter, Jimmy. *Keeping Faith: Memoirs of a President.* New York: Bantam Books, 1982.

Gromyko, Anatoly, ed. *Africa Today: Progress, Difficulties, Perspectives.* Moscow: USSR Academy of Sciences, 1983.

Kennan, George. *Russia and the West Under Lenin and Stalin.* New York: The New American Library, 1961.

VanAlstyne, Richard W. *The Rising American Empire.* New York: W. W. Norton and Company, 1974.

Vance, Cyrus. *Hard Choices: Critical Years in American Foreign Policy.* New York: Simon and Schuster, 1983.

Articles

Akinyemi, A. B. "Nigerian-American Relations Re-examined." In *Survey of Nigerian Affairs, 1976–1977,* edited by O. Oyediran, 105–114. Macmillan Nigeria Publishers Ltd., 1981.

Ate, B. E. "Nigeria Needs a New Oil Strategy." *Nigerian Forum* (March-April 1984): 80–87.

———. "The Presence of France in West-Central Africa as a Fundamental Problem to Nigeria." *MILLENNIUM* 12 (2) (Summer 1983): 110–126.

———. "United States Africa Policy After Carter." *Nigerian Forum* 1(1) (March 1981): 14–21.

Coker, Christopher. "Neo-Conservatism and Africa: Some Common American Fallacies." *Third World Quarterly* 5(2) (April 1983): 283–299.

Crocker, Chester A., et al. "Missing Opportunities in Africa . . ." *Foreign Policy* 35 (Summer 1979): 142–161.

Delancey, Mark W. "Nigeria: Foreign Policy Alternatives, Background Notes at the Beginning of Civilian Rule." Mimeographed. Washington, D.C.: Department of State, October 3, 1979.

Easum, Donald B. "Nigerian-American Relations." *Africa Report* (July-August 1981): 52–53.

Herskovits, Jean. "Dateline Nigeria: Democracy Down, Not Out." *Foreign Policy* 54 (Spring 1984): 171–190.

Huntington, Samuel P. "American Ideals Versus Institutions." *Political Science Quarterly* (Spring 1983): 1–37.

Jay, Peter. "Regionalism as Geopolitics." *Foreign Affairs* 58(3) (1979): 485–514.

Kitchen, Helen. "On Safari—Again." *Orbis* (Winter 1982): 855–858.

Lake, Anthony. "Africa in a Global Perspective." *Department of State Bulletin* 77 (July-December 1977), Washington, D.C.

Mazrui, Ali. "Nigeria and the United States: The Need for Civility, the Dangers of Intimacy." *Orbis* (Winter 1982): 858–864.

Obasanjo, Olusegun. "Africa's Needs." *Foreign Policy* (Winter 1984): 80–91.

Thompson, W. Scott. "U.S. Policy Toward Africa." *Orbis* (Winter 1982): 1011–1024.

Tucker, Robert W. "The Role of Defense in the Foreign Policy of the Reagan Administration." *The Jerusalem Journal of International Affairs* 7(1-2) (1984): 47–56.

Young, Andrew. "The United States and Africa." *Foreign Affairs* 59(3) (1979): 648–666.

Quarterlies and Periodicals

Foreign Affairs 58(3) (1979).
New African (February 1979): 58–61.
Newsweek (March 3, 1981).
Nigerian Forum (March 1981; October 1982).
Orbis (Winter 1982).

Newspapers

Daily Sketch (Ibadan), 1978–1983.
National Concord (Lagos), 1982–1983.
The Guardian (Lagos), 1982–1983.
The Punch (Lagos), 1981–1983.

Index